# THE TRANSPARENT SOCIETY

*Will Technology Force
Us to Choose Between
Privacy and Freedom?*

David Brin, Ph.D.

ADDISON-WESLEY
*Reading, Massachusetts*

Many of the designations used by manufacturers and sellers to distinguish their products are claimed as trademarks. Where those designations appear in this book and Addison-Wesley was aware of a trademark claim, the designations have been printed in initial capital letters (e.g., Kindercam).

Library of Congress Cataloging-in-Publication Data
Brin, David.
    The transparent society : will technology force us to choose between privacy and freedom? / David Brin.
       p.    cm.
    Includes bibliographical references and index.
    ISBN 0–201–32802–X
    1. Freedom of information.   2. Privacy, Right of.
    3. Responsibility.  I. Title.
JC598.B75   1998
323.44'8 — dc21                      98–5310
                                            CIP

Addison-Wesley is an imprint of Addison Wesley Longman, Inc.

Jacket design by Steven Brower
Text design by Karen Savary
Set in 11 point Electra by Carlisle Communications, Inc.

1 2 3 4 5 6 7 8 9-MA-0201009998
First printing, April 1998

Addison-Wesley books are available at special discounts for bulk purchases. For more information about how to make such purchases in the U.S., please contact the Corporate, Government, and Special Sales Department at Addison Wesley Longman, One Jacob Way, Reading, MA 01867, or call (800) 238-9682.

Find us on the World Wide Web at http://www.aw.com/gb/

*To Popper, Pericles, Franklin, and countless others who helped fight for an open society . . . and to their heirs who have enough courage to stand in the light and live unmasked.*

There is not a crime, there is not a dodge, there is not a trick, there is not a swindle, there is not a vice which does not live by secrecy.

JOSEPH PULITZER

Sunlight is said to be the best of disinfectants.

JUSTICE LOUIS BRANDEIS

# CONTENTS

# PART I
# A NEW WORLD

*There's no going back, and there's no hiding the information. So let everyone have it.*

ANDREW KANTOR

# CHAPTER ONE

# THE CHALLENGE OF AN OPEN SOCIETY

*Sacrificing anonymity may be the next generation's price for keeping precious liberty, as prior generations paid in blood.*

HAL NORBY

*You're wondering why I've called you here. The reason is simple. To answer all your questions. I mean—all. This is the greatest news of our time. As of today, whatever you want to know, provided it's in the data-net, you can know. In other words, there are no more secrets.*

JOHN BRUNNER,<br>THE SHOCKWAVE RIDER, 1974

This is a tale of two cities. Cities of the near future, say ten or twenty years from now.

Barring something unforeseen, you are apt to be living in one of these two places. Your only choice may be which one.

At first sight, these two municipalities look pretty much alike. Both contain dazzling technological marvels, especially in the realm of electronic media. Both suffer familiar urban quandaries of frustration and decay. If some progress is being made in solving human problems, it is happening gradually. Perhaps some kids seem better educated. The air may be marginally cleaner. People still worry about overpopulation, the environment, and the next international crisis.

None of these features is of interest to us right now, for we have noticed something about both of these twenty-first-century cities that *is* radically different. A trait that marks them as distinct from any metropolis of the late 1990s.

Street crime has nearly vanished from both towns. But that is only a symptom, a result.

The real change peers down from every lamppost, every rooftop and street sign.

Tiny cameras, panning left and right, survey traffic and pedestrians, observing everything in open view.

Have we entered an Orwellian nightmare? Have the burghers of both towns banished muggings at the cost of creating a Stalinist dystopia?

Consider city number one. In this place, all the myriad cameras report their urban scenes straight to Police Central, where security officers use sophisticated image processors to scan for infractions against public order — or perhaps against an established way of thought. Citizens walk the streets aware that any word or deed may be noted by agents of some mysterious bureau.

Now let's skip across space and time.

At first sight, things seem quite similar in city number two. Again, ubiquitous cameras perch on every vantage point. Only here we soon find a crucial difference. These devices do *not* report to the secret police. Rather, each and every citizen of this metropolis can use his or her wristwatch television to call up images from any camera in town.

Here a late-evening stroller checks to make sure no one lurks beyond the corner she is about to turn.

Over there a tardy young man dials to see if his dinner date still waits for him by a city fountain.

A block away, an anxious parent scans the area to find which way her child wandered off.

Over by the mall, a teenage shoplifter is taken into custody gingerly, with minute attention to ritual and rights, because the arresting officer knows that the entire process is being scrutinized by untold numbers who watch intently, lest her neutral professionalism lapse.

In city number two, such microcameras are banned from some indoor places . . . but not from police headquarters! There any citizen may tune in on bookings, arraignments, and especially the camera control room itself, making sure that the agents on duty look out for violent crime, and only crime.

Despite their initial similarity, these are very different cities, representing disparate ways of life, completely opposite relationships between citizens and their civic guardians. The reader may find both situations somewhat chilling. Both futures may seem undesirable. But can there be any doubt which city we'd rather live in, if these two make up our only choice?

## TECHNOLOGY'S VERDICT

Alas, they do appear to be our only options. For the cameras *are* on their way, along with data networks that will send a myriad images flashing back and forth, faster than thought.

In fact, the future has already arrived. The trend began in Britain a decade ago, in the town of King's Lynn, where sixty remote-controlled video cameras were installed to scan known "trouble spots," reporting directly to police headquarters. The resulting reduction in street crime exceeded all predictions; in or near zones covered by surveillance, crime dropped to one-seventieth of the former rate. The savings in patrol costs alone paid for the equipment in a few months. Dozens of cities and towns soon followed the example of King's Lynn. Glasgow, Scotland, reported a 68 percent drop in crime citywide, while police in Newcastle fingered over 1,500 perpetrators with taped evidence. (All but seven pleaded guilty, and those seven were later convicted.) In May 1997, Newcastle soccer fans rampaged through downtown streets. Detectives studying video tapes picked out 152 faces and published 80 photographs in local newspapers. In days, all were identified.

Today, over 300,000 cameras are in place throughout the United Kingdom, transmitting round-the-clock images to a hundred constabularies, all of them reporting decreases in public misconduct. Polls report that the cameras are extremely popular with citizens, though British civil libertarian John Wadham and others have bemoaned this proliferation of snoop technology, claiming, "It could be used for any other purpose, and of course it could be abused."

Visitors to Japan, Thailand, and Singapore will see that other countries are rapidly following the British example, using closed circuit television (CCTV) to supervise innumerable public areas.

This trend was slower coming to North America, but it appears to be taking off. After initial experiments garnered widespread public approval, the City of Baltimore put police cameras to work scanning all 106 downtown intersections. In 1997, New York City began its own program to set up twenty-four-hour remote surveillance in Central Park, subway stations, and other public places.

No one denies the obvious and dramatic short-term benefits derived from this early proliferation of surveillance technology. That is not the real issue. In the long run, the sovereign folk of Baltimore and countless other communities will have to make the same choice as the inhabitants of our two mythical cities. *Who will ultimately control the cameras?*

Consider a few more examples.

How many parents have wanted to be a fly on the wall while their child was at day care? This is now possible with a new video monitoring system known as Kindercam, linked to high-speed telephone lines and a central Internet server. Parents can log on, type "www.kindercam.com," enter their password, and access a live view of their child in day care at any time, from anywhere in the world. Kindercam will be installed in two thousand day-care facilities nationwide by the end of 1998. Mothers on business trips, fathers who live out of state, even distant grandparents can all "drop in" on their child daily. Drawbacks? Overprotective parents may check compulsively. And now other parents can observe *your* child misbehaving!

Some of the same parents are less happy about the lensed pickups that are sprouting in their own workplaces, enabling supervisors to tune in on them in the same way they use Kindercam to check up on their kids.

That is, if they notice the cameras at all. At present, engineers can squeeze the electronics for a video unit into a package smaller than a sugar cube. Complete sets half the size of a pack of cigarettes were recently offered for sale by the Spy Shop, a little store in New York City located two blocks from the United Nations. Meanwhile, units with radio transmitters are being disguised in clock radios, telephones, and toasters, as part of the burgeoning "nannycam" trend. So high is demand for these pickups, largely by parents eager to check on their babysitters, that just one firm in Orange County, California, has recently been selling from five hundred to one thousand disguised cameras a month. By the end of 1997, prices had dropped from $2,500 to $399.

Cameras aren't the only surveillance devices proliferating in our cities. Starting with Redwood City, near San Francisco, several police departments have begun lacing neighborhoods with sound pickups that transmit directly back to headquarters. Using triangulation techniques, officials can now pinpoint bursts of gunfire and send patrol units swiftly to the scene, without having to wait for vague telephone reports from neighbors. In 1995 the Defense Department awarded a $1.7 million contract to Alliant Techsystems for its prototype system SECURES, which tests more advanced sound pickup networks in Washington and other cities. The hope is to distinguish not only types of gunfire but also human voices crying for help.

So far, so good. But from there, engineers say it would be simple to upgrade the equipment, enabling bored monitors to eavesdrop through open bedroom windows on cries of passion, or family arguments. "Of course we would never go that far," one official said, reassuringly.

Consider another piece of James Bond apparatus now available to anyone with ready cash. Today, almost any electronics store will sell you night vision goggles using state-of-the-art infrared optics equal to those issued by the military, for less than the price of a video camera. AGEMA Systems, of Syracuse, New York, has sold several police departments imaging devices that can peer into houses from the street, discriminate the heat given off by indoor marijuana cultivators, and sometimes tell if a person inside moves from one room to the next. Military and civilian enhanced vision technologies now move in lockstep, as they have in the computer field for years.

In other words, even darkness no longer guarantees privacy.

Nor does your garden wall. In 1995, Admiral William A. Owens, then vice chairman of the Joint Chiefs of Staff, described a sensor system that he expected to be operational within a few years: a pilotless drone, equipped to provide airborne surveillance for soldiers in the field. While camera robots in the $1 million range have been flying in the military for some time, the new system will be extraordinarily cheap and simple. Instead of requiring a large support crew, it will be controlled by one semi-skilled soldier and will fit in the palm of a hand. Minuscule and quiet, such remote-piloted vehicles, or RPVs, may flit among trees to survey threats near a rifle platoon. When mass-produced in huge quantities, unit prices will fall.

Can civilian models be far behind? No law or regulation will keep them from our cities for very long. The rich, the powerful, and figures of authority will have them, whether legally or surreptitiously. And the contraptions will become smaller, cheaper, and smarter with each passing year.

So much for the supposed privacy enjoyed by sunbathers in their own backyards.

Moreover, surveillance cameras are the tip of the metaphorical iceberg. Other entrancing and invasive innovations of the vaunted *information age* abound. Will a paper envelope protect the correspondence you send by old-fashioned surface mail when new-style scanners can trace the patterns of ink inside without ever breaking the seal?

Let's say you correspond with others by e-mail and use a computerized encryption program to ensure that your messages are read only by the intended recipient. What good will all the ciphers and codes do, if some adversary has bought a "back door" password to your encoding program? Or if a wasp-sized camera drone flits into your room, sticks to the ceiling above your desk, inflates a bubble lens, and watches every keystroke that you type? (A number of such unnerving techno-possibilities will be discussed in chapter 8.)

In late 1997 it was revealed that Swiss police had secretly tracked the whereabouts of mobile phone users via a telephone company computer that records billions of movements per year. Swisscom was able to locate its mobile subscribers within a few hundred meters. This aided several police investigations. But civil libertarians expressed heated concern, especially since identical technology is used worldwide.

The same issues arise when we contemplate the proliferation of vast databases containing information about our lives, habits, tastes, and personal histories. As we shall see in chapter 3, the cash register scanners in a million supermarkets, video stores, and pharmacies already pour forth a flood of statistical data about customers and their purchases, ready to be correlated. (Are you stocking up on hemorrhoid cream? Renting a daytime motel room? The database knows.) Corporations claim this information helps them serve us more efficiently. Critics respond that it gives big companies an unfair advantage, enabling them to know vastly more about us than we do about them. Soon, computers will hold all your financial and educational records, legal documents, and medical analyses that parse you all the way down to your genes. Any of this might be examined by strangers without your knowledge, or even against your stated will.

As with those streetlamp cameras, the choices we make regarding future information networks—how they will be controlled and who can access the data—will affect our own lives and those of our children and their descendants.

## A MODERN CONCERN

The issue of threatened privacy has spawned a flood of books, articles, and media exposés—from Janna Malamud Smith's thoughtful *Private Matters*, and Ellen Alderman and Caroline Kennedy's erudite *Right to Privacy* all the way to shrill, paranoid rants by conspiracy fetishists who see Big Brother lurking around every corner. Spanning this spectrum, however, there appears to be one common theme. Often the author has responded with a call to arms, proclaiming that we must become more vigilant to protect traditional privacy against intrusions by faceless (*take your pick*) government bureaucrats, corporations, criminals, or just plain busybodies.

That is the usual conclusion—but not the one taken here.

For in fact, it is already far too late to prevent the invasion of cameras and databases. The *djinn* cannot be crammed back into its bottle. No matter how many laws are passed, it will prove quite impossible to legislate away the new surveillance tools and databases. They are here to stay.

Light *is* going to shine into nearly every corner of our lives.

The real issue facing citizens of a new century will be how mature adults choose to live—how they can compete, cooperate, and thrive—in such a world. A transparent society.

Regarding those cameras, for instance—the ones atop every lamppost in both city one and city two—we can see that very different styles of urban life resulted from just one decision, based on how people in each town answered the following question.

*Will average citizens share, along with the mighty, the right to access these universal monitors? Will common folk have, and exercise, a sovereign power to watch the watchers?*

Back in city number one, Joe and Jane Doe may walk through an average day never thinking about those microcameras overhead. They might even believe official statements claiming that all the spy eyes were banished and dismantled a year or two ago, when in fact they were only made smaller, harder to detect. Jane and Joe stroll secure that their neighbors cannot spy on them (except the old-fashioned way, from overlooking windows). In other words, Jane and Joe blissfully believe they have *privacy*.

The inhabitants of city number two know better. They realize that, out of doors at least, complete privacy has always been an illusion. They know anyone can tune in to that camera on the lamppost—and they don't much care. They perceive what really matters: that they live in a town where the police are efficient, respectful, and above all accountable. Homes are sacrosanct, but out on the street any citizen, from the richest to the poorest, can both walk safely and use the godlike power to zoom at will from vantage point to vantage point, viewing all the lively wonders of the vast but easily spanned village their metropolis has become, as if by some magic it had turned into a city not of people but of birds.

Sometimes, citizens of city number two find it tempting to wax nostalgic about the old days, before there were so many cameras, or before television invaded the home, or before the telephone and automobile. But for the most part, city number two's denizens know that those times are gone, never to return. Above all, one thing makes life bearable: the surety that each person knows what is going on, with a say in what will happen next. And has rights equal to those of any billionaire or chief of police.

This little allegory—like all allegories—may be a gross oversimplification. For instance, in our projected city of "open access," citizens will have ten thousand decisions to make. Here are just a few examples:

- Since one might conceivably use these devices to follow someone home, should convicted felons be forbidden access to the camera networks?

- Might any person order up a search program, using sophisticated pattern-recognition software to scan a throng of passersby and zero in on a specific face? If such "traps" could be laid all over town, a lot of fugitives might be brought to justice. But will individuals ever again be able to seek anonymity in a crowd? Will people respond by wearing masks in public? Or will safety ultimately come when people unleash their own search programs, to alert the watched about their watchers?

- When should these supercameras be allowed indoors? If cameras keep getting smaller and more mobile, like wasp-size drones, what kind of defenses might protect us against Peeping Toms, or police spies, flying such devices through the open windows of our homes?

The list of possible quandaries goes on and on. Such an endless complexity of choices may cause some citizens of city number two to envy the simplicity of life in city number one, where only big business, the state, and certain well-heeled criminals possess these powers. That elite will in turn try to foster a widespread illusion among the populace that the cameras don't exist. Some folk will prefer a fantasy of privacy over the ambiguity and arduous decisions faced by citizens of city number two.

There is nothing new in this. All previous generations faced quandaries the outcomes of which changed history. When Thomas Jefferson prescribed a revolution every few decades, he was speaking not only politically but also about the constant need to remain flexible and adapt to changing circumstances, to innovate as needed, while at the same time staying true to those values we hold unchanging and precious. Our civilization is already a noisy one precisely because we have chosen freedom and mass sovereignty, so that the citizenry itself must constantly argue out the details, instead of leaving them to some committee of sages.

What distinguishes society today is not only the pace of events but also the nature of our tool kit for facing the future. Above all, what has marked our civilization as different is its knack for applying two extremely hard-won lessons from the past.

*In all of history, we have found just one cure for error—a partial antidote against making and repeating grand, foolish mistakes, a remedy against self-deception. That antidote is criticism.*

Scientists have known this for a long time. It is the keystone of their success. A scientific theory gains respect only by surviving repeated attempts to demolish it. Only after platoons of clever critics have striven to come up with refuting evidence, forcing changes, do a few hypotheses eventually graduate from mere theories to accepted models of the world.

Another example is capitalism. When it works, under just and impartial rules, the free market rewards agility, hard work, and innovation, just as it punishes the stock prices of companies that make too many mistakes. Likewise, any believer in evolution knows that death is the ultimate form of criticism, a merciless driver, transforming species over time.

Even in our private and professional lives, mature people realize that improvement comes only when we open ourselves to learn from our mistakes, no matter how hard we have to grit our teeth, when others tell us we were wrong. Which brings us to our second observation.

> ### Alas, criticism has always been what human beings, especially leaders, most hate to hear.

This ironic contradiction, which I will later refer to as the "Paradox of the Peacock," has had profound and tragic effects on human culture for centuries. Accounts left by past ages are filled with woeful events in which societies and peoples suffered largely because openness and free speech were suppressed, leaving the powerful at liberty to make devastating blunders without comment or consent from below.

If neo-Western civilization* has one great trick in its repertoire, a technique more responsible than any other for its success, that trick is *accountability*. Especially the knack—which no other culture ever mastered—of making accountability apply to the mighty. True, we still don't manage it perfectly. Gaffes, bungles, and inanities still get covered up. And yet, one can look at any newspaper or television news program and see an eager press corps at work, supplemented by hordes of righteously indignant individuals (and their lawyers), all baying for waste or corruption to be exposed, secrets to be unveiled, and nefarious schemes to be nipped in the bud. Disclosure is a watchword of the age, and politicians have grudgingly responded by passing the Freedom of Information Act (FOIA), truth-in-lending laws, open-meeting rules, and codes to enforce candor in real estate, in the nutritional content of foodstuffs, in the expense accounts of lobbyists, and so on.

Although this process of stripping off veils has been uneven, and continues to be a source of contention, the underlying moral force can clearly be seen pervading our popular culture, in which nearly every modern film or novel seems to preach the same message—suspicion of authority. The

---

*For a discussion of this term, and many other terms, tangents, and ways to explore this book's topics, please see the notes beginning on page 336.

phenomenon is not new to our generation. Schoolbooks teach that freedom is guarded by constitutional "checks and balances," but those same legal provisions were copied, early in the nineteenth century, by nearly every
new nation of Latin America, and not one of them remained consistently
free. In North America, constitutional balances worked only because they
were supplemented by a powerful mythic tradition, expounded in story,
song, and now virtually every Hollywood film, that any undue accumulation of power should be looked on with concern.

Above all, we are encouraged to distrust government.

The late Karl Popper pointed out the importance of this mythology in
the dark days during and after World War II, in *The Open Society and Its Enemies*. Only by insisting on accountability, he concluded, can we constantly
remind public servants that they *are* servants. It is also how we maintain
some confidence that merchants aren't cheating us, or that factories aren't
poisoning the water. As inefficient and irascibly noisy as it seems at times,
this habit of questioning authority ensures freedom far more effectively than
any of the older social systems that were based on reverence or trust.

And yet, another paradox rears up every time one interest group tries to
hold another accountable in today's society.

> *Whenever a conflict arises between privacy and accountability,*
> *people demand the former for themselves and the latter*
> *for everybody else.*

The rule seems to hold in almost every realm of modern life, from special prosecutors investigating the finances of political figures to worried
parents demanding that lists of sex offenders be made public. From merchants anxious to see their customers' credit reports to clients who resent
such snooping. From people who "need" caller ID to screen their calls to
those worried that their lives might be threatened if they lose telephone
anonymity. From activists demanding greater access to computerized government records in order to hunt patterns of corruption or incompetence
in office to other citizens who worry about the release of personal information contained in those very same records.

Recent years have witnessed widespread calls to "empower" citizens
and corporations with tools of encryption—the creation of ciphers and secret codes—so that the Internet and telephone lines may soon fill with a
blinding fog of static and concealed messages, a haze of habitual masks and
routine anonymity. Some of society's best and brightest minds have begun
extolling a coming "golden age of privacy," when no one need ever again
fear snooping by bureaucrats, federal agents, or in-laws. The prominent
iconoclast John Gilmore, who favors "law 'n' chaos over law 'n' order," re-

cently proclaimed that computers are literally extensions of our minds, and that their contents should therefore remain as private as our inner thoughts. Another activist, John Perry Barlow, published a widely discussed "Declaration of Independence for Cyberspace" proclaiming that the mundane jurisdictions of nations and their archaic laws are essentially powerless and irrelevant to the Internet and its denizens (or "netizens"). Among the loose clan of self-proclaimed "cypherpunks," a central goal is that citizens should be armed with broad new powers to conceal their words, actions, and identities. The alternative, they claim, will be for all our freedoms to succumb to a looming tyranny.

In opposing this modern passion for personal and corporate secrecy, I should first emphasize that I *like* privacy! Outspoken eccentrics need it, probably as much or more than those who are reserved. I would find it hard to get used to living in either of the cities described in the example at the beginning of this chapter. But a few voices out there have begun pointing out the obvious. Those cameras on every street corner are coming, as surely as the new millennium.

Oh, we may agitate and legislate. But can "privacy laws" really prevent hidden eyes from getting tinier, more mobile, and clever? In software form they will cruise the data highways. "Antibug" technologies will arise, but the resulting surveillance arms race can hardly favor the "little guy." The rich, the powerful, police agencies, and a technologically skilled elite will always have an advantage.

In the long run, as author Robert Heinlein prophesied years ago, will the chief effect of privacy laws simply be to "make the bugs smaller"?

The subtitle of this book—*Will Technology Force Us to Choose Between Privacy and Freedom?*—is intentionally provocative. As we'll see, I think such a stark choice can be avoided. It may be possible to have both liberty and some shelter from prying eyes.

But suppose the future *does* present us with an absolute either-or decision, to select just one, at the cost of the other. In that case, there can be no hesitation.

Privacy is a highly desirable *product* of liberty. If we remain free and sovereign, we may have a little privacy in our bedrooms and sanctuaries. As citizens, we'll be able to demand some.

But accountability is no side benefit. It is the one fundamental ingredient on which liberty thrives. Without the accountability that derives from openness—enforceable upon even the mightiest individuals and institutions—how can freedom survive?

In the information age to come, cameras and databases will sprout like poppies—or weeds—whether we like it or not. Over the long haul, we as a people must decide the following questions:

*Can we stand living exposed to scrutiny, our secrets laid open,
if in return we get flashlights of our own that we can shine on
anyone who might do us harm—even the arrogant and strong?*

*Or is an illusion of privacy worth any price, even the cost of surrendering our own right to pierce the schemes of the powerful?*

There are no easy answers, but asking questions can be a good first step.

## THE PRIVACY WE ALREADY HAVE

Much of this chapter up to now appeared earlier as a published article and has since been perused online by interested parties around the globe. Their varied comments opened my eyes to a wide range of opinions about freedom, privacy, and candor. From philosophers to steelworkers, it seems that each person views such things differently. Especially privacy, which, like the fabled elephant fondled by a dozen blind sages, is described uniquely by each beholder.

Even legal scholars cannot agree what the word means. American judicial rulings tend to treat privacy as a highly subjective and contingent commodity, a matter of trade-offs and balanced interests, whereas freedom of speech and freedom of the press are defended with sweeping judgments of broad generality. Some reasons for this difference will be discussed in chapter 3, where privacy is examined from many angles and shown to be the exquisite desideratum that it is. Indeed, without some privacy, we could scarcely function as humans. A chief aim of this book is to explore whether—and how much—privacy can be safeguarded in a coming era of cameras and databases.

Alas, although it seems intuitive to protect privacy by erecting *barriers* to information flow, there may be good reason to question that assumption. Although I shall put off a more involved discussion until later, let me briefly illustrate with a restaurant analogy.

We all know it is possible to be alone, or hold intimate conversations, in a public place. It bothers people to be stared at, especially while eating, yet we dine in crowded restaurants all the time, fairly secure that most of the eyes surrounding us aren't looking our way, at least not very often. We don't achieve this confidence by wearing masks, or because laws require other customers to wear blinkers and blindfolds. Mutual civility and common decency play a role, but not alone.

An added factor that helps deter people from staring is *not wanting to be caught in the act.* The embarrassment accrued by a voyeur caught observing you is greater than your chagrin at being seen by the voyeur with asparagus in your teeth. Open visibility seems to favor defense over offense.

All right, it's not perfect, but it works overall.

Now suppose we try to improve things by passing laws and sending forth regulators with clipboards commanding all restaurants to erect a maze of paper *shoji* screens to keep customers from ogling other patrons. Will this prevent people from staring, or encourage them? Without any plausible likelihood of getting caught, might voyeurs use technology, in this case poking tiny holes, to penetrate the "protective" curtain? No longer deterred, could peepers stare with impunity?

The restaurant analogy is just a thought experiment. But it suggests that there is no dichotomy between accountability and privacy. Rather, you may need one to get the other.

## WHAT LIES AHEAD

We must cover important ground before getting to the kernel of the argument over transparency. So chapter 2 begins by comparing the bright new information age with other highly vaunted "eras" that left disappointment in their wake. Cynical observers already predict the same demise for the swaggering epoch of silicon and electrons, yet new cybernetic tools *may* help bring a time of unprecedented opportunity, assisting hard-pressed humanity with pragmatic solutions to many vexing problems.

Chapters 3 and 4 explore the nature and practical limits of privacy, how it is perceived by the law, and the looming question of whether information is a commodity that can be owned, focusing especially on the role of copyright protection to promote openness and creativity.

Ultimately, the big choices must be made by citizens, who will either defend their freedom or surrender it, as others did in the past. Chapter 5 examines some peculiar traits of neo-Western civilization, a quirky and amorphous global super society that fosters eccentricity and ego the way other cultures have extolled obedience or physical courage. Chapter 6 then considers how lessons of accountability may apply to everyone from cops to social rebels, as we learn to "watch the watchmen."

Along the way, in secondary interludes following each numbered chapter, we will take a look at several topics of survival in the information age, including the worrisome problems of photographic fakery and computerized extortion, as well as the ongoing question of whether we should concentrate on ideals, or on what works.

(End notes, references, and supplementary material for each chapter can be found in a section at the back of this book.)

Chapter 7 gets into "nitty gritty" issues concerning encryption (secret codes) and anonymity, two prescriptions that are highly touted by some of society's best and brightest cyberphilosophers. Chapter 8 covers some pragmatic problems, such as the controversy concerning names, passwords, Social Security numbers, and national ID cards.

Any honest person must consider the possibility that he or she might be mistaken, so chapter 9 is where I do that. Among other things, I discuss whether mathematicians think encryption can really offer security against data spying by the biggest government computers. The chapter also covers a range of possible ways in which "transparency" might turn into a nightmare, especially if my sanguine views of the advantages turn out to be wrong.

Finally, chapters 10 and 11 will expand the context of discussion to encompass the security of global civilization, pondering whether we at last have the tools to avoid the errors that toppled so many societies in the past.

But first, let's consider the nature of open societies.

## THE GHOST OF PERICLES

We live in a time that spills over with contradictions. Extraordinary wealth gushes alongside grinding poverty. Episodes of horrific bloodshed contrast starkly with unprecedented stretches of peace, in which billions of living human beings have never personally experienced war. Within a single life span we've seen great burgeonings of freedom—and the worst tyrannies of all time. To find another era with as dramatic a range of highs and lows, you might go back twenty-five centuries, when another "golden age" posed towering hopes against cynicism and despair.

Like the world of today, classical Athens featured profound bursts of creativity in science, culture, and the arts. But above all, the vision we tend to retain is that city's brief adventure in democracy, a brave experiment that lasted just a little while and would not be tried again in a big way for two millennia.

Even staunch fans of Athenian democracy admit it was imperfect by present-day standards; for instance, women, slaves, and those not born in the city had few rights. Yet its relative egalitarianism was impressive in an age of hereditary chiefdoms and arbitrary potentates. Across centuries of darkness, from that democracy to this one, the lonely voice of Pericles spoke for an open society, where citizens are equal before the law and where influence is apportioned *"not as a matter of privilege, but as a reward for merit; and poverty is not a bar. . . ."*

The virtues of this notion may seem obvious to modern readers. Today, citizens of many nations—those that I call neo-Western—assume that principles of equality and human rights are fundamental, even axiomatic (though they are often contentious to implement in practice).

So it can be surprising to learn just how rare this attitude was, historically. In fact, Pericles and his allies were roundly derided by contemporary scholars. Countless later generations of intellectuals and oligarchs called democracy an aberration, ranking it among the *least* important products of the Athenian golden age. Even during the Italian Renaissance, Niccolo Machiavelli had to mask his sympathy for representative government between the lines of *The Prince,* in order to please his aristocratic sponsors. After Athens's flickering candle blew out during the Peloponnesian War (431–403 B.C.E.), none was more eager to cheer the demise of democracy than Plato, the so-called father of Western philosophy. He wrote:

> The greatest principle of all is that nobody should be without a leader. Nor should the mind of anybody be habituated to do anything at all on his own initiative; neither out of zeal, nor even playfully. . . . In a word, he should teach his soul, by long habit, never to dream of acting independently, and to become utterly incapable of it.

Partly due to the influence of Plato and his followers—and for reasons discussed in chapter 5 of this book—the democratic experiment was not tried again on a large scale until the era of Locke, Jefferson, and Madison.

We all know in our hearts that freedom cannot survive such assaults, unless it is defended by much more than good intentions. For a time, in the middle of the twentieth century, it looked as if the Athenian tragedy might happen again, when constitutional governments seemed about to be overwhelmed by despots and ideologues. Writing under the shadow of Hitler, and later Stalin, Karl Popper began *The Open Society and Its Enemies* by appraising the relentless hatred for empiricism and democracy that Plato passed on through his followers all the way to Hegel—a philosophical heritage of self-serving, tendentious incantations (or "reasoning") whose hypnotic rhythms were enthusiastically adapted by innumerable rulers, from Hellenistic despots to Marxist-Leninist commissars, many of them using contorted logic to justify their unchecked power over others.

Looking back from the 1990s, when democracy seems strong—though hardly triumphant—we can only imagine how delicate freedom must have seemed to Popper, George Orwell, Aldous Huxley, and others writing in the 1940s and 1950s. Did they feel the ghost of Pericles hovering over their shoulders as they worked? Would the candle blow out yet again?

Scanning history, those writers could see only a few other brief oases of relative liberty—the Icelandic Althing, some Italian city-states, the Iroquois Confederacy, and perhaps a couple of bright moments during the Roman Republic, or the Baghdad Caliphate—surrounded by vast eras when the social pyramid in every land was dominated by conspiracies of privilege. Ruling elites varied widely in their superficial trappings. Some styled themselves as kings or oligarchs, while others were priests, bureaucrats, merchant princes, or "servants of the people." But nearly all used similar methods to justify and secure the accumulation and monopolization of privilege.

One paramount technique was to control the flow of information. Tyrants were always most vulnerable when those below could see and hear the details of power and statecraft.

Today, the light appears much stronger than in Popper's day, and new technologies such as the Internet seem about to enhance the sovereign authority of citizens even further. Yet the problem remains as fundamental and worrisome as ever: *What measures can we take to ensure that freedom, instead of being a rare exception, will become the normal, natural, and stable condition for ourselves and our descendants?*

In fairness, this same unease motivates many of those who oppose the notion of a "transparent society." They share the apprehension Orwell conveyed so chillingly in *Nineteen Eighty-Four*: that freedom may vanish unless people promptly and vigorously oppose the forces that threaten it. So from the start, let me say to them that we are not arguing about goals, but rather the best means to achieve them.

That still leaves room for disagreement, for instance, over whether the sole peril originates from national governments, or whether dangerous power centers may arise from any part of the sociopolitical landscape. Moreover, we differ over which tools will best help stave off tyranny. Metaphorically speaking, some very bright people suggest that citizens of the twenty-first century will be best protected by masks and shields, while I prefer the image of a light saber.

These glib metaphors may cue readers that I won't be presenting an erudite or academic tome on the same level as Popper's *The Open Society and Its Enemies*, and that is certainly true. I shall not claim to prove or demolish any broad social rules. Above all, this book does not push an absurd overgeneralization that candor is always superior to secrecy! Only that transparency is *underrepresented* in today's fervid discussions about privacy and freedom in the information age. My sole aim is to stir some fresh ideas into the cauldron.

If we have learned anything during the hard centuries since Pericles and his allies tried to light a flickering beacon in the night, it is that we owe our hard-won freedom and prosperity to an empirical tradition—in science, free markets, and the rough-tumble world of democracy. Only mathematicians can "prove" things using pen and paper. The rest of us have to take our ideas pragmatically into the real world and see what works.

In other words, this is not a book of grand prescriptions (though some suggestions are offered). I plan chiefly to discuss underutilized tools of openness and light that have served us well in the past.

## STRONG PRIVACY

Before getting to those suggestions, we need to establish some context about today's public debate over privacy. In keeping with the theme of this book, I rank the players and their arguments according to what effect their proposals would have on the flow of information in society.

Take Megan's Law, for example. Under a 1994 U.S. federal mandate, all fifty states have begun publishing registers of sexual offenders, which will lead eventually to a nationwide database. California provides this information on a CD-ROM disk that can be viewed at most police head-quarters, letting parents, school officials, and other interested parties survey over 65,000 names (and many photos) for "potential molesters" who may live or work in their area. Activists supporting this system portray it as a way to ensure accountability in an area of life where a single mistake can lead to tragedy.

Foes of the measure, including the American Civil Liberties Union (ACLU), claim that the rights of former prisoners are violated by this registry, which can be regarded as a nonjudicial additional penalty slapped onto the sentences of convicts who have already paid their debt to society. Opponents also cite anecdotes in which individuals suffered because they were erroneously listed, showing that innocents can be harmed by hastily and overzealously opening spigots of potentially faulty data.

As far as this book is concerned, the relative merits of Megan's Law are not at issue. Rather, this struggle simply serves to illustrate two opposing traits that appear in countless other modern privacy disputes.

> **A.** *One party believes that another group is inherently dangerous, and that its potential to do harm is exacerbated by secrecy. Therefore, accountability must be forced upon that group through enhanced flow of information.*
>
> **B.** *The other party argues that some vital good will be threatened by heightened candor, and hence wants the proposed data flow shut down.*

Watch for this pattern as we go along. We shall see that it is almost ubiquitous when people take a stand on knowledge disputes. In chapter 7, for instance, we'll discuss many and varied "Clipper" proposals that have been floated by the FBI and other federal agencies concerned about the potential of data and voice encryption to conceal criminal or terrorist activities behind a static haze. Officials worry that widespread use of electronic ciphers will thwart traditional surveillance techniques, such as court-ordered wiretaps, enabling dangerous villains to conspire in security and secrecy. They want to retain the level of vision and accountability that they traditionally held in an era of crude analog phone lines.

A coalition of groups, including the Electronic Frontier Foundation (EFF) and the Electronic Privacy Information Center (EPIC), joined numerous journalists and private persons to lambaste the Clipper proposals, depicting them as encroachments by government on freedom and privacy in cyberspace. Often, they couched the threat in dramatic terms, as the opening move in a trend toward a Big Brother dictatorship. In any event, they point out that the FBI seeks a data flow enhancement that would go just one way, *to* government officials.

In this example, the FBI's proposal fits pattern A, while their adversaries fill position B. But these roles are often reversed! Take the ongoing struggle faced by anyone seeking documents from a federal agency under the Freedom of Information Act (FOIA). Although many officials are forthcoming and cooperative, others react with hostility against any attempt to enforce accountability. They drag their feet, cite national security, and sometimes use privacy concerns to justify noncompliance.

It can be fascinating to watch the very same players take turns performing roles A and B, without any apparent awareness of irony or inconsistency. Some groups justify this conditional attitude toward information flow by assuming that government will always and automatically be wrong, whether it is trying to open a data spigot or attempting to close one down.

The same pattern can be seen in other areas of modern society. For instance, when a corporation starts spying on its employees, tracking every computer keystroke, timing each phone call, reading everyone's e-mail, and logging trips to the bathroom, managers justify these actions as essential for efficient conduct of business and to ensure staff accountability. Opponents decry such practices as violating basic human rights, calling for a shutdown of the offensive data flow.

Those same opponents then turn around and file suit to force release of proprietary company documents—for the public good, of course—seeking to widen the particular spigot that they choose.

These issues will all be discussed later. I am not making value judgments at this point, only noting a consistent pattern that will help us explore why we often take one-sided positions, self-righteously demanding far more openness from our opponents than we want applied to ourselves.

Matters of privacy, accountability, and freedom are often judged first and foremost on the basis of whose ox is being gored.

In the following chapters, I use a catch-all phrase, "strong privacy advocates," to label those who are most outspoken against "transparency." From the start, let me state that this term oversimplifies a wide range of groups and individuals. For instance, many ACLU members do not share the generalized antipathy toward government that is a common premise of "cypherpunk" activists like Hal Finney and Tim May. Although liberals and libertarians both see themselves staunchly combating dire threats to freedom, they often find themselves vigilantly facing in opposite directions.

As we'll see later, the prescriptions proposed by those I put in this camp also cover a wide range. For instance, some groups like the ACLU lobby for new legislation to prevent misuse of private data by corporations and snooping government agencies. This is sometimes called the "European model," since members of the European Union have been extremely active in setting up rules and regulations to govern who has the right to collect, withhold, or control the use of personal information. At one extreme of this trend are those who demand legal recognition that individuals have a basic right of ownership over any and all data about themselves: no one should be able to use any fact or datum concerning you—not even your name—without your explicit permission.

Supporting a quite different approach are some of the most vivid and original thinkers of the information age. John Gilmore, Esther Dyson, John Perry Barlow, and others on the (roughly) libertarian wing were in the vanguard fighting against both the Clipper proposal and the Communications Decency Act. Seeing little need or value in new laws, they hold that technology will be a key factor in defending liberty during the coming era. Fresh tools of encryption and electronic anonymity will protect individuals against intrusive spying by others, and especially by the state. What they demand, therefore, is that government stand back and not interfere as a myriad anonymous personae and enciphered secrets throng across the dataways.

Taking this attitude to far greater extremes are the "anarcho" libertarians, such as financier Walter Wriston, who take pleasure in predicting a virtual end to all government, opening an age of unbridled and anonymity-shrouded individualism.

Straddling the cypherpunks and lobbyists are some of the newer online privacy groups, for example, EPIC and the Center for Democracy and Technology, which support crypto-technologies while still seeking to influence laws and regulations, a mix that sometimes leaves them seeming to pull in two directions at once. Others, like the Privacy Rights Clearinghouse (PRC), emphasize a strictly pragmatic approach. A book by PRC project director Beth Givens offers copious practical advice about how "little guys" can use today's legal protections to take some control of their credit ratings, their medical records, or whether their names will proliferate endlessly across countless irritating mailing lists.

This short compilation leaves out many other players, but it is enough to illustrate a single trait shared by all, the belief that modern concerns about freedom and privacy can often be solved by some specific or general reduction in the flow of information, or by making the stream flow in just one direction. Whether they advocate new laws, technologies, or practical savvy, each would empower people and groups to conceal things. For want of a better term, "strong privacy" will have to do.

In fact, I admire many of these advocates for their intelligence, passion, and concern. We would all be a lot worse off if they weren't out there, pitching their ideas.

In some cases, they are probably right.

But there is another side to the issue. One that needs to be heard.

## OTHER VOICES

I am not the only one speaking for transparency, the notion that we may all benefit by carefully *increasing* two-way information flows. In addition to the names mentioned earlier in this chapter, some others should be noted.

Jack Stack, already a business legend for transforming his manufacturing company from red ink to splendid profitability, hit best-seller lists in the mid-1990s with his book *The Great Game of Business: Unlocking the Power and Profitability of Open-Book Management,* in which he advocates letting all of a company's employees view the ledgers. By welcoming input and oversight from every level, he claims, managers profit from a much wider pool of criticism and good ideas. This doesn't mean giving up executive authority, but it does engender in staff at all levels a sense of personal identification with team success—even when the "team" consists of several thousand employees. Stack's simple argument shrugs aside all theory. He makes no pretensions to ideology. His basis for open-book management is pragmatic. It works in good times, and especially well in hard times. It is a formula for success.

Unfortunately, as we'll see in chapter 5, it takes maturity and willpower for any kind of authority figure to loosen the reins of control, even when doing so clearly serves the greater good. Despite the popularity of his book, Stack is swimming against powerful currents of human nature.

On the other hand, didn't I just spend the first half of this chapter implying that transparency is inevitable?

Late in this book, we'll examine whether any single scenario about tomorrow seems compellingly likely. Personally, I think the jury is still out. But there is one celebrated author who contends that our fate has already been decided. According to cartoonist-humorist Scott Adams, we are destined for a world of universal vision, whether we like it or not. In *The Dilbert Future,* Adams offers a look at the next century that is at once both earnest and bitingly sardonic. Exploring many of the same themes as this book—for instance, the notion that professional news reporters will be replaced by swarms of amateurs with cameras—Adams takes into account likely breakthroughs such as ubiquitous video, DNA matching, and cybernetic scent-bloodhounds before reaching the following conclusion:

> *"In the future, new technology will allow the police to solve 100 percent of all crimes. The bad news is that we'll realize 100 percent of the population are criminals, including the police."*

Adams then makes the hilarious extrapolation that every human on the planet will eventually land in jail for minor crimes, except the world's smartest person who, since she was too clever to get caught, must thereafter bear the tax burden of supporting everyone else in prison, forever. Like Mark Twain and other great humorists, Adams uses outrageous exaggeration to raise serious issues—in this case how we may respond when our smallest peccadilloes become public knowledge. Will we become a society of frantic finger-pointers and blamers? Or might we learn to "chill out" when everyone realizes that people who live in glass houses are unwise to cast stones?

At the opposite end of the "seriousness" spectrum from Adams, we find Dartmouth physicist Arthur Kantrowitz and philanthropist-investor George Soros, who have taken up the cause Karl Popper championed a generation ago and are campaigning that an "open society" is healthiest when it lives up to its name. Both men have been vigorous in promoting the notion that free speech and transparency are not only good but absolutely essential for maintaining a free, creative, and vigorous civilization.

Kevin Kelly, executive editor of *Wired* magazine, expressed the same idea with the gritty clarity of information-age journalism: "The answer to the whole privacy question is more knowledge. More knowledge about who's watching you. More knowledge about the information that flows between us—particularly the meta-information about who knows what and where it's going."

In other words, we may not be able to eliminate the intrusive glare shining on citizens of the next century, but the glare just might be rendered harmless through the application of more light aimed in the other direction. Nor is Kelly alone in this opinion among cyber-era luminaries. Even some of the bright people I labeled earlier as "strong privacy advocates"— Esther Dyson and John Perry Barlow, for instance—have publicly mused that transparency might be preferable, if only it could somehow be made to work. Said Barlow: "I have no secrets myself, and I think that everybody would be a lot happier and safer if they just let everything be known. Then, nobody could use anything against them. But this is not the social norm at the moment."

If transparency is the requisite condition in science, democracy, and free markets, it should come as no surprise that economists—who work at the nexus of all three—find openness appealing. Many economists now lean toward attributing most kinds of injustice, bureaucracy, and societal inefficiency to *asymmetric information flows*—where one person or group knows something that others don't. Pick an institution, and these economists will talk about how the structure was chosen in response to some information-related problem. When they examine causes of "market failures" (things that make simple markets handle problems poorly) these experts list uneven knowledge right at the top. Other reasons, such as lack of complete competition, inability to commit, public goods, and externalities, would be relatively easy to fix, via either contracts or politics, if we all had symmetric information.

"In that case," says Robin Hanson, an economist at the University of California, Berkeley, "we'd each know how much we expect to gain or lose in a change. We could negotiate such changes in ways that made everyone feel better off than before."

Hanson cites the following familiar problems: *war*, caused by one side guessing wrong about the other's power or determination; *lack of trade*, often due to buyers' unwillingness to admit how much they want something; *going to trial*, like war, attributed to misreading what the other side would settle for; *law enforcement*, costly and overbearing because the police don't know who did what crimes; *status consumerism*, buying visible but less valuable goods to show others that we can; *the collapse of mutually beneficial negotiations*, being afraid that someone else knows something we don't, and if they agree to a proposal, it must be because it favors them in some way we haven't realized; *monopoly*, causing losses because the monopolist can't discriminate price perfectly and charge each person what it's worth to them; and *rat races*, working too hard to convince employers that we really want success. All of these problems arise because of limited or restricted information flows. With improved knowledge on all sides, many governmental and nongovernmental organizations might lose their purpose, lose their constituencies, and possibly fade away.

Caltech professor John O. Ledyard points out that "asymmetric information conveys a monopoly position on the holder of the information that markets cannot easily overcome."

Although they generally favor transparency, economists warn that information flows should be opened up *evenly*, lest one side or another gain unfair advantage during the transition—a gradualist approach that is supported throughout this book.

Finally, there are groups and individuals who believe in action, rather than words, and providing the tools of transparency to those who need it most. For example, the Witness Program donates video equipment and training to human rights groups around the world, from Nigeria, Rwanda, and Bosnia to Guatemala and Haiti. According to Witness cofounder Peter Gabriel, "a camera in the right hands at the right time can be more powerful than tanks or guns. Let truth do the fighting." Other groups concentrate on U.S. inner cities, helping create neighborhood watch programs to combat both crime and unprofessional police practices. Meanwhile, Transparency International fights corruption by promoting open legal and business practices around the world.

All of these efforts are aimed at making things better by increasing, rather than decreasing, the flow of information and forging a path into the future that takes advantage of light, as if the right to *see* will be as vital tomorrow as the right to bear arms was yesterday. Nevertheless, they would have little chance of success without help from powerful social forces. Chapters 5 and 6 look at some trends in our strange, quirky civilization that lean strongly toward rambunctious openness. If transparency is not "inevitable," at least we are bound for interesting times.

## THE CONCERNS OF NORMAL PEOPLE

Theory is fine, but in the long run society's course will be determined by regular folks, whose concerns strike close to home. Here are some of the apprehensions expressed by people who have written to me.

> Is my boss recovering and reading all my deleted e-mail messages at work? Is my supervisor metering my coffee breaks?

> Will my medical records be shared with every insurance company and every employer I submit an application to? Might my *neighbors* somehow snoop the records of my therapist?

> I'm worried about my dossier, kept by some secretive credit bureau. How will reciprocal transparency protect me from the countless databases that already have my name and Social Security number?

> Can "openness" ever work both ways—applying equally against the powerful—in a world that's suddenly filled with cameras?

Finally, there is the message I received from one woman reflecting a somewhat different perspective.

> I don't care so much about privacy. What have I got to hide that would interest anybody? And even if they did learn everything about me, why should I care? No, what bothers me is the same kinds of things that fret most of the people I know. My family's

safety, with crime all over. Not knowing or having any say in what's happening each day to my kid in school, if he's being beaten up or offered drugs. If I'm being robbed by the companies and politicians, or if some maniac is going to swerve around the next corner at ninety and splatter my brains. We live in "gated-community" prisons, afraid of strangers, afraid to let our kids play in the street. Ask me what I'd trade, to have these worries lifted off of me!

All our fancy social speculations won't matter if we can't address the concerns of people like this, who feel beleaguered enough to talk about "trading" something for more security, or a little less fear. Later, we'll talk more about this notion of *trade-offs*, one of the most insidious, troubling logical fallacies of our day, the widely held idea that danger is a *price* we all must pay for freedom. For now, let me just say that I won't exchange my liberty—or anyone else's—for security. I surely won't give up essential privacy: of home, hearth, and the intimacy that one shares with just a few.

But that is a far cry from maintaining a so-called right to skulk in shadows and act against others anonymously—a fictitious right that shelters nearly all the predators who make this a wary, suspicious age, fueling both the growth of government and a rising obsession with personal safety.

Suspicions that may snuff out the bright hopes of a coming "infotopia."

So much for practicing what I preach: letting the reader know what to expect. I'll close this introductory chapter now with a final thought.

***It is hard for recent cave dwellers to transform themselves into smart, honest, and truly independent creatures of light.***

For millennia, philosophers have told us we could do it by *willing* ourselves to behave better, through faith, or by obedience to strict codes of conduct. Those prescriptions never worked well, not all by themselves, and they proved almost useless at thwarting truly malignant men bent on harming others. But now, at last, we seem to have hit on a pragmatic tool more in keeping with our ornery natures.

Accountability.

All right, it still has some kinks to work out. We cave folk are new at this sort of thing—just a few centuries along the road of democracy, and only decades exploring diversity as a paramount virtue.

It's unclear, as yet, how far this road will take us. Nevertheless, one fact should grow apparent soon.

We'll all stumble a lot less if we can see where we are going.

# THE END OF PHOTOGRAPHY AS PROOF OF ANYTHING AT ALL

*There was once a kingdom where most people could not see. Citizens coped with this cheerfully, for it was a gentle land where familiar chores changed little from day to day.*

*Furthermore, about one person in a hundred did have eyesight! These specialists took care of jobs like policing, shouting directions, or reporting when something new was going on. The sighted ones weren't superior. They acquired vision by eating a certain type of extremely bitter fruit. Everyone else thanked them for undergoing this sacrifice, and so left the task of seeing to professionals. They went on with their routines, confident in a popular old saying.*

*"A sighted person never lies."*

• • •

One of the scariest predictions now circulating is that we are about to leave the era of photographic proof. For generations we relied on cameras to be the fairest of fair witnesses. Images of the Earth from space helped millions become more devoted to its care. Images from Vietnam made countless Americans less gullible and more cynical. Miles of footage taken at Nazi concentration camps confirmed history's greatest crimes. A few seconds of film shot in a Dallas plaza in November 1963 set the boundary conditions for a nation's masochistic habit of scratching a wound that never heals.

Although there have been infamous photographic-fakes—trick pictures that convinced Sir Arthur Conan Doyle there were real "fairies" and Mary

Todd Lincoln that her husband's ghost hovered over her, or the ham-handedly doctored images that Soviet leaders used to erase "nonpersons" from official history—for the most part scientists and technicians have been able to expose forgeries by magnifying and revealing the inevitable traces that meddling left behind.

But not anymore, say some experts. We are fast reaching the point where expertly controlled computers can adjust an image, pixel by microscopic pixel, and not leave a clue behind. Much of the impetus comes from Hollywood, where perfect verisimilitude is demanded for on-screen fictions and fabulations like *Forrest Gump* and *Jurassic Park*. Yet some thoughtful film wizards worry how these technologies will be used outside the theaters.

"History is kind of a consensual hallucination," said director James Cameron recently. He went on to suggest that people wanting to prove that some event really happened might soon have to track closely the "pedigree" of their photographic evidence, showing they retained possession at all stages, as with blood samples from a crime scene.

•    •    •

*One day a rumor spread across the kingdom. It suggested that some of the sighted were no longer faithfully telling the complete truth. Shouted directions sometimes sent normal blind people into ditches. Occasional harsh laughter was heard.*

*Several of the sighted came forward and confessed that things were worse than anyone feared. "Some of us appear to have been lying for quite a while. A few even think it's funny to lead normal blind people astray!*

*"This power is a terrible temptation. You will never be able to tell which of us is lying or telling the truth. Even the best of the sighted can no longer be trusted completely."*

•    •    •

The new technologies of photographic deception have gone commercial. For instance, a new business called Out Takes recently set up shop next to Universal Studios, in Los Angeles, promising to "put you in the movies." For a small fee they will insert your visage in a *tête-à-tête* with Humphrey Bogart or Marilyn Monroe, exchanging either tense dialogue or a romantic moment. This may seem harmless on the surface, but the long-range possibilities disturb Ken Burns, innovative director of the famed public television series *The Civil War*. "If everything is possible, then nothing is true. And that, to me, is the abyss we stare into. The only weapon we might have, besides some internal restraint, is skepticism." Skepticism may then further transmute into cynicism, Burns worries, or else, in the arts, into decadence. To which NBC reporter Jeff Greenfield added: "Skepticism may itself come with a very high price. Suppose we can no longer trust the evidence of our own eyes to know that something momentous, or something horrible, actually happened?"

There are some technical "fixes" that might help a little—buying special sealed digital cameras, for instance, that store images with time-stamped and encrypted watermarks. But as we'll see in chapter 8, that solution may be temporary, at best. Nor will it change the basic problem, as photography ceases to be our firm anchor in a sea of subjectivity.

•   •   •

*This news worried all the blind subjects of the kingdom. Some kept to their homes. Others banded together in groups, waving sticks and threatening the sighted, in hopes of ensuring correct information. But those who could see just started disguising their voices.*

*One faction suggested blinding everybody, permanently, in order to be sure of true equality—or else setting fires to shroud the land in a smoky haze. "No one can bully anybody else, if we're all in the dark," these enthusiasts urged.*

*As time passed, more people tripped over unexpected objects, or slipped into gullies, or took a wrong path because some anonymous voice shouted "left!" instead of right.*

•   •   •

At first, the problem with photography might seem just as devastating to transparency as to any other social "solution." If cameras can no longer be trusted, then what good are they? How can open information flows be used to enforce accountability on the mighty, if anyone with a computer can change images at will? A spreading mood of dour pessimism was lately distilled by Fred Richtien, professor of photography and multimedia at New York University: "The depth of the problem is so significant that in my opinion it makes, five or ten years down the road, the whole issue of democracy at question, because how can you have an informed electorate if they don't know what to believe and what not to believe?"

•   •   •

*Then, one day, a little blind girl had an idea. She called together everybody in the kingdom and made an announcement.*
*"I know what to do!" she said.*

•   •   •

Sometimes a problem seems vexing, till you realize that you were looking at it the wrong way all along. This is especially true about the "predicament" of doctored photographs and video images. We have fallen into a habit of perceiving pictures as unchanging *documents,* unique and intrinsically valid in their own right. To have that accustomed validity challenged is unnerving, until you realize that *the camera is not a court stenographer, archivist, or notary public. It is an extension of our eyes. Photographs are just another kind of memory.*

So cameras can now lie? Photographs can deceive? So what? *People* have been untrustworthy for a very long time, and we've coped. Not perfectly. But there are ways to deal with liars.

*First,* remember who fooled you before. Track their credibility, and warn others to beware. "Your basis cannot be looking at the reality of the photograph," says Andrew Lippman, associate director of the Massachusetts Institute of Technology (MIT) Media Lab. "Your basis . . . has to be in the court of trust."

*Second,* in a world where anyone can bear false witness, try to make damn sure there are *lots* of witnesses!

•   •   •

*"Here," said the little girl, pushing bitter fruit under the noses of her parents and friends, who squirmed and made sour faces.*

*"Eat it," she insisted. "Stop whining about liars and go see for yourselves."*

•   •   •

In real life, the "bitter fruit" is realizing that we must all share responsibility for keeping an eye on the world. People know that others tell untruths. Even when they sincerely believe their own testimony, it can be twisted by subconscious drives or involuntary misperceptions. Detectives have long grown used to the glaring omissions and bizarre embellishments that often warp eyewitness testimony.

So? Do we shake our heads and announce the end of civilization? Or do we try to cope by bringing in *additional* testimony? Combing the neighborhood for more and better witnesses.

One shouldn't dismiss or trivialize the severe problems that will arise out of image fakery. Without any doubt there will be deceits, injustices, and terrible slanders. Conspiracy theories will burgeon as never before when fanatics can doctor so-called evidence to support wild claims. Others will fabricate alibis, frame the innocent, or try to cover up crimes. "Every advance in communications has brought with it the danger of misuse," says Jeff Greenfield. "A hundred years ago, publishers brought out books of Abe Lincoln's speeches containing some words he never spoke. Hitler spread hate on the radio. But today's danger is different."

Greenfield is right. Today *is* different, because we have the power to make photographic forgery *less* worrisome.

Because even pathological liars tend not to lie when they face a high probability of getting caught.

Would we be tormenting ourselves over the Kennedy assassination today if fifty cameras had been rolling, instead of just poor Abraham Zapruder's? Suppose some passerby had filmed Nazi goons setting fire to the Reichstag in 1933. Might Hitler have been ousted, and thirty million lives saved? Maybe not, but the odds would have been better. In the future, thugs and provocateurs will never know for certain that their sneaking calumny won't be observed by a bystander or tourist, turning infrared optics toward those scurrying movements in the shadows.

We are all hallucinators to some degree. So now our beloved cameras may also prove faulty and prone to deception? At least they don't lie except when they are told to. It takes a deliberate act of meddling to alter most images in decisive ways. Cameras don't have imaginations, though their acuity is improving all the time. In fact, when their fields of view overlap, we can use them to check on each other. Especially if a wide range of people do the viewing and controlling.

As citizens, we shall deal with this problem the way members of an empirical civilization always have, by arguing and comparing notes, giving more credibility to the credible, and relying less on the anonymous or those who were caught lying in the past. Discerning truth, always a messy process, will be made more complex by these new, flawed powers of sight. But our consensual reality does not have to become a nightmare. Not when a majority of people contribute goodwill, openness, and lots of different points of view.

Again, *cameras are simply extensions of our eyes.*

If you're worried that some of them are lying, tradition offers an answer: more cameras.

We'll solve it by giving up the comforting blanket of darkness, opening up these new eyes, and sharing the world with six billion fellow witnesses.

CHAPTER TWO

# THE AGE OF
# KNOWLEDGE

*But all the conservatism in the world does
not afford even a token resistance to the
ecological sweep of the new electronic
media.*

MARSHALL MCLUHAN, *UNDERSTANDING MEDIA*

*Although only a few may originate a pol-
icy, we are all able to judge it.*

PERICLES OF ATHENS

## TRANSFORMING TECHNOLOGIES OF THE PAST AND FUTURE

Each human generation seems to have a fulcrum—a pivot around which
fateful transformations revolve. Often, this has less to do with the struttings
of kings and statesmen than with technology. We speak of Stone, Bronze,
and Iron Ages. There were eras of steam and coal. Some historians already
look back with nostalgia on the brief, glorious "petroleum century."

These epithets benefit from hindsight, but it is quite another thing to
speak accurately about the future. Shortly after the discovery of nuclear fission, enthusiasts gushed that the *atomic era* would produce energy too cheap
to meter. That promise fizzled, along with the early advent of a *space age*. Yet
pundits seem undeterred, always moving to the next glittering bauble.

Nowadays, yet another alluring, emblematic phrase heralds a new social epoch: "The Information Age." Almost daily, another book or article

appears, written by some modern Pangloss, forecasting unalloyed wonder in the years ahead. Electronic conduits will unite home, factory, and school to the digital assistant on your wrist. All the world's databases and libraries will merge into a universal network. Telecommuting will solve traffic jams and improve parenting. Barren shopping malls will be refitted to house the homeless, once we learn how convenient it is to roam digital catalogs, purchasing everything we need from the comfort of home.

Today's business pages fill with news of mergers as companies line up strategic partners—telephone companies with computer firms, cable television operators with movie studios, and so on—reorganizing like mad to compete in a century when knowledge will be the most precious commodity.

When it will be like money. Like power.

Even after putting aside the most extravagant hype, one cannot but be impressed with the pace of real events on the main express lane of the information superhighway: the Internet. Tens of millions of people have hooked up, with more signing on each day. All you need is a personal computer and a "portal" for your modem to dial. A small monthly fee grants you access to memory banks scattered around the globe. With appropriate software it is simple to point and click your way across the sea of information available on World Wide Web. Anyone can learn to navigate this ocean, whose exotic offerings range from ridiculous to the truly sublime.

- You can download satellite weather photos or space images from a NASA site, or stroll through museums on five continents, summoning digital renderings of paintings or relics.

- Physicians—and increasingly patients—routinely call up databases linking hospitals and medical schools that contain the latest information about disease, diagnosis, and treatment.

- The Human Genome Project maintains its catalog of *Homo sapiens* DNA on-line. Elsewhere in cyberspace, biologists list the family trees of all known animal and plant species.

- In just a year, the proportion of U.S. senators and representatives with Web pages went from single digits to nearly 100 percent. Countless agencies and officials exploit the new medium to communicate with clients and constituents. Most newly released government documents appear first on the Internet, then on paper.

- Businesses use globalized computer services: 24-hour customer assistance hotlines are answered in Ireland when it is late at night in North America because international telecommunications are now cheaper than paying overtime; contract programmers in India make overnight changes in databases and fix bugs in time for the following day's business in London and New York; Barbados has a flourishing data entry, medical transcription, and litigation support industry, receiving raw material by overnight courier and sending back finished products electronically.

Other services include electronic access to movie reviews and concert schedules, travel reservations, employment and self-help forums, merchandise catalogs, and online encyclopedias. Millions join discussion groups to confer about common interests, from feminism to medieval languages, from recipes to *Star Trek*, from esthetics to pornography. Some interactive fantasy games involve hundreds or thousands of individuals at a time, all immersed in ornate dungeon adventures or murder mysteries. Above all, millions exchange electronic mail (e-mail), conveying everything from terse notes to glossy documents and video, casting messages across oceans and continents at nearly the speed of light. With rapid binary voice transmission, some users even bypass traditional phone systems, holding cheap conversations over communication lines once designed to carry only computer programs.

Some parts of cyberspace are primly organized. Full-service companies such as Prodigy or America Online (AOL) might be likened to middle-class villages with tidy libraries, shopping malls, and friendly but firm cops on each corner. (Watch your language. No spitting, please.) In contrast, countless bulletin board systems operate out of private homes, offering sites dedicated to specific interests, passions, or perversions. These small outfits are like frontier trading posts scattered across a prairie, sometimes with a saloon attached. No rail or stagecoach access. Supply your own horse.

Local governments have joined the rush to go online. Systems pioneered by Cleveland and Santa Monica—letting residents read city council minutes, file complaints, or pore through the main library catalog—have spread with astonishing speed to a majority of cities in the nation.

Then there are the Big Boys. Like railroads in the 1870s, Microsoft, Pacific Bell, AmericaWest, AT&T, Time-Warner, and others hear the call of cash flowing through new conduits. They envision new toll roads, where money can be made the same way fortunes were built from the telegraph and telephone—by charging small amounts, trillions of times. Suddenly, the extensive physical rights of way owned by gas companies, cable television operators, electric utilities, and rail corporations have become incredibly valuable as paths for data transmission. Those lacking earthly rights of way scramble for alternatives, filling the sky with hordes of low-altitude relay satellites to offer a new era of wireless communication.

Finally, there is the Internet itself, sometimes grandly (but parochially) called the National Information Infrastructure (NII), which is in fact a nebulous, ill-defined thing, with traits unlike any commercial business or government institution. While its origin, core elements, and philosophical basis are American, the Internet has swiftly transcended national boundaries. Some liken it to an "interstate highway system" for information, but that analogy misses nearly all of the network's outstanding features. If other dataways are like villages, saloons, or railroads—dotting or crisscrossing a frontier—the Internet might be compared to the landscape itself. To the hills, streams, natural contours, and passing clouds.

Any effort to explore the concept of a transparent society should begin here. Not because the Internet is the revolutionary event of all time. Most of the transformations we will discuss in this book—for example, the proliferation of cheap video cameras, or the advent of perfect photographic fakery—would have happened anyway. Issues of privacy, openness, and accountability were already on the agenda, with or without the advent of computer networks. But the Internet has clearly multiplied the pace of change, bringing matters to a head much more rapidly. This may turn out to be a good thing, since it forces us to come to grips with the future now, instead of letting it come upon us in a shambling, deceptive crouch.

So in this chapter and the next, we will talk about *context*—how the stage was set for the quandaries and decisions we now face. Above all, we have to know what the Internet is, and where it came from.

Today's computer interconnection network has roots stretching back to 1945, when Vannevar Bush, who helped oversee the Manhattan Project, wrote an article entitled "As We May Think," claiming that scientific ingenuity in the postwar era should focus on new tools for thought. He called for a system of links and trails between islands of information—using text, images, and sound. Bush called the device performing this role a *memex*. Marc Andreesen, designer of Mosaic and Netscape, looks back upon Bush as a prophet who addressed "fundamental ideas we are still trying to realize today."

The Internet's earliest physical implementation began as an experiment to enhance the effectiveness of government scientists and engineers promoted by the U.S. Defense Advanced Research Projects Agency (DARPA) in the 1960s, when investigators used to ship crates of magnetic tape across the continent to the few computers with enough power to solve intricate technical models. Even a small error in software coding might take weeks of back-and-forth shuttling to fix. But visionaries foresaw a day when researchers in Berkeley might transmit programs by high-speed cable to a computer in Los Alamos, making corrections in real time. The experiment began with just four linked computers, around the time that men first walked on the moon.

DARPA had an ulterior motive in developing this valuable research tool. A motive that would fundamentally affect all the networks that followed, and perhaps alter society forever. Ironically, this fantastic device for peaceful rambunctiousness arose out of bloody-minded contemplations, then called "thinking about the unthinkable."

Pondering what to do during and after a nuclear war.

Back in 1964, Pentagon officials asked the Rand Corporation to imagine a transcontinental communication system that might stand a chance of surviving even an atomic cataclysm. Since every major telephone, telegraph, and radio junction would surely be targeted, generals were desperate for some way to coordinate with government, industry, and troops in the field, even after a first strike against U.S. territory.

Rand researcher Paul Baran found that such a survivable system was theoretically possible. It would be a *dispersed* entity, avoiding all the classic principles of communications infrastructure, such as central switching and control centers. Instead, Baran reasoned that a system robust enough to withstand mega-calamity ought to emulate the way early telephone companies proliferated across New York City a century ago, when wires were strung from lampposts to balconies and fire escapes. The early jumble of excess circuits and linkages seemed inefficient, and that chaotic phase passed swiftly as phone companies unified. But all those extra cables did offer one advantage. They ensured that whole chunks of the network could be (and often were) ripped or burned out, and calls could still be detoured around the damage.

In those days, long-distance call routing was a laborious task of negotiation, planned well in advance by human operators arranging connections from one zone to the next. But this drudgery might be avoided in a dispersed computer network if the *messages themselves* could navigate, finding their own way from node to node, carrying destination information in their lead bits like the address on the front of an envelope. Early theoretical work by Alan Turing and John Von Neumann hinted this to be possible by allowing each part of a network to guess the best way to route a message past any damaged area and eventually reach its goal. In theory, such a system might keep operating even when others lay in tatters.

In retrospect, the advantages of Baran's insight seem obvious. Still, it remains a wonder that the Pentagon actually went ahead with experiments in decentralized, autonomous message processing. Certainly the Soviets, despite having excellent mathematicians, never made a move to surrender hierarchical control. The image of authorities ceding mastery to independent, distributed "network nodes" contradicts our notion of how bureaucrats think. Yet this innovative architecture was given support at the highest levels of the U.S. establishment.

Why did generals and bureaucrats consent to establish a system that, by its nature, undermines rigid hierarchical authority? Whenever I ask this question, modern Internet aficionados answer that "they must not have realized where this would lead." But even early versions of the Internet showed its essential features: hardiness, flexibility, diversity, and resistance to tight regulation. A more reasonable hypothesis may be that some of those who consented to creating the nascent Internet were influenced by Vannevar Bush, and had an inkling that they were midwifing something that might ultimately distribute authority rather than concentrate it. The critical moment came when a decision was made to let private networks interconnect with the government's system. Steve Wolff of the National Science Foundation presided over this delicate era, as systems like Uunet, Csnet, and the anarchic Usenet linked up, taking matters beyond the point of no return.

Whether it was fostered by visionary thinking or pure serendipity, the chief "designer" of this astonishingly capable and flexible system has clearly been the system itself. Some even say it illustrates the post-Darwinian principle of "pre-adaptation," under which traits that served an organism for one purpose may emerge later as the basis for entirely new capabilities. (For example, the fins of some fish later became adapted as legs.) Indeed, the high autonomy of the Internet's many segments might be viewed as letting each node create its own micro-ecology of users, programs, and services. These then transact with others in ways that start to resemble the stochastic and competitive behaviors of organic life. None of it might have been possible in a hierarchically designed system.

Putting aside such extravagant speculations, we do know that a crucial decision to seek robustness, even at the cost of classical security and control, was to have consequences far beyond those early worries about nuclear conflict. In a great paradox of our time, the deep rifts dividing humanity during the Cold War ultimately led to a supremely open and connecting system. The same traits responsible for the Internet's hardiness in the face of physical destruction seem also to protect its happy chaos against attempts to impose rigorous discipline, a point illustrated in a popular aphorism by John Gilmore: "The Net perceives censorship as damage, and routes around it."

I plan to reconnect with this thought in later chapters, for it bears directly on the issue of a transparent society. Censorship can be seen as just one particular variant of secrecy. In the long run, the Internet and other new media may resist and defeat any attempt to restrict the free flow of information. While some hope to fill the Net's electronic corridors with anonymity and cryptic messages, they might find they are ultimately thwarted by the nature of the thing itself.

From humble beginnings, mighty entities grow. After the first crude network came online, more agencies tied into the embryonic ARPANET. The National Science Foundation (NSF), the National Aeronautics and Space Administration (NASA), and many universities added their own innovative structures. E-mail thronged alongside more formal data streams, as workers exchanged official and private messages, or set up niches of "cyberspace" to explore ideas beyond the limits of their study grants. Off-duty techs played midnight chess with colleagues half a world away. Discussion circles, or newsgroups, staked out a territory called Usenet, a vast informal zone where interested parties could roam at will, exchanging information, rumors, and argument. Official authority was never very clear on the growing Internet. In lieu of some rigid, controlling agency, ad hoc committees achieved consensus on standard communications protocols, such as the system of address designations assigned to each linked computer node.

Word eventually spread among people outside government and academe. Businesses and private citizens heard about a universe of sophisticated wonders that had been created by scholars, and clamored to be let in. Companies formed to act as gateways to the data cosmos. The Net explosion began. And with it, proclamations of a new age for humankind.

## PROJECTIONS OF CYBERNETIC PARADISE

Amid speculative talk of 1,500 channels on your television set, interactive movies, brain-to-computer links, and virtual reality, one can lose track of which predictions are tangible and which seem more like "vapor." Some very smart people can get swept up by hyperbole, as when John Perry Barlow, a cofounder of the Electronic Frontier Foundation, declared the Internet "the most important human advancement since the printing press." Barlow later recanted, calling it simply the most important discovery since *fire*. Nor was he the sole prophet acclaiming an egalitarian realm of unlimited opportunity for all, just around the corner.

As the number of users grows geometrically, some anticipate that by 2008 the Net might encompass the entire world population. In his 1993 book *Virtual Reality*, Howard Rheingold called for redefining the word *community*, since in the near future each sovereign individual may be able to sift among six or more billion souls, sorting by talent or avocation to find those compatible for consorting with at long range, via multimedia tele-presence, in voluntary associations of shared interest. No longer will geography or birth-happenstance determine your friendships, but rather a natural affinity of passions and pastimes.

Some pundits emphasize transnational features of an electronic world, predicting the end of the nation state. (See "A Withering Away?" after chapter 9.) Others proclaim the Internet a modern oracle, enabling simple folk to query libraries, databases, political organizations, or even corporate and university researchers, at last breaking the monopoly of "experts" and empowering multitudes with the same information used by the decision-making class. (See "A Century of Aficionados" later in this chapter.)

Projecting this transcendent imagery forward in time, science fiction author Vernor Vinge foresees computerized media leading to a cultural-technical "singularity." When each person can share all stored knowledge, and exchange new ideas instantly, every field may advance at exponential rates, leading to a kind of human deification, a concept elaborated by UCLA researcher Gregory Stock in *Metaman: The Merging of Humans and Machines into a Global Superorganism.*

This transcendent notion of apotheosis through technology is not new. It is illustrated by Benjamin Franklin's 1780 letter to the chemist Joseph Priestley. "The rapid progress true science now makes occasions my regretting sometimes that I was born so soon. It is impossible to imagine the heights to which may be carried, in a thousand years, the power of man over matter."

What might Old Ben have thought of his heirs' accomplishments in a mere quarter of that time?

Inevitably, all this gushing hype has led to a backlash. In a recent book, computer scientist Clifford Stoll coined the term "silicon snake oil" to describe the recent ecstatic forecasts about electronic media. Despite his background, Stoll urged skepticism toward the more extravagant arm waving of Net enthusiasts, whose high-tech razzle-dazzle may distract users from building relationships with the real people around them. Taking Stoll's objection further, University of California Professor Philip Agre warns that each major advance of the industrial age was associated with fits of transcendentalism, in which enthusiasts rushed eagerly to blur the distinction between themselves and the machines, and then between their favorite machinery and the world. (We mentioned earlier the fervor and disappointment that accompanied first nuclear fission and then space flight.) Agre says this peculiar mental aberration most often arises in bright, excitable males who, faced with complex social problems, seem drawn to miraculous solutions tinkered out of inanimate matter. Matter that is more easily understood than cantankerous, complex human beings.

At the opposite extreme, we see waves of *Luddite* reaction, featuring antitechnology tirades by people who see devils (or at least soullessness) in the machines and call fervently for a nostalgic return to "better" days.

Others foresee a danger of societal collapse resulting from our fragile, computer-dependent civilization falling prey either to some unexpected software glitch or to deliberate sabotage. This new era is especially rattling to the military and intelligence communities, for whom strict control of information used to be justified by a life-or-death need to retain their competitive advantage. The cultural transformation that these communities face in coming years will be all the more difficult, says strategic analyst Jeffery Cooper, "because the military must build its core competencies and forge its competitive advantages from tools that may be available to all." (See chapter 10.)

Is it possible to make sense out of these contrasting views—from brilliant to gloomy—about our electrified future? History certainly does warn us to be wary whenever a new communication technology arrives on the scene. While some seek to uplift humanity, others skillfully seize each innovation, applying it to the oldest of all magical arts—manipulating others.

Take the introduction of Gutenberg's working printing press, which ended the medieval control over literacy long held by the church and nobility. This invention liberated multitudes to shatter old constraints and sample provocative ideas. It also freed demagogues to cajole with new slanders, spread effectively via the printed word. According to James Burke, author of *Connections*, the chief short-term beneficiaries of printing turned out to be religious factionalism and nationalism. The following two centuries illustrated this, as Europe drifted into waves of unprecedentedly savage violence.

More recently, in Germany of the 1930s, *Junker* aristocrats thought they could control the firebrand Adolf Hitler because they owned the newspapers. They were mistaken. Nazis went *around* the press, reaching vastly greater masses with the hypnotizing power of radio and loudspeakers. To people freshly exposed, without the technological immunization that often comes with familiarity, these new media seemed to amplify a skilled user like Hitler, making him appear larger than life.

New communications technologies also have the potential to undermine authority. In prerevolutionary Iran, followers of the Ayatollah Khomeini bypassed the shah's monopoly over radio and television by smuggling into the country one audiocassette per week. Khomeini's sermon, soon duplicated a thousandfold, was played at Friday services in countless mosques, preparing for the storm to come.

Fax machines came close to serving the same insurrectionary function in China, during the Tian An Men uprising. A few years later, fax and Internet connections helped foil the 1991 attempted coup in the last days of the Soviet Union. Members of the old guard briefly tried to reinstate rigorous one-party rule by seizing central organs of communication, but found themselves neatly bypassed by new media.

Some effects go far beyond the merely political. Television plays no favorites, serving tyrants and educators alike, carrying both culture and propaganda, truth and lies, pandered drivel and deep insights. Innumerable nature programs have given urban citizens a better feel for ecological matters than their farmer ancestors who actually toiled on the land, thus boosting support for farsighted environmental policies. On the other hand, overuse of television effectively shortens the active life span of a sedentary "couch potato" by more years than he saves by voting for clean air laws.

So it often goes with the fruits of science. New communication arts prove at once both empowering and potentially manipulative of the common man or woman. As for the vaunted Internet, both messianic utopians and pessimistic critics may be missing the point. Amid all the abstract theorizing, why aren't we asking important, pragmatic questions, such as what will happen when personal computers become so cheap that citizens of the poorest Third World nations will have readier access to data than food or clean water?

We are bound for interesting times.

> *Nothing makes me happier on a sunny day than to think of how wrong I've been in the past. The old fears of people like me that technology leads to totalitarianism and cultural sterility do not come true. The computer, the fax, the car phone, the answering machine, all seem to lead to a more civilized life, affording us greater privacy and freedom, not less.* GARRISON KEILLOR

## A PASSION TO BE DIFFERENT

New media are important to the transformation that is taking place. But all by themselves, such technologies as the Internet will not determine our fate. Whether they wind up enhancing freedom or become all-seeing tools for Orwellian oppression will largely depend on the attitudes that prevail among millions of our fellow citizens. And so next we'll explore whether there is both the will and the mettle to maintain an open society.

• • •

Throughout recorded history, countless human clans and nations exhibited a tendency toward xenophobia. Ancient myths and legends are filled with warnings against strangers, from *Little Red Riding Hood* (don't tell your business to hairy beasts you meet in the woods), to the tale of *Coyote and the Green Buffalo* (watch out for tricks pulled by the tribe over the hill). In many tongues the word or phrase that meant "human being"—someone whose violent killing would be murder—was reserved for initiated members of the tribe. While relatively primitive technology may have kept wars somewhat less bloody in olden times, chronicles show that they were also much more frequent.

None of this should be surprising. The chief factor governing how well people tolerate outsiders appears to be their ambient level of fear. Under ceaseless threat of starvation or invasion, it was natural for our ancestors to be suspicious of strangers—and toward those *within* a community who did not act in normal, predictable ways. Kings often found it useful to bolster this reflex, fostering dread of some external or internal group to promote social cohesion and control.

I do not say any of this to insult past cultures. Far from it. Studying them rouses poignant sympathy for people coping under hard circumstances. As anthropologist Joseph Campbell pointed out, we gain insight into the human condition by studying the lore of our ancestors. Still, little good comes from romanticizing the past under a blur of nostalgia. We faced a long, hard road getting here. And along the way it was especially harsh to be a stranger—or an eccentric within one's own culture. Being different often had dire, even fatal consequences.

Elsewhere I have discussed a striking characteristic of our own neo-Western civilization—a salient feature of the last fifty years that has so far escaped much comment—arising from the unprecedented wealth and peace lately experienced by certain parts of the world. In large sections of the Americas, western Europe, Japan, Australia, and some other lucky regions, several generations have grown up with (on average) very little experience of hunger or foreign invasion. Despite justified continuing public angst over poverty, crime, and external threats, our day-to-day fear level is arguably the lowest experienced by any mass polity since humans first strode upright.

This may seem at odds with the unease depicted in newspapers and on television. Villainy and violence are still widespread. (We'll see how a transparent society may bring these rates down.) Yet most historical accounts show that citizens of other days were accustomed to far greater levels of daily disorder and death. Revisionist anthropologists have shown, for instance, that on a per capita basis even the !Kung bushmen of the Kalahari Desert, renowned for their gentleness, experience a statistically higher intratribal homicide rate than denizens of downtown Detroit. Some researchers estimate that 20 to 30 percent of males in preindustrial societies died at the hands of other males.

To gain perspective, consider what fraction of the readers of this book may have ever lived a whole month worrying their children might starve. What portion have recently seen a dead body in the course of normal community life? Experienced hand-to-hand combat on a battlefield? Trod the smoldering ruins of a sacked town? Witnessed firsthand an overlord exerting capricious power of life and death over underlings? Oh, surely a few readers have (this is still a dangerous world). But in almost any prior society, any average person would have answered each of these questions with a shrug, "Of course I have, and often."

(At one level this is just a tautology. Other cultures lacked reliable contraception, yet despite high birthrates their numbers never reached today's billions. Our vast—and possibly world-threatening—population decisively testifies to a reduced death rate.)

Despite such statistical reassurance, we wring our hands, unsatisfied. Our standards keep rising—as they should! We want peace and long lives. Any danger should come by our own choice—on a ski slope perhaps, or free-falling at the end of a bungee rope. Even a small chance of being mugged is unacceptable to people who count on being hale and hearty at ninety. Still, despite this inflation of perception, ordinary citizens know we are safer than other generations.

An intriguing result of declining fear is a society where tolerance has become one of the paramount stated virtues. Our culture's definition of "citizen" has expanded for generations—first from aristocrats to all white male landed farmers, then to all white males, then to all adult males, then to all adults . . . and so on. Children, once considered chattel property, have acquired a nearly full suite of rights. This agenda of expansion is taken very seriously, especially by groups just experiencing inclusion, or whose improving economic status has not kept pace with their increased liberties and expectations. Impatience with difficult stages in the process can lead to dramatic or violent episodes of social criticism. Even people who agree on the fundamental desirability of tolerance frequently deride each other over differences in preferred technique for achieving the same end (for example, whether affirmative action programs redress old injuries or serve to perpetuate racialism as an unfair means of judging people).

Today, large segments of the population push inclusiveness further still, calling it "murder" to slay a dolphin, or an ape, or members of a threatened species—even species that our hard-pressed ancestors considered vital food sources.

Please understand that I am not talking only about the subcultural phenomenon called "political correctness." Whether or not some people take this process to extremes, or even become caricatures of hypertolerance, is quite beside the point. No ideological wing owns this phenomenon, though many political partisans would have us think they do.

So involved are we in the ongoing struggle over details that scarcely anyone bothers to note how this entire agenda contrasts with the paranoia that was typical of our forebears. But in fact, our otherness-obsession is culturally extraordinary, perhaps unprecedented. While most Hollywood films treat authority figures as objects of (at best) contempt, the other lesson pushed by popular media appears to be the desirability of diversity. From television sitcoms to earnest news programs, the constant message is that different cultures enhance the overall richness of a complex world society. Those watching nature shows soon learn that Earth's ecological balance relies on continued genetic diversity. Each lost species is portrayed as harming the planet's overall health and, inevitably, our own.

A low ambient fear level fosters not only empathy but enlargement of our *time* sense. When the near future seems less hazardous, we feel free to cast our thoughts further ahead, contemplating not just immediate needs but also those that our grandchildren, and even *their* grandchildren, might face. Peter Schwartz, president of the Global Business Network, put it this way.

> More and more people, whether or not they think they are in control of their lives, feel as if their actions have consequences. They feel more entwined with the global community. They thus are learning to look at the future of the world, and at each other. People who engage in this process become less dangerous; they begin to take everyone's interest at heart.

What does all of this have to do with a transparent society?

Without doubt, the new media-saturated world will have some traits that increase citizens' exposure and acceptance of different cultures. Other features of the twenty-first century Net may foster fear and the creation of intolerant new tribes. I will talk about how both trends relate to transparency in later chapters. But for now, let's focus on a particular type of tolerance. Not of foreigners or outsiders, but of unorthodox individuals and groups *within* our own society.

The unusual and idiosyncratic. The eccentrics among us.

Romantic images of the past may lead some to imagine that oddballs and exceptional people were respected in antiquity, but this was seldom true. Wealthy aristocrats could sometimes afford bizarre interests or affectations. But for the most part, sameness was a paramount civic virtue. We look back admiringly on individuals like Michelangelo and Galileo, whose ideas triumphed despite suspicion and oppression by their peers. But they were geniuses, recognized even in their own times, and nonetheless faced dire troubles for their uniqueness. How many of their eccentric contemporaries were squelched by poverty, inquisitions, or the stifling oppression of distrustful neighbors?

Listening to modern artists and writers, you might think conformity is just as prevalent in the final years of the twentieth century. Aggrieved individuals decry the leveling influence of mass media and bland "white bread" culture without seeming to notice the irony that nonconformists are among the most admired and best-paid members of contemporary society! Instead of being repressed for their defiance, they are often rewarded in direct proportion to the degree that they startle, divert, or outrage. In other words, they are entertainers. Heroes of an exceptional age, whose propaganda mills tell young people it is romantic and admirable to "be different," and to "believe in yourself, no matter what others say."

I know this well, having found my own well-paid niche in this economy of eccentricity. I was raised to seek out unusual thoughts and points of view. To search always for amazing notions others may have overlooked, and to depict them in entertaining ways. I'm doing it right now.

And yet, in a society that mass-produces would-be social critics and individualists as if from an assembly line, it can be humbling to realize just how normal this endeavor is. There is nothing especially unusual about such a quest. It is what I was trained to do.

So, in all probability, were you.


Out of millions brought up under this "dogma of otherness," some applied their unleashed creativity in the world of new media. Is it just coincidence that the silicon revolution burgeoned near the birthplace of "flower power"? Or that some who rode with Ken Kesey in the Electric Koolaid Schoolbus later established pioneering outposts on the cybernetic frontier? Almost no one foresaw the personal computer. Certainly not the big shots at IBM or Burroughs. But society acquired the PC and other wonders because a cohort of young minds were indoctrinated to seek novelty where standard organizations never looked.

Would another culture put up with the likes of Stewart Brand, always poking at stagnant structures, from state government to the stuffy profession of architecture? Would Steve Jobs or Andrew Grove be billionaires in an economy based on inherited advantage? Where else might happy magicians like Howard Rheingold and Kevin Kelly be more influential than establishment priests or scientists? Would important power brokers hang on the words of Esther Dyson, Sherry Turkle, and Dorothy Denning if this culture did not value original minds? Listening to such remarkable individuals, one can tell they know how lucky they are. Few other cultures would reward oddball iconoclasts whose sole common attribute is a hatred of clichés.

They are dedicated to preserving and enhancing the social features that enable eccentrics like them to exist. Especially freedom.

In other words, out of pure self-interest, they are just like millions of their fellow citizens—fiercely devoted to liberty. Defenders of an individual's right to be unique.

If you are reading this book, you probably agree. With freedom, tolerance, and progress our consensus goals, we may differ only over *how* to preserve and enhance them.

Ah, but there's the rub!

In future chapters we shall see what noisy battles erupt around that question of how.

> Alice laughed. "There's no use trying," she said: "one can't believe impossible things."
>
> "I daresay you haven't had much practice," said the Queen. "When I was your age, I always did it for half-an-hour a day. Why, sometimes I've believed as many as six impossible things before breakfast."
>
> LEWIS CARROLL, *ALICE IN WONDERLAND*

## A CENTURY OF AFICIONADOS

If eccentricity is to be a factor in preserving an open society, it can't be limited to the rich, the talented, or any other elite. The new attitudes must encompass millions.

Despite some cherished stereotypes, not all of our neighbors are "couch potatoes" glued to their television remote controls. Millions are active in their communities, in scouting or volunteer work, or in their kids' schools and sports teams. Moreover, each weekend multitudes spend enough time and money on personal avocations to match a small country's gross domestic product. Activities range from garage crafts like carpentry, to intensive gardening, to collecting, to restoring that old Chevy Impala. According to one survey, the number of senior Americans participating in athletic sports has gone up by 73 percent in the last decade alone. A 1997 CNN poll showed that 40% of Americans pursued some outdoor activity.

Sport fishermen spend $38 billion annually. Photographic-sightseers shell out an additional $26 billion.

Some pastimes stretch the meaning of the word *hobby*. When Ted Turner wanted to do a film about the Battle of Gettysburg, he put out a call to Civil War reenactment clubs, inviting seven thousand members to bring their own muskets, equipment, and expertise—already organized in companies and fanatical about historical verisimilitude—in order to create a vivid rendition of Pickett's Charge. Other amateurs in "anachronism societies" adeptly resurrect medieval arts, so that mail-order catalogues now offer everything from gargoyles to whole suits of armor. Spinning wheels and weaving looms have seen a resurgence, despite (or perhaps because of) the continuing cheap availability of mass-produced textiles. And thanks to individual riding enthusiasts, there are more horses—and blacksmith services—in the United States today than in the era of the cowboy.

Folk dance groups, costume aficionados, and cooking clubs concentrate on any ethnicity you can name. And every year science fiction fans hold over a hundred conventions across the world—gatherings that range from erudite discussions of technology and literature all the way to fully attired plenary sessions of the Klingon Language Institute.

According to an American executive of the American Association of Association Executives, America alone has more than 140,000 national, regional, and local organizations, from sober professional societies to others created for pure satire. Some names prompt ironic smiles, like the Society of Loners, or the Association in Opposition to Human-Animal Hybridization. Others, like the earnest but awkwardly named Marine Mammal Stranding Center, involve hundreds of eager volunteers who will race to help save creatures that their ancestors would gleefully have butchered on the shore.

The Internet has expanded this trend many times over. Now an accountant who happens to be the only person in Duluth with a zeal for Japanese Nō theater can swiftly find others who share her interest, across half a dozen continents. In fact, any list of Usenet groups reveals a dizzying array of modern preoccupations, each roiling in its corner of cyberspace, involving anywhere from a dozen to tens of thousands of participants. (Sections devoted to fans of rock groups account for more traffic and memory capacity than the whole Internet of just a decade ago.) New Age sects, already flourishing like dandelions, have taken to the Web like a well-manured meadow.

What impulses drive this trend? Theories have been presented, ranging from dour to optimistic. Perhaps millions are so alienated from the modern world that they seek refuge in small "tribes" whose rituals, though ornate, are somehow comforting and offer a sense of belonging. Becoming expert in some small area of arcane lore may redress the feeling of being lost amid the dazzling complexities of modern science. That is one view—and it surely explains some aficionados, who dive into "hobbies" to escape the pressures of life.

But then there are others, each, in the words of Walt Whitman, "singing what belongs to him or her and to none else," whose passion for excitement and self-driven expertise seems like anything *but* withdrawal from a challenging modern world. Technical advances in scores of fields are now driven by enthusiasts. Take parachuting, where amateurs keep coming up with half-mad innovations like face-jumping, skyboarding, and formation dives in which complex cluster patterns are created by as many as two hundred highly skilled maniacs at a time. Or the daring breakthroughs in flight led by people like Paul MacReady and Burt Rutan. Or the sixty fanatics who set forth from the Canary Islands last summer, aiming to race across 2,700 miles of open ocean in rowboats, a "tradition" in which, despite high-tech designs, one in nine past participants never reached shore again.

The effect is especially visible in science, where part-time naturalists have collected valuable data for decades, according to Shawn Carlson, head of the Society for Amateur Scientists. For example, despite having high-tech satellites, weather agencies rely more than ever on timely reports from widely scattered volunteer stations, both ashore and at sea. When it came to maintaining stocks of rare plant types, in case some new disease might strike a major food crop, experts had been swamped until the laborious task was partly assumed by private gardeners with a fetish for growing rare or exotic varieties.

In June 1997 an event took place with important implications we'll explore in this book. An ad hoc association linked over ten thousand personal computers and workstations across North America to crack the Data Encryption Standard (DES). Three years earlier, a similar effort assailed the RSA-129 encryption code, succeeding "about a trillion years ahead of schedule," according to one surprised observer. Encryption experts make excuses in retrospect, but this pair of surprise breakthroughs has two implications: (1) consortiums of amateurs may be formidable, and (2) we should be wary when "experts" blithely assure us that their favorite encryption system is foolproof.

Astronomers like Caltech's Elinor Helin, who catalogs drifting asteroids and comets, have long been helped by cadres of amateur sky watchers privately scanning the heavens. Once, these seekers had to painstakingly memorize constellations in order to find new objects. But today some robot backyard telescopes open at dusk, check the weather, and then start hunting automatically, sifting CCD images for telltale glimmers that could make their owners briefly famous. Other aficionados transform satellite dishes into radio observatories, participating in a worldwide network for amateur SETI, the Search for Extra-Terrestrial Intelligent life. These last examples are noteworthy because they use the same technologies we spoke of in chapter 1, applying sophisticated surveillance tools for unusual ends. And whatever techniques or devices the rich can afford now, the rest of us may have soon after. In a few years, the sky will be watched as never before by armies of individuals pursuing their own private, passionate interests, sharing expertise over fiber-optic cables with like-minded enthusiasts, challenging the professionals on their own turf.

A few decades from now there will be ten billion people on the planet, and computers as sophisticated as today's mainframes will be cheaper than transistor radios. If this combination does not lead to war and chaos, then it will surely result in a world where countless men and women swarm the dataways in search of something special to do—some pursuit outside the normal range, to make each one feel just a little bit extraordinary. Through the Internet, we may be seeing the start of a great exploration aimed outward in every conceivable direction of interest or curiosity. An expedition to the limits of what we are, and what we might become.

Some very smart people might disagree with this appraisal. For instance, while Pulitzer Prize–winning historian Daniel Boorstin has spoken admiringly about the spirit of *amateurism* (whose Latin root is *amare*, "to love") he perceives this spirit declining in a world of narrow professionals and bureaucrats. He has addressed this theme as an invited speaker at symposiums and informal gatherings of enthusiastic eclectics from around the world, the sort who flock to resort hotels and university conference centers in order to share interdisciplinary insights and cross-fertilization of ideas. As the popularity and accessibility of such gatherings grow, they create spin-offs, increasing the number of venues where eager renaissance men and women can temporarily put aside their specialties, trade diverse new ideas, and collectively bemoan the decline of liberated open-mindedness. In other words, the world can be ironic.

*Assuming that I am right, and the pessimists are mistaken, almost nothing of recognized value that is now known about the human past or present will ever again be lost.*

From oral folktales, to ritual dances of recondite cults, to subvariant musical themes, or conspiracy-oriented interpretations of history—however obscure or crackpot a topic or activity might be, our culture will stash it away, protect it, cherish it. This great preservation won't be accomplished by some haughty ministry of culture, but with strangely chaotic efficiency by countless private individuals probing each dimly lit corner of human knowledge, seeking some small niche where even a "nobody" might become a world-class expert. A big fish in a small pond.

> *Information wants to be free.*    POPULAR SAYING ON THE INTERNET
>
> *Information wants you to give me a dollar.*    BRUCE STERLING

## AN AGE OF PASSIONS

Back in the days of Charles Dickens, the word "innovation" was often used as an insult. Today on the other hand many people identify themselves by the thing that makes them feel different or special. To call someone average is to be contemptuous, implying that they are part of the despised "masses."

In later chapters we will explore how a civilization of aficionados might flourish, especially with some useful new tools. For instance, credibility "tags" may dog those who preach or bring us news. Predictions registries will help separate those who have good track records for being right from those whose charisma is matched only by their hot air. With alternative venues for innovation, new ideas and artworks may percolate, rising to renown by quality alone, without advertising, thus bypassing the mavens of culture who now wield such power over which artists, actors, or writers prosper, and which fail. Arenas for responsible debate could help satisfy society's growing appetite for accountability in an era when mistakes will grow more costly and lies will become much harder to hide.

On the other hand, the future will not lack for challenges and dangers. If nearly all valid or important wisdom from the past and present winds up being stored and valued, so will misinformation, lies, and slanderous half-truths. While ethnic crafts and amateur science promote wholesome diversity, calumnies like the *Turner Diaries* will also keep circulating, reproduced by cheap electronic means, infecting yet more fragile minds and egos with the same cruel madness that brought ruinous destruction to Oklahoma City in 1995.

Of course it is by tolerating such forces, which proudly avow to hating tolerance and diversity, that our system proves its essential strength. Yet one recalls with unease the words of historian Will Durant: "Great empires often bring about their own demise through excessive adherence to their own central principles."

This issue will be a major focus of the next chapter. For it can be a mistake to extrapolate too much from present trends, especially when the curve you're looking at seems to accelerate ever upward. In the long run, this time of eccentricity may be seen as a fluke—when a favored generation lived high off the earth's remaining surplus until the consumer economy finally collapsed, leaving our grandchildren in the same state as our ancestors, harassed by immediate perils, fearful and intolerant, with no free time to spare from the incessant struggle to survive.

That may happen, but I am betting we'll pull off a chain of miracles. Barring something unforeseen, we may see a flowering of commerce, information, creativity, and ideas. An age when even the most august expert will have to keep looking over his or her shoulder, as hordes of well-informed citizens catch every undotted "i" or missing minus sign. A time when bureaucrats and committees will lose much of their authority, because countless tasks will be augmented—or even taken over—by voluntary associations of passionate devotees.

The next one hundred years may come to be called the "century of amateurs."

If so, it will happen because we made it possible for many hopeful new trends to continue.

Because we unleashed the full range of human potential into a transparent society.

# CITIZEN TRUTH SQUADS

One of the pastimes most peculiar to the nineties is amateur sleuthing. We are all familiar with examples of private individuals videotaping some news-worthy event—from natural disasters and crimes in progress to rogue cops in the act of harassing citizens. The new genre of "reality"-based television has created an ever-hungry market for interesting footage, while other cap-tured images go straight to the Web, circulating without aid or interference by professional media experts. This trend is bound to multiply in the future. Or, as humorist Scott Adams put it, "Thanks to the ubiquity of video cameras and the Internet, every citizen will be a reporter."

We have already seen how human rights groups are providing equip-ment to dissidents and activists overseas, to record and combat abuses of state power. In the section "Guarding the Guardians" in chapter 6, we will discuss efforts under way in America and other Western nations to make sure that police authority becomes difficult to abuse.

But video serendipity only brushes the surface of a phenomenon that has major long-range implications. Take, for example, just a few of the sophisti-cated amateur truth squads that have sprouted on the Internet to collect or correlate both facts and innuendos, sometimes bypassing or even refuting more official sources.

- Both ad hoc and established consumer groups have started to use the Web to expose a new generation of scams and con artists (www.scam-busters.org), reveal fraud (www.fraud.org), or provide archives of con-sumer information (www.ConsumerReports.org).

• G-TWO (Get the Word Out) is a grassroots Internet service developed by Eric Nelson, a San Diego State University premed student and Marine Corps reserve staff sergeant. "I like to uncover that which is hidden," says Nelson, who relies exclusively on open-source, unclassified material. When rebels took over the Japanese ambassador's residence in Peru in December 1996, an e-mail request went out over several computer networks requesting photographs and a floor plan of the residence where hostages were being held. The information was available ten minutes later.

• Tired of waiting for state officials to start posting campaign finance information on the Web, Kim Alexander of the California Voter Foundation collated a list of the biggest contributors prior to that state's November 1996 elections and made the results available at www.calvoter.org. The subsequent media coverage about last-minute donations earned Alexander a James Madison Freedom of Information Award.

• Paul McGinnis, a test engineer from Huntington Beach, code named Trader, assembles and correlates public information to publish his own detailed estimate of the Pentagon's black budget. Meanwhile, Steve Aftergood's "Secrecy and Government Bulletin" exposes weapons problems and cost overruns.

• Alt.folklore.urban is the umbrella site for a cluster of news groups that specialize in debunking legends, urban and otherwise. (For instance, Procter & Gamble apparently does not pay tithes to the Church of Satan, and pet alligators flushed down toilets are not living in sewers.) There is also alt.folklore.science which debunks science myths, such as the misconception that people would explode into a cloud of red blood if exposed to the vacuum of outer space. Meanwhile, Web publications like the "Groom Lake Desert Rat" pursue every conceivable conspiracy scenario, ensuring that even refuted rumors achieve a kind of immortality.

Taken by themselves, these private efforts at truth-descrying don't amount to very much. But multiply them by the hundreds of others that already exist, or the tens of thousands that soon will, and they illustrate how a century of amateurs pertains to transparency. Throughout this book, we will glimpse new, alternative information pathways, some based on the Internet's inspired chaos, that tend to bypass older structures of central command and control. These may unleash new creativity (see chapter 8), ensure accountability (see chapter 6), or even produce new forms of governance (see "A Withering Away?").

Or else, lacking any unifying purpose or sense of shared citizenship, this trend may worsen the centrifugal forces tearing us apart.

One factor could help determine the outcome—whether it all happens in the open, under the light.

## CHAPTER THREE

# PRIVACY UNDER SIEGE

*Individuals are sacred. The world, the
state, the church, the school, all are
felons whenever they violate the sanctity
of the private heart.*

BRONSON ALCOTT

*Little in life is as precious as the freedom
to say and do things with people you love
that you would not say or do if someone
else were present.*

JANNA MALAMUD SMITH

## EMBATTLED CITIZENS

The previous chapter depicted a civilization arming itself with tools of
openness, diversity, and accountability, a theme that will be taken up again
later in the book. But other factors may prove critical in determining our
future, for instance, whether people can maintain their spirit and morale
in a technological age that keeps thrusting challenges their way. Ours is a
nosy era, in which each day seems to force more intrusions—by governments, corporations, ex-lovers, busybodies, news reporters, or worrisome
strangers—encroaching on our sense of serenity and solitude.

Later in this chapter we will talk about privacy in more general terms—
how it affects people personally, and how the law has (or has not) adjusted

to safeguard it in the modern era. We will also broach an idea that at first may seem contradictory and counterintuitive: that "reciprocal transparency" may be our best hope to enhance and preserve a little privacy in the next century.

But first, some context will be essential in order to grasp how many pressures are already squeezing us, even before the millennium clock turns over. The following examples offer a fragmentary cross-section of disquieting modern quandaries.

### Big Brother

More than 1,500 employees of the U.S. Internal Revenue Service have been investigated or disciplined since 1989 for using government computers to browse through tax returns of friends, relatives, neighbors, enemies, and celebrities. Recently, President Clinton signed the Taxpayer Browsing Act, threatening up to a year in jail for anyone convicted of abusing access for personal reasons, and further oversight procedures were on the docket in late 1997. New supervision software will help enforce the ban—by *surveilling employees* each time they access a tax return.

Reacting to spy scandals, such as the Aldrich Ames affair, the administration and Congress collaborated on legislation that may subject up to three million people with access to government secrets to snap inspections of their bank statements, credit histories, and foreign travel records. The initial aim, to detect those who betray their country for money, might have the ancillary effects of (1) deterring other types of corruption and bribery and (2) subjecting federal employees to a level of glaring intrusion unprecedented in modern times.

The federal government is helping coordinate and develop new databases aimed at helping states enforce their own laws—to find parents who depart and abandon child support payments, to catch fugitives from state justice, to check backgrounds of gun buyers under the Brady Law, to track registered sexual predators, and so on. As yet, these databases are not linked, but few doubt they will be.

The U.S. Postal Service sells change-of-address card updates to direct-mail marketers and businesses that correlate consumer information. Does this mean you won't be able to escape the "junk mail catalog from hell," even by the drastic measure of selling your house and moving away?

While these examples seem less horrid in detail than the flagrant dossier gathering, callous break-ins, nefarious blackmailings, and other abuses performed during J. Edgar Hoover's tenure at the FBI, they make up for this through their overpowering pervasiveness and the vast, correlating power of computer databases. For instance, will increased use of citizens'

Social Security numbers (SSNs) become so entrenched and universal that Americans wind up having the long-dreaded "national ID card" at last?

Fingerprint systems are being used in many locales to prevent welfare recipients from filing under multiple names. Escrow and credit companies, along with many banks, now demand thumbprints to prove identity. A nationwide fingerprint clearinghouse, activated by the FBI in 1996, promises to process inquiries electronically in seconds, rather than days, meaning that use of this identification technique will no longer be restricted to dangerous felons but may spread to include us all. (We will discuss SSN abuse and fingerprinting further in chapter 8.)

This list of concerns only scratches the surface. Nor are federal agencies the sole potential abusers of government power. Many citizens find local officials much worse; for example, one man recently won a five-year lawsuit for defamation against a former assistant police chief who allegedly used official computers to obtain facts about him as part of a personal vendetta. The problem of petty local "microtyrants" can be exacerbated by lack of attention from media and rights organizations, who traditionally focus their attention on the national level. As one expert confided, "This sort of thing is going on all the time. It's a kettle waiting to explode."

### Spying in the Workplace

In countless offices, employers can monitor telephone calls, peruse e-mail messages, and even retrieve supposedly "deleted" files without an employee's knowledge. Clerical workers are watched by diligent programs that count the number of keystrokes they type per minute and time their coffee breaks to the second. The ACLU claims that this type of monitoring violates rights, hurts employee morale, and lowers productivity. Yet, as will grow clear in this chapter, numerous courts have ruled that subordinates do not enjoy the same constitutional protection against intrusive supervision by private employers as they have against the government.

In late 1997, a survey of 906 employers found that 35 percent conducted one or more types of close electronic surveillance on their workers. When less invasive kinds of electronic monitoring were included, the figure rose to 63 percent. Most companies employing more than a couple of dozen workers now demand a pre-employment drug test before hiring. (An estimated $1.2 billion was spent on drug testing in the United States during 1992, the latest year tallied.)

Many corporations can access their employees' medical records. Some use this power to cut costs by helping workers with wellness programs and exercise facilities. Others discriminate based on health, or force high-risk employees to pay higher insurance premiums.

### The Commercialization of Personal Information

Almost any commercial action we take can provide information on our buying patterns and lifestyle choices: dialing a toll-free number, subscribing to a magazine, using a credit card, starting a business, purchasing from a catalog, donating to charity, buying a car, sending in a product warranty registration card, using frequent-flier miles for a vacation, booking a hotel reservation, using a grocery store club card, obtaining a home loan, joining a health club, belonging to a church or temple. Simply clicking on a site on the World Wide Web may wind up creating a "biography" about you. After coming home from the hospital maternity ward, a new mother is besieged by baby magazines and advertisements for infant-care goods. The purchaser of a new home automatically receives coupons from hardware stores, interior designers, and contractors. Have a serious accident, and you'll start receiving solicitations from lawyers.

In 1990, Lotus Corporation offered *Marketplace: Households*, a CD-ROM containing transaction-generated information (TGI) on the buying patterns and incomes of 120 million Americans. A firestorm of protest forced Lotus to withdraw the product, though ironically *Marketplace* would only have provided the same access for small businesses that big companies already enjoy. AOL, the nation's largest private online service, confirmed that it was compiling the names and addresses of its subscribers and packaging lists with demographic information to sell to marketing companies and manufacturers. (Subscribers who do not want their names released may specify by sending a message to AOL.) Mark Rotenberg, director of the Electronic Privacy Information Center (EPIC), based in Washington, D.C., says that subscribers go from "being in the AOL chat room to the AOL fishbowl." All of this raises a question:

*How much of the above do you find objectionable? How much of your objection is due to real, tangible harm—and how much of it is "on principle"?*

Solveig Singleton, director of information studies at Washington's influential Cato Institute, considers all the fury over corporate "info gluttony" to be overwrought. "Businesses that collect data on customer profiles usually do so because they are trying to sell something. As human motives go, this is not an especially sinister one." That is one point of view. We will hear from others in the next chapter dealing with the question of who owns information.

The Internet makes it easy to obtain personal information about other people, such as their driving record, whether they own a house, or their marital status. According to Carole Lane, author of *Naked in Cyberspace: How to Find Personal Information Online*, "Most people would be astounded to know what's out there. . . . In a few hours, sitting at my computer, beginning with no more than your name and address, I can find out what you do for a living, the names and ages of your spouse and children, what kind of car you drive, the value of your house and how much in taxes you pay on it."

The California legislature recently voted to limit access to voter registration information and the computer tapes of a Los Angeles County municipal court docket, although this type of information was always kept public in order to hold government accountable. But the new law, like many others, does little to inhibit access by major corporations. There are so many loopholes that anyone with a little know-how can skirt the provisions.

And some will gladly provide this expertise. An industry of "how to" manuals has arisen, catering to those seeking to learn tricks for finding out information about the other guy—or to protect their own privacy. A company called CDB Infotek compiles data from a multitude of local, state, and federal public records, adds private-sector data, and sells the sorted reports to its subscribers. Much of this information was already available at places like your local county hall of records. Anyone willing to spend enough time and energy could look such things up on their own. It is the relative ease of availability that now makes this accessibility seem chilling to some people, opening the way to casual browsing by their neighbors, or possibly would-be burglars. In response, groups such as the ACLU have set up task forces to track abuses, publishing books and providing Internet-based archives to help citizens research their rights.

### Credit Ratings

This special kind of corporate information gathering merits a category all its own. Equifax Corporation, positioning itself to be the premier information storage, processing, and retrieval company for the twenty-first century, carries personal information on nearly every resident of the United States. Their systems include the Consumer Credit Database, motor vehicle records, and Equifax Check Services. (Recently spun-off units do research for auto and home insurance companies.) Critics complain that Equifax sells personal information as widely as possible, with few controls on dissemination, or checks on the accuracy of its data. While the press routinely reports lurid cases of erroneous records fouling up individuals' lives through mistaken identity or unjust use of unreliable information, Equifax responds by claiming that its high overall statistical accuracy benefits the economy as a whole, helping both credit and capital flow swiftly to those who need and deserve it.

Whether it is done by Equifax or a competitor, nearly all consumers are branded by a "score," based on their past credit history, purportedly predicting how readily they will repay their bills. This score is used to judge mortgage, insurance, auto, department store, and small-business loans. In their supposedly color-blind impartiality, such ratings have actually been used to help quash racial and other kinds of discrimination. Yet the scorers employed by these private companies keep their methods secret, thereby making it hard to spot errors or patterns of bias. The Federal Trade Commission recently decided that it could not force the firms to disclose their methods to consumers.

Things used to be worse. Two decades ago, before passage of the Fair Credit Reporting Act, TRW Information Systems and Services (now Experian) and other industry leaders claimed that it was essential to maintain secret records, predicting that the sky would fall if their subjects ever saw the contents of their own files. Despite such self-serving rationalizations, public ire prompted laws letting individuals peruse their credit dossiers for a small fee. Instead of predicted chaos, the result was increased accountability, accuracy, and efficiency.

Now a new wave of suspicion, stoked by fresh horror stories, seems to be forcing movement toward the next plateau of transparency. Responding to public pressure, Equifax lately claimed a heightened devotion to protecting consumer data from errors and abuse. "Every person has the right to personal privacy consistent with the demands and requests he or she makes of business," states a bronze plaque in corporate headquarters. "Every person is entitled to have his or her privacy safeguarded through the secure storage and careful transmission of information."

Yet those troubling anecdotes continue growing in number. A study of credit bureaus by *Consumer Reports* magazine found that half of all files examined held some inaccurate information. One out of five files contained major mistakes that could "ruin a person's credit rating." Subsequent studies have since shown smaller error rates, but results remain high enough to be worrisome.

Even if the system were perfect, citizens must ponder whether it is wise to entrust companies like Equifax with quasi-governmental powers, while allowing them to retain the low accountability of a private company.

### Identity Theft

"It'll be the next growth industry in crime," said Ontario privacy commissioner Ann Cavoukian. Unlike simple credit card fraud, whereby a thief rings up charges until the card is canceled, identity theft is akin to a felon stealing *who you are*. A clever swindler starts by using just a few bits of personal information, perhaps your full name and SSN, to access Internet databases and thereby obtain your address, telephone number, driver's license number, and so on. The swindler can then apply for credit using your good name, run up bills, take over bank accounts, rent apartments, buy cars, and at times even take out mortgages. Some victims find out about this frighteningly personal violation only months later, after receiving angry calls from collection agencies. One brash con artist impersonated Seattle Congressman Jim McDermott for months, running up large bills.

The important legal point about identity theft is that, unlike the accused in criminal cases, who have "reasonable doubt" on their side, victims of credit fraud bear the burden of proving they are not the individuals who incurred the debts and rang up the purchases in question.

Bronti Kelly of Temecula, California, found himself repeatedly turned down for jobs in retail. Finally, he learned that the Stores Protection Association, a private firm that carries out background checks on job applicants, was telling each potential employer he had been arrested for shoplifting. It turns out that months earlier someone had taken Kelly's wallet. Caught swiping goods from a store, the thief gave Kelly's ID to credulous and careless police officials, thus initiating his nightmare.

In fact, the creation of false identities has a long tradition. According to MIT sociology professor Gary T. Marx, "Life in urban society, with extensive interactions with strangers, requires that we rely on factors such as uniforms, licenses, credentials to establish identity, resulting in great potential for fraud. . . . There may be more than 500,000 Americans with fraudulent credentials, diplomas, even questionable medical degrees."

### Tracking

For years now, some drivers have hidden primitive radio tracking units aboard their cars, to be triggered if the vehicle is ever stolen. These devices have resulted in many recoveries, as well as the breakup of major theft rings. Newer versions can locate themselves with Global Positioning System (GPS) signals and even dial home via the car's cell phone. A similar feature now being installed on many laptop computers will dial an Internet-based reporting service the next time the modem is connected if the user does not keep entering a monthly code word.

With the spread of high-tech toll roads, tens of thousands of automobiles now carry small transponders that let the "smart highways" log each driver's position, redirect traffic, ease congestion, and send commuters sweeping past toll booths without stopping. It also means that a computer somewhere "knows" where drivers get on the highway, where they get off, and when. Privacy advocates worry how this information might someday be gathered, correlated, and possibly used to track specific persons.

In one experiment, the Florida Department of Corrections awarded a five-year contract to Pro Tech Monitoring to create SMART (Satellite Monitoring and Remote Tracking), using GPS units and wireless networks to monitor tamper-resistant ankle bracelets worn by sex-crime malefactors.

These examples of "transponder tracking" are only the beginning of a trend. Bracelet devices are now sold to anxious parents, who tag their kids before visiting a crowded shopping mall. A city in Australia mandates that "curfew bands" be attached to troublemaking teens. Most veterinarians now offer to implant tracking chips painlessly under the skin of pets, enabling rapid recovery by owners, and one California city *requires* the tagging of any animal processed by the city for neutering, or picked up as a stray.

Some imaginative civil libertarians worry about a time when subdural transponders might be routinely required for insertion in all citizens, a concern I discussed in my 1979 novel *Sundiver.* Just because a new technology hasn't been abused yet, that is no guarantee it won't be.

### Advanced Sensors

Under discussion at the A.C. Nielsen company (the television ratings folks) is their recent patent of a system that would marry cheap digital cameras with face recognition systems to track movement of specific customers down supermarket aisles, correlating this data with information collected at the checkout counter.

As we discussed in chapter 1, technologies of vision and surveillance seem to be looming from all directions. Some, like putting plastic taggants in explosives, seem inevitable and so obvious that the public wonders with perplexity about politically motivated delays. Others seem more problematic.

Several new types of concealed-weapon detectors would let police officers ascertain, from a distance of ten to thirty feet, whether a suspect is armed, letting officers "frisk" for weapons without having to approach or touch the person, or even from the safety of their squad car. Officers might drive down a street and search everyone nearby for weapons. Because they are "contraband specific" and do not make body images, few court challenges are expected. Yet requiring citizens to "assume the risk" of observation by whatever technology the government can command raises serious questions. For instance, Pacific Northwest National Laboratory reportedly developed a millimeter-wave imager that "sees" through textiles but is blocked by metal, plastic, and skin. From across a room it can produce a remarkably detailed nude picture of an oblivious, fully clothed person. Airport security might be a potential application if this device is introduced, especially as criminals and terrorists continue to develop plastic weapons that escape discovery by today's metal detectors. And yet, questions abound. Will a bashful public demand separate aisles for men and women? Or that all operators be elderly ladies? If this technology leads to "X-ray spectacles," straight out of adolescent fantasy, will citizens develop an intense interest in metallized undergarments?

Extrapolating just a few years, one can conjure up pictures of a future that is either hell or utopia—depending on who you imagine is controlling the machinery.

### Media Abuse

When does a private life become a news story? Putting aside for now the matter of paparazzi photographers swarming around the rich and famous, dozens of cases are pending nationwide against broadcasters who put ordinary people on television without their permission or knowledge. A recent explosion of reality-based shows such as *Cops* and *Rescue 911* has led to camera crews accompanying police and ambulance workers. Faces of people are frequently obscured if their permission is not granted, but not always. One woman was filmed in a ditch, pinned inside her family's overturned car, moaning in pain, and even begging to die. She was tended by a paramedic wearing a microphone. A cameraman also taped her helicopter trip to the hospital, which was broadcast on a syndicated show about real-life rescues. When the woman sued the show's production company for invasion of privacy, a Los Angeles appeals court ruled that she had a potential right to privacy in the helicopter, but not the ditch, which was a public place. "Involuntary public figures, such as accident victims, lose their right to privacy, not only in regard to the accident itself but, to some extent, to other information as well," said the judge. Not all such suits fail, however. In another case, where camera crews followed paramedics into a bedroom and taped failed efforts to revive a heart attack victim, the man's widow later settled out of court for $400,000.

### Private Eyes

In olden days, the average customer who hired private detectives might have been some shady character or jealous spouse. Today, a burgeoning industry caters to worried parents, anxiously checking up on teens who may be getting involved with drugs, slipping into gangs, or just "running with the wrong crowd." Actor Carroll O'Connor typified this attitude when he was interviewed after his son, Hugh, committed suicide amid drug-related problems. "I should have spied on him. Tapped his phone," O'Connor said. "There are no ethics in a war."

This tense matter encapsulates many issues we are covering in this book, such as "the toxicity of ideas" (chapter 5) and the whole question of accountability. Do loved ones have a natural right to yank their children back from a precipice, even against their will? If so, who is to define where the precipice is? Where does protective accountability leave off and where does repression of eccentricity begin?

"I hope every teen in America suspects there's a P.I. following him," said a private eye while tracking a youth, during an episode of the CBS documentary show *48 Hours*. The same show covered the growing use of at-home drug test kits by parents, who are either tyrannically meddlesome or else desperately clutching at straws, depending on your point of view.

### A New Kind of Harassment

In June 1997, on the eve of a major series of Federal Trade Commission hearings concerning online privacy, the EPIC released a study of one hundred top sites on the World Wide Web. Although many of these sites captured personal information from visitors and users, the study reported that virtually none had privacy policies that complied with globally accepted privacy standards. Those that did have privacy policies rarely made them easy to find.

University of California at San Diego Professor Phil Agre describes an irksome encounter with one Internet site. It began when his e-mail box suddenly began filling with puzzling "requests for an autograph." Eventually, the problem was traced to a "celebrity e-mail addresses" service on a "white pages" Web site that permits Internet users to look up personal information about a large number of people. (The site is funded by advertising.) Both miffed and intrigued, Agre probed deep into their online presence. Finally, below a list of their two dozen corporate partners, he found the following statement:

> Our Commitment to Privacy
> [This company] is committed to protecting its customers' privacy. Anyone who does not want to be listed in either the telephone or e-mail directory can request to be removed, and a separate database is maintained to prevent them from ever being accidentally re-added to the directory. In addition, we promise never to sell or trade our users' address information and believe it is essential to protect our users from unsolicited commercial e-mail and mass marketing.

Agre attempted to make use of this policy, writing to most of the company officers. After many delays, he finally received repeated promises that he would be removed. Yet for another year, his name and address continued to be advertised on their Web pages. Agre concludes, "We can learn some lessons here. One is that the world's best privacy policy is worthless unless it is followed. . . .[I]t is not reasonable for a company to profit by causing nuisances for innocent people."

And sometimes it can be more than a nuisance, as in the case of a woman in Burbank, California, who ordered a maternity catalog when she became pregnant. A barrage of additional catalogs ensued, along with baby-product samples, calls from baby photographers, and offers from diaper services. Unfortunately, she had a miscarriage. But despite her best efforts, the mail and calls kept coming, especially around the date the baby would have been due, many of them offering "congratulations."

Two years later, she was still receiving painful birthday cards from merchants eager to sell products for a toddler who never was.

### Medical Records

Once upon a time, a patient's records consisted of papers in a manila folder, kept in the doctor's office and "encrypted" in the physician's indecipherable handwriting. Health workers were guided by professional standards that mostly prevented disclosure of patient information, except on a need-to-know basis. The old ways also meant that seeing a specialist involved awkward, complex paper shuffling. Records were often late, illegible, or misplaced.

Computerization has resulted in a quicker and vastly more knowledgeable care delivery system—even if it sometimes feels less human. But standards and procedures have not kept up with this speedy availability of information. Computerized medical databases cross state lines, though laws regulating the confidentiality of patients' medical records vary widely. In America, the files are largely controlled by insurance companies or health maintenance organizations (HMOs), and are often unavailable to patients. Medical database information is sometimes bought and sold without the patient's knowledge or consent.

There is a lot of legitimate worry about so much knowledge and power being monopolized by "faceless" bureaucracies. Some people fear social discrimination, lack of access to insurance, or poor employment prospects if medical histories or psychological treatments are revealed. Few matters seem so personal as the intimate details about our frail, aching, or aging bodies.

Yet even this area features some remarkable examples of modern candor. For political candidates, elected officials, and especially the president, medical records are now often released as a matter of routine. We have come a long way since the days when Franklin D. Roosevelt's wheelchair-bound condition because of polio was carefully shielded from the public. Today, detailed medical press releases are issued regarding even the president's minor procedures—treatment for a sprain, a mole removal, or even his weight loss program.

The trade-offs can at times seem impossible. For example, public health workers have long relied on tracking medical histories to help control the spread of infectious diseases. Smallpox was obliterated worldwide through such detailed sleuthing, identifying disease victims and tracking others they may have infected. Doctors, dentists, and nurses claim they need to know if patients are HIV-positive, so that they can take necessary precautions. Conversely, patient advocacy groups demand that they should know if doctors are HIV-positive. But the advent of AIDS aroused powerful forces driving hard for redoubled confidentiality, and even downright secrecy, a campaign that was reinforced each time ignorant or intolerant people overreacted, such as when Ryan White, a young hemophiliac infected with the HIV virus, was forced out of public schools in Kokomo, Indiana.

"Our private health information [is] being shared, collected, analyzed and stored with fewer federal standards than video store records," said Donna E. Shalala, secretary of health and human services in the Clinton administration. Many lawmakers of both parties are demanding better protections, but few have concentrated on the details, which are bound to be wrangled over by lobbyists for powerful interests, from the insurance industry to the ACLU and the American Medical Association (AMA). At first, we may see an incremental approach, mandating adherence to some basic privacy protocols, such as the Open Profiling Standard (OPS) that has begun to take hold in a few areas of the Internet. Such efforts might at least assure consumers access to their own records and impose sanctions against flagrant distribution of personal data without a treatment-related need. Two long-range possibilities being discussed include a centralized medical database accessible to health care workers, or a "smart card" carried by the patient containing up-to-date medical records. Both have provocative implications for the future.

### Safeway Is Watching You

Nowadays in the United States, most supermarket chains will issue a "club" card to anyone who asks for it. Shoppers wave the card before the cashier's UPC reader in order to qualify for special bonuses, customized coupons, and discounts off the retail price. Polls show that a substantial fraction of customers understand the implication: that the store may now correlate their purchases in a growing database in order to perceive buying patterns and better anticipate their clients' needs. In effect, the company uses point-of-sale discounts to "buy" information that may enable it to provide better service and compete more effectively. Some privacy advocates find it chilling to picture a big corporation knowing the detailed contents of every shopping cart. Yet the cards prove increasingly popular, indicating that most people simply don't care. Their blithe attitude may be based on two factors.

First, even if strangers know which brand of dog food I purchase, it is hard to imagine how they could possibly use the data to harm me. (This may be less true of items like pregnancy test kits, hemorrhoid creams, and so on.)

Second, it is comforting to know that we can always stop using the club card, or even put aside checks and credit cards. In other words, if it ever seems important to do so, we can fall back on cash, which is safely anonymous.

Or can we? Already there are legal and practical limits to how much cash merchants will accept without becoming darkly suspicious. And now, a proposal looms on the horizon that may have radical implications about the beloved anonymity of greenback currency. Faced with sophisticated counterfeiting efforts that are allegedly subsidized by hostile nations, and acknowledging that the total flow of cash through worldwide criminal activity now exceeds the budgets of all but a dozen nations, planners are suggesting that the next generation of currency be equipped with "super barcodes" for instant scanning and identification at any bank, and later at any commercial point of sale.

While greenbacks have carried individual serial numbers for a long time, it seems quite another matter for each one to be scanned and tracked many times in a given day, with the information tallied and correlated in one vast, omniscient database! The notion of tracing the path of every crumpled dollar bill in a staggeringly huge economy might seem impossibly daunting at first. And yet, most of the monetary value exchanged in modern transactions is already electronic, leaving detailed trails for modern sleuths to follow.

In effect, each of the new bills would have an individual identity, or a name, to be logged during every purchase or exchange. The implications of such a change are diverse and multifarious. For instance, it has long been pointed out that most street crime depends on the anonymity of cash. If victims could report the specific ID numbers of every bill that was stolen from them—allowing alerts to go off the next time they were spent—it would result in the swift capture of many culprits, perhaps reducing violence on the streets as much as those vaunted cameras we mentioned in chapter 1.

But on the other hand, how would we feel if and when cash anonymity was lost, resulting in a world where every transaction we made was followed around by electronic ghosts, whispering a chorus of details? No matter how hard we tried to maintain the old anonymity—by using shrouds of encryption to scatter the specters and hide the details of our electronic commerce—would we ever be completely sure that someone else, with more powerful software, could not reassemble those ghosts, and persuade them to tell all?

### Feeling Naked

Worst of all are the intrusions that strike close to home. The ones that aren't offensive just in abstract, or in principle, but because they glaringly, or even dangerously, shatter or erode the quality of people's lives. The problem is best presented in anecdotes, each with a human face attached.

In 1989, an obsessed fan stalked and murdered television sitcom star Rebecca Schaeffer after hiring a private investigator to obtain the actress's address from California's Department of Motor Vehicles. New laws have supposedly narrowed access to these records. Still, this has not slowed the spread of both legal and illicit "telltale" databases about public figures. The old practice of selling maps to the movie stars' homes has burgeoned into a flurry of colorful, fan-maintained Web pages, offering excruciating details about every aspect of the lives of these public figures.

A San Francisco man was recently caught secretly videotaping other men showering at an athletic club. Police were at a loss how to charge him. He wasn't trespassing, he filmed no lewd acts or juveniles, and he wasn't selling copies, so the taping itself apparently violated no laws. Finally they charged him with breaking the state's anti-eavesdropping act, since the tape's audio track recorded members' conversations.

These incidents, and those we talked about earlier, scarcely begin to illustrate the range of modern threats to privacy. A few snowflakes start adding up to look like an avalanche. One can see why some privacy advocates worry that we're entering an era when our most personal information may be seized at any moment and transmitted to a million curious strangers, or to our bitterest rivals, or possibly to some nameless agency with all the caring accountability you might find in a tale by Kafka, Heller, or Dostoyevsky. While some, like the Privacy Rights Clearinghouse, offer practical advice, other activists have begun suggesting that it is time for "another revolution."

And yet, these new tools also offer so many advantages and benefits! Will it be possible for us, as a confident civilization, to find a balance?

Weighing heavy on the scales will be our perception, and the underlying reality, of privacy.

*We shall have very sane reactionaries at all periods warning us to remain in the natural and primitive state of humanity, which is usually the last stage but one in their cultural history.*

J. D. BERNAL, *THE WORLD, THE FLESH AND THE DEVIL*

*We have reached a point in America where our private lives are grotesquely public.*  RICHARD DREYFUSS

## THE ENCHANTMENT OF THE PAST

Back in the 1960s, long before anyone imagined how thoroughly computers would pervade civilization, Vance Packard warned in *The Naked Society* of a coming age when privacy might be taken away by the inexorable logic of ravenous bureaucracies. Some modern observers believe Packard's prediction has already been fulfilled, and that the purgatory of ubiquitous cameras depicted in George Orwell's *Nineteen Eighty-Four* looms ahead. Indeed, many respond to these pressures by seeking shelter in nostalgia, harking back to the blissful simplicity of another time.

Were things actually better in the past? Nostalgic reminiscence is often notoriously misleading, especially when it comes to earlier states of privacy. In countless societies, common folk had little recourse if those higher on life's pyramid wanted to come snooping, whether these superiors were Prussian clerks, Confucian mandarins, feudal lords, or parish priests.

Nevertheless, the United States has always featured a thread of cultural aversion toward official scrutiny. Americans often led undocumented lives, especially on the frontier. Historians estimate that it was 1930 before 90 percent of births were recorded. An official U.S. passport did not exist before 1914, and was not consistently required of citizens returning from foreign travel during peacetime until the 1950s. Certainly, the amount of data that people have to enter on forms—in order to qualify for jobs, Social Security, credit, or education—seems to have burgeoned beyond anything our ancestors would recognize.

And yet, this impression of increasing nosiness may be misleading. For instance, in every U.S. census since the first one in 1790, officials demanded answers to a range of inquiries that might today be considered obnoxious or insolent, concerning everything from extreme details of your racial ancestry, to any family history of "lunacy," to specifics regarding the shape and size of your children's heads. In fact, the list of census questions to be asked of an average citizen in the year 2000 may be one of the shortest since surveys began.

Of course, today's federal government does not rely solely on census data. (Nowadays it has lots of alternative sources of information.) A better perspective on the past might be achieved by browsing through newspaper clippings from almost any small town in America, from roughly the 1840s to the middle of this century. Modern sensibilities might be shocked by how widely and invasively the events of people's lives were covered by the local press, often with purple, judgmental prose, in journals that almost always unabashedly favored local patrician families. (Those who consider Rush Limbaugh to be uniquely talented at diatribe surely never read the disagreeably vivid Fenno and Freneau harangues, waged between Federalist and Democrat newspapers in Jefferson's day.)

Was there ever "privacy" for women, or members of minority groups, who often had to get cosignatures from a property-owning white male when they wished to enter a legal contract? Certainly, anyone who has traveled extensively in the Third World, or who grew up in a small town, knows one of the singular truths about human nature: that it has always been hard for people to hide personal affairs away from the curiosity of gossiping neighbors.

One needn't delve too deeply into the past to find rampant and repeated abuse of power by public authorities; for example, during the "idyllic" American 1950s and 1960s, Hoover's FBI reportedly sent tapes of Martin Luther King's infidelities to his wife, in a conspiratorial effort to drive him to suicide. From 1952 until 1979, the Chicago police routinely and offensively strip-searched female prisoners, even those detained for minor traffic violations. Legal immigrants had to register at frequent intervals at local police stations. At the height of the McCarthy hearings, those tarred by innuendo were forced to undergo severe and biased questioning—and sometimes had difficulty getting minimal police or fire protection.

From the perspective of a later era, modern law enforcement professionals look back on such attitudes and policies with disgust. And yet, the image of a better, more innocent past continues to hold sway in the public mind. Janna Malamud Smith, author of *Private Matters*, commented on this fallacy of perspective, the assumption that prior generations lived in some paradise of reticence and respectful seclusion, safe from meddlesome officials and nosy villagers alike.

> Much that is written about privacy is premised on the idea that privacy, once plentiful, is only now endangered. While privacy is endangered, it was hardly a staple in the past, when most people had little. . . . Privacy offers emotional and psychological opportunities that, far from having been continually present and now endangered, are in fact quite new, an exploration just beginning.

In other words, even if nostalgia is misguided, and there was no *golden age of privacy* in the past, that does not mean we must resign ourselves to putting up with all the recent outrages and irritations listed earlier in this chapter.

Okay, so privacy may be newer than we thought. The version we picture in our minds—featuring true individual sovereignty, secluded sanctums, plus a dash of voluntary anonymity—may be a recent innovation. Still, isn't it the very essence of progress that people should get what they want? And if we now desire this new kind of privacy, should we not—as independent citizens—be able to get ourselves some?

Don't we need privacy now more than ever, in order to stay free?

That question goes to the heart of this book. Yet we will put it aside for now. Before getting to our core argument—whether shadows or light will most effectively defend liberty—we should finish laying more groundwork, first by briefly talking about the law, and then by taking some excursions into important dilemmas of human nature.

> *We can complain all we want about Big Brother, but when we wrested our reputations from human memory and turned them over to far less judgmental computer circuits and phone lines—vanquishing those nasty old village snoops who might keep us from living out our hearts' desires—reputation remained as important as ever. The difference is that even as we have downplayed its significance—whether out of honest egalitarianism or excessive individualism—we have consigned it to the banal, impersonal testing ground of supermarket checkout stands and pre-employment background checks.*
>
> JEFFREY OBSER

> *Let's say that someday technology will allow anybody to find out every possible thing about my life. I can compensate by being so uninteresting that nobody could survive the process of snooping on me without lapsing into a coma.*
>
> SCOTT ADAMS, *THE DILBERT FUTURE*

## PRIVACY AND THE LAW

Although this book is actually about the benefits (and perhaps inevitability) of reciprocal candor, booksellers will almost certainly rack it in their section on books devoted to privacy. Nowadays, with so much angst being expended over the issue, enough writers and commentators have offered their own learned remarks on the subject to fill entire shelves with the latest offerings. One of the better recent books, Ellen Alderman and Caroline Kennedy's *The Right to Privacy*, deals with this issue from the perspective of American legal tradition, using case studies to cover a wide range of judicial precedents. For instance, although the constitutions of many nations explicitly contain such a right, the word *privacy* is not mentioned even once as such in the oldest and most famous modern national charter, the Constitution of the United States of America. The closest thing to such a promise can be found in the Fourth Amendment of the Bill of Rights, which forswears any violation of "The right of the people to be secure in their persons, houses, papers and effects, against unreasonable searches and seizures."

The U.S. Supreme Court has interpreted the Fourth Amendment as protecting a person's "reasonable expectation of privacy"; but that leaves a lot of room to wriggle in almost any direction. For instance, courts severely limit citizens' privacy privilege against law officers looking at their property from the air, or noting illegal activity that some other passerby might see from the street. Likewise, banking records are not strictly protected, since the customer implicitly waives some privacy by sharing information with the bank corporation. The same logic limits the extent to which telephone records, or trash, are protected against inspection. Underage students still live in uncertain limbo, with their privileges constantly being revised and fine-tuned by courts trying to balance individual rights against the needs of society to protect and constrain the young.

Moreover, it should be noted that the Constitution only formally protects citizens against actions *by the state*. The Fourth Amendment has almost no application to behavior of individuals, corporations, or the press. To regulate such private activities, governments must pass explicit statutes, or else citizens may seek recourse in the murky, precedent-based world of common law, called torts.

In what may come as a surprise to many Americans, there appears to have been very little formal protection of privacy during its purported golden age, the era of the wild west. Only in 1890, as the frontier was closing down, did glimmers of the modern approach appear, in an article written by Samuel D. Warren and Louis D. Brandeis (later a Supreme Court justice). Reportedly prompted by Warren's outrage over a malicious gossip column, this influential essay argued for a "right to privacy" that applied to civil injuries, thus creating an inherent power to sue others for "invasion of privacy."

The fundamental basis of this tort, as proposed by Warren and Brandeis, was that the pressures of an increasingly frenetic and technological society could be kept bearable only if individuals possessed an enforceable *"right to be let alone."* That phrase, more than any other, lies at the core of the privacy issue, as it is now seen by modern American jurists. (This legal definition may differ somewhat from the way privacy is envisioned by a layperson.)

As an associate justice, Brandeis later got a chance to promote this opinion further while dissenting in *Olmstead v. United States* (1928), and his influence in this area has grown ever since, as illustrated in a famous 1967 case, *Katz v. United States,* which established the right to be secure in one's private conversations as part of the interest protected by the Fourth Amendment. Later, in a landmark 1992 case, *Doe v. City of New York,* the Supreme Court unanimously declared that it recognizes *two* kinds of privacy. One is the right to make fundamental decisions (as in the case of abortion) without undue external interference. This class of privacy, based fundamentally on Brandeis's concept of the right to be let alone, covers what I call personal sovereignty. The second class, less fully explored even today, covers an individual's rights, authority, and obligations when it comes to avoiding the disclosure of personal information.

Let me take a step back at this point and confess that I'm not an attorney or legal scholar. Still, it is possible for an educated citizen to follow the general outlines of modern American privacy law as it continues to evolve across the end of the twentieth century. Of particular interest is Dean William Prosser's 1960 analysis of the privacy tort, which divides it into four categories.

**1.** *Intrusion* covers the violation (physical or otherwise) of another person's solitude in a highly offensive manner, for example, barging into the hospital room of a suffering victim and taking a picture over his or her objections.

**2.** *Disclosure of private facts* relates to the publicizing of highly offensive private information about someone that is not of legitimate interest to the public. This tort is entirely separate from libel and slander, which are covered by explicit statutes. Under the "private facts" tort, one can be held liable for damages *even if the disclosed information was true.* It should be noted that this tort is questioned by many legal scholars, with some states rejecting it entirely. Some others use "newsworthiness" as a test to determine whether a suit may proceed. It is also important to note that public figures can find no recourse in this principle.

**3.** *False light* is the act of portraying someone in a harmful manner, such as using the person's photo to illustrate a newspaper story about pedophilia, even if it is never explicitly stated that this individual was accused of the crime.

**4.** *Appropriation* consists of taking another person's name, likeness, or other identity-related data for unapproved use. This might apply to identity theft, as discussed earlier, although there are already laws against fraud. (See chapter 4 regarding who owns information.) Or it might also be used to seek redress against a company using a sports figure's likeness in advertising without her permission. (In this case, a public figure has *greater*-than-average protection.)

It should be noted that invasion-of-privacy lawsuits were rather rare before 1960, but after Prosser's article became influential, floodgates appeared to open. A new "right" became widely (and often indignantly) defended across the American landscape. And yet, Prosser's four categories are far from universally accepted. Nor have we begun to see more than a glimmer of their implications for the electronic age.

Although much of the legal activity surrounding privacy is taking place in the turbid realm of torts, there has also been some legislation by statute. For instance, when Judge Robert H. Bork was nominated to the U.S. Supreme Court, some journalists obtained his video rental records, presumably to learn if he had kinky tastes. Outraged by this intrusion, Congress passed the Video Privacy Act, outlawing this narrowly specific invasion of privacy. As yet, there is no comparable protection for books or periodicals, or even our medical histories. The Fair Credit Reporting Act gives individuals access to their records and limits disclosure of credit files. The Telephone Consumer Protection Act regulates telephone solicitations, and the Driver's Privacy Protection Act limits the release of motor vehicle records. But these laws are riddled with exceptions allowing "routine use" and the divulging of protected information for "legitimate business needs." Alderman and Kennedy sum up the situation thus: "As even a partial list of privacy laws indicates, they address a hodgepodge of individual concerns. The federal statutory scheme most resembles a jigsaw puzzle in which the pieces do not fit."

State laws sometimes try to fill in, but for the most part they are just as woefully scattershot. Anyway, they prove next to useless when it comes to matters in cyberspace, where there are no state, or even national, boundaries.

What all this shows is that the legal definition of privacy is still not chiseled in stone. More than a hundred years after Warren and Brandeis called for a right to privacy, the outlines of such a general, overarching principle remain downright murky. Even as we plunge into the electronic age, legal scholars keep hedging, backtracking, and disagreeing over the constantly shifting borderline between the essential interests of the individual and the practical needs of an urban state.

This chaos is especially noteworthy when we compare it to the way certain other rights, especially that of free speech, are treated as quasi-religious essences and defended with rulings that are fierce in their sweeping, uncompromising clarity. Robert Bork is among the many jurists who have called privacy a "derived" right, not a basic one, like free speech.

What does tend to come through many recent privacy decisions is the following:

1. The "right to be let alone," to go about our lives free from unreasonable interference by external forces, has become somewhat accepted as a guiding principle of common law.

2. A ruling of "unreasonable interference" is more probable if the plaintiff faces actual harm or active obstacles to exercising personal sovereignty. It is much less likely to be accepted if complainants merely do not like others knowing things about them.

3. The pragmatic outcome of a case—which party is hurt and by how much—generally matters at least as much as any all-encompassing precept. An invasion of privacy is often whatever *seems* unduly invasive according to the standards of reasonable contemporary citizens.

## PRIVACY LAW IN ALLIED NATIONS

What are the legal traditions in other parts of the neo-West? Privacy is not seen quite the same way, even in countries that share many common values. The European approach to privacy matters may in some ways seem more relaxed than in the United States. Many nations make income tax records public, for example, without much apparent harm or resentment. Sweden gives citizens a unique identification number that tracks them all their lives.

Other aspects of privacy receive more thorough protection, to the point of being guaranteed in national constitutions. Many European countries, as well as Canada, Australia, New Zealand, Hong Kong, and Japan, have created an office of privacy commissioner, something unseen in the United States. In 1980, the Organization of Economic Cooperation and Development (OECD) adopted Guidelines on the Protection of Privacy and Transborder Flows of Personal Data, whose goal was to "harmonize national privacy legislation and, while upholding such human rights, [to] at the same time prevent interruptions in international flows of data."

In 1998, a further evolution of the OECD's Guidelines will go into effect with the European Union's (EU) Directive on Protection of Personal Data. This edict aims to establish "a stable regulatory framework to enable the movement of personal data from one country to another, while at the same time ensuring that privacy protection is 'adequate' in the country to which the data is sent. If the recipient country has not established a minimum standard of data protection, it is expected that the transfer of data will be prohibited."

At this point it seems unlikely that American standards will be "adequate" in time, posing the possibility that transfer of personal data from EU countries to the United States may be disrupted.

## "PRACTICAL OBSCURITY"?

Many kinds of government data have traditionally been accessible to the public, especially to diligent researchers willing to spend considerable time and energy driving from courthouse to city hall, then to the local federal building, then to the hall of records and back again. These open files generally include property tax records, voter rolls, and committee minutes, as well as the daily log of pleas, prosecutions, and arraignments at each widely dispersed courtroom. While such archives might be restricted in many other nations, the basic principle behind free access in America is the same one underlying this book, namely, accountability. Even before the computer was invented, any citizen with the requisite passion, intelligence, skill, and free time might collate enough information to prepare a case against a corrupt administrator, nailing him either for malfeasance or some outrageous error, even if the authorities *formally* charged with the official's supervision had failed at their task.

High officials have always felt profound ambiguity toward this tradition. Even as august and respected a leader as postwar Secretary of State George Marshall once said that he approved of democracy highly ". . . though I suffer from it greatly." As we saw at the end of chapter 2, and will explore further, our system encourages the unleashing of countless amateur sleuths and activists, each self-righteously determined to foil some perceived outrage and insistent on accessing all the tools they need to prove their point.

Elected and appointed officials, being human, naturally resist being held accountable in such a confrontational fashion. Even those with a clear conscience typically drag their feet, for instance, by delaying compliance with requests filed under the Freedom of Information Act (FOIA). They cite national security, or claim forgetfulness, or fail to budget for compliance (resulting in yearlong queues for even simple questions), or use "spin control" to avoid giving direct answers that might be taken out of context. Above all, many are terrified by the latest trend of computerized and rapid public access to all "open" records.

Many of the files that used to take teams of researchers days and weeks to pore through, laboriously visiting scores of locales, can now be scanned by online search engines, delivering swift and accurate correlations. This development understandably frightens some bureaucrats, who foresee hordes of news reporters and dilettante activists swarming over every document, peering to find the slightest mistake. Desperate for an excuse to impede this floodlight of enhanced accountability, some officials have grasped at a convenient and popular rationale, privacy.

Some years ago, while investigating possible illegal campaign contributions, CBS news correspondent Robert Schackne applied under FOIA for a set of raw FBI criminal data that were officially part of the public record. The FBI refused, and the agency's position was subsequently sustained by the U.S. Supreme Court on the grounds that Schackne's trawling violated the personal privacy of those listed in the database. Writing for the majority, Justice John Paul Stevens noted that while most of the material contained in the FBI's rap sheets was public, private citizens had hitherto benefited from their "practical obscurity." "There is a vast difference between the public records that might be found after a diligent search of courthouse files, county archives and local police stations throughout the country and a computerized summary located in a single clearinghouse," Stevens wrote in the 1989 *Justice Dept. v. Reporters Committee* decision.

Which means that it was all right to make paper records available, because they were effectively inaccessible to all but the most determined, or those rich enough to hire paid researchers. As far as the common man or woman was concerned, the records might as well be located on the Moon—and this situation was a *good* thing, according to Stevens.

But computer accessibility came along, threatening this happy equilibrium. If unchecked, the tools would prove intolerably invasive.

To the plaintiffs in the 1989 case, the message sent by this decision was evident. The First Amendment is great, as long as there is no efficient means of carrying it out. Indeed, a number of jurists and legislators have proposed to solve the computerization problem by establishing a new legal principle: *that access to electronic records should be roughly equivalent to their availability on paper.* Presumably, this might be done by resetting your modem down to a mere 15 baud, whenever you connect to one of these bad but open databases.

As absurdly Luddite as the proposal appears at first sight, matters are actually far worse, since powerful entities—big corporations, government bureaucrats, or anyone with official connections—already have access to the electronic data stores, and no initiative will cut *them* off. In effect, an opportunity to greatly improve the flow of light and accountability is being used instead as an excuse to *reduce* it. Using privacy as a shield, members of a threatened Brahmin class seek to freeze the world as they were accustomed to it—a slow-paced realm of quaint filing cabinets, acid-tongued clerks, and manila folders redolent of dust and termites. Presumably, the same scholars would also rule that financial transactions should move no faster than when we all pulled heavy coins from leather purses.

True, the databases can be abused, and they contain a multitude of errors (see examples in the first part of this chapter). Privacy *will* be put under some stress if people become expert at perusing the whole range of public documentation. Basic rethinking may be appropriate concerning which kinds of personal information can be released, and when. Proposed systems like Open Profiling and TRUSTe show how some believe we can implement fair information practices—though with transparency in mind, we should err on the side of openness.

All of that can be negotiated, as long as the result puts average citizens on even ground with MegaCorp, Inc. But deliberately fostered "obscurity" is no solution. Rather, it is a craven refusal to seek a solution. Errors can be corrected only after being discovered, and the best way to prevent abuse is to let everyone in equally, shining light on all potential abusers of trust and forcing them to realize that they are being watched, even as they peer at others.

What does this all mean? When it comes to privacy, there are many inductive rules, but very few universally accepted axioms.

If we cannot count on jurists to define privacy for us, or legislators to supply realistic protections for it, those tasks will largely be our responsibility during the decades and generations to come. Judges and scholars have trod lightly along this path for one reason above all others: as the years go by it is a free citizenry, not only in America but throughout the neo-West, that will ultimately decide how much priority to give the matter.

In the long run, it will come down to us, deciding what we want.

> *The right to privacy includes a sense of autonomy, a right to develop a unique personality and living space, and a right to distinguish one's own persona from everyone else's.*
>
> ROBERT ELLIS SMITH

## PRIVACY AS A PERSONAL GOAL

Well, then, what should we want?

Philosophers have also been at work—quite separately from legal scholars—attempting to palpate, measure, and encompass the concept of privacy. For example Alan Westin, in his influential work *Privacy and Free-dom*, described four kinds: solitude, anonymity, reserve, and intimacy.

The most complete form of privacy, *solitude*, is about seeking separation from your fellow humans and being secure against intrusion, observation, or interruption, free to "let your hair down" and do what you would not do if there were a chance of being watched. This may involve anything from routine toiletry all the way to shouting out the rage against the world that all of us feel now and then but some never dare express in public. Most people find enforced or protracted solitude intolerable, but when undertaken voluntarily it can be essential for creativity, a sense of freedom, or restoring the soul.

To be *anonymous* is to be unnamed, unnoticed, part of a crowd. In an urban setting, anonymity can provide many of the same benefits as solitude, letting us stroll down a busy street content that no one is likely to be looking at us at this precise moment. Yet, in the anonymous context *we* can be people watchers, or express feelings we might suppress if those nearby knew our name. While this kind of privacy leaves hooligans and criminals unaccountable, anonymity also shelters a shy person from having to guard every word. Lost amid the mob at a sports stadium, she can yell her head off as she might never dare to, back among family and friends.

*Reserve* could be illustrated by an elegant person who is detached and dignified—or else by the pimply kid sitting across from you on a bus, withdrawn behind headphones into his own private world. Such people are not necessarily anonymous. You may know their names. Yet by choice they are not entirely *there*. They withhold opinions and confidences, preserving them to share with others, or at another time. Even the most extroverted among us wants the option to choose, moving back and forth across a spectrum of reserve.

Westin's fourth state, *intimacy*, is the opening of a door between two gardens, a merging of realities, even as the rest of humanity is barred from taking part. If the gist of all types of privacy is choice and control, then intimacy—the choice of whom to share with, how much, and for how long—is its purest form. Or, as Janna Malamud Smith puts it, "The virtue of privacy, as I have come to understand it, is not in isolating people, but in allowing them temporary space in which they may accomplish important human tasks that are otherwise thwarted."

This is just a summary, and Westin is not without critics in privacy circles. But the capsule version presented here may prove useful to our work in this book. If I sound sympathetic to all four types of privacy mentioned above, the reader should not be surprised. As a human, I recognize all these needs in myself, and can extrapolate that they also apply to the other bipedal beings around me who are striving, shouting, and hurting. Moreover, to be an eccentric in this world is to have special needs and cravings for solitude, anonymity, reserve, and intimacy. There is just one salient point to add:

*All of these deeply human desiderata are enhanced by freedom.*

Despite sharing the world with more than six billion pairs of sapient eyes on a planet where every square meter appears to have been explored or exploited, and where cities teem increasingly with cameras, it can reasonably be argued that most citizens of the affluent neo-West have more access to Westin's four privacies than their ancestors ever did. Although life's frenetic pace seems to press from all sides, things were hardly any better for our farmer forebears. At least we *do* have headphones, private bedrooms, the sealed enclosures of our automobiles, several thousand square miles of urban and rural landscape within an hour's drive, and telephones to reach that special intimate friend, even when he or she lives half a continent away.

A majority of us can close the door to our rooms now and then, making it hard to imagine how our ancestors lived in crowded one-room cottages or multifamily apartments. Moreover, unlike the chiefs, kings, and priests of past eras, today's authorities are severely limited in their power to intrude.

There is a reason for this; the same reason that jurists almost consistently rule with lightning zeal on issues of free speech, even while they have such a hard time defining the outlines of a "right to privacy." It is because the two are not equivalent. While free speech seems an indivisible, immiscible right that must be preserved with absolute clarity for liberty's sake, privacy appears to be more like a liquid, a delicacy that free people can pour for themselves, as much or as little as they choose. I have said this elsewhere, and will make the point again: Privacy is a wonderful, highly desirable *benefit* of freedom. As sovereign citizens, we can debate the details among ourselves, and then choose to vote ourselves some.

On the other hand, there can be few compromises when it comes to protecting the underpinnings of liberty. Those foundations will crumble unless they are guarded with fervent vigilance. Without both individual freedom and distributed sovereignty, all our vaunted modern privacy would vanish into legend, consigning us back to the oppressive feudal villages or despotic collectives that less fortunate men and women knew all their lives.

*There is a growing consensus that if the jumble of state and federal statutes, consumer pressure, and self-help is to be unified into meaningful privacy protection in the digital age, then we will have to do more than pass a law. The law in general, and each of us in particular, will have to make some fundamental adjustments in the way we think of personal information and electronic communication. In doing so, we will ultimately have to change our idea of what we can reasonably expect to keep private.*

ELLEN ALDERMAN AND CAROLINE KENNEDY

## RECIPROCAL TRANSPARENCY

Bearing in mind all we've learned, let's go back to the problems described at the start of this chapter—modern quandaries and threats to privacy in our turn-of-the-century world. A careful reappraisal shows that most of these examples share two common traits.

**1. The Reflex Response.** The way some activists suggest dealing with any problematic situation is to *shut down the information flow.* To pass some rule impeding somebody else from acquiring or sharing a particular type of data. In other words, to prohibit a specified kind of knowing.

Alas, we'll see in chapter 5 that this type of "solution" conflicts fundamentally with human nature. We are, at our core, information pack rats and inveterate correlators. We hunger for news, facts, and rumors—especially when they are forbidden! In this attribute, the rich and powerful, and major corporations, are no different from the rest of us.

The predictable consequence? If one kind of data acquisition is made illegal, you can be certain that someone will be doing it anyway on the sly, and possibly turning its dissemination into yet another highly profitable criminal enterprise, one that must be policed by yet another bureaucracy.

Here is a little philosophical exercise that can sometimes be instructive. When dealing with so-called obvious solutions to fundamental issues, always try to imagine what might happen if we extrapolate the recommended trend to some extreme degree. For instance, consider a hypothetical world in which *free speech* reached levels of absurd exaggeration. To most of us, the resulting image would be of a place that is noisy, frenetic, and perhaps even scandalous—but despite all that, also productive and free. An overdose of free speech might be nasty, but hardly fatal.

Now consider the "obvious solution" that is nearly always applied to privacy problems. Selective censorship. One bureaucracy to regulate *this* kind of information, and another agency to monitor *that* kind of data. Laws forbidding you to know this or tell that. The trend doesn't have to be extrapolated to any logical extreme before the mind starts to reel.

Conclusion: If you start forbidding people from knowing things—for example, telling physicians what they may and may not learn about their patients' health—then take care. It might be effective for a little while, but soon you could find yourself embarked down a dangerous river, one whose *reductio ad absurdum* terminus is hell.

And yet, many of the examples cited earlier in this chapter seem to hint at a possible alternative, already discernible within the problem itself.

**2. Reciprocal Transparency.** Among the aims of this book is to present a second entire class of solutions to privacy issues, whose approach is not to close down information flows, but rather to compensate by opening them wider. For instance, if some company wishes to collect data on consumers across America, let it do so only on condition that the top one hundred officers in the firm must post exactly the same information about themselves and all their family members on an accessible Web site.

Right now, an ever-increasing number of companies are using electronic means to monitor their clerical employees, to a degree that no keystroke goes uncounted. No pause for breath goes unmetered. This may seem objectionable and Orwellian to modern folks. It is also completely inevitable. As managers acquire such powers of supervision, justifying it all as "optimization," we could begin an endless struggle to regulate these practices, creating a vast *apparat* of antagonistic government inspectors, shop stewards, and company human resources experts.

Or else, as Professor Gary Marx suggests, we could try simply forcing higher-ups to share the accountability—and the pain. "While I am certainly not an advocate of unrestrained monitoring," Marx says. "It does seem only fair that . . . the same methods and technologies be applied to managers."

Instead of introducing hairsplitting rules and a dour bureaucracy to enforce this principle, the desired result could be achieved by letting unions, stockholders, or even individual workers file suit for the enforcement of a simple reciprocity rule, or tort. In fact, Marx suggests, the case for monitoring executives is much greater because their performance is more crucial to company success, and because their errors (or illegal activities) may have far greater consequences. "We might even adopt a principle that the more central a position and the higher the costs from poor performance, the greater should be the degree of monitoring. The credibility of those who advocate monitoring increases to the extent they are willing to apply the same technologies to themselves."

Likewise, if some institution establishes a drug-testing program, justified on grounds of both security and safety, it might be both fair and pragmatic to make all managers submit to the same snap inspections, and to ensure that the program checks for illicit chemicals currently fashionable among the aristocratic class. If it is feared that insurance companies might be prejudiced against clients based on their family genetic histories, why not supplement antidiscrimination laws by requiring the executives of any firm wishing to use gene-based data first to submit themselves and their immediate relations to all available genetic tests, and publish the results?

It isn't perfect, but at least there might be a bit less hypocrisy, and a tad more sympathy.

Let's suppose for a moment that I am right about those cameras—an infestation of stationary lenses, and even flying drones, that may soon fill the skies over every city. Which measure is more likely to help us secure our homes against invasions by new, high-tech Peeping Toms who send tiny, remote-controlled wasp cameras into our bedrooms: yet another unenforceable *law?* Or instead providing folks with high-tech tools of transparency that might detect and track those invasive little robot spies all the way back to their impudent pilots? Few people do anything in their bedrooms that would be more embarrassing to reveal than the shame that might befall such perverted voyeurs when their acts are shouted forth.

As with any criminal activity, it is not the ferocity of punishment that deters, *but the certainty of getting caught.* Through reciprocal transparency, we might enforce fairness simply by using one of the oldest and most famous parables, "Judge not, lest ye be judged." Fairness would be compelled not by exhortation and regimentation but by demanding equal application of the Golden Rule.

"It's a very schizophrenic time," says Sherry Turkle, professor of sociology at MIT, adding, "We have very unstable notions about the boundaries of the individual."

She might also be talking about the conflict between prescriptions (1) and (2) above, apparently opposite approaches to ensuring fairness in the coming century. Opposition between these two philosophies already deeply divides the community of electronic age rights activists. For example, Marc Rotenberg, director of EPIC, supports the European model of an agency set up to provide legal protections and enforce regulations, but members of the Cato Institute and many EFF activists prefer a hands-off approach.

I won't be doctrinaire and try to claim that the reciprocal transparency alternative will always be right for every modern dilemma. There will surely be times when the only viable solution to some problem is to forbid the collection, distribution, and/or storing of certain kinds of knowledge, at least for a limited time. My chief argument is that we should avoid doing this *routinely*, as a dubious but addictive habit. In principle, an open society sees information flow as a good thing, to be hampered only in the presence of strong evidence that harm cannot be prevented by any other means.

Having said that, let me strengthen the argument for reciprocal transparency by, paradoxically, pointing out some potential flaws and weaknesses!

- Reciprocity may be rendered ineffective if one side simply doesn't care what others know or think of them. Some judgmental types may try to make themselves "immune" to reciprocity by coming clean with gaudy confessions, then zealously seeking to redeem others the same way. Such behavior has already been exhibited in our era by some gays who have come out of the closet and proceed to "out" others. Similar fervid morals campaigns are waged from the opposite end of the political spectrum by some whose religious sanctimony makes them feel righteously immune to rebuke, freeing them to lash at others without restraint.

- Companies may start recruiting executives from the ranks of the "squeaky clean" rather than for their management skills (a situation that has been happening to politicians for a long time). These administrators could pass all forms of scrutiny, and thus feel free to pass judgment on others.

- Even if two sides have equivalent information, there will still be inequality in their ability to act upon the data. ("We already know our bosses do nothing, so spying on them won't help.") The relative powerlessness of one side might spur greater efforts at coalition building—or it could result in apathy or despair.

These are reasonable criticisms of an admittedly imperfect idea. Yet none of these pragmatic worries is a devastating refutation in principle. And as we shall see in later chapters, each objection has one or more feasible solutions. In any case, reciprocity is more equitable and less complicated than regulation. Even if such measures are only partly effective, they will leave us at least a little better off than before. That is how empirical civilizations solve problems—one practical step at a time.

Anyway, what seems appalling at this point, so near the close of the twentieth century, is that whenever dilemmas erupt concerning privacy, only one class of solutions seems to dominate. The reflex reaction—to try and squelch others from knowing things—may fit human nature, but it is still a dour, suspicious, and ultimately futile approach. Even if those "others" are people you don't approve of very much.

For the record, let me emphasize that I am *not* arguing for people to abruptly go naked or to unilaterally foresake traditional forms of privacy. Certainly transparency can only work if it happens in a manner that people call "fair." Whenever some outsider asserts a need to peer at you, it is only proper to demand: "First show me yours, before I show you mine!" This holds doubly when the inquisitive party is some government official or agency.

What I am suggesting is that in the future, whenever we argue over how to deal with some vexing problem involving information and justice, we should at least consider how the second class of solutions might apply. Reciprocal transparency solutions that involve pushing aside stuffy drapes rather than shutting them, opening a door instead of slamming it, and above all letting *more* air flow through, rather than less.

The next chapter is about a matter that some readers may find a little dry, the problem of *intellectual property* in this new electronic age. Chapter 5 will then return to some flamboyant speculations about human nature and our rambunctious, amazing civilization. Later in this book we will cover specific aspects of the modern debate over privacy and anonymity in the Internet era, going into controversies like the "Clipper chip" imbroglio, in which the U.S. government sought the power to eavesdrop on encrypted conversations and data transfers. The firestorm reaction to that proposal, and others like it, illuminates many of the issues raised in this chapter, showing how widespread perceptions of privacy collide with matters of public well-being.

In exploring these matters, we'll see that some vituperative shouting matches are based on simple misunderstandings, whereas other disagreements appear so fundamental that compromise of any sort may be anathema to either side.

# THE ACCOUNTABILITY MATRIX

*"No man is so fond of freedom himself that he would not chuse to subject the will of some individuals of society to his own."*

OLIVER GOLDSMITH, *THE VICAR OF WAKEFIELD*

In 1996 the famed muckraker and consumer advocate Ralph Nader was the presidential candidate of California's Green Party. At one point, after lecturing earnestly about the need to hold corporate officials accountable for every nefarious transaction and scheme, Nader was asked why he refused to publish his own financial records, as all other candidates had done. Without irony, Nader replied that his own bank and tax statements were private, and by refusing to comply he was making an important gesture for liberty. This despite the fact that he was running for the most powerful office in the land, and the one most urgently in need of relentless scrutiny.

Such unidirectionality of righteousness, so typical of our era, illustrates how people can be trusted to hold their foes accountable but are seldom as scrupulous in applying the same standards to themselves.

Information can flow in various ways that provoke people subjectively and powerfully, depending on their point of view. For instance, self-interest attracts us to any new development that increases our power to see others, especially our opponents, the better to observe their actions and stratagems. It is quite another matter when something comes along that makes *us* more naked and visible to our foes! Consider how this is illustrated in the following matrix.

85

| 1. TOOLS THAT HELP *ME* SEE WHAT *OTHERS* ARE UP TO | 2. TOOLS THAT PREVENT *OTHERS* FROM SEEING WHAT *I* AM UP TO |
|---|---|
| 3. TOOLS THAT HELP *OTHERS* SEE WHAT *I* AM UP TO | 4. TOOLS THAT PREVENT *ME* FROM SEEING WHAT *OTHERS* ARE UP TO |

Now, where it says "others," go ahead and insert some person or group, such as "government" or "aristocrats" or "corporations"—perhaps your worst foe, or whomever you perceive as a dangerous power center in the world. You are likely to call "good" any device, law, or technical advancement that enhances the effectiveness of categories 1 and 2. In contrast, whatever comes along that increases the effectiveness of 3 and 4 may raise your discomfort level, if not ire.

Illustrating this, EFF cofounder John Gilmore has been outspoken about restricting government's ability to conceal (through tools like FOIA), while also curbing its ability to see (by promoting encryption and denying the FBI court-ordered access to the coded communications of suspected criminals).

> The US government attracts a lot of people who like wielding power. We limit the power of our government for the health of our society. . . . We've seen what happens when states get those powers. We get governments that can't be voted out of office, that must be run out with guns; administrations that torture people, dictators who steal from their citizens. We get reigns of terror, inquisitions, star chambers, political prisoners, J. Edgar Hoovers.

Gilmore's statement sounds prudent. Government *does* attract the power hungry (though so do other walks of life). But historically, the ability of governments to oppress has always depended on maintaining a *one-way* flow of information. Kings, tyrants, and parties in power above all concealed things from the citizenry at large. In contrast, one would be hard pressed to show that restricting the amount of information flowing *to* government has more than a marginal impact on preventing the arrival of tyranny.

In fact, there is a vivid counterexample: *us.* Despite uncountable flaws in our contemporary neo-Western world, there has never been a major urban society in which individuals of all social classes had more freedom than we do today. This is true despite the fact that our government knows far more about its citizens than any other in history. The one factor making this possible has been reciprocity of information flow.

Each time government acquired new powers of sight, citizens seized another tool for enforcing transparency and accountability *from* government. From open-meeting laws, to special prosecutors and conflict-of-interest prosecutions, to whistleblower protections, to financial disclosure codes and the vaunted FOIA, we have (so far) successfully used such tools to thwart the potential of tyranny that is inherent in any coercive bureaucratic system. Moreover, this was accomplished not by blinding our officials but by granting them the vision they claimed to need, and then insisting that they walk around (metaphorically) naked, observed, supervised, and forced to account for each marginal abuse of power.

Chastened by the Watergate experience, citizens seem to know almost instinctively that it is better to shine too much light than too little. Witness the so-called scandals that have transfixed U.S. news media in recent years. Would any past Speaker of the House have received so much attention for minor improprieties as Newt Gingrich did for letting a Republican think tank pay for a minor lecture course? In former times, would anyone have bothered a First Lady for firing some members of the White House travel office? And yet, I am not saying that lesser peccadilloes should be dismissed! Increased scrutiny and raising of standards may irk public officials who as a consequence find themselves living in a searchlight glare, with minor infractions receiving the attention of felonies, but that seems a small price to pay for the vigilance freedom requires.

And the trend continues. As terrorists, criminals, and bombers go more high-tech and lethal, each new heinous act will prompt government appeals for greater surveillance powers. Perhaps citizens will refuse these requests nine times in a row—until something truly grievous happens. Then, in the ensuing dread and panic, a frightened public will grant those new powers. No indignant posturing or bleating about sacred privacy rights will prevent it.

But we can make sure baby won't be thrown out with the bath water, *by doing the same thing we've done all along.* By demanding that officials be scrutinized every bit as much as they scrutinize us.

Two millennia ago Juvenal posed the riddle, "Who shall watch the watchman?"

There is just one answer. We all will.

•   •   •

Going back to the accountability matrix, one can take almost any contemporary privacy issue and see people choosing different boxes, depending on their point of view. As Ralph Nader vividly illustrated, any effort either to restrict or open up a data spigot is judged good or evil subjectively. When we enhance our own "privacy," this may be seen by others as a sneaky attempt to keep them in the dark, a conspiratorial veil that might conceal threats to their liberty.

Nowhere is this tendency more apparent than on the Internet, where the semi-official dogma is openness and liberty, but where unpopular opinions are often greeted with vicious attacks and masked retribution. *Wired* magazine columnist Jon Katz posed the problem in October 1996: "What exactly does freedom of speech mean here? Are we only to post opinions that young, angry males like, or things we all agree are politically correct?" Describing the behavior of many "netizens" whose subjective ethics fit the accountability matrix perfectly, Katz complained that: "Freedom of speech seems to mean we get to say whatever we want whenever we want. If people don't like it, tough. But hostility, personal attacks, and flaming, have, in some ways, already done more harm than the CDA (Communications Decency Act) ever could."

Is this inevitable? Does human nature have to conflict with maturity and good sense?

Each of us would *personally* call boxes 1 and 2 good, and boxes 3 and 4 bad. But if our aim is to live in a society that is fair and free, the tools needed by our commons will be those favoring boxes *1* and *3*, enhancing our ability to hold others accountable, and their ability to do the same to us.

The most dangerous trends, laws, and technologies are those promoting boxes 2 and 4, pitting citizens against one another in an arms race of masks, secrets, and indignation.

## CHAPTER FOUR

# CAN WE OWN INFORMATION?

*I find the prospect of documented lives a
little chilling, but some people will warm
to the idea. One reason for documenting
a life will be defensive. If someone ever
accused you of something, you could
retort: "Hey, buddy, I have a documented
life . . . I can play back anything I've ever
said. So don't play games with me."*

BILL GATES, *THE ROAD AHEAD*

*There are some things man was not
meant to know.*

H. P. LOVECRAFT

Privacy is not the only reason that people are frantic to control information. An even stronger motive stirs bitter efforts to dominate streams and reservoirs of data, not only on the Internet but wherever else the tributaries lead. That motive is *revenue*.

It has become fashionable to call information the "money of the future," a new take on the old adage that knowledge is power. Perceiving a potential for profit, corporations and individuals are now laying claim to all sorts of facts, as well as strings of words, bits, or sounds. Thus we see professional sports leagues attempting to assert exclusive property over game scores. Movie studios seek new copyright rules so broad and proactive that they could conceivably outlaw personal computers (as possible tools for copying infringement). Government agencies try to fund themselves by selling to favored private firms the sole right to distribute public records digitally. Software vendors demand laws to make "shrink-wrap licenses" as fully enforceable as freely entered agreements. And publishers of noncopyrightable (because noncreative) works such as telephone directory white pages lobby for new legal protections so sweeping that the National Academy of Sciences condemned them as potentially stifling to research.

According to Pamela Samuelson, professor of law and information management at the University of California, Berkeley, "These examples show how the ongoing revolution in information technology is affecting older views of intellectual property, in ways that are being felt far beyond the computing field."

Such anecdotes only hint at the complexity of future "ownership" dilemmas. For instance, our own bodies were built according to plans coded in complex molecular packets of deoxyribonucleic acid (DNA), called genes. Each of us, except for identical twins and other clones, has a unique genetic pattern that is intrinsically one of the most personal things anyone can know about us. Does this mean a sovereign citizen should therefore *control* any scientific or commercial use of the specific patterned sequence of coded letters representing his or her DNA? No act of creativity or investment risk was undertaken by the individual making such a claim, nor does he or she undergo any tangible sacrifice or loss if some medical institute applies that code to produce some useful product. Nevertheless, shouldn't the "source" individual share in the proceeds? Might he or she even claim the power to withhold permission—refusing to share information that could save another person's life?

Are personal data a commodity? Are individuals endowed by their Creator, or by natural law, with an innate proprietary power over the words, images, and factual details of their lives? According to privacy scholars Arthur Miller, Alan Westin, and Ken Laudon, this broad theory of data ownership may offer an effective legal weapon against inquisitive governments and corporations, especially if people could bring charges of "theft" against a commercial database that compiles their address or Social Security number, or anyone else who gathers private information without permission. Communications attorney Anne Wells Branscomb, in her 1994 book *Who Owns Information? From Privacy to Public Access*, proposed that "our names and addresses and personal transactions are valuable information assets worthy of recognition that we have property rights in them." That sentiment is echoed by the ACLU in its Take Back Your Data campaign, pushing for legislation allowing individuals to prevent others from using their personal information, and basing this in part on inherent property rights. Taking a radical approach, P. Michael Nugent, general counsel for technology and intellectual property for Citibank, proposed two fundamental rights: control over personal information and a "right to be unknown," a pair of assertions we'll see again in chapter 7.

Australian privacy scholar Roger Clarke is among those opposing this approach.

> Information as a *commodity* is one of my pet hates. Most people think it's a turkey of an idea. The property notion began with real estate, and migrated, with some difficulties, to chattels. To extend it to replicable intellectual ephemera is pointless, and doomed to failure. The useful convention is to recognize *interests* in data, and in the case of personal data to recognize a very strong interest on the part of the data subject.

Even Clarke's views appear somewhat radical compared with the present legal situation in the United States, where courts have tended to rule that consumers who engage in commercial transactions with companies have essentially chosen to go public with any information they provided, and thereafter have no reasonable expectation of control over that data — except as provided for in specific statutes. (We described some of these current and proposed laws in chapter 3.)

Where society finally lands along this continuum will be vitally important to life in the future. A generalized principle of data ownership, if carried to its logical conclusions, would almost certainly produce a citizenry that spends half the next century in courtrooms, filing indignant injunctions to keep other people from sharing this or that snippet of knowledge without permission — in other words, a permanent entitlement program for lawyers. On the other hand, it can be galling to see huge commercial interests profit from the income-generating value of our personal data, without making token efforts to share the proceeds, or even a modicum of dignity, with those who have a stake in those flickering bits and bytes.

At first glance this can be seen as yet another example of the ongoing struggle between passionate theoreticians and pragmatists, those who believe in *essences* versus those who concern themselves with the *effects* on real people and cultures. Later, we'll address this point head-on, continuing the 2,500-year-old tussle between Plato and Pericles to the verge of a new millennium. But by now it should be clear that this book — whose central thesis is that liberty will be better protected by light than by shadows — deals with freedom and other important matters from a perspective of practical empiricism.

What works? What practical measures have already helped this society achieve elevated levels of wealth, education, and openness, with greater diversity and more individual liberty than any of its predecessors? Which other measures may be needed for our newest commons, the Internet, to grow and thrive, transforming itself into a tool for better things to come?

It is time to take a fresh look at the rules that society uses to coordinate the ownership of informational property.

*That ideas should spread freely from one to another over the globe, for the moral and mutual instruction of man, and improvement of his condition, seems to have been peculiarly and benevolently designed by nature, when she made them, like fire, expansible over all space, without lessening their density at any point, and like the air in which we breathe, move, and have our physical being, incapable of confinement or exclusive appropriation. Inventions then cannot, in nature, be a subject of property.*

THOMAS JEFFERSON

## THE END OF COPYRIGHT?

In the middle ages, artisan guilds kept tight control over various technical and mechanical arts, restricting them for exploitation only by acknowledged master tradesmen. Others who wanted to use these forbidden crafts had to do so clandestinely—and so a great many people did exactly that. Later, the principle was expanded, as kings created monopolies to reward favored supporters and maximize revenue from various overseas ventures. For instance, when the British monarchy granted "patents" to the Hudson Bay Company and the East India Company, the objective was to funnel all British trade in these regions through an exclusive set of corporate officers (with the king a silent partner). In effect, it was an application of state force with the sole aim of preventing competition.

History shows that this scheme seldom worked very well. In response to such exclusions, many clever and daring entrepreneurs took the traditional recourse open to those who are excluded by law from trade: they went underground. As smugglers and black marketeers they created a second economy that thrived in parallel to the official one—untaxed and unsupervised—prompting the Crown to spend far more on patrol ships and other enforcement measures than it gained through lavishing favoritism on patent holders. Nor do these superficial losses begin to measure the damage resulting from a general concomitant increase in crime and disrespect for law. In time it became evident that this kind of patent regulation was both foolish and self-defeating.

Late in the seventeenth century, a second theory began circulating, a notion almost diametrically opposite to the one underlying the East India Company, or the exclusivity of medieval guilds. This notion proposed using patents to *increase* openness, encouraging all commercial activity to come out of the shadows and stimulating the fastest possible sharing of technical advances for the benefit of all society.

How would such a miracle be achieved? Until this time, patents were synonymous with monopoly, forcing others who wanted to use the forbidden thing (an invention, or a trade route) to do so surreptitiously. In response, to prevent cheaters from stealing their techniques, inventors often went to great lengths to keep their innovations secret. But now reformers suggested turning the whole process on its head. They would return the word *patent* to its original meaning (having to do with something being open or apparent, as in "patently obvious"). The power of the state would not be used to enforce exclusive franchises, but rather to make certain that inventors and other creators *were rewarded for sharing.*

The means to do this would be a well-regulated market, or clearinghouse, allowing individuals to stake claim to their novel techniques for a fair but limited time, and license the rights in exchange for reasonable royalties. Under this system, the main goal was never to guarantee profits for inventors! Instead, profit would simply be a vehicle for achieving the real aim, which was to make sure that knowledge was openly shared, as quickly as possible, and that economic activity would take place in the open, where it could be taxed.

The Statute of Anne, enacted in Britain in 1710, was the first national law to attempt this approach. Almost eighty years later, after some further evolution of thinking on the subject, the United States Constitution empowered Congress to pass laws "to promote progress of science and useful arts." Benjamin Franklin was among those intimately involved in designing the Patent Office according to principles of maximized transparency. Since these beginnings, and despite many flaws, the system has worked admirably in many nations.

During any generation, the test of any system for regulating intellectual property has always been to what extent most innovators are tempted to keep their advances secret, in order to retain an advantage for a while, until competitors finally discover or duplicate them. Most inventors and other creators in the West eschew this tantalizing option, choosing instead to file for patents, counting on modest but reliable commissions for their accomplishments. This high level of participation proved the system was doing its job. Hence the spread of patent-based expertise accelerated, benefiting all.

A similar idea lay behind *copyrights*, which reward creativity of a different sort — stringing words together in unique and meaningful sequences, or generating other original works of subjective art. The more interesting or captivating a creation is perceived by others, the more income its writer or artist should receive, normally through royalties, a per-sale share in retail proceeds. But again, over the long run, it is society and consumers that profit most from such relatively open exchange.

Indeed, most authors also spend a large part of their lives "consuming" works that other scribblers produce, so they benefit from that side of the deal, too. In the metaphor of a commons, patent and copyright law enable creative people to "graze their sheep openly" and sell the wool for a fair price, without fear of losing the whole herd to the next big bully who comes along.

Alas, what works well during one generation may need fine-tuning — or even a major overhaul — in the next. Today we can see signs of immense strain in this traditional structure of law, originally designed as one of the greatest tools for openness.

- Intellectual Property (IP) law was originally meant to foster public disclosure and dissemination of new ideas, but one new trend pulls in the opposite direction. Trade secrets have been getting increased honor and protection, both under the U.S. Economic Espionage Act of 1996 and through the willingness of courts to grant major damage awards to plaintiffs in trade secret misappropriation cases (for example, a $57 million award was recently assessed against Polaris and Fuji for unapproved use of an electronic fuel injection system). But the trade secret strategy denies the public its quid pro quo of public disclosure in exchange for legal protection of the inventor's rights. Ironically, this returns us to the more ancient approach, encouraging secretive monopolies of knowledge, and backing those monopolies up with the full force of state power. New bills, under consideration during the 1998 congressional session, would take this trend further.

- Although a special court was established in 1980 to gather and focus the attention of technically minded jurists on patent matters, even these well-educated judges can nevertheless be boggled by increasingly arcane scientific terminology. They often fall back on presiding over a "war of the wizards," duels between expert witnesses who sometimes win cases based more on their charisma and legerde-main than on the detailed specifics of scientific priority. All too many out-of-court settlements are based purely on the cost of litigation, since according to one patent attorney, "being right or wrong has almost nothing to do with whether you sue or get sued." This trend, too, results in many innovations going unpatented as companies seek to protect them instead as trade secrets.

• There has always been a singular and worrisome problem with patent law—that it offers a mechanism for the thwarting of new ideas if a patent holder refuses to license the patent for a reasonable royalty. While individual inventors seldom do this (and licensing is manda-tory in some countries), large U.S. corporations have been known to suddenly and frenetically research a promising new field—or buy some innovative small firm—with the sole aim of preempting com-petition, getting a patent lock on relevant techniques, and then seal-ing the new processes away, never to be used. This can be especially tempting when the company's investment in older technologies amounts to billions of dollars.

• A strategy used until recently by U.S. companies wishing to corner a technology niche was to keep what were known as "submarine patents" in their portfolios. The contents and even the existence of patent applications were secret until final issuance, so companies would do everything in their power to delay prosecution of an appli-cation with very broad claims, filing repeated "continuation" applica-tions to reset the clock, thus ensuring that it had a secret application constantly pending as it watched its competitors develop new product lines. (The United States is in the process of adjusting its procedures toward international norms, making this harder to do.)

Inventors are not the only ones feeling strain. Artists, authors, and other creative people approach this coming age with justifiable trepida-tion, because one of its most exciting features is also among the most deeply disturbing. Unlike any of the physical objects we desire—food, shelter, space, companionship—information can be copied countless times, at negligible cost.

• The publishing industry was shaken recently when the establish-ment journal *Atlantic Monthly* ran an article casting doubt on the fate of magazines and books in the information age. It compared the value of printed text to tomes distributed on the Internet, concluding that digital media had advantages that could, in the long run, outweigh the tangible "touch and feel" of paper. Those advantages include trivial ease of duplication, bringing into question the whole income system that publishers and authors have relied on for two centuries.

• Raising new fears is a new kind of photocopier with an attachment that automatically turns the pages of a book. This means that a volume can be plopped on the platen and left in place to be copied. Publishers believe that, until now, the sheer drudgery of standing at a hot machine, turning pages, had heretofore deterred many, causing them to prefer spending a few dollars for a legal version from the bookstore.

• By some estimates, computer software companies lose a dollar to pirated copies for every dollar of legitimate sales. According to former U.S. Labor Secretary Robert Reich, in mid-1994 China alone was responsible for producing an estimated 75 million unsanctioned compact discs per year, all but two million exported to other countries. Similar horror stories indicate that a majority of music recordings on compact disc and videotapes of movies on sale in South Asia, Africa, and large parts of the Americas were never licensed or sanctioned by the copyright owners.

The recent General Agreement on Tariffs and Trade (GATT) achieved concessions from nations such as Taiwan and Thailand, which had formerly served as havens for illicit duplication. And software companies fight back with various innovations. Frequent updates make it in the best interest of a heavy user to register with the company in order to be kept current, and the need for technical support keeps many users willing to stay legal.

But this war has barely begun. The big "content owner" media companies—from movie and recording studios to book and software publishers—worry about the new era ahead. Above all, they fear that widespread use of digital technology will enable vastly greater numbers of people to copy just about anything. The *Creative Incentive Coalition* (CIC) is a powerful trade group whose membership roster reads like a *Who's Who* of "content providing" giants, including Microsoft, the Motion Picture Association of America, the Association of American Publishers, and the Software Publishers' Association. The CIC has been vigorous in pursuing changes to both national and treaty law, in order to better protect the billions of dollars that flow through corporations whose lifeblood is their intellectual property. Their greatest success so far has been persuading the Clinton administration to support the National Information Infrastructure Copyright Act (NIICA), whose aim is to plug some of the leaks before they become a hemorrhage of lost profits.

This proposal, if fully enacted, would practically eliminate the customary practice of "fair use," which currently allows copies to be made without payment or permission under certain conditions including research, teaching, journalism, criticism, parody, and library activities. Courts have also interpreted fair use to include the simple act of taping a television program in the privacy of one's own home for purposes of time-shifted viewing, as well as many other little actions that we now take for granted in daily life: browsing through a book before deciding whether to buy it; photocopying a magazine article to share with a friend; selling or giving away a copy of a book, after having paid once for the original purchase. In fact, without the fair use doctrine, I would have been crippled in the writing of this book. Of more than one hundred quotations and references that I drew from various sources, I had to seek permission to use only about half a dozen of the longer ones. The burden on academic researchers and nonfiction writers will become insupportable if they have to extract an okay from—or negotiate a fee with—every single person whose words they want to cite.

But the NIICA's reach extends farther. Early drafts of the bill have interpreted existing copyright law as being violated if users made temporary reproductions of copyrighted matter in their computers' working memory, even to peruse a page on the World Wide Web. That would brand *any* digital transmission of a work as an attempt to distribute the work to the public. Service providers such as America Online and Prodigy would have to enforce strict pay-per-use rules. Moreover, the NIICA is perceived as a precursor of the Global Information Infrastructure (GII) which the World Intellectual Property Organization (WIPO) contemplates will supplement the Berne Convention.

Despite the list of the NIICA's titanic corporate sponsors, its advocates nevertheless portray this bill as the chief hope and defense of the little guy. When anybody with a scanner can upload a comic strip and send it to a hundred friends or "subscribers," the profession of cartoonist starts to look like a threatened species. According to the CIC, the livelihoods of millions of freelancers will be endangered if reforms are not made at once.

In response to what they see as draconian proposals in the NIICA, the Digital Future Coalition (DFC) was formed, drawing membership from the Computer and Communications Industry Association, the Electronic Frontier Foundation, the National Education Association, and various library societies. Note that all of these organizations serve as data *conduits*. Unlike copyright owners, they would naturally perceive their self-interest to lie with open access. The stated aim of DFC is to prevent any oppressive restrictions on the open flow of information.

At one level, this can be seen as a clash between two cultures: on the one hand, the business community is accustomed to payment on a per-use basis; on the other hand, the academic and cybernetic communities are used to general access. According to Anne Branscomb, the common assumption by Internet aficionados when it comes to copyright is, "What is yours is mine."

While at first the DFC may resemble a "David" in contrast to the CIC's well-funded "Goliath," their relative strengths are not properly measured by the amount of raw cash behind each side, nor even by which one has the support of the White House. In fact, the DFC has a far stronger ally, the world press corps, whose hostility toward NIICA has been reflected in most news stories and editorials dealing with the subject. Moreover, the DFC has the advantage of inertia. People are already accustomed to fair use. It is very doubtful in the short term that citizens will accept being hounded for pennies each time they photocopy a clipping, browse a Web page, or crib a brief quote from Kurt Vonnegut, Jr., to use in a speech before the local rotary club.

What might happen if the conduit companies and content owners ever get together? Stranger things have happened. Howard Rheingold, author of The Virtual Community, worries about this possibility when the Internet is commercialized. "If the company that carries the communication also creates the content, are they going to discriminate against competing content?" Rheingold believes they will if they are allowed to. It could be the worst possible combination of both worlds.

On copyright, the EFF and its allies seem to be pushing hard for "transparency." On the other hand, as one of the "little guy" authors, I have a lot to lose if novels and nonfiction works are routinely pirated, so that we freelance writers are reduced to the honorable penury now enjoyed by poets. The benefits of copyright have outweighed the disadvantages for centuries, and a heavy burden of proof falls on those who suggest this should change.

As in the Clipper dispute (see chapter 7), the back-and-forth shouting over NIICA often winds up being expressed in apocalyptic terms, with both sides depicting themselves as defenders of truth and freedom. If the CIC does not get its way (they say), millions of little daily thefts will wind up corrupting civilization. Creative industries will collapse, authors will have to get day jobs, and we will all be left poorer for it.

Not so, cry defenders of the status quo. Members of the DFC depict an awful prospect if proposals like NIICA are implemented—an era when citizens must keep dropping quarters into the great Viewmaster of Life, an interminable drudgery of expense and inconvenience, simply in order to exercise the gracious power of sight.

NIICA is hardly the only modern storm brewing over copyright. A recent report by the U.S. National Academy of Sciences warns of a worldwide trend to grant commercial companies exclusive access to scientific data gathered at taxpayers' expense, and then to sell the data to scientists and other companies. "Full and open access to scientific data should be adopted as the international norm," the committee's report concludes. Private companies would not have a monopoly on the original dataset, but might charge fees for organizing or improving the data.

An ongoing effort to formulate new portions of the Universal Commercial Code may result in the licensing of information being handled in much the same manner as commerce in tangible goods. This effort, while less publicly notorious than NIICA, could have effects that are just as far-reaching, especially in the area of "noncreative" information, such as telephone directories.

Another ominous copyright war has been taking place between the Church of Scientology (CoS) and its critics. No battleground on the Internet has been more bitter than alt.religion.scientology, a Usenet discussion group where take-no-prisoners attacks rage between defenders and detractors of that organization. Among the alleged dirty tricks employed are forged messages, "cancel-bot" programs dispatched to delete the other side's postings, and the use of litigation to suppress free expression. In one famous case, a former CoS minister was accused of illegally acquiring and posting confidential CoS documents. In an aggressive legal campaign, CoS attorneys went to Finland and forced the owner of the world's most renowned "anonymizer" remailer to expose the name of the person distributing purloined material. Following this coup, rulings by one judge in the United States resulted in seizure of a private individual's computers, as well as his arrest and prosecution on several felony counts. The rationale was that the CoS retain, under copyright control, the right to disseminate their own "creative works" as they see fit.

This case offers fascinating reading and insight into all sorts of late-twentieth-century quandaries, including freedom of speech and religion. But we will concentrate on a single ominous implication relating to openness. Traditionally, the aims of patent and copyright law were twofold: first, to encourage the greatest possible sharing of knowledge and, second, to ensure that creators derive fair market value for artistic or technical innovations. The two goals were ranked in this order for reasons that go back to the origins of the American republic. (See next section.) But recent cases involving the CoS appear to run in the opposite direction.

At one level, CoS officials had a legitimate case to seek monetary damages commensurate to income they might otherwise have received, had the documents never been stolen and "netcast." But these were *clandestine and concealed* documents. Some were never meant for publication in any form. Others were strictly reserved for sale to acolytes who take a series of expensive preparatory courses. Concealment in this case is justified in part on the basis that the documents contained concepts that would prove harmful if perused by unprepared minds. (See the section in chapter 5 on the "toxicity of ideas.")

One effect of this case has been to realign the law so that it encourages and rewards secrecy, a reversal of the fundamental principles underlying copyright. The abstract purity of property rights now comes ahead of the practical goal of maximizing openness. Even more astonishingly, a federal judge ruled recently that Internet access providers can be held liable for copyright violations committed by one of their users if they know that illegal copyright infringement of CoS-related material is taking place. In fact, none of this need ever have happened. CoS had other recourses—accusing its hacker-enemies of crimes such as computer tampering and theft, for instance—besides sending us all down a questionable road and using state power to punish people just for knowing things.

This forbidding trend can be seen burgeoning in many walks of life, for instance, when corporations force executives and other employees to sign nondisclosure compacts, agreeing in advance to penalties if they divulge company secrets to outsiders. Sometimes this normal business practice crosses the line from reasonable accountability to absurd persecution or concealment of alleged crimes, as in the famous case of Jeffrey Wigand. That former biochemist at Brown & Williamson Tobacco Company released documents indicating possible perjury by the presidents of several major tobacco corporations (when under oath before Congress they denied knowing of the likely addictive effects of nicotine). Though depicted heroically on news programs such as *Sixty Minutes*, Wigand was beset by legal charges stemming from alleged betrayal of his nondisclosure agreement, as well as an orchestrated campaign to discredit him by investigating all aspects of his life and publicizing potentially embarrassing personal information. This campaign was dropped as part of a tentative deal the tobacco companies struck with the attorneys general of several states early in 1997. But its effect on Wigand cautioned other would-be whistle-blowers.

While the basic meaning and purpose of copyright are endangered by some who would plunge us back toward a secret-ridden past, there are others who wish to eliminate it entirely, calling copyright an impediment to virtuous openness.

## REMEMBERING ORIGINAL GOALS

Thomas Jefferson's original draft of the Declaration of Independence used the phrase "life, liberty and property," which was amended, partly under the influence of Benjamin Franklin, to the more familiar "life, liberty and the pursuit of happiness."

Why the change? Among other reasons, it appears to have happened because there was no consensus among the Founders that property should be enshrined as a fundamental right. To be sure, most of them were property holders who wanted some due-process ownership protections, such as later found their way into the U.S. Constitution. But for the most part the Founders showed remarkable reticence toward defending property ownership as a rigid postulate. Unlike free speech, which was enshrined as a central or fundamental right, property became a contingent right—like privacy.

One can argue that this path was chosen because the Founders were largely pragmatists. As with copyrights and patents, they tended to look at desired *outcomes* rather than mythologized essences. From a strictly practical point of view, "fundamental" rights must be defended without compromise, because they become useless if diluted. Even a little diminution makes them ineffective. This is obviously true of freedom of speech.

But contingent rights, while highly desirable, can be balanced in trade-offs among individuals, groups, and the state, without necessarily tumbling down a slippery slope to tyranny. They can be malleably adjusted by each generation to suit its own circumstances, after which sovereign citizens can then freely debate whether the results justify further changes.

(While it is acknowledged that purists will find the above paragraph loathsome, this republic was not established by purists, but by the greatest assemblage of Enlightenment-era empiricists to gather in one place.)

When it comes to patents and copyright, the practical social goal has always been to encourage maximal openness and minimal secrecy. Profits for the owners of a creative work are of secondary concern, except as incentives to encourage creative effort and rapid sharing.

But as we see in this chapter, recent cases show a dangerous reversal of priorities. Property rights are placed first, and enforced in ways that encourage the clandestine caching of information away from public view. The aim is no longer to enhance the sharing of learning and skills, or even to maximize economic benefit to owners. Rather, the law is used in these cases to ensure that citizens of a free commonwealth will be prevented from knowing certain things, whether they would be willing to pay for the information or not.

Lee Daniel Crocker, a member of the Extropians futurist society, typified this view when he recently suggested that true accountability can take place only if "tag commentary" is taken to its logical conclusion. People who criticize a specific work on the World Wide Web should be able to "tag" that site with a compulsory "back-link" that will notify any future visitor about the critic's censure—whether or not the author wants his Web page to carry any disparaging tags. (In effect, such a tagged alert would say, "When you finish reading what this fool has to say, come on over to this address and listen to somebody who disagrees!") Like the aggressive so-called truth squads who follow opposing politicians around to refute their stump speeches, these contentious datalinks would stalk and harry a rival's works, remaining attached to them, like remoras or lampreys, as long as electrons flow through the conduits of the Internet. (One primitive but positive example of tags might be the blurbs on book jackets.)

This notion—a level of transparency so radical that even I find it hard to swallow—would be fundamentally thwarted by existing copyright laws, which protect the cohesive integrity of a creator's work. Hence, Crocker and others propose ending the "fiction" of copyright altogether! Strong medicine, and perhaps unnecessary, if tag commentary systems were designed properly. Some proposed implementations of the Platform for Internet Content Selection (PICS) might enable critics to let back-link citations float *outside* the formal boundaries of any message or Web page. That way, creative content would continue enjoying the protection of copyright, while the less formal, tagged portion would connect to whatever caveats outside observers might want to append.

Let's assume that unavoidable back-linked tag commentary does eventually become a routine part of cyberlife. In that case, controversial books like this one will almost certainly be among the earliest works to be dogged by relentless little annotations and rebuttal references, swarming and sniping like jackals trying to corner a water buffalo.

Fair enough. In that case, let me go down in history as one of the first authors formally to welcome such attention to one of his works. After all, it's only accountability—something that operates in both directions, by the way. Here you go, boys. Here's an ankle. Give it your best shot.

*It is a fiction, devised by those whose interests are best served by a more sharing society, that information wants to be free. Users may want it to be free—and in the short run, much can be saved by denying compensation to those who have devised the systems and done the work—but if we as a society do not make sure that providers are compensated for their efforts, the information age may turn out to be a short-lived footnote to history.*

ANN WELLS BRANSCOMB

## A FUTURE FOR COPYRIGHT?

Lest anyone misunderstand when I urge that tomorrow's dataways remain unfettered and clear, this means easy *availability* of information. It does not imply anarchy or never having to pay for what others worked to produce. If we are to retain the time-honored benefits of copyright—enabling creative groups and individuals to remain in business—it will require society to accept that some kinds of proprietary interest in data clearly *can* be claimed, at least for a limited length of time.

This is consistent with a transparent society. In a world of openness and accountability, one might still assert that "information created by (or about) me is mine. I may not be able to conceal it, but you should pay a reasonable standard fee if you make use of it."

But how? We've already seen that digital duplication offers a formidable threat to any system based on copy-by-copy sales. Can pragmatic ideas offer a way out of such a fix?

First, let's acknowledge that the CIC (the wealthy "bad guys" in the NIICA debate) actually have the best case in principle. Ideally, some means *should* be found for intellectual property to be compensated in proportion to the amount that it is used by people and institutions in the world. Even so, the approach taken by CIC lawyers is catastrophically flawed. By insisting on criminalizing so many harmless traditional behaviors, they are following an ancient and discredited path—one that will only foster disdain for the law and drive the real information economy underground.

A much better approach would use *positive* measures to attract society toward a system based on fair payment. This might be accomplished in a number of ways:

1. Developing technology to make pay per use reliable and convenient.

2. Creating one or more commercially distinct zones within cyberspace, which people can visit to test and grow familiar with these payment schemes, while sampling therein some truly distinct and original entertainment experiences they can find nowhere else.

3. Demonstrating some of the proposed new techniques of encrypted uniqueness verification that can be embedded in each customer's use-copy of a given work. Since every person entering the special

entertainment zone will already have agreed by contract to abide by certain rules, it will be legitimate to track leakages back to the source and then charge for damages. A "telerighted" document might even contain embedded applications capable of informing its publisher about its subsequent use.

**4.** Exhibiting willingness to live with slack, by abiding by current standards of fair use and not hollering theft over someone download-ing a JPEG image of Mickey Mouse. For many years, the music indus-try has tracked play-lists of radio stations, accruing per-use royalties through BMI and ASCAP, while at the same time recognizing that they would look foolish trying to charge for songs played by local ama-teur bands. There should also continue to be generous provisions for researchers, educators, and other traditionally protected information users. In other words, a sense of scale—and basic human decency— might go a long way toward legitimizing the notion of fair payment for goods received.

**5.** Developing such trials to the point where people trust they won't be bled dry simply for exercising the privilege of looking around. The system should be so easy to use, and so readily capable of being self-audited by customers that the payment of a penny here for a news arti-cle and a penny there for a cartoon becomes too trivial to perturb the average person, even when they settle their monthly bills. In other words, pay per use must never deter a hardworking citizen from using electronic media to explore and grasp the world. (For example, par-ents today buy Disney videos that are so inexpensive that few are ever tempted to make copies. Sales are in such fantastic numbers that only an executive who is certifiably compulsive would care about the exceptions.)

**6.** Making pay-per-use sites attractive for major creators to publish, exhibit, or perform there first, inducing more customers to visit, and so on—thereby establishing acceptance of the pay-per-use principle through attraction, instead of by enlisting state power to impose it everywhere at once.

Beyond all this, executives of the big American content-producing companies might pause in their moral dudgeon, take some deep breaths, and note that the United States spent half its existence, until the early 20th century, as a *net importer* of intellectual property. Once upon a time, Amer-ica was known as a major center of pirate printing presses, to the exasper-ated wrath of European publishing houses. Therefore, while we should continue seeking pragmatic solutions to piracy—both overseas and domestic—it might be more dignified to do so without taking on the appearance of pompous hypocrites.

### An Economy of Micropayments?

I cannot predict whether such an experiment would succeed, though using a "carrot"—or what chaos theorists call an "attractor state"—offers better prospects than the coalition's present strategy of saber rattling and making hollow legal threats. In fact, the same approach might be used to deal with other aspects of "information ownership," even down to the change of address you file with the post office. Perhaps someday advertisers and mail-order corporations will pay fair market value for each small use, either directly to each person listed or through royalty pools that assess users each time they access data on a given person. Or we might apply the concept of "trading-out": getting free time at some favorite per-use site in exchange for letting the owners act as agents for our database records. It could be beneficial to have database companies competing with each other, bidding for the right to handle our credit dossiers, perhaps by offering us a little cash, or else by letting us trade our data for a little fun.

Proponents of such a "micropayment economy" contend that the process will eventually become so automatic and computerized that it effectively fades into the background. People would hardly notice the dribble of royalties slipping into their accounts when others use "their" facts—any more than they would note the outflowing stream of cents they pay while skimming on the Web.

But Hal Finney, senior engineer with Pretty Good Privacy, Inc., one of the leading encryption software companies, doubts the process would be anywhere near so gracious or smooth. "I see every possible piece of information about your neighbors and your society being gathered into little pools, with price tags and jealous bureaucrats making sure that you don't know anything you haven't paid for." Similar doubts have been expressed by Microsoft vice president Nathan P. Myhrvold.

Despite having worked out the above scenario for an experiment in micropayments, I agree with Finney and Myhrvold. My *best* recommendation for the future would err in favor of openness, and not sweating the small stuff. While hard work and creativity deserve fair rewards, I see no point in charging some mail-order company a penny for my address. Nevertheless, an economy of micropayments is one possible destination on our horizon. If so, it could be either an accountant's dream or a nightmare, depending on the details. In any event, it would hardly be the worst place for us to wind up. At least information would flow. Creators would be encouraged. And we would all get to share in whatever's going on.

•  •  •

At the opposite end are those who believe that all efforts at copyright control—even using the venerable tools of a well-regulated market—will ultimately fail. Indeed, the odds seem stacked against any effort to keep people from making digital copies whenever they want. For all their money, power, and motivation, members of the CIC may be thrashing against technological inevitability. "Like dinosaurs in a tar pit," derided one eloquent hacker, who laughed at the notion of anyone forcing him to pay for something acquired electronically. He went on to quote one of the oldest, most revered, and by now most hackneyed Net aphorisms: *"Information wants to be free."*

Perhaps. But still there remain a couple of options to consider.

Brad Templeton, chairman of Clarinet News Service, made an interesting comment when asked whether he was troubled by customers making copies of their downloads and broadcasting them across the Net: "One of the reasons Clarinet does not have a big problem with piracy is that you can't steal our clippings and post them without running a substantial risk of getting caught *by other customers*. People on the Internet will report you."

In other words, Templeton relies on a basic human trait: *people don't like seeing others get away with something*. Where customers are already paying for a service they appreciate, watching someone else steal the same service can raise ire. There is nothing new in this. Despite all the money retail chains spend on new surveillance devices, their most important defense against shoplifting has always been the general goodwill of customers who report suspicious activities.

This trait makes it especially urgent for the CIC not to persist in its initial strategy. For if harsh threats drive normal people to an underground info-market, simply in order to continue harmless fair use practices, those citizens will cheer more serious copyright violators, rather than tattle on them. In other words, the accountability desperately sought by CIC members may be achieved, but only in an atmosphere of trust.

An even more laid-back vision is seen in the phenomenon of "shareware," which is akin to an honor system. Small-scale software designers often publish their works for free copying via the Internet. First-time users see an appeal saying, in effect, "If you like this program, please send $10 to me at the following address."

To the amazement of cynics, this actually works! At least to a degree that compares well with semiannual appeals by the Public Broadcasting System. A hefty minority of shareware users feel obliged—through guilt, morality, or perhaps loyalty toward a "commons" they revere—to pay for the ideas and work of others, even when no threat stands behind the request for payment.

Of course this seems no way to run a large-scale business. Nor is it easy to see the principle applied to other realms of creative endeavor. Can you envision shareware applied to art? Or to a casually viewed television show?

Well, maybe not in the short term, but in the long run . . . ?

Socially and psychologically, the phenomenon of shareware depends on two things: relative wealth and a sense of shared citizenship. People like to feel good about themselves. If it isn't too onerous or expensive, they will gladly pay a little. Different people will have diverse standards, and the whole effect may prove meaningless if the new era becomes centrifugally sundered into a myriad microscopic "cybertribes," self-centered and mutually suspicious, so that all sense of shared civilization vanishes.

And yet, as we will see, such a breakdown is not written in the stars. People can still prevent it. If we do manage to preserve and enhance the requisite sense of wealth and citizenship, expanding them to include a worldwide polity, there may yet be a chance to see something both strange and marvelous—a culture where people pay royalties to creators *because it seems the right thing to do.*

Before deciding how likely that may be, we should take a diversion through chapter 5 to see how the debate over transparency sinks its roots deeply into gritty, cantankerous, ever-fascinating human nature.

# AN OPEN SOCIETY'S ENEMIES

*I myself am a big fan of information flows remaining free
from restraints imposed by government, but have no objection to restrictions imposed by the private sector using
property, contract law, or technology.*

SOLVEIG SINGLETON, DIRECTOR OF

INFORMATION STUDIES, CATO INSTITUTE

*Why has government been instituted at all? Because the
passions of men will not conform to the dictates of reason
and justice without constraint.*

ALEXANDER HAMILTON

This book, together with its argument for general transparency, is based on
several assumptions. Among the most important is that liberty can face peril
from any part of the sociopolitical landscape, and therefore light should shine
in all directions. This point is central, because so many of those who support
widespread anonymity and encrypted communications—libertarians, free-
market republicans, cypherpunks, and various allies—see those tools as vital
bulwarks against one paramount source of danger: government.

If government truly *is* the sole credible threat, then it would be appropriate to demand unevenness in the flow of information. To prevent abuses
of power, we would be obliged to (1) force officials to work in the light,
closely scrutinized by all citizens (on this we agree), and (2) *blind* the state,
denying it many powers of sight by using masked communications and
shielded identities, lest officials collect and abuse data about citizens. We

would do this even if it reduced government efficiency or effectiveness, as a bulwark against tyranny.

Elsewhere, I discuss several flaws in this reasoning, for instance, the lack of any historical evidence that blinding an already accountable government ever resulted in greater safety or freedom. (Weak-blind governments that swiftly gave way to horrid tyrannies include 1917 Russia, 1926 Italy, 1933 Weimar Germany, 1936 Spain, and 1948 China—hardly a resounding endorsement for this prescription!) In this section, however, I will address that other core assumption, the notion of a single threat to liberty.

At one level, this is yet another example of the ongoing struggle between Platonic idealism and brass-tacks empiricism. Is it reasonable to call *all* governments inherently vile, because a fraction of them performed beastly acts? Georgetown University Professor Dorothy Denning thinks not.

> I tend to be a pragmatist and am skeptical of anything that appears idealistic while not being grounded in experience. Many people argue that governments are inherently dangerous and use as evidence Nazi Germany and Communism. While I don't dispute that, it seems that many of the horrors resulted from pursuing some ideal society. Perhaps those governments that are well grounded in what works, and what does not . . . survive and uplift their people.

While I share Denning's distrust of grand generalizations, I will stipulate along with her that governments are, by their very essence, extremely dangerous concentrations of power in need of special scrutiny. So, for the sake of argument, we shall let a leading cypherpunk/libertarian, Hal Finney, define the terms for discussion: "Standard libertarian analysis of government defines it as that institution in society which can legitimately exercise the use of force and coercion. Government is unique in that it can use force against you. Corporations can only operate through persuasion."

For this reason, Finney contends, government must be held to a much higher state of accountability than corporate interests. This is already the case in the United States and most major nations in the neo-West. Elected officials are answerable to voters. They face more rigorous regulations, codes of conduct, and routine scrutiny than the officers of any company.

As they should! Institutions armed with police and military power—all the way to nuclear weapons—must be watched with great care. The worst crimes of history were performed under the color of state authority. And "authority," as we'll see in the next chapter, is a word we have been taught to hate. A careful reader will note that throughout this book I never call for removing any practical means of dividing, supervising, or devolving government power into units that will keep it harmless. In fact, I recommend numerous ways to increase the accountability of state officials by combating the fallacy of secrecy, and by adding new methods of transparency and light.

As cyberspace entrepreneur Esther Dyson prescribes, "Our best defense [against government spying] is offense. Spy back! We need the ability to follow more closely what governments are doing."

Where I part with cypherpunk dogma is in proposal number (2) on page 108. Even most libertarian scholars concede that government is ideally a *tool* that can enable free people to enhance and protect their liberty. If there remain other power centers that might endanger liberty, blinding government may offer those cliques the very darkness that they need to conspire against freedom, or even seize the tool of state power for their own purposes.

MIT Professor Gary Marx expressed this unease in a formal way.

> *Restrictions on government are not a sufficient guarantee of freedom. Taken too far, they may guarantee its opposite, as private interests reign unchecked. For Orwell, the state and the economy were synonymous, and the threat to liberty was only from big government. But in our age of large and powerful nongovernment organizations, a broader view and new legal and policy protections are required.*

Or, as explained more tersely by Texas businessman Steve Jackson, "Nasty types will avoid whatever branch of human life *is* under a spotlight, in order to seek manipulative power in the shadows."

So the basic question is critical. *Do* other dangers lurk? Are some freedom lovers so obsessed with defending against one potential enemy that they are leaving the ramparts unguarded against others?

•   •   •

First, let's get rid of one common misconception implied by Hal Finney's remark, that the only likely alternative threat is corporations.

Surveys certainly do show that people rank Big Business high on any list of obnoxious power centers. In fact, major companies fare worse than government when it comes to popular rating of specific faults like deceit, venality, and pollution. One recent poll showed that insurance companies are trusted less than a quarter as much as Congress! When it comes to personal privacy, corporations are often far more callous at disregarding the rights and feelings of common folk. We discuss many of these matters elsewhere.

Nevertheless, here we are talking about direct threats to constitutional democracy, and even people who despise capitalist big shots can be pretty skeptical of any notion that the directors of Texaco and Microsoft are about to wage war against Washington, or stage a coup to take over the United States! It doesn't seem likely to most of us that Procter & Gamble will try to set up an Orwellian state.

But this dismissal may be much too blithe, for the following reasons:

1. The limited liability stock company is a fairly recent innovation, having emerged at a time when states were already strong.

2. Corporations *have* behaved in tyrannical and oppressive ways, for example, when the Dutch East India Company, the British East India Company, and Belgian King Leopold's private "development" company in the Congo all engaged in profoundly murderous acts of repression. Any visitor to Central America will hear many a local citizen lodge similar accusations against the United Fruit Company, for activities early in this century.

3. When we think of government as a tool that can sometimes be seized by private parties for their own benefit, it is easy to cite countless examples of corporations wielding undue influence over legislation or the administration of laws, for example, in areas of trade, defense appropriations, "sweetheart" regulations, and "corporate welfare."

4. The human storybook is rife with tales about *other* enemies of freedom, whose past deeds make these corporate peccadilloes look like child's play.

Let's turn the issue around with a simple exercise. Name all the bright moments you can, in the long struggle of humanity. Write them down on a piece of paper. Then, next to each one, describe what brought it crashing down.

Naturally, such a list will vary, depending on how you define "bright." Some people admire flashy kings and conquerors, or ages when potentates hired sculptors and had stirring monuments built. I happen to be partial to periods when people were free to argue, create, move about, trade, and even change social classes by virtue of their own accomplishments. Times when leaders were chosen for qualities other than bloodlines or violence. By that standard, bright eras were rare. In chapter 1 I mentioned a short list: pastoral Iceland, a couple of Renaissance city-states, the Iroquois Confederacy, and a stretch or two during the Roman Republic. Let's add a few brief examples in the Middle East and India, and of course Periclean Athens, brief epochs when individuals competed somewhat fairly, leveraged labor with innovation, tolerated diversity, and spoke their minds.

*Somewhat fairly.* At best, these cultures were deeply flawed. But compared with the surrounding tribes and empires, they shone. Until, after a fleeting springtime, each sank back into a winter of tyranny. Occasionally, the cause was external invasion, or plague, or perhaps a societywide loss of nerve. But most often the demise followed a familiar, dismal pattern. A cohort of enterprising leaders would rise (perhaps proud to have done so by their own efforts). Then, once in power, they connived to close what had been open, to change the rules so that newcomers would find the same climb harder. In other words, they formed a conspiracy of power, an oligarchy.

Examples include the takeover of Florence by the Medicis, or the gradual entrenchment of a few family cliques in the Republic of Venice. There were coups by the Roman patrician class and civil service paralysis in imperial China. Napoleon in France, Porfirio Diaz in Mexico, and countless other dictators betrayed popular assemblies to install a narrow cabal of friends and relatives in power. In later years, despite the liberality of official constitutions, we have seen oppression by the top two thousand families of the Soviet *nomenklatura*, staunch resistance by the ruling classes in Victorian Britain to the stirrings of social mobility, and the machinations of American "robber barons," who nearly sealed their grip on power before the turn of the last century.

This pattern grows out of a very strong human impulse to grab any opportunity to be a ruler. In fact, the aristocratic will has opposed open societies in nearly all epochs. As time passed in Rome, for instance, imperial law required that all men stay rigidly in their social class of birth, no matter what their talents or abilities. An edict promulgated by the Japanese Shogun Hideoshi forbade any peasant from rising to samurai rank by merit, as Hideoshi himself had done. Caste rules in Egypt, Persia, India, China, Indonesia, Meso-America, Africa, and countless other civilizations all had the same aim: hindering those who were low on the vast social pyramid from sending up their brightest sons and daughters to compete fairly with the heirs of the mighty. Above all, tyrants passed rules ensuring that people could not vigorously hold their rulers accountable.

In contrast to past brief glimmerings, our own recent run of freedom is impressively long and deep. For instance, the United States has managed for two centuries to prevent takeover by a true ruling class—one able to enforce its whim without constraint by due process, or the need to negotiate with other social classes. And yet, a heritage of dark suspicion seems justified when one looks across six thousand years at all the betrayals that brought down other hopeful beginnings.

Now it is possible to argue that conditions are different today. We live in an era when most power seems to be held by formal social structures such as governments and corporations, which makes it seem a bit quaint to talk about "conspiratorial cliques." This book, however, is about dramatic changes in the world that may transform all the rules. (See the section at the end of chapter 9, "A Withering Away?")

Lessons from the fall of liberty in Florence, Rome, and Athens *may* be irrelevant. Those days may be over, and good riddance.

And yet, who bears the burden of proof? Those who would still worry about liberty's age-old enemies—aristocracies, oligarchies, and mobs? Or those who say, "Don't worry, those bad old guys are long gone."

We should stay wary of dangers in all directions, until it is demonstrated for a fact that the historic perils are no more. The burden of proof is on those who say that now we can leave those ramparts undefended.

• • •

This topic deserves much more thorough discussion than we can go into here. But a few pertinent points merit repetition.

• Freedom had enemies long before nation states or modern corporations were invented.

• Those enemies gave themselves many names—from Communists to nobles to merchant princes—but their techniques were remarkably similar: form a tight-knit "in group," conspire in secret, manipulate the system, choose the right moment to stir up the rabble, take over the reins of state authority, and then clamp down.

• If "government" is a tool, we have seen that tool all too often taken over by one party, then used against others.

The last point is important. An essential difference between freedom and tyranny is *who* controls state power. The very same bureaucracies can be brutal or benign, depending on whether they are in the grip of a cliquish party or supervised and wielded by a diverse, confident, and pragmatic citizenry. We shall talk more about this later. But for now let me suggest that the instrumentalities of government should be carefully watched, but not reflexively or unthinkingly crippled.

We own these tools. We may need them, trim and well oiled, in order to deal with other ancient, but still dangerous, foes.

# PART II
# MINEFIELDS

*In my course I have known and, according to my measure, have cooperated with great men; and I have never yet seen any plan which has not been mended by the observations of those who were much inferior in understanding to the person who took the lead in the business.*

EDMUND BURKE

## CHAPTER FIVE

# HUMAN NATURE AND THE DILEMMA OF OPENNESS

*Every society imposes some of its values
on those raised within it, but the point is
that some societies try to maximize that
effect, and some try to minimize it.*

IAIN M. BANKS

*Well sure the government lies, and the
press lies, but in a democracy they aren't
the same lies.*

ALEXIS A. GILLILAND

## THE FAILURE OF EXHORTATION

There is a lesson to be learned by listening to some folks who claim to have been abducted by UFOs. Many of these people solemnly insist they got a parting gift at the end of their nocturnal ride. A benefaction of wisdom from the alien visitors.

What wisdom? What sage advice do "abductees" report receiving from little silver savants? Here is the great insight that some proclaim after their cosmic encounters:

**Be nice to one another.**

Now I have no objection to that admonition (even if it does sound hypocritical when purportedly coming from secretive outer space kidnappers). In fact, all by itself, the message sounds pretty good. There are a couple of problems, though.

**1.** We've heard the same thing preached innumerable times before.

**2.** It doesn't work.

At least, it doesn't work all by itself. Anyone who has dealt with groups of twelve-year-old boys can testify that author William Golding had it right in his classic novel *Lord of the Flies.* Pleading and preaching do little good unless accompanied by keen-eyed, pragmatic guidance. Against the urges of emotional, self-interested, conniving human beings, exhortation is futile if not backed up by other elements such as *persuasion, example,* and *accountability.*

In fact, great teachers—from Moses and Confucius all the way to John Lennon and "the famous Bill and Ted"—have always urged us to "be excellent to each other." But in most cases the message was also accompanied by lists of prescribed (and proscribed) behaviors, meant to fill in the details, regulating tribal activities and laying down sanctions to oblige compliance. In very general terms, the list often went something like this.

- If you are a properly anointed leader, take care of your followers. See to their needs, and don't abuse your privileges—at least not very much. At least not enough to make the peasants rebel. Above all, safeguard your inheritance and never let upstarts threaten your power.

- If you are a follower, be respectful to those above you. Give them loyalty, obedience, plus a share of your crops. And your sons, of course. For war.

- Treat your immediate neighbors with courtesy. Follow ordained rituals and traditions in order to keep friction in the village at a minimum level.

- Conform. Do not deviate from accepted social norms.

- Bribe the sage or witch doctor. Propitiate unseen powers.

- Be wary of strangers. Watch out for deviants in the tribe.

- Work hard. Respect your elders.

- Try to be nice. Cooperate. Get along.

Now, human beings surely are imperfect rascals. In any clan or hamlet the rules were often broken when people thought they could get away with it. Nevertheless, members of almost any culture I am familiar with would recognize the list of adages given above and call most of them pretty obvious.

To a contemporary neo-Westerner, on the other hand, the list provokes mixed feelings. We want to ask questions, define terms, pick and choose among the rules, propose an amendment or two, and maybe reject some items altogether. Especially when it comes to that business about conformity. And regarding leaders, we think it only fair that the guy on top should earn his spot, account for how the taxes are spent, and then get out of the way when his turn is done.

Moreover, unlike nearly every prior culture, we believe that the leader can be a "she."

Modern people take for granted countless attitudes that would seem bizarre to our ancestors. After all, isn't it only human nature for leaders to resist being brought down to the rank of commoners? In most cultures there were major advantages—in health, wealth, and reproduction—to staying on top and making sure your kids stayed up there, too. Today, the often shameless way that many politicians squirm to hold slivers of power reflects this ancient pattern.

The "Paradox of the Peacock," which I briefly referred to in chapter 1, illustrates this point with an example from nature.

In their native forests, peafowl are best able to move around—seeking food and avoiding predators—if they are small, fast, and camouflaged. Those are exactly the traits adopted by the sensible females. So why is the male peafowl so garishly colored? Because, despite the risk, inconvenience, and metabolic cost, his plumage offers one overpowering advantage to any single peacock. It demonstrates his own particular fitness, enabling him to win mates and reproduce. Only peacocks who possess those garish traits get to have descendants.

In other words, what benefits the individual leader nearly always prevails over what is good for the group. So it is for peafowl—and so it has been for human civilizations through most of history.

What is healthy for a nation? *Accountability*. Many minds and talents working to solve problems through a market of ideas. Since no single ruler can ever spot all errors, especially his own, open criticism helps a nation evade disasters.

What is healthy for a king, high priest, or tyrant? The exact opposite! Criticism is inherently dangerous to those perched at the privileged top of a pyramid. It can undermine absolute authority, and even lead to rebellion. So it was seldom allowed.

Countless examples illustrate this tragic paradox between the needs of the one and of the many. By suppressing dissent, Stalin ensured that tens of millions of his countrymen and -women died for his cumulative blunders. But from his point of view, it was still a good idea. Because by crushing dissenters, *he* got to stay in power. Nor was Stalin an exception in the dreary litany of human dictatorships. What was good for the leader nearly always triumphed over the collective health of the commonwealth.

One factor that exacerbates this situation is the problem of lying.

Recent ethological studies of apes and other animals show we aren't the only creatures who practice deceit. Conniving members of other species — apes, dogs, and monkeys, for example — have been observed pretending, feigning, and misleading others of their own kind, while seeking some advantage having to do with sex, food, or hierarchy. Nevertheless, as Robert Wright points out in *The Moral Animal*, natural selection must have especially rewarded this trait in humans in order for us to become such excellent liars. "We are far from the only dishonest species," explains Wright, "but we are surely the *most* dishonest, if only because we do the most talking."

Moreover, one of the most fascinating and effective kinds of lying is self-deception. As humans, we are gifted with strong egos and remarkable imaginations, a combination that makes it all too easy for a person to see exactly what he or she already wants to see. We construe the remarks of other people, up or down, depending on which interpretation best suits our predisposed leanings, generally choosing whatever version makes us feel better about ourselves, and contemptuous of our foes. So-called logic is used to craft ornate ideologies that defy all science and common sense, yet still hypnotize millions.

Unless restrained, this *triumph of the subjective* has especially noxious effects on leaders. Tyrants seldom see themselves as oppressors, often justifying their absolute rule as a beneficent reign, essential for good order and decency to prevail. Since they punish disagreement, despots get a warped view of reality, seldom receiving clear accounts of problems until it is too late.

Matters are a little different now. After millennia of hard experience, we have learned some practical lessons.

> *If criticism is the best known antidote to error . . .*
> *and leaders naturally hate criticism . . .*
> *then clearly a society is best served by ensuring that*
> *leaders cannot suppress or evade critical appraisal.*

In other words, free speech should be viewed as sacred and inviolable *not* simply for its own sake, but for utterly pragmatic reasons. Only through an active, vibrant, noisy ferment of criticism can blunders be discovered before they bring nations crashing down. Moreover, we can never tell in advance *which* criticism will later prove right; therefore, we must allow, foster, and even encourage all the criticism we can get.

This excursion into human nature applies to our debate over a transparent society. As a culture, we face problems that rush toward us at great speed—from energy crises and new kinds of pollution to terrorism, cloning, and reliance on frail computer software. As lag times between cause and effect keep shrinking, our best efforts invariably bring about unintended consequences. Mistakes can wreak damage ranging from mere millions of dollars all the way to possible *ecocide*, effective destruction of the earth's functioning biosphere.

Amid this ferment, critics and complainers sometimes seem insufferable. Not all criticism is on target! History and life experience testify that most of the screeching, self-righteous, mutually contradictory stands taken by raucous advocacy groups eventually wind up being labeled drivel, or at best tendentious exaggeration. Yet ideally, that should not matter! In the free market of ideas, charge and countercharge should carom and collide under the gaze of a detached and bemused citizenry until some truth pops out.

Take one anecdote: the Alaska Pipeline. Engineers working for ARCO now admit that flaws in their initial design might have wrought catastrophe, but attacks by implacable environmental organizations during public hearings forced them back to the drawing board until they could make a convincing case that all plausible failure modes were accounted for. The redesigned pipeline was eventually built and, said one engineer, "We have both oil and caribou."

Over the years, contemptuous cynics keep proclaiming that "the public" is shallow and incapable of taking a long view. But then what happened in the late 1970s, when chemist Sherwood Rowland expressed concern about an esoteric decline in the parts-per-million concentration of a trace corrosive gas in the ethereal zones a hundred thousand feet above the South Pole? The "hole" in the ozone barrier (protecting Earth against harmful ultraviolet radiation) at first struck reporters as far too abstruse for public consideration, until waves of average people expressed deep concern. Investigations were launched, scientists debated heatedly, and soon international agreements largely curbed the particular pollution at fault. An imperfect solution, but remarkable nonetheless.

Are such examples of open debate, followed by constructive consensus, less frequent in the 1990s? Leaders of some advocacy groups do seem more interested in being right than in finding solutions. Courteous debate is out. Demonizing your opponent is in.

This problem hasn't gone unnoticed. A new movement is afoot. People and political parties are all talking about a *return to civic virtues*, calling for a resurrection of manners, preaching that we should learn to get along. In other words, we ought to "be nice to one another."

Have we come full circle, then? Are we back to admonishing people? Asking them to be good, for goodness' sake? Kings and priests used to enforce civility at sword point. But short of calling in troops, will it really be effective to exhort activists—high on self-righteousness endorphins—to calm down, take turns talking, and maybe listen to the other guy for a change?

Of course not!

Exhortation, all by itself, is not the answer. It never was, no matter how often and poetically it's been tried.

> *Never attribute to malice what can be explained by stupidity.*
> *Don't assign to stupidity what might be due to ignorance.*
> *And try not to assume your opponent is the ignorant one—until you*
> *can show it isn't you.*                                  M. N. PLANO

## VIRULENT IDEAS

For about a week in early 1997, frenetic helicopters buzzed around my home. They were swarming toward an elite community beyond the next hill where three dozen people had just taken their own lives, attempting to follow their charismatic leader to the next astral plane aboard a cometary spacecraft. Pinned by television camera lights, residents of Rancho Santa Fe voiced dismay that their sanctuary had been invaded *twice*—first by a strange cult that lived for months unnoticed in their midst, and again by throngs of newsfolk, peering at their patrician enclave from both ground and air. This episode epitomized many trade-offs between secrecy and transparency, above all an age-old debate over the toxicity of ideas.

Are ideas inherently dangerous?

Perhaps more than any other question, this one is crucial to determining whether humans can or should maintain privacy—and indeed, whether we can or should remain individually free. It is an ancient quandary.

One side maintains that people are innately frail, pliable, and prone to brainwashing. Unless carefully guided, humans all too easily adopt unwholesome beliefs and behaviors that could undermine everything a civilization holds dear. For example, Plato preached that much art, even certain passages in Homer, tended to have an evil influence upon the young and accordingly, in his ideal state, should be banned. Countless myths and legends have preached that knowledge can be dangerous or destructive, for example, Eve and the serpent, or Pandora and her box. The theme is repeated in many familiar works, from *Paradise Lost, Faust,* and *Frankenstein* all the way to *Star Trek III: The Search for Spock.* Most past societies preached tradition and fidelity to ancestral ways.

When alien or unconventional concepts did arise among the masses, kings and priests often squelched such outbreaks ruthlessly. In some cases—as when the Roman Empire crushed Judea, or when the Tokugawa Shoguns suppressed Japanese Christians, or when the Chinese imperium smashed the rebellious Tai'pings—defense of orthodoxy was justified as a matter of public hygiene, to protect society against infection by something virulent or poisonous. When Senator Joseph McCarthy led witch-hunts against fellow citizens who had even glancingly touched the contagion of communism, the ensuing hysteria was couched as a war of quarantine against a mortally communicable ideology.

Such fears have not always been unfounded! History is rife with novel ideas that seemed to spread like pandemic fevers, sweeping older creeds aside and creating new priestly castes—who then devoted themselves to defending the *next* status quo. The sudden advance of Marxist oligarchies in Russia and China, though somewhat less ominous than McCarthy's followers claimed at the time, was certainly frightening for contemporaries to behold. Other examples might include the way both Islam and Orthodox Christianity abruptly transformed themselves from persecuted sects to established state religions and then went about curbing predecessor faiths, as well as smashing any subsequent apostasy to come along.

Various theories have been submitted to explain this pervasive pattern, which recurred on every inhabited continent. Is doctrinal purity a tool used by ruling classes to control and manipulate subject populations? Is it a useful way for nations to maintain cohesion against external influences? Recently some creative thinkers, inspired by microbiology, have suggested that we look beyond nations, tribes, or leaders to the ideas themselves. In his seminal work *The Selfish Gene*, Richard Dawkins coined the term *memes* to describe "self-replicating ideas."

In brief, Dawkins suggests that certain concepts may invade host organisms (human minds) in much the same way that viruses hijack the cells of a living body, reproducing avidly, and then causing those hosts to react prejudicially against competing memes. In other words, ideas may sometimes evolve traits that enhance their own reproductive success, independent of their hosts' better interests. In human terms, this might explain why so many religions have "exclusionary rules," dismissing other theologies as heresy and demanding that children be guarded against exposure to conflicting doctrines.

It hardly matters whether "memes" have any basis in fact (at one time the concept of viruses was considered far-out) or if they just metaphorically depict the way many tribes doggedly clenched their core beliefs despite great hardship. Either way, we can recognize an ancient and recurring tendency for people to react paranoically toward foreign notions—a penchant to believe that gullible citizens must be protected, and their thoughts kept pure, lest they fall into evil ways.

Is this pattern universal? If it were, little more need be said. We would be doomed by our basic temperaments to endless petty squabbles over picayune ideological differences, until the end of time. Fortunately, human nature isn't that simple.

In fact, there is another way in which people sometimes react to novel concepts—not with paranoia, but with delight.

*The technological shock to our moral systems means that we are going to have to teach our children that the locus of control must be in their heads and hearts—not in the laws or machines that make information so imperviously available. Before we let our kids on the Internet, they had better have a solid moral grounding and some common sense.* HOWARD RHEINGOLD

### Maturity

From Spinoza to Montaigne to Chief Sequoia, rare dissenters have argued that a confident, enlightened person cannot be harmed by mere words. According to their minority belief, children can be raised with critical reasoning skills so that, as they mature, they will be able to evaluate new ideas with a mix of curiosity and skepticism, culling what is wrong or harmful while incorporating the rest into an ever-expanding intellectual panorama.

This attitude is quite opposite to the "frailty thesis." One might call it the "maturity argument," since it posits that we can learn from our mistakes (and those of our parents), growing wiser, in effect inoculating ourselves against the deleterious effects of bad ideas, while remaining open to good from any source. Goethe called this *tätige skepsis*, a skeptical but open-minded willingness to consider new or alternative views.

"The flip side of living in *tribes* is living in the world—in the *kosmos*," says computer scientist Stefan Jones, in another approach to the same idea.

> *Cosmopolitanism* is Maturity's eccentric brother; the bohemian uncle who drops by with weird gifts for the kids and lots of strange stories. *Aunt Frailty* wants to throw away the shrunken heads and the brass lamp with naked people on it, and tries to put the kids to bed early before Cosmo has had a few and starts talking about his visit to the Yoshiwara and the time he ate dog. But *Mother Maturity* lets the kids listen from the stairs and secretly pulls the gifts out of the trash before collection day. Maturity certainly keeps a wary eye on Cosmo. On the other hand, she doesn't want her kids to turn out to be dullards, like their cousins.

In fact, the very notion of a liberal education is aimed at creating just the sort of thoughtful, curious, aware, and judicious person who can operate as a sovereign, independent-minded citizen of a free commonwealth—a model so successful that it is all too easy to forget how revolutionary it was, just a little while ago.

These two views of the toxicity of ideas have been battling for a long time, though in most traditional cultures the contest was one-sided. Even in the neo-West, where the maturity thesis has gained belated prominence, large constituencies still hold to older views of human nature. A belief that information can be dangerous pervades all boundaries of class, ethnicity, or politics. While the "religious right" pushes to expurgate prurient or racy content from mass media in order to protect families and children, an equal devotion to censorship now burgeons from many radicals of the left, for example, academic feminists who impute a direct causal link between pornography and aberrant or abusive male sexual behavior. Whatever the relative merits of their arguments, it is fascinating to witness alliances between the likes of Andrea Dworkin and Jerry Falwell, each of them proclaiming the same fundamental belief: that some wise elite should hold sway over what others see and hear. Clearly, superficial political differences matter less than deeper, shared assumptions regarding human nature.

Yet despite such vehement recidivist coalitions, we have clearly entered a new era. For the first time, a major society has based its legal code, education system, and mass media on the maturity thesis. In particular, the essential protections of the United States Bill of Rights are rooted in a belief that free individuals can be trusted to weigh contrasting arguments and reach conclusions that, if imperfect, will at least be right often enough to justify governance by universal franchise. Although the framers of the Constitution did insert elements meant to slow down the momentary passions that sometimes surge like fevers through a populace, their trust in mass sovereignty was nevertheless unprecedented in human annals. If anything, that belief has grown stronger with each passing generation.

Closely related to the issue of toxicity is another long-running dispute — over whether evil manifests itself only in what people do, or in their thoughts as well. Some cultures, religions, and psychologies teach that "thinking it is the same as doing it." Others say that the mind is where we do experiments, contemplating possibilities and outcomes in order to choose which ones we will then try to put into effect. It is our outward behavior that affects other people, and so becomes their legitimate concern. But the world within belongs to each of us.

Fealty to the latter attitude is widespread among "netizens," and was recently expressed by John Perry Barlow.

> Action is what the body does, over which physical authority may be exercised. In cyberspace, I might threaten to kill you, [but] in New York, I can slit your throat. This is why I said [to governments] in my declaration that "we must declare our virtual selves immune to your sovereignty, even as we continue to consent to your rule over our bodies." I'm not seeking to evade legal responsibility for our physical actions. But rendering the depiction of crimes criminal is an effort to extend government authority beyond the physical into the mental.

At this point the reader might guess my bias in this ancient argument. With both heart and intellect, I avow that the free flow of ideas is vital to civilization. Moral and pragmatic factors support my belief (for example, the role of criticism as a vital antidote to error). Yet I admit that another reason underlies my fidelity to openness. I admire candor and despise censorship because I was raised that way.

Here we reap a harvest of irony. For if a majority of modern citizens believe in the maturity thesis and are trying to raise their children to have open, autonomous minds, this has happened largely because *we* were taught these values by a relentless campaign of public instruction, conveyed through mass media.

We mentioned this briefly in chapter 1. In novels, films, and popular music, it is nearly always the eccentric, the curious, or the unconventional who get favored treatment. Movies from *Altered States*, to *Aladdin*, to *Thelma and Louise*, have repeatedly conveyed the same message:

> *Make up your own minds. Question authority.*
> *Be open to things that are new and strange.*

That's the irony. If we citizens are becoming more independent and open-minded, the change came only after some of the most persistent propaganda in history! Propaganda that so romanticized individualism and idiosyncrasy that many citizens now base their self-worth on how different they are from everybody else.

In other words, those of us who defend openness, claiming that people needn't be coddled or steered, should honestly concede that we were guided toward this belief by one of the strangest and most intense sales campaigns ever seen. One whose roots are only now starting to be explored.

The debate between frailty and maturity continues today in confrontations over public policy issues exemplified by the Communications Decency Act (CDA). Passed in 1996 by the Republican-dominated Congress and signed by President Clinton, this legislation established criminal penalties for distributing "indecent" material over the Internet in ways that might allow minors access. When the CDA was argued before the United States Supreme Court, one aspect in dispute was whether Internet-based services such as America Online should be viewed as "common carriers," which are not responsible for content, or whether their role is more that of "publishers," answerable if some client uses their channels to pander or commit libel.

At that level, the arguments may seem picky and recondite. But the fundamental issue can be expressed more simply. As *Newsweek* correspondent Steven Levy put it,

> Here is the nub: in cyberspace, the most democratic of mediums, should priority be given to allowing adults to exercise their constitutional right to speech? Or, as the CDA dictates, should they have to curb their expression—even certain constitutionally protected speech with redeeming social value like sex-education, highfalutin nude art, and George Carlin comedy routines—so that Net-surfing children will not be exposed to so-called patently offensive content?

No two goals could seem more archetypal and worthy than protecting children and ensuring free speech. To find such values in apparent conflict reinforces the fact that we live in a complex and imperfect world. But now at least we can see the argument in a new light—as a classic face-off between the maturity and frailty models of human mental life. Typically,

## PROPAGANDIZED TO REBEL?

I have made the counterintuitive argument that we are "raised to rebel" before many audiences, and it nearly always provokes the same response.

"How can you say the media are pro-individual?" Someone demands. "We're told over and over again to conform!"

To which I respond with a challenge. "I'll bet you can't cite a single popular book or film from the last decade whose professed message is conformity. Yet we could stay here all night listing famous novels, movies, and TV shows revolving around a single idea: that it is admirable to be independent-minded, eccentric, even defiant. Consider one of the most celebrated motion pictures of the last generation, Steven Spielberg's *E.T.*, whose chief moral is that modern children should hide an alien from their own freely elected tribal elders! Can you name any other people who taught their kids such lessons? That other is better than self? That rebellion can be more honorable than obedience? That independent thinking is admirable, even when mistaken, and that authority should always be held in deep suspicion?"

Soon, audience members are shouting titles of favorite books, from *Catcher in the Rye* to *On the Road,* and a plethora of films whose heroes disdained every hierarchy in order to go their own way. Popular authors—from Koontz, King, and Clancy to Atwood and Anderson—all seem to worry unrelentingly about potential oppressors. Yet many in the crowd remain grim-faced, finding it unpleasant to imagine that their own fierce independence could have come about this way, as something they were spoonfed all their lives, as natural and wholesomely American as Wheaties.

I sympathize. It hit me the same way—a revelation that poses more questions than it answers. Like how did such a bizarre propaganda campaign come about in the first place?

We'll return to this point later, but for now it is enough to note the irony, as rich as any in our complex human stew, that we individualists were *taught* to believe in ourselves, and in our powers as free-thinking, autonomous beings.

Nor is the battle over, by a long shot! It remains forever tempting to fall back on older views of human nature, especially the ego-gratifying assumption that the great mass of our fellow citizens are fools, easily gulled and needing protection against the deadly influence of noxious ideas. It is harder to contemplate that many others, even our political opponents, may be quite a bit like us. Equally cantankerous. Equally bent on autonomy. And equally determined to protect their uniqueness, as important to them as life itself.

with passionate voices rising on both sides, the most extreme proponents of each philosophy denounce their rivals as evil harbingers of a looming dark age.

At the same time, there are pragmatic compromisers. Before the Supreme Court rendered its decision on the CDA, Deputy Solicitor General Seth Waxman held that adults could still access any kind of material they desire, even if offensive content is banished from open areas of the Net, by joining private online clubs with passworded entry for those eighteen and older. Responding for the American Library Association, the ACLU, and other plaintiffs, attorney Bruce Ennis conceded that parents might have an interest in monitoring what their kids view, but maintained that this issue should be handled by adults and guardians installing supervisory software in their homes and schools, to bar offensive stuff coming in from the outside world.

Both suggestions were (and remain) seriously flawed. But for our purposes here, the interesting point is to notice *how* they differed. One side put the burden of assertive effort on would-be users, requiring adults to perform a complex act of volition in order to see. The other side contended that the Internet's default condition should be openness. Those wishing to limit the kinds of words and images entering their homes should be the ones burdened with a chore of taking active steps to avert the family gaze.

This particular battle ended in June 1997 when, as nearly everyone expected, the Supreme Court threw out the CDA, basically agreeing with federal appeals Judge Dalzell, who earlier wrote:

> ... the Internet may fairly be regarded as a never-ending worldwide conversation. The Government may not, through the CDA, interrupt that conversation. As the most participatory form of mass speech yet developed, the Internet deserves the highest protection from government intrusion. Just as the strength of the Internet is chaos, so the strength of our liberty depends upon the chaos and cacophony of the unfettered speech the First Amendment protects.

This rejection could hardly have been couched more emphatically. It was a typically ferocious (and predictable) defense of free speech. Yet, it was no final victory by the maturity view over darker models of human nature. As surely as the sun rises, or as innovations have unintended consequences, both sides will soon be back, pugnaciously debating whether people are innately vulnerable to bad ideas, or if we can trust them to handle such inputs with good sense.

The argument won't end soon, because neither side can ever prove it is completely right.

Despite all the moral posturing and charges of "censorship" and "immorality" flung at each other, what the disputants fall back on is an endless stream of anecdotes.

- In Amsterdam, twelve children aged eight to eleven are injured (one blinded) by grenades they built from instructions downloaded from the Internet. In New York teens are poisoned following a bad recipe for kitchen-made drugs.

- In Birmingham, a nine year old exploring the Web reads an article about pedophilia and correlates it with things he witnessed going on next door, realizing that his unhappy best friend is being abused. His resourceful use of open information leads to three children being rescued from an intolerable home.

It goes both ways. For every case study of a child traumatized by some scandalous speech or image, there are a myriad counterexamples of children who withstood far worse onslaughts of verbal or pictorial offensiveness, and reacted only by growing more resilient, with all the inquisitive skepticism that makes truly sovereign citizens. And yet, for every group of junior high students who avidly discuss modern events, welcome diverse viewpoints, and seek wide-ranging evidence to improve their models of the world, you can also come up with some band of adult nitwits—people well past supposed maturity who should know better—who nevertheless swallow implausible myths and self-righteous clichés, about long disproved ethnic stereotypes, or purported Washington Beltway conspiracies, or the fatuous UFO aliens worshiped by those poor cultists who killed themselves just a mile from my home.

Returning to the Heaven's Gate tragedy, one is struck by incongruities, such as how well educated many of the deluded victims were, or how their ideology mixed hatred of authority with utter obedience to a single leader. In some ways they differed radically from comparable sects—gruesome Jonestown, Japan's terrifying *Aum Shinrikyo* cult, or the dour Branch Davidians. (The Gaters' final fling? Visiting Las Vegas, Sea World, and various amusement parks.) And yet, none of these disparities masks the essential, common thread.

For some people, ideas can indeed be lethal.

There is no satisfying conclusion. No encompassing generalization, except to reiterate that humans are complex. No smug ideology ever encompassed the range of our quirks—the highs some can reach, or the lows that others plumb. In an open society some vulnerable folks are sure to be traumatized. But if we choose paternalistic (or maternalistic) guidance, it will only guarantee that our brightest feel stifled and muzzled; and our culture will be much poorer for it.

What are parents to do? While aiming to teach our kids critical judgment and mental self-reliance, we know that those skills don't show up overnight, even in a home that encourages skeptical enquiry. Though details will be debated endlessly across generational lines, anyone with a grain of sense knows that children should not see or hear some things till they are older. One can be on the side of openness without wanting sadistic images floating on one's television screen, or weeping over the demise of "Joe Camel" cigarette ads.

And yet, despite our lack of a perfect answer, there can be no equivalence between those two ancient, conflicting worldviews. While compromise and flexibility may be called for on a daily basis, one basic assumption should underlie society's approach to the information age. In the long run, defensive shrouds simply don't protect us as well as agility, the capacity to appraise and reevaluate as we go along. People acquire good judgment through practice, even if a milieu of ongoing uncertainty makes citizens feel queasy at times.

We must choose the maturity thesis. Not because it is inherently right, or because it works for everyone. (It doesn't.)

We must choose it because it is our only hope.

*There is the tradition of the young outsider challenging conventional wisdom. However, in real life it is always difficult for really new ideas to be heard. Such a victory is almost impossible in a hierarchical structure. The usual way a new idea can be heard is for it to be sold first outside the hierarchy. When the project is secret, this is much more difficult.*

ARTHUR KANTROWITZ

## A CIVILIZATION OF "T-CELLS"

Faculty and students at Sonoma State University, in California, spent the last two decades pursuing a venture called Project Censor: The News That Didn't Make the News. Their ambitious aim? To scan for significant stories and events that sank below the public's radar screen, instead of receiving the attention they deserved. Members of every academic department monitor more than seven hundred "minor" press sources, from scientific journals to gazettes of the radical left and extreme right, sifting for worthy items that somehow escaped the attention of the national press. This effort culminates in a synopsis of the year's most seriously underreported events.

The members of this small university campus appear to have found themselves an interesting niche venture with some real social utility. Because many mainstream reporters subscribe to Project Censor's annual summary, some items on the "neglected" list get another look. In other cases, online discussion groups take up the cause, continuing to probe slighted issues through the voracious channels of cyberspace. Even some pundits of old-style newspapers and broadcast networks laud this effort, calling it a useful annual resifting, a way to help make sure the regular media don't miss anything truly important.

So far, so good. But the Project Censor coordinators don't stop there. Not content with simply listing underappreciated stories, they go on to *diagnose* why some events may not be covered as thoroughly as they deserve to be. According to Peter Phillips, assistant professor of sociology at Sonoma State, some of these potential scoops were squelched because of pressure applied by corporate interests, for example, when big-time advertisers threatened to pull their accounts from media outlets that dared carry muckraking articles about their products. In one case, a Chicago television station that began airing stories about the real (and inexpensive) contents of overpriced cosmetics hurriedly yanked the series when a large commercial account complained. In other cases, blame is attributed to government pressure or coercion, as when NASA purportedly swayed newspeople from widely discussing the space agency's plans to launch the Cassini space mission with 72 pounds of highly toxic plutonium fuel aboard. Though encased in high-tech armor, this substance could theoretically have endangered the populace of south Florida if the rocket had blown up. Project Censor members ascribed the lack of public outcry only partly to direct government intimidation, adding that media outlets can also fall prey to patterns of laziness and social suasion.

Naturally, some mainstream journalists take exception to this appraisal. Bernard Kalb of CNN responded that submitting to commercial or bureaucratic pressure "is not what working journalists do. For the most part, they are feisty, skeptical and committed." In other words, Kalb believes that no power broker can reliably suppress a big story once the basic facts leak beyond a very tight inner circle. Surely the fondest dream of any ambitious correspondent is to achieve the career-making coup of a startling exposé. Many stories would never have been revealed without undercover journalism, a tradition that goes back more than a century; during the 1880s, Nellie Bly, a courageous reporter for *New York World*, got herself committed to a mental institution in order to expose the horrors of New York City's lunatic asylums. Ever since then, investigative journalists have been nosing around for hints and clues leading to the next ripening scandal, or the next sensational story.

It is certainly tenable that advertisers and politically connected publishers wield undue influence over various periodicals, from time to time. For this reason some cutting-edge publications, notably *Consumer Reports* and *Whole Earth Review*, refuse advertising in order to safeguard their vaunted reputation for credibility. Nevertheless, such meddling can be counterproductive. In a competitive environment, the chief effect will be to drive the best reporters away to other journals, where freedom of inquiry is the common culture. In other words, suggests Kalb, if some stories fail to reach general awareness, it may be because the public did not find them compelling in the first place.

Why do some news reports provoke great interest, while others languish in obscurity? The preceding two contrasting explanations, posed by spokesmen who each seem quite convinced of their point of view, present an engaging dichotomy.

What these arguments over Project Censor actually illustrate is a distinct aspect of our neo-Western civilization that I call "social T-cells."

For a helpful analogy, let's take a brief detour into the realm of biology. The body of any large vertebrate animal contains billions of component cells, each performing a variety of roles. Most stay primly in place throughout their life spans, providing chemical or structural services. Others, such as red blood cells, roam all over the place, delivering nourishment or transporting waste. Every day, your body comes under threat from contaminants and invading parasites. Furthermore, throughout the organism, cells occasionally "go crazy." For some reason these rogues abandon selfless devotion to the whole, instead setting forth on a campaign of individual aggrandizement and unrestrained reproduction that is called cancer.

Whatever the nature of these varied threats, they are all *errors* that must quickly be overcome by an effective immune system, or else life's delicate balance will be forfeit. We all know how catastrophic it can be when the immune system becomes deficient, as in AIDS, or grows hyperactive, as in lupus or some forms of arthritis, mistaking the body itself for an enemy, attacking and savaging healthy organs. For many reasons, immunology has become one of the most important fields of modern medicine.

Now, if some human engineer had been asked to design a strategy for defense and error correction, he or she might be tempted to create a central information center, with a master control program, constantly comparing the body's current status with some ideal condition, and then sending out proxies with specific instructions to repair any deviation. Such a hierarchical approach may sound logical. (So logical, in fact, that it was used as the model for "planned" economies such as the Soviet Union.)

But that is not the way living organisms do it. Instead, our bodies throng with semi-independent agents, caroming randomly through the blood and lymph networks, sniffing for trouble like lone marshals of the old West. Chief among these roving deputies are white blood cells, especially "T-cells," whose mission is to detect threats on the spot and emit a chemical summons for help, so that the problem can be counteracted before it gets out of hand.

T-cells are not generalists. In fact, a human body comes equipped with countless subtypes, each of them tuned to recognize just a narrow range of potential perils. Every day, our lives depend on having an adequate variety of these little troubleshooters, and on having the right ones drift randomly toward each new danger zone, arriving in the nick of time. For the most part, it is a startlingly effective technique for dealing with organic or cellular errors, one that is far more flexible than relying on central control.

This protection depends, above all, on having an unobstructed circulatory system. One that lets these T-cells and other error-correcting agents into every corner of the body to deal with potentially mortal dangers as quickly as they occur.


How do immune systems relate to Project Censor? Or to transparency, for that matter? Recall the keystone epigram of this book.

**How do immune systems relate to Project Censor? Or to transparency, for**

*Humans have found one fairly reliable antidote to error: criticism.*

Elsewhere I discuss the great irony this poses. Free speech and open criticism are good for a nation, helping it discover mistakes before they bring lethal consequences; and yet those qualities so threaten national leaders that kings, priests, oligarchs, and demagogues have always suppressed criticism to varying degrees.

Criticism might be viewed as a civilization's equivalent of an immune system. Moreover, it cannot be mandated or levied from some high source. The capriciousness of human nature means that any central intervention, even by a well-intended ruler, will inevitably wind up squelching the most desperately needed criticism of all, a critique aimed at those on top. Instead, a healthy immune system must be distributed, dispersed, and based on an almost random overlapping of function, so that if one agent fails to detect a festering problem, there is a good chance it will be uncovered by the next one to come bumping along.

Moreover, our bodies show yet another type of inherent "wisdom." Those swarming T-cells that go scurrying around looking to *detect* errors are not the same cells principally in charge of *eradicating* them. A separation of roles between detection and enforcement is a principle that will come up later in this book.

Perhaps now we can see how all this is relevant. In social terms, our contemporary neo-Western civilization already throngs with the *human equivalent of T-cells*, independent-minded persons who are well educated, skeptical, and driven by pumped-up egos to the point where their most devout goal is to find and reveal some terrible mistake or nefarious scheme. This category enfolds a lot more than news reporters, activists, and professional muckrakers. Any of you reading this book can probably close your eyes and envision quite a few friends or colleagues whose personalities exhibit some of the following traits:

- strongly held opinions
- a belief that he or she can see patterns in some field of knowledge (such as the news) that others are too obstinate or ignorant to perceive
- a distrust of certain (and perhaps all) types of authority
- profound faith in his or her own unique individuality

Perhaps you recognize, or even proudly avow, many of these traits in yourself. If so, it hardly makes you exceptional. For most citizens of contemporary America and many other subcultures of the neo-West, these personality attributes are the very ones that have been drilled into them from a very early age.

This point, though already discussed, merits reiteration. The characters we find admirable in books and films often exhibit driven individualism and have difficulty accepting regimentation by formal organizations. They are irked by rules and routines, and above all display suspicion of authority. This archetype is copied in such endless profusion that the "lonely rebel" might by now have become the most dreadful of clichés. But in fact, it seems to have escaped the notice of most social observers that the principal moral lesson carried by neo-Western media is scorn for stodgy establishments of any stripe.

Is this really new? Didn't some past myths and legends carry threads of rebellion?

Perhaps a thread or two. Odysseus was a rule breaker, though the penalties were dire. His family suffered, and all who followed him died. Moreover, he never defeated the gods who inflicted such capricious punishments. Likewise, Romeo and Juliet could hardly be thought of as prevailing, the way so many modern rebels are depicted overcoming the social barriers to love. The protagonists of *Candide, Pride and Prejudice,* and *The Iliad* all had spells of railing against the constraints surrounding them—and then went about living according to the fixed overall conventions of their time. Even Swift's wonderful and prescient Gulliver battled an unjust social order through parable. His triumph was spiritual and metaphorical.

Modern audiences want something more explicit and decisive, whether the hero loathes all vile authorities (*Catch 22*), or happens to be a cop whose bosses are corrupt or inept (*Dirty Harry*). It isn't that there must always be a happy ending. The reader or viewer can accept occasional tragedy, even the death of a protagonist, just so long as some oppressor is perceived as losing.

Nor is this unswerving message restricted to popular movies and novels. Radicalized professors of both the left and right recite the same themes by rote on any North American university campus, often denouncing in righteous tones the very institutions that give them subsidized and tenured perches from which to hurl scathing critiques. While specific intellectual arguments may range from cogent to specious across the political spectrum, what so many strikingly share is contempt toward some "establishment," an indignant scorn that they strive to teach their students.

We will postpone trying to analyze the whys and wherefores of this exceptional phenomenon, perhaps for another book. For now, it is fascinating just to concentrate on results. So caught up are we in the details of our individual opinions that we may completely miss this common current running beneath our most vociferous political arguments, a theme that unites many of those who see each other as political foes.

In the United States, a typical voter who is politically *right* of center worries about *accumulations of undue power* by officious academics or faceless government bureaucrats.

From the viewpoint of voters who are somewhat *left* of center, the transfixing danger is *accumulations of undue power* by conniving aristocrats and faceless corporations.

When expressed this way, it seems rather sad that both sides scarcely recognize a deep-seated political reflex they share—especially since both parties have legitimate points! Governments *and* aristocrats have long track records of oppressing people. Both merit close scrutiny by corps of eager critics.

It is important to note here that the details often do not count. What matters is that millions of people feel a passion to be different. To poke at dangerous secrets and experience heroic pride when they uncover some mistake, or thwart a nefarious scheme. This personality trait is diffusive, meaning that those who are most truly independent of mind will inevitably grow uncomfortable as part of a herd. Needing individuality, they often strike forth in some unusual direction, seeking to distinguish themselves from the despised mob.

The fact that people have contempt for conformity does not mean that they don't conform! Any more than having a declared faith in individualism will automatically make someone unique. You have only to walk on any university campus in Europe or America to see that members of the most rebellious element, the surly "bohemian" crowd, nearly all dress with incredible similarity, expressing their scorn for "mundanes" in terms that hardly vary from mouth to mouth, or campus to campus. The *otaku* social rebels in Japan also exhibit this trait. As commentator Richard Raynor put it, "Most teenagers are innate conservatives. Their rebellion happens, if at all, by the numbers, whether numbers are written by Elvis Presley, Jim Morrison, or Snoop Doggy Dog." The same holds true for many other modern tribes. While the ideology is individualistic, there remains a deep-seated human drive to be part of a group. To be different— just like your friends.

And yet, the ideology *is* powerful. If just 1 percent of North Americans eventually succeed in achieving some degree of bold difference in their lives, that results in three million true individuals, whose genuine uniqueness will change their communities, as well as civilization.

In other words, the aforementioned propaganda campaign could not have been better designed to spawn several generations of frenetic T-cells, rebounding all over the place, zealously pouncing on every error they can find, both real and imagined. In many cases, they do it for their own egos' sake. And yet the effect, in the long run, is to supply civilization with copious amounts of wildly diverse criticism—the only known antidote to error.

*The right to be heard does not automatically include the right to be taken seriously.*                    HUBERT H. HUMPHREY

## DUDGEON ADDICTION

It seems that the Pleasure Principle is back from the dead. This once discarded theory held that humans and animals behave in certain ways because those actions *feel* good. For much of the twentieth century, the notion was abandoned in favor of behaviorist concepts propagated by B. F. Skinner, or more recent cognitive theories. Only now are neuro-chemists finding that a great many of the things we do are reinforced by the release of psychoactive molecules in our brains. Many of life's most wholesome joys, such as listening to music, or watching a sunset, or pro-voking a baby's wide smile, actually trigger waves of endorphins, enkephalins and other substances, which are responsible for the warm feelings that come over us when we experience our favorite things. There is no shame in discovering this about ourselves. Knowledge about detailed processes does not diminish any of the joy, nor make it less gen-uinely good. It just means that we are starting to understand how we remain addicted to the best parts of life.

This discovery also sheds new light on the whole issue of illegal or abused drugs, many of which are crude substitutes for those very same nat-ural pleasure chemicals. In other words, people who use heroin may do so because they never learned better ways to activate the same molecular receptors that spark and flare inside the rest of us during expressions of love, or exercise, or the gratifying employment of a skill.

There is a third way to excite these pleasure centers. Humans can learn to trigger the release of endorphins and other natural chemicals in the body by voluntarily entering certain mental states. For instance, ever since the days of William James, it has been known that deep religious faith can have similar physiological effects on believers, across nearly all boundaries of doctrine and creed. Studies of experts in the arts of meditation have shed light on the agreeably detached conditions that they enter by volition, enabling some aficionados to develop shortcuts using computerized biofeedback equipment, training themselves to achieve pleasurable levels of (non)consciousness almost at will.

One particular mental state seems quite effective at enabling individ-uals to self-administer these psychotropic chemicals on a massive scale. *Self-righteousness* is an especially heady condition that all of us have expe-rienced at one time or another. Those who are honest will admit there is something sickly-sweet and alluring about *knowing* you are right, while others are terribly wrong. However many unpleasant or anxious feelings may accompany a crisis, righteousness is one side effect that can imbue a person with sensations of romantic virtue, and the satisfaction of feeling like a martyr, or the lonely champion of a pious cause.

For some, this mental state is not rare or occasional. It can be as addic-tive as any other reinforced pleasure. Look in the eyes of the most self-right-eous people you know, even those whose opinions you share. Whether or not they are achieving success in their crusades, one trait that many exhibit is an outward impression of being "on a high." Under these conditions, it is hard for people to notice their own mistakes, or even towering hypocrisies—such as when the livid radio personality G. Gordon Liddy indignantly vowed to shoot down any conjectural federal agent who might come breaking into his office . . . despite the fact that Liddy's own sole claim to notoriety on this planet was for having been caught as an incompetent burglar on behalf of a corrupt federal president. Liddy's irate tunnel vision is hardly exceptional. It illustrates an addictive trait that may be more common in our society than dependencies on alcohol, drugs, or tobacco.

It may seem twisted, but amid their struggles, many self-righteousness junkies seem to be having one helluva good time.

Now please don't get me wrong. I am hardly one to get judgmental toward self-righteous people! Over the course of more than forty years, I have wallowed in the same state all too often. My aim here is not to cast stones, but to discuss one of the more vivid aspects of human nature—one that has beneficial uses, from time to time. Indeed, like so much of bio-chemistry, the effects can be positive, when applied in moderation.

Take the "social T-cells" I described a little while ago. For many icon-oclasts, the adversarial rough and tumble of their creative or error-seeking quest can get rather sticky, or even dangerous. After all, there *are* mighty forces out there who hate having their mistakes exposed. These forces often lash out, despite all the rules that are supposed to protect freedom of speech. For criticism to penetrate every crevice and capillary of society, our lonely T-cells often need some extra incentive to keep on fighting for the truth (as they perceive it). Beyond possible career or monetary compensa-tions, they may also require the pleasure-reward of sanctimony.

A certain amount of self-righteousness can put fire in your belly, mak-ing you more willing to face great odds to make your point, or even tilt at windmills. When this formidable mental state mixes with an ideology of rebellious individualism, the result can be a potent cocktail, fortifying some lonesome dissenter to stand on street corners shouting, "Wake up!" to a distracted or indifferent society.


And yet, the amount of heat in a person's voice bears almost no relation to how right they are. The two factors seem almost orthogonal, unrelated to each other. Passion may provide force and motivation, but truth can only be tested in the open marketplace of debate, experimentation, and the relentless experience of daily life.

In fact, despite positive uses, who can deny that self-righteousness has drawbacks, pushing nonconformists into states of bitter rage, alienated from everyone around them, rancorously paranoid and derisive of the very society that trained them to be proud individuals? (Sometimes such persons mask their egomania behind a shield of indignant "professionalism.")

Biologists and physicians have a name for what happens when white blood cells scorn the organism they were made to serve, tearing loose the bonds of commensal life, attacking healthy tissue and bringing on a general collapse. The condition is a type of cancer called leukemia.

When disdain of authority becomes bilious hatred, the result may be not a helpful dissenter but a calamitous traitor, such as Timothy McVeigh. In his published letters, the convicted Oklahoma City bomber repeatedly exulted in his own "exceptional" intelligence and insight, expressing not only wrath over purported government schemes but also delighted pride in being among the only ones to "see through their propaganda and lies." McVeigh's need to feel special was so profound, and his contempt for his fellow citizens so deep, that he cut himself off from every bit of feedback or criticism—anything that might have helped him notice the horrible error sloshing through his endorphin-soaked brain—the error of rationalizing a foul criminal act, the murder of 162 innocent neighbors and children.

What makes this so pathetic is that McVeigh's own nature and personality disproved his paranoic fantasy, since his special illness was a deeply American product of the very culture that he despised as a "regimented" fascist dictatorship. In fact, we might ponder how lucky we have been so far, having trained several hundred thousand young men to become expert with explosives (in the military), after having weaned them on suspicion-of-authority messages. Given such a volatile blend, are we blessed that Oklahoma City happened just once, and that most angry rebels express their rage as they should, through words?

That fact may offer solace while we endure the ever-growing murmur of sullen suspicion that often seems to drown all common sense. Especially in the United States, where a poll taken by the Scripps-Howard News Service in July 1997 found that a majority of citizens affirmed some belief in government conspiracy theories. For instance, a third of those surveyed gave credence to the notion that FBI agents "deliberately" set fire to women and children, in broad daylight and in front of news cameras, at the Branch Davidian compound in Waco, Texas, in 1992. A whopping 51 percent of respondents called it either "very likely" or "somewhat likely" that federal officials were directly responsible for the assassination of President Kennedy.

Even retractions do little good, such as when the man who first accused the U.S. Navy of shooting down TWA flight 800 told CNN that he had fabricated the story "to give the government a black eye by any means that looked opportune. . . . TWA 800 was just a vehicle for my larger agenda." Ian Goddard, who identified himself as a libertarian and investigator into various purported government plots, apologized not only to the families of the victims but also "to those who believed in my efforts who are now upset with me for my change of mind."

"Paranoia is killing this country," commented Curtis Gans, executive director of the Washington-based Committee for the Study of the American Electorate, in response to the Scripps-Howard survey. Oklahoma Governor Frank Keating echoed that sentiment. "Maybe people are watching too many Oliver Stone movies. What we see on movie screens these days demonizes government agencies and public officials. Free institutions cannot survive this kind of cynicism."

Are Gans and Keating right? Does a plague of excessive, indignant imagination threaten the very life of the republic?

I don't think so. Not yet. Surveys tend to overstate their case, since modern folks will often express interest in any intriguing idea or notion, trying it on for size. Hence other surveys reveal substantial overall confidence in our shared institutions.

Anyway, the benefits gained from suspicion of authority outweigh the disadvantages. Our ongoing freedom and economic success testify to the effectiveness of error-correcting systems, imperfect as they are. So does the fact that species extinction rates in North America, though still excessive, have declined to among the lowest on any continent.

At least now there is a useful model for the "militia phenomenon" currently infesting the United States. After raising several generations to enjoy the role of defiant dissenters, it can hardly be surprising that some "T-cells" fixate on bizarre scenarios and conspiracy theories—everything from government hangars filled with captured aliens, to melaninist or neo-Nazi styles of racism, to swarms of black U.N. helicopters bent on conquering the world. In 1997 alone, the number of Web sites devoted to hate groups and related subjects increased 300%.

Under these conditions, it's not hard to see how some of the most imaginative and self-righteous might actually convince themselves that they live under tyranny, instead of the mildest and most tolerant continental-scale culture the world has ever seen. One that is so patient and broad-minded that it will forbear any kind of vituperative speech, protecting the privilege of millions to be wrong so that we may all benefit from a few who turn out to be right.

*The best argument for open-book management is this: the more educated your work force is about the company, the more capable it is of doing the little things required to get better. . . . The odd part is that nobody hates surprises more than the manipulative control freaks who practice old-fashioned, secretive, need-to-know management. [Yet] that way of operation virtually guarantees a steady stream of surprises, because people don't have the tools they need to forecast and project, to live up to their commitments.*

JACK STACK, *THE GREAT GAME OF BUSINESS*

## A CIVILIZATION IMMUNE TO ERROR?

All this talk about *immune systems combating error* may strike some readers as too optimistic, given how many grievous faults plague us, from law and policy to our chaotic personal lives. As a youth in 1968, I learned how deeply a nation can wound itself with war, assassination, injustice, and hate. Nowadays, like my neighbors, I often mutter during the television news, despairing over the obstinacy of political leaders who cling to rigid orthodoxies instead of applying pragmatic solutions to problems ranging from drugs to gun control. Yet who can look back at the litany of awful mistakes that regularly toppled smug empires and proud cities without recognizing that something has changed? At last rulers must undertake most of their decisions in the open, subject to observation and comment by a broad spectrum of unabashed citizens. Among businesses, a new trend toward internal trust and openness among executives and employees has begun bearing fruit for those companies brave enough to resist age-old bullying habits of hierarchy and domination.

This new "immune system" may be imperfect (the animal kingdom had eons to perfect the biological counterpart) but at least we started noticing some dangers, like ozone depletion and species extinction, long before the trends grew too severe. Passionate advocates and antagonists swarm around each problem, hollering so loud we can't ignore the peril, even when we squeeze our eyes shut and hope it goes away.

The trend is especially important given society's growing complexity and the rapid pace of change. Science and technology *must* progress swiftly, in order to offer any hope of solving the world's problems. Still, with every advance, new questions and dilemmas burst forth to confound even a culture filled with large numbers of college graduates. As the recent furor over potential human cloning showed, it takes time for people to listen, argue among themselves, overreact, learn some more, and finally start making the sort of practical, as-we-go decisions that may (with luck) take us into the twenty-first century in fairly decent shape.

The same truth applies when we find ourselves arguing about human rights with tyrannical nations. So far, it has proved rather futile to sermonize at dictators, preaching moral justifications for freedom of speech. As we'll discuss later (chapter 10, "Global Transparency"), the rulers of modern China and other authoritarian regimes need only counter with protestations of cultural sovereignty, accusing the West of trying to impose its own social values on the world.

Exhortation is a pallid and mostly unavailing approach to achieving change—a fact that applies even more to nations than it does to individuals. But suppose instead we take a different strategy toward such old-fashioned ruling cliques. What if we explain that we seek freedom for their subject peoples *because it is vital for our own safety's sake?* Because a nation that lacks free speech and open criticism will inevitably make dire errors, misjudge threats or opportunities, and even launch adventures that it cannot possibly win. (The 1990 invasion of Kuwait by Saddam Hussein was a prime example. Or go back and revisit similar blunders by Hitler and Stalin.) Although the more resilient, error-correcting cultures will almost certainly "win" such future clashes, the cost could be enormous, making vast pain our common lot on earth.

How much better if such huge mistakes can be avoided in the first place! Toward that end, we will all be much safer if the citizens of every nation can stand erect and speak freely to their leaders.

I am not the first to mention this fact—that the great strength of neo-Western civilization rests not on its ethereal ideals and justifications but upon its foundation of hard-as-stone pragmatism. Jean François Revel, author of *Democracy Against Itself* and *Without Marx or Jesus*, expressed it thus: "Democracy's practical superiority derives from the fact that it is the only system which, through trial and error, can become aware of its mistakes and correct them. Totalitarianism cannot correct itself: it is forced to follow its logic until the final catastrophe."

The irony here is that our relative immunity against fallacy is in large part carried out via the adversarial tug and push of countless indignant, righteous, and often narrow-minded individuals, many of whom would be anything but tolerant or democratically inclined if by some magic or intrigue they ever achieved coercive power. The service they provide for the rest of us—the calm, relatively contented majority—cannot be overstated.

And yet, one might be forgiven for nursing a favorite little daydream—that perhaps just once a month, say at noon on the thirtieth day, each of us might pause amid our irate protestations against what we see as wrong, take a deep breath, and recite the following sentence aloud:

### I am a member of a civilization.

All our talk about immune systems and "social T-cells" resonates with the core topic of this book, transparency, for these metaphors illustrate two basic things about our fascinating new world.

1. Openness and candor are essential for the survival of any civilization, especially a global throng of over six billion human beings.

2. Many aspects of openness are already so deeply rooted in the system that nothing will ever tear them out. At least, not without surgery so brutal that it would take the annihilation of millions.

The main question may be whether we can fine-tune this fractious, rambunctious system, so that useful criticism will not be drowned out beneath floods of screeching rudeness and the memic equivalents of cancer. Toward such a goal, endeavors like Sonoma State University's Project Censor set a good example. We needn't affirm their more extravagant charges of widespread corruption in mainstream news media in order to credit the project with worthy service, providing an annual list of topics meriting further investigation—a menu for hungry T-cells—and letting would-be heroes of openness pick and choose from an array of causes to which they can devote their untapped, fervent energies.

The example of the NASA Cassini mission seems to illustrate the point. Within weeks after Project Censor published its list of underreported stories, a surge of interest focused on that space endeavor, from both media reporters and suddenly aroused advocacy groups. None of them seemed to notice purported "pressure" from NASA hierarchs to squelch the story. But by the time Cassini launched (without mishap), a thorough national discussion of the pros and cons had taken place.

As if aware of this synergistic need for open debate, the United States Supreme Court in January 1998 unanimously stripped automakers, tobacco companies, and other firms of a method they were widely using to stifle "whistle-blowers" who release internal documents or testify about corporate misbehavior. According to this ruling, nondisclosure agreements in one state cannot be applied in ways that block important testimony in another, opening yet another crack in the walls that corporations have erected to keep secrets and stave off accountability. (Similar whistle-blower protections have applied to federal workers for many years.) In other words, information, the life blood of both commerce and justice, must be allowed to flow.

Let me reiterate. It does not matter what fraction of T-cells are right in their worried search for errors to assail. In fact, as society improves, the percentage may decline! (Or else we may keep raising our standards, pouncing on errors that seemed too "minor" to notice in the past.)

In the long run, efficiency is not urgent. What counts is that every important decision should get sniffed, argued over, and poked at from all sides before it can be put into effect, thus hopefully preventing yet another major tragedy of unintended consequences. The vital thing to note, as we conclude this chapter, is that the new-style social immune system thrives on passion, and even large doses of overwrought ego, but that hatefulness and self-righteousness are less beneficial. Viewed over the long run, they are often early signs of *metastasis* by a promising T-cell. Its transformation from potential savior into a virulent kind of predatory parasite.

That's probably all right. As long as we live in a relatively transparent society, *other* T-cells will often swarm in to neutralize the danger. (We will see this illustrated in the next chapter, in a story about struggles between two computer hackers.) And yet, it seems a pity for so much energy and angst to be wasted.

Is it too much to hope that someday perhaps all the angry young men and women will finally see how valuable and integral they are to a society they claim to despise?

Would we spend so much time, effort, and money *training* them to be rebels, if that were not the case?

# ESSENCES AND EXPERIMENTS

*People are flexible enough to make any theory look good
for a while. What is impossible to be sure of, though, is
how much the theory might have limited what people could
have become. . . . The self-congratulatory fallacies of artificial intelligence are similiar to the ways in which communists fooled themselves into believing they had found the
key to paradise, while actually they had only blinded themselves to their own humanity for a time.* JARON LANIER

Imagine an encounter between two of history's greatest minds, each defending his own view of reality.

PLATO: *Our senses are defective; therefore, we cannot discover truth
through experience. That chair, for instance. Despite all your gritty
"experiments," you will never determine what it is. Not perfectly.*

*Therefore give up! Empiricism is useless. Seek the essence of truth
through pure reason.*

GALILEO: *You're right. My eyesight is poor. My touch is flawed. I will
never know with utter perfection what this chair is.*

*Nevertheless, I can carve away untruths and wrong theories. I
can demolish fancy "essences" and epicycles and disprove self-
hypnotizing incantations. With good experiments—and the helpful
criticism of my peers—I can find out what the chair is not.*

•  •  •

Neuroscientists have learned that a baby approaches birth with far more brain cells—and more links *between* those cells—than he or she will require. While learning important life tasks, the child does not add new synapses. Rather, she culls those that are unneeded.

Instead of a nervous system that is a "blank slate," we begin life with countless mutually contradictory possibilities already written. A majority must be eliminated for the remaining connections to do useful work. In other words, learning is as much about *editing* as about creating new ideas.

But we already know this! Pause and let your own mind free-associate for a time. Freud elucidated how each of us carries a roiling storm of thoughts, some pertinent, and a great many others that seem to whirl in and out with no apparent meaning or correlation to the business at hand. Every waking moment, we perform semiconscious editing tasks, winnowing this tempest of associations down to a manageable roar. One secret of effective creativity is to do this *just right,* so that enough cunning images, nifty juxtapositions, and eerie correlations get through to inspire new ways of viewing old problems. Nevertheless, it is principally by culling innumerable useless notions that we arrive at a few that seem worth keeping, or even acting on.

As it is in our brains and the whirling maelstroms of our thoughts, so it is with science. Karl Popper and others have shown that discovery is not about coming up with a grand, idealized theory and then "proving it true." Instead, research tends to be a messy process. Each hypothesis breaks up into dozens of subtheories, each with different implications that can then be tested on the lab bench, or in the field. Half of a scientist's job is to come up with experiments that might disprove a favorite theory and then honestly perform those experiments—or invite others to do so. This is called "falsification," and it amounts to the ultimate act of honesty. A scientist says:

> *Here is my cherished model of the world. And here is a list of potential experimental results that would prove it wrong! I challenge anyone to check it out. If none of these results happen, that does not necessarily mean my model is right . . . but it will grow unlikely that I'm wrong!*

Now read Plato—*Phaedrus,* or *The Republic*—or any other articulate promoter of a persuasive, idealized dogma, from Karl Marx to Ayn Rand. There is no similarity between their version of Truth (with a capital *T,* perfect and unassailable) and the tentatively true (always lowercase) models of science. This is especially pertinent when it comes to ideal models of human nature.

In chapter 5, I presented some metaphors, wild and entertaining results of combining facts with correlated observations (for example, all that talk of "social T-cells"). I hope they lent some insight to phenomena such as the surge of pro-eccentricity propaganda and suspicion of authority. But that is a long way from contending that any of it is perfectly true! The most gruesome crimes in history were committed by parties and ideologies that professed to have genuine, unassailable pictures of how human beings function. For example, Hegel taught that nothing is real except the "whole" or "absolute" . . . a perfect society that all of history will inevitably and tendentiously move toward. (His image of predestined perfection was the contemporary Prussian state of his own time. It was the duty of individuals to serve that state.) Fascists and Leninists extrapolated this idealism to justify the worst regimes of this century. Of course their simplistic pictures nearly always ignored the vast range of women and men who would never fit their neat philosophies.

These exceptions angered Stalin, Hitler, and other tyrants, who did not like falsification. Not one bit. They treated all competing ideas, or even slight deviations from dogma, as "toxic."

That point is especially relevant to this book because so many arguments boil down to a continuing face-off between pragmatism and idealism. Admittedly, most of the idealists in the next few chapters are far from being tyrants. Indeed, most are devoted, in their own ways, to fighting vile accumulations of power, and to offering prescriptions for safeguarding liberty. There is nothing wrong with this. But when people start believing in the perfect reality of their metaphors, they take footsteps down the path of Plato and so many others. A path that has, in the long run, led to more harm than good.

Recall the quotation from Jaron Lanier that began this section. Go back and replace "artificial intelligence" with "crypto-anarchy," and Lanier might be describing the latest techno-transcendentalist fetish—a passionate belief that all will be well if only we pledge our faith and trust to encrypted chains of bits and bytes, managed by algorithms of chaste mathematical purity. We shall see that this latest techno-religion is no different from the others that preceded it. At best it is an exaggeration that ignores practical problems. At worst it is deeply dehumanizing.

Plato was right about one thing. We can never learn what is flawless or unblemished with our senses alone. But the devastation wrought by idealists in the past shows how easily we can also lie to ourselves *within* our imaginative minds. Reason is an excellent tool for generating hypotheses. But it is in the world of hard, gritty practicality that honest folks test their favorite ideas, modify them under the helpful heat of criticism, carve away errors, and join others in developing systems that work.

Systems that may even be somewhat true.

CHAPTER SIX

# LESSONS IN ACCOUNTABILITY

*Conscience is the inner voice which warns us that someone may be looking.*

ATTRIBUTED TO H. L. MENCKEN

*Make up your minds that happiness depends on being free, and freedom depends on being courageous.*

PERICLES OF ATHENS

For an open society to be flexible and error-resistant, it must deal with all kinds of messy or harsh problems that face people in daily life. And not just normal people, but those who are angry, alienated, or on the edge. Societies have always sought to reinforce those human traits they found worthwhile, and to diminish those deemed injurious. In a culture based on diversity and appreciation of eccentricity, there should be a lot of the former, and just a few of the latter. But we can still expect a need for law, and restraints applied upon those who would do harm.

In this book, we emphasize accountability as a tried-and-true technique for minimizing disaster in a complex society, and mutual transparency as a useful means to ensure accountability. This chapter will deal with a few examples, some of them taken from the new electronic world of video cameras, multimedia, and computerized communications. But the principles apply almost anywhere.

Later, chapters 7 and 8 will plunge into the cutting-edge debates over encryption, anonymity, and secrecy. We shall also continue the ongoing discussion of whether our governments will keep playing a role in helping us ensure a decent civilization, or whether a time has come to cast loose the bonds of our past and plunge into an uncertain future, when it will be everyone for themselves.

## A NEW "COMMONS"

Back in the European Middle Ages, there existed in England tracts of common lands, fields no one owned that could be used by anyone in the neighboring community. Unwritten rules of sharing evolved, sometimes enforced by a feudal lord, but often mediated by consensus among the farmers and herdsmen themselves.

Garrett Hardin's influential study *The Tragedy of the Commons* describes what happened when the medieval order began breaking down. Rising population, improved farm technology, and accelerating commerce put pressure on communal lands. Individuals saw personal benefit in grazing their herds on the commons till every scrap of greenery was eaten. Water was diverted, trees felled, and lumber taken without the earlier forest-tending practice of coppicing. In other words, the logic of unbridled competition began to prevail. If it wasn't your land, your short-term incentive was to use up the common resource before others did.

Lest any misconstrue, I am not preaching nostalgia for the Middle Ages, a time of ignorance, largely dominated by brutal feudal overlords. Nevertheless, the old commons is often cited as an example of innocent communal sharing that collapsed with the arrival of commercial resource exploitation.

This has happened elsewhere. Events in Asia and the Americas were not too dissimilar. Even today, companies are known to pay pennies on the acre to lease federal lands in the western United States, exploiting the General Mining Act of 1872 to plunder a region's minerals and then departing, often leaving spoilage in their wake. Similar complaints are raised about ranchers' subsidized overgrazing of the public range. An international example is the way several dozen nations subsidize expensive fishing fleets, which are rapidly depleting overharvested ocean stocks.

Can a parallel be made with today's information superhighway? At first sight, the Internet seems to run on an ad hoc basis, almost like a "commons." Some official groups, such as the National Science Foundation (NSF), used to exert sway over the major infrastructure, for instance, the on-ramps and loading yards called network access points. But the NSF gave up control several years ago to concentrate on developing technologies for the next phase. In fact, most of the key decisions are now made by informal groups. For instance, the Internet Engineering Task Force (IETF) mediates technology standards and seeks consensus among major users, while another licensed group governs the allocation of domain names, the closest thing to a formal bureaucracy that many users encounter on the Net. Although commercial services restrict their own sections of cyberspace to members and clients, the Internet itself has grown far too diverse, with too many alternative pathways, for anyone to claim real dominion. It operates as a collective virtual frontier, where all may roam pretty much as they please, so long as they have a port of entry.

To some who have pondered this, the analogy with a medieval commons falls short of describing the blithe chaos of today's burgeoning dataways. After all, information can be duplicated endlessly and at no cost, a trait not shared by pasture or farmland. According to futurist Bruce Sterling:

> The Internet's "anarchy" may seem strange or unnatural, but it makes a certain deep sense. It's rather like the "anarchy" of the English language. Nobody rents English, and nobody owns English. As an English-speaking person, it's up to you to learn how to speak English properly and make whatever use you please of it (though the government provides certain subsidies to help you learn to read and write a bit). Otherwise, everybody just sort of pitches in, and somehow the thing evolves on its own, and somehow turns out workable. And interesting. Fascinating even. Though a lot of people earn their living from using and exploiting and teaching English, "English" as an institution is public property, a public good. Much the same goes for the Internet. Would English be improved if "The English Language, Inc." had a board of directors and a chief executive officer, or a President and a Congress? There'd probably be a lot fewer new words in English, and a lot fewer new ideas.

While Sterling's allegory is enthralling, it implies that the networks consist only of information—abstractions, words, and data. Equally important, and binding this new realm to the real world, is the hardware—fibers, cables, switching yards, and nexus points of silicon memory. These are the equivalent of gates, fences, and flowing streams—points of high value that stand out from the rest of the landscape. Today, a kind of chaos does reign across fields of throbbing electrons, letting individuals ramble across worldwide databases almost free of regulation. But will this last long when vital pieces can be owned? Here the parallel with language breaks down.

Like its medieval counterpart, the electronic commons emerged from step-by-step evolution of makeshift techniques among a small number of neighbors—from "goofy, Jolt cola–swilling UNIX freaks" to generals, foundation heads, and Nobel laureates. There is a mythology that the Internet took everybody by surprise, springing like Athena from the brow of Zeus. But surely some of these people realized that the routes they laid down would be used for more than exchanging research data. From the start, engineers fiddled ways for the embryonic Internet to be even more wild and free.

Today it is a truly international commons, growing at phenomenal rates. The eager millions signing up are no longer intellectuals. They come from all walks of life. Many of the trends people worry about—flame wars, spamming, child pornography, chaotic and unverified rumors—are symptoms of the centrifugal forces sundering contemporary society at large. Already there are widespread calls for order, for organization and structure, for legislation and a bureaucracy to enforce rules of the road for the Infobahn. Some topics discussed in other chapters—the Communications Decency Act and the Clipper chip controversy—relate to this trend.

No wonder the netizens are frightened. Above all, they denounce anything they see as a threat to one of the great emancipatory events of modern life, the opening of an untamed frontier with possibilities as fertile and hope-filled for its settlers as the old West seemed to a prior generation. So what if this independence, this precious sovereignty, is newer than the youngest Net user, a surprise gift few dreamed of as recently as ten years ago? It is a fact of life that any liberty, once enjoyed, swiftly becomes essential, a requisite as vital to happiness as food and air.

Are we about to see another "tragedy of the commons"? Ask the dour pessimists who haunt many electronic discussion forums, unsurprised by any depths society might plumb, the way cynics from Molière to Kerouac used to mutter warily in smoky coffee houses. To them, Garrett Hardin's scenario is already unfolding, only this time over a span of months, rather than centuries. Indeed, popular "*cyber*punk" books and films often project tomorrows that have more in common with the nightmares of Dickens and Orwell than the fabled innocence of a Saxon village—bleak tales of stalwart individuals struggling for niches between gray mansions of faceless, unassailable power. The twenty-first-century worlds depicted by authors like William Gibson, Pat Cadigan, and Walter Jon Williams are dominated by vast corporate entities that have parceled out the cybernetic realm, erecting razor-sharp fences and for-profit channels that only a few brave hackers dare infiltrate, at great peril.

We will revisit these disturbing visions later. Some may come true, if history is our guide.

On the other hand, I see no reason why history must recapitulate. Making analogies to long-ago events in feudal England may be apt as a thoughtful warning, but our civilization already has traits that go far beyond simple parables about medieval farming villages. And we are more knowing, far mightier folk than our ancestors were, as they would surely have wanted us to be. It should be possible at this date to think, argue, innovate, and compromise until we find ways to make this dream greater and more startling than ever. Something diverse, free, and immune to the tragedies that ruined other "commons" in the past.

> *I see no way around our predicament; neither the quest for a spartan "sustainable" existence nor reliance on the forces of the marketplace will release us. . . . I am not arguing against change, but for a modest, tentative and skeptical acceptance of it.*
>
> EDWARD TENNER, WHY THINGS BITE BACK: TECHNOLOGY AND
> THE REVENGE OF UNINTENDED CONSEQUENCES

## THE RISKS PEOPLE WILL ENDURE

Sometimes it can be hard to get a clear image of the wants and fears that worry denizens of the modern era. Contradictions abound. For instance, although a 1993 Harris poll found that 83 percent of Americans were concerned about privacy, Steven E. Miller, author of *Civilizing Cyberspace: Policy, Power and the Information Superhighway*, concedes that "there are those who feel that the public's concern for privacy is like the River Platte, a mile wide but only an inch deep." Though his book vigorously promotes strong privacy, Miller notes that people routinely trade personal information for convenience or a few dollars of savings, even offering names of "friends and families" to commercial users, if it benefits them.

How can we explain this ambivalence between expressions of deep concern and a reality in which so many individuals seem cavalier about releasing details of their personal lives?

One way that academics and pundits often handle such discrepancies is with contempt—by assuming that people are too lazy or stupid to behave as active and knowing players in the social drama. They view citizens as puppets, jerking to strings pulled by dark forces, an attitude typified by the following statement: "Shorn of the ability to enter into relationships of responsibility and trust, individuals will tend to gravitate towards a safe average, suppressing their individuality and creativity in favor of a thoroughgoing orientation to the demands of an omniscient observer." In this example, the authors were specifically arguing that surveillance systems (like "smart" highways that speed traffic along while tracking vehicle locations via transponder) contribute to a corrosive atmosphere of distrust, fatalism, conformity, and declining citizenship skills. But the same attitude—a convention of portraying people as sheeplike and craven—pervades countless other social commentaries. (We explored some roots of this habit in chapter 5.)

For the sake of argument, I will stipulate that the above statement can be true, under certain conditions. People probably *do* shrink inward when surveillance is pervasive and relentlessly "top down" in orientation, such as in a true dictatorship, or in oppressive corporations that spy on their employees. Conformity is a classic survival reaction when people live in an ambience of terror and observation by unaccountable authorities. Chapter 9 illustrates several scenarios showing how high-tech repression may invade our future. On the other hand, we shall see in this section that feelings of distrust and fatalism do not tend to dominate when transparency is reciprocal, nor when people retain a sense of participation and control.

Scorn is both unnecessary and inadequate to explain the contradictions that modern people exhibit in daily life. Rather, such incongruities of attitude and behavior reflect the dynamic way in which citizens are trying to strike a balance amid tectonic shifts that may presage a new society. Science has shed light on this process through the fascinating field of risk analysis.

For many years, actuaries and officials at insurance companies and government regulatory agencies have tried to appraise *danger* in all corners of society, from airlines and automobiles to food safety and prescription packaging. In a sense, this is fine T-cell activity, since our institutions should endeavor to help us all thrive safely. And it is easy to see the success that some efforts have achieved, such as delivering clean water supplies, providing safer cars, and reducing pollution in our rivers and skies. We live longer and travel with more confidence, because many varied hazards are sniffed out by those with the expertise to find them.

Some may object in principle that we should not be coddled by bureaucrats, or that the free market (*caveat emptor*) could protect us better still. But contentious issues of paternalism will be dealt with later. (See the section on "public feedback regulation" in chapter 8.) Right now we should focus on the evolving way in which researchers have come to view the concept of risk and how people respond to it.

Until recently, most models were based on classical decision theory, supplemented by the later game theory that John Von Neumann developed after World War II. These are essentially mathematical approaches to betting—calculating odds for success or failure when contributing factors are either well known, or partly unknown. For instance, a problem called "the prisoners' dilemma" explores how two parties might behave when each can make a quick, temporary score by betraying the other, or else both might prosper, moderately but indefinitely, by deciding to cooperate. Over the years, many institutional leaders have studied various aspects of game theory, hoping to optimize everything from war scenarios to business plans.

Only there remained a mystery—how to make risk analysis fit the behavior of normal people! It seemed that men and women on the street were acting only partly according to principles of game theory when making decisions about investments, travel, or whether to take that chancy new job on the coast. A good example is *flying*. Everyone knows the well-publicized, reassuring statistic that traveling on regularly scheduled airlines is much safer, on a per-mile basis, than riding in an automobile. Yet countless people feel more nervous on planes. Some researchers condescendingly dismissed such deviations from theory, calling them irrational or psychological, as if that made them any less relevant. Finally, fresh studies found the answer, and it turned out not to be so unreasonable after all.

It seems that people internalize the perceived risk in any situation—whether through prim statistics or overheard anecdotes—and then multiply in a factor having to do with how much *control* they have over the situation. In other words, folks are willing to experience greater risk behind the wheel of a car, because their destiny remains partly subject to their own will. Personal action might adjust the risk, upward or downward, even in an accident that is someone else's fault. In contrast, passengers have a sense of powerlessness on an airplane, relying on the skill and professionalism of many strangers, from pilots to mechanics to the manufacturers of critical components on which their lives will depend for several hours, until the wheels touch down. It is all very well to advertise how well that chain of competence seems to work—the safety record of air travel is emblematic of a marvelous and ingenious civilization, filled with adults who take pride in their work—but that doesn't completely erase the creepy feeling that comes from surrendering command over one's fate to others.

According to the Environmental Protection Agency's risk summary, other factors that are known to affect public perception of risk include "certainty and severity of the risk; the reversibility of any health effect; the knowledge or familiarity of the risk; whether the risk is voluntarily accepted or involuntarily imposed; whether individuals are compensated for their exposure to the risk; the advantages of the activity; and the risks and advantages for any alternatives." Above all, people hate being exposed to dangers that might strike out of nowhere, without warning. They will accept much greater risks from other activities in which they feel they have some sense of control. An example is athletics, in which amateur participants know-ingly pit their dexterity and pride against very real odds of injury, and some-times even death.

Factoring in this insight, new models of risk assessment correlate much better with the value and/or dread that members of the public assign to cer-tain dangers. It explains why citizens who refuse to tolerate even statisti-cally insignificant perils from contaminated food deeply resent bureaucrats for overregulating the design of ski equipment and motorcycle helmets, or blocking access to fad vitamins, or interfering in the "extreme sports" craze, since (they argue) people should be able to risk their own necks, if they know the danger and proceed with open eyes.

What the risk assessment experts have concluded—and this should be obvious to anyone with common sense—is that people feel better when they can see what's going on, and have some sovereign mastery over deci-sions that affect their lives. They want information, and the power to act on it. That is the very essence of accountability.

This reaction to lack of control is especially clear when it comes to *crime*. Despite declining rates of serious felonies, gated communities and guarded buildings are proliferating. Private security forces in the United States now outnumber public police officers, while people increasingly seek diversion in "home entertainment centers" instead of clubs or cinemas. Although most citizens of the neo-West arguably live more secure against violence than members of almost any other mass polity in history, this sta-tistical reassurance does not comfort as much as it should, because so much crime today happens by surprise. Although many felons do know their vic-tims, it is the anonymous assailant who creates the most widespread general unease. The stranger who might jump out of nowhere and turn a life upside down in moments. This is why mugging, carjacking, child snatching, and terrorism rank so high on lists of public concerns. This unease has been amplified by mass media, which exploit fear of surprise attack in both dra-mas and news shows, so that many people living in low crime areas feel they can maintain a sense of control only by keeping their kids indoors, putting bars on the windows, and seldom venturing out after dark.

Strong privacy advocates—especially those promoting encryption and anonymity—may deny that this phenomenon is a direct physical corollary of their message, so I will let the reader decide whether a philosophy that relies on *cybernetic* gates, walls, and coded locks is any different in its underlying basis—fear.

I do not mean to ridicule those who have alarms in their homes, or who take reasonable precautions in a society awash with guns. (If things really are inexorably heading that way, I will do the same!) Yet, one can ask whether it would not be better for citizens to *reclaim* their neighborhoods, their cities, and even the night. To do this, they don't have to chase all the buskers and bikers and panhandlers and colorful weirdos off the streets. God forbid! If the aim is simply to regain a sense of safety, all we need is a means to distinguish real villains from harmless freaks. And the way to do that is not by stereotyping people according to their appearance. It is by *knowing their names.*

And if they want to know yours in return? So what?

We will continue with the subject of crime, and its opponents, in the next section. But first let us reiterate: there is no inherent incongruity in the fact that people are both concerned about privacy and at the same time blithely willing to reveal lots of information about themselves. Esther Dyson, author of *Release 2.0,* draws a parallel with evolving twentieth-century attitudes toward the acceptability of body exposure in fashion, pointing out that it used to be indecent to reveal a navel, or even an ankle, in public. Today, twenty-year-old men skim past ubiquitous lingerie ads in the newspaper with barely a flicker of their eyes. So it may be with personal data, according to Dyson, in the electronic age to come.

> *"As people feel more secure in general on the Net, they will become accustomed to seeing their words recorded and replayed. They will no longer feel uncomfortable being on display, since everyone around them is on display too."*

A key element in the coming years will not be the *extent* of information flow (or vision, or even surveillance) as much as the degree of *powerlessness* that people may feel at any moment, in any given situation. Humans certainly do get depressed in situations where they lack feelings of involvement and control. On the other hand, we can soundly reject the contempt expressed by those commentators and academics who depict their fellow citizens as sheep, incapable of grasping the reins of their own destiny.

The overwhelming counterexample — again — is us. No other populace has ever had so much known about them, both in groups and as individuals — and no populace has ever been so cantankerously individualistic or free. We have done this by assertively retaining the sovereign powers of sight and control. Such a society is a long way from deserving anyone's contempt.

> *We need to calibrate our idealism for what is possible. So I do not propose that corruption, confusion, or deception can be eliminated, but merely that they can be controlled so that they aren't catastrophic.*                JARON LANIER

## GUARDING THE GUARDIANS

We can illustrate how tools of accountability may offer most citizens increased confidence and control by applying those tools to the gritty world of crime and law enforcement.

In July 1997, as a portent of bigger steps to come, the San Diego County Sheriff's Department began equipping all deputies with pocket tape recorders, requiring them to turn on the devices during encounters with the public. Meanwhile, in some ethnic neighborhoods of New York, San Francisco, and Los Angeles, small bands of activists have set up ad hoc surveillance committees, using inexpensive video cameras to drive out local criminals—and to keep an eye on the police. Any modern citizen would have to be catatonic to miss this particular trend. Ever since the infamous Rodney King case, when out-of-control cops were videotaped beating a suspect after an adrenaline-drenched, high-speed chase, law enforcement personnel have grown ever more aware of this yin-yang situation: cameras can point both ways. Almost nightly, the public sees examples of transparency at work, either helping public officials track down perpetrators, or else catching misbehavior by the officials themselves.

- Television shows such as *America's Most Wanted* have surprised their severest critics. Despite a crude, sensationalist approach, their contribution to the apprehension of violent criminals is significant and growing.

- Dashboard-mounted video cameras have become fixtures in many constabularies, capturing vivid images of traffic infractions and more serious offenses, as well as occasionally nailing the police officer for brutal or unprofessional behavior.

- In 1996, a woman who was kidnapped in a carjacking secretly recorded the subsequent desperate conversation with her abductor, who then sadly became her killer. Her courage and presence of mind poignantly helped police to find the man responsible.

This recalls the trend discussed in chapter 1, afoot in countless municipalities, to install cameras on a myriad street corners. It seems quite unstoppable, both in the democratic neo-West and in more authoritarian cultures. The fundamental question, who *controls* the cameras, will determine whether citizens of each town remain sovereign and free. Right now, the chaotic manner of implementation in the United States appears to be resulting in considerable transparency, with nearly as much light shining on public guardians as on those they are sworn to protect. But results have been patchy, and there will be many twists and turns before a new equilibrium is reached, some time in the next century.

One writer, Sandy Sandfort, posed an intriguing possibility. What if it were possible to have a fair witness next to every police officer in the world? Perhaps by equipping a police helmet with camcorder, plus chips to track an officer's location and even record his or her bodily movements. Would this result in improved safety and conviction rates, *plus* a heightened degree of police professionalism?

At MIT, dynamic young technologists such as Steve Mann have spent several years developing the next step in electronic omni-accessibility. *Wearables* are tiny computer transceivers that combine the attributes of a pager, dictaphone, music player, camcorder, cell phone, laptop computer, and modem in a single portable unit, enabling a person to stay linked to the Internet even while strolling down a boulevard. Early versions combined camera and monitor into garish goggles (like those in a Buck Rogers movie) plus a bulky backpack stuffed with circuit boards. But each year the contraptions grow smaller, lighter, and more subtly incorporated into conventional clothing accessories. Recent models barely stand out from an ensemble of a baseball cap plus heavy sunglasses, except for a thin cable trailing down the back to a strangely bulging pair of pants. Mann's prototype scans his surroundings, transmitting images in moments. He can download a map of his location, find information about the building he is looking at, or look up any topic from the vast archives of the World Wide Web.

Generally speaking, this innovation seems like a logical compression of standard office tools into a nifty and portable device for the next century. But for our purposes, the fascinating aspect is what wearables imply about mutual transparency. Steve Mann says, "This apparatus suggests that shopkeepers and customers, police and ordinary citizens alike, must respect the possibility that they could be caught on camera."

It shouldn't be forgotten that many in society worry about the police, often with cause. Race relations in several American cities have been harmed by rogue officers who use their badges to mask brutality. Nor is it unheard of for departmental intelligence units to employ unscrupulous tools—illegal wiretaps, coerced confessions, planted evidence, and untrustworthy informers—to target individuals or groups they don't like, as when the FBI's Cointelpro project forged letters and infiltrated civil rights and antiwar organizations in the 1960s and 1970s. Although any fair-minded observer would give our society credit for increasing the proportion of police officers who are skilled and impartial, this problem will not vanish by exhorting or wishing it away. As Gary T. Marx observes, such abuses are not confined solely to despotic societies; they can happen anywhere that you mix adrenaline, testosterone, firearms, and a lack of accountability.

But now imagine the scene a few years in the future, say at 2 A.M. on Sunday morning, as a patrolling officer pulls over some young man for a traffic violation in one of our tension-filled neighborhoods. The cop worries about a potentially violent encounter with the burly teen. The youth has just been at a party, listening to friends gripe about how many of their peers were rousted by the heat this month. It is a tense situation, ripe for another urban tragedy.

Picture the patrolman approaching the vehicle. A lens on his shoulder swivels, sending images straight to precinct HQ.

"Would you please get out of the car, sir?" he asks.

Standing, the youth reveals a similar device on *his* shoulder, winking away as the *true-vu* unit transmits this encounter for storage in his inexpensive home computer-VCR. Peering at the constable's badge, he says—"Well, hello, Officer . . . 56467. What seems to be the problem?"

Will the result of such camera standoffs be increased rates of conviction for the guilty? A decline in false arrests of the innocent? A sudden upsurge in exaggerated (if sarcastic) courtesy on our city streets? Perhaps all of the above? Already, T-cell activity has combined with easy Web access to promote groups we mentioned earlier, in the section "Citizen Truth Squads" (after chapter 2); for example, Copswatch and the Police Complaint Center, eagerly collate reports and videotaped footage from all over the United States, sometimes setting up their own private sting operations to catch rogue cops in the act.

These efforts are hardly unbiased. They don't have to be, in order to take part in the push-pull of accountability, or to let anyone who wants to get involved help "watch the watchmen."

I can hardly begin to guess at all the consequences, which will surely surprise even far-seeing pundits. Nevertheless, it cannot be repeated too often that the cameras *are* coming. Urban face-offs between implacably wary lenses will become the rule, especially wherever there is tension over rights, or laws, or even touchy dignity. Real criminals may have more to worry about. The innocent may have less to fear. And our agents of authority will share the glare of accountability. A glare that will make the job better for any cop who acts like a skilled professional, but hellish for thugs in uniform.

The scenario just described—a citizenry empowered by cameras—may lessen our concern about street criminals and uniformed bullies. But what about other worrisome centers of power and latent oppression? The corporate heads, media snoops, silk-collar thieves, and federal agents with their sweeping powers of court-sanctioned scrutiny and high-tech surveillance? If accountability tools are to help free citizens maintain morale and sense of control, we may have to keep an eye on all of them.

One particular class of influential individuals tends not to see itself as a "worrisome power center." I refer to a burgeoning technological elite, many of whom prefer to call themselves "brave rebels," and would resent being ranked among the mighty. Yet in their proficiency, their disdain for rules, and their vast diversity of character and integrity, members of this new Brahmin caste merit being listed among the most vigorous and commanding authors of the society we shall wind up living in. This prospect may be hopeful, for these people include some of the brightest products of our boisterous civilization; or it may be ominous, since hardly anybody, even inside government, is qualified to keep an eye on the "cyberaristocracy," a new elite class whose members can prowl at will through the digital jungle, like predatory cats. Masters of either justice or deceit, depending almost purely on their own inclination or whim.

> *I freely and openly confess that I am a cyberpunk, but there's nothing new about it. Counter culture is a very old thing, as old as industrial society. I don't control how others who call themselves cyberpunks behave. Every Bohemia has a criminal element. There are guys there who are not healthy.* BRUCE STERLING

## HACKED TO BITS

Hackers are individuals who use extraordinary skill (or dogged persistence) in manipulating software to infiltrate restricted computer systems. A sort of Robin Hood mythology has grown up around these nerdly outlaws, depicting them as libertarian heroes who pierce fences that others would throw up across the open data range, fighting for their belief that "information wants to be free." Popular films such as *War Games* and *The Net* portray admirable loners who improve the world by overcoming and revealing either mistakes or the nefarious plans of dark organizations.

A number of books have explored this netherworld at the edge of both technology and the law—for example, *The Hacker Crackdown* by Bruce Sterling, *At Large* by David Freedman and Charles Mann, and *Masters of Deception* by Michelle Slatalla and Josh Quittner. Some writers take pains to distinguish "cyberjocks" who cruise the dataways in a spirit of fun-loving curiosity, careful to avoid doing harm, from others who aim to steal, vandalize, or demonstrate a sense of power and superiority, labeling the latter "crackers." John Markoff of *The New York Times* used the terms "Hacker A" and "Hacker B" to make a similar distinction.

A clumsy but brutal example of the second type, showing that threats don't always come from a techno-elite, was described by Dixie Baker, chief scientist with Science Applications International Corp. (SAIC). The thirteen-year-old daughter of a hospital clerk copied the computer records of several emergency room patients and then phoned those patients to inform them they were HIV-positive. Hearing this false news, one expectant mother terminated her pregnancy. In some cases, sophisticated data-protection systems may help prevent such tragedies. On the other hand, what precaution will reliably keep every bored teenager from poking at an open terminal, while waiting for a parent to get off work?

A more sophisticated case of harm done via computer was the September 1996 assault on Panix (Public Access Network Corp.), the oldest company providing Internet access to New York City residents. It was driven near bankruptcy by a cracker who tied up the company's lines for a week with dozens of false—and untraceable—information requests every second, revealing the power that can be wielded by unaccountable individuals, avenging some real or imagined affront. Nor is the phenomenon limited to any city or nation. A few years ago, Vladimir Levin, a biochemistry graduate in Russia's St. Petersburg, allegedly stole $12 million from Citibank using his laptop. He was arrested, and now awaits extradition to the United States. "People wondered how he could do it without knowing English. It's because once you are in, it was like using a calculator," claimed one fellow hacker.

What suggestions have been made for dealing with this problem? As usual, they divide into two major classes. Some would clamp down on information flows, adding one "firewall," or keyword-protected layer, after another. This kind of solution may prove necessary in many cases, as a basic matter of improving technology, removing flaws, and correcting newly discovered failure modes. But as a general principle, such an approach is yet another manifestation of the venerable fallacy of security. Some of the best experts think complex expensive shields and firewalls simply create a false sense of complacency. "All the security in the world will not help if employees keep their passwords in an unlocked desk drawer," remarked Tsutomu Shimomura, a systems expert with the San Diego Supercomputing Center.

A different approach is to try working with the Internet's inherent strengths. Instead of acting only to prevent intrusions with ever-greater layers of "armor," some experts emphasize making sure that saboteurs and thieves are detected and caught. Such accountability can happen if measures are instituted to make sure that little happens in your portion of the Net without leaving a spoor. That way, if one operator proves incompetent at protecting a system, others might take over and pick up the trail. (Not everyone is a genius.)

"There is no strength in security through obscurity," said Michael Merrit, a department head with AT&T, addressing the need for cooperation. "If we don't work together, Hacker B will inevitably break into our systems."

Working together sounds a lot like reciprocal transparency—keeping a protective eye not just on your own house but on your neighbor's as well. If nothing can happen on the Net without leaving a trace, those who do harm can be held accountable. Sometimes by the authorities. But perhaps more often by some private individual with a sense of citizenship.

In other words, by "Hacker A."

Just such a situation became national high drama when U.S. media were riveted by the hunt for Kevin Mitnick. Through the first half of 1994, word spread that a "dark side" hacker was prowling about, using clever methods of remote penetration to invade supposedly protected computer systems, stealing files (such as twenty thousand customer credit card numbers from the large Internet provider, Netcom), and filching private programs from the cream of the Internet community. Marshals and FBI agents spent fruitless months hunting Mitnick, who often left derisive notes, taking apparent joy in taunting his hapless opponents, an egotistical trait that eventually brought his downfall; for it led to his decision to take on Tsutomu Shimomura, already a legend at tracking down cyberspace predators. At that point, Mitnick met his match.

"He wasn't very hard to catch," Shimomura later said, after directing a team of agents and technicians who pierced the fugitive's cover using old-fashioned electronic engineering techniques that completely bypassed Mitnick's complex veil of encrypted identities. It seemed that expertise in one area—software coding—was not enough to shelter the computer outlaw, who forgot that nearly every security system (including his own) comes equipped with side and back doors. In this case, he guarded the pulse coding of his cell phone but forgot that each unit is a radio transmitter, with its own quirks that can be traced.

There are other examples. Clifford Stoll, author of *Silicon Snake Oil*, also wrote the fascinating *Cuckoo's Egg*, about his own experience hunting down a rogue international hacker-spy in much the same way as Shimomura did. As Kevin Mitnick learned, no clever set of masks and false IDs will protect a bright fool who tries to take on the whole world, single-handed. "Cancers" will almost inevitably attract the attention of healthy and creative social T-cells.

Some may call this approach vigilantism, but it can be argued that society's "immune system" will deal with such problems more flexibly than any rigid police organization, whose blunt methods and goliath scale can turn a cracker into a martyr or hero.

At least, that is the theory. It is still much too early in the game to know how things will actually play out in the coming decades. Chapter 9 discusses some features that are needed to prevent transparency from devolving into a pattern of vicious witch-hunts.

One can understand why hackers are often perceived as romantic figures. Right after *Newsweek* published a pictorial story on the Mitnick case, the charismatic Shimomura received so many electronic fan letters and marriage proposals that the University of California at San Diego's e-mail system crashed for several days. Other computer wizards have become cult figures after rushing to defend their idea of Internet purity, for example, when several hacker "digilantes" sabotaged Cyber Promotions, Inc., one of the most hated e-mail advertisers, or "spammers." These colorful fellows certainly deserve some of the extensive coverage they have been given.

Nevertheless, hackers will get short shrift in this particular book about the information age. True, their aim might superficially seem compatible with "transparency." In fact, some of the best hackers are admirable figures who tread lightly as they poke away at sophisticated networks, uncovering flawed security systems, gleefully sharing their "trade secrets," and sometimes exposing felonies. On the other hand it is delusive to give this subculture paramount credit for ushering in a dawn of accountability. Although some hackers are merry extroverts, relishing sunlight, others secretly access hidden knowledge in order to savor private victories over the establishment, reveling in a virtuosity that sets them apart from both those in authority and the common herd. It is a familiar syndrome that we discussed in chapter 5, where we showed that the ire expressed loudly and eloquently by angry young men can be almost orthogonal to how right or wrong they are.

In other words, hackers are behaving exactly the way we—through shared media messages—trained them to do. As randomly programmed social T-cells, their talents and obsessions range from ridiculous to sublime. Some will make headlines through nasty acts of sabotage—until they are caught. Others will surely discover and expose horrid errors or villainous schemes, revealing the news in time to save us all.

It seems a worthwhile bargain, justifying some tolerant forbearance by the rest of us.

And that, despite their romantic aura, is all the attention we'll pay hackers.

## THE END OF CIVILITY?

Dear Fellow E-Mail User:

This is to inform you that your mailbox has just been riffled by EmilyPost, an autonomous courtesy-worm program released by a group of netizens anonymously concerned about the decline of manners in cyberspace. In brief, dear neighbor, you are not a polite person. EmilyPost's syntax analysis subroutines show that a high fraction of your net exchanges are heated, vituperative, even obscene. Of course you enjoy free speech. But excessive nastiness is ruining the Net for everybody. EmilyPost homes in on folks like you and begins by asking them to consider politeness.

For one thing, your credibility would rise. (EmilyPost has checked your favorite bulletin boards, and finds your ratings aren't high. Nobody is listening to you!) Moreover, courtesy can foster calm reason, useful debate, and even consensus. We suggest introducing an automatic delay into your mail system. Communications are so fast these days, people often blurt anything that comes to mind, forgetting the gift of tact. If you wish, you may use one of the public domain delay-and-reconsider programs included in EmilyPost, free of charge.

On the other hand, should you insist on continuing as before, disseminating nastiness in all directions, we have equipped EmilyPost with other options you'll soon find out about. . . .

This little vignette, taken from my novel *Earth*, was written back in 1987 as far-out speculation about computer networks five *decades* in the future. Little did I expect it would come true in a tenth of that time! Since then, I've been told that "courtesy worm" programs already roam the dataways — some even named after my fanciful EmilyPost — illustrating just one possible response to what many are calling a major electronic social disease.

Then again, some people don't like the idea of self-appointed "courtesy police." When science fiction author and journalist Bruce Sterling read about EmilyPost, he penned the following amusing retaliatory missive to represent how certain parties on the Net will surely react.

Dear Milksop Creep:

We have hacked EmilyPost to insert the word "fullacrap-fatass" randomly into everything you write from now on.

signed,

Anonymous Darkside Hackers

. . .

P.S. Vigilantism cuts both ways, jerk!

Today's Internet is plagued by countless individuals who seem intent on making nuisances of themselves, flying into abusive, self-righteous tirades known as "flames." Electronic conversations seem especially prone to misinterpretation, suddenly and rapidly escalating hostility between participants, or else triggering episodes of sulking silence. When flame wars erupt, normally docile people can behave like mental patients suffering from coprolalia, a version of Tourette's syndrome. Typing furiously, they send impulsive text messages blurting out the first vituperation that comes to mind, abandoning the editing process of common courtesy that civilization took millennia to acquire. (Hence the fad expression "Net-Tourette.")

Other assaults are less impulsive and more deliberately vicious. In a variant that recently led to arrests in California and Michigan, some sociopathic network users made a fervid avocation of tracing the e-mail addresses of famous people, no matter how well protected by pseudonyms, and harassing them in a manner reminiscent of the "stalking" of movie stars. In another example, a group calling itself alt.syntax.tactical, or AST, strove for some years to start out-of-control flame wars as part of an organized campaign. This clique sought renown by sending graphic messages about cat-killing to a group of feline lovers. To an erotic pictures group, its members posed as outraged Puritans demanding censorship; and in an Olympics newsgroup, a member masqueraded as a loutish caricature of an overly patriotic Canadian fan, in order to inspire hatred by American readers. An excerpt from their manifesto reveals smug rationalizations.

> What is important is that each individual brings into this their own brand of inspired mischief. In some ways it is innocent. In some ways it is completely destructive. . . . On most levels, it is entertainment; but there is an element here that allows individuals to become their own experts in propaganda, manipulating hundreds or even thousands of people to believe that what they are reading is real, when in fact it is absurd, incorrect, made up.

We probed the roots of this phenomenon in chapter 5, seeing how easily culturally promoted individualism can turn into solipsism, especially when combined with self-righteousness and a frail ego. Alas, understanding a phenomenon does not make it go away, nor does it prevent sociopaths from doing capricious harm.

Sometimes the aim goes beyond pranksterism, as when individuals created a Web page asserting that Earthlink, a fast-growing Internet provider, was connected with the Church of Scientology. (As we saw earlier, hostility toward the CoS, whether deserved or unjust, is rampant among Internet aficionados.) The effort to tie Earthlink's chairman Sky Dayton with CoS hierarchs involved fine-tuning a slur page with all the same keywords as Earthlink's official home page, so that anyone seeking information about his company through a simple search engine would also automatically call up the accusation. With similar tricks, a disgruntled former employee of K Mart started a vivid Web site titled "K Mart Sucks." Then there is a story, reported in the *New York Times*, of someone creating a Web page with a URL address nearly identical to the 1996 "Pat Buchanan for President" site. Visitors found a screen similar in appearance to the genuine article — but featuring a swastika motif.

Dirty tricks have a long history in politics, as in the rough-and-tumble of life in general. Are any of these examples essentially different from stunts pulled by Donald Segretti in 1972 on behalf of the Nixon campaign? Nowadays, at least in theory, the target of any such attacks can respond swiftly with rebuttals or outright refutations. In a perfect world, especially with "tag commentary" (see chapter 8), this would result in "an efficient information market." One lawyer-activist with the Electronic Frontier Foundation suggests we may never again have to worry about libel, because in years to come the truth will supposedly chase down and slay any calumny or lie.

But this view may be far too sanguine. Even if the Net becomes adept at openness and transparency, few readers will devote the energy to peruse each datum and weigh the evidence concerning every nasty rumor. Who has the time? In cyberspace, the most frequent data-handling mode is rapid *skimming*, as users race from spot to spot, sampling, forming quick impressions that often enter the unconscious and plant deep roots, then moving on. Inevitably, some damage is done. We tend to think that "where there's smoke, there must be fire." (See the discussion of "data smog" in chapter 9.) According to author Robert Wright, "On the Web, anyone can construct a 'shadow identity,' a slanderous characterization, that sticks to your cyberidentity like glue." It can be done by an ex-husband, former lover, fired employee, and so on. You can instantly post rebuttals and countercharges, yet the smear may still affect people's impressions.

In truth, none of this should seem surprising. Esther Dyson, publisher of *Release 1.0* newsletter, notes that the Internet "is suffering from the same pathologies that affect our daily lives: fraud, incivility, unwelcome advertising, harassment, and even virtual rape. While some netters believe [it] will change human culture, we believe that net culture so far has reflected a small segment of the population, and it will change more toward the mainstream as the mainstream joins the net."

In other words, things have come a long way from when the principal traffic consisted of prim, honorable exchanges of scientific ideas and data among a few thousand intellectuals. "It's a real test of whether something this large can be managed on a cooperative or voluntary basis," adds Roger Karraker, host of a First Amendment conference on the Well, a Sausalito-based online service. "It's very clear one or two obnoxious individuals have the power to inconvenience hundreds of thousands of people. I don't know where it will end."

Fortunately, destructive hacker-attacks and deliberate slander campaigns are relatively rare. Still, a list of *other* Net-civility breaches, compiled by Australian computer scientist and privacy scholar Roger Clarke, can look daunting. They include information overload, rumor and accidental mis-information, negligent or intentional defamation, plagiarism, inadequate care with data, trawling for personal information, harassment, mail bomb-ing, obscenity, incitement, impersonation, surveillance, spamming, abuse of intellectual property rights, hacking, releasing software worms or viruses, breaching security, obscuration, and some kinds of anonymization.

Despite this extensive catalog, ranging from accidental lapses of good manners all the way to serious crimes, most rancor on the Net falls into the mundane category of short-tempered grouchiness, enough all by itself to make some pine for the good old days, when we wrote letters on paper and were thus compelled by time to moderate our responses. On the tele-phone, voice tones sometimes conciliate, compensating for rash words. But while e-mail is terrific for exchanging terse bullets of useful information, it seems almost designed to exaggerate misunderstandings because it con-tains no visual or aural cues, what linguist Peter Farb calls *paralanguage*, to soften or clarify. While hurriedly clearing a packed *in box*, one can eas-ily leap to wrong conclusions about a correspondent's intent, or see a smear that was not there, or give a message the worst possible interpretation, and then lash out as one never would in personal proximity.

Some have called for modification of slander and libel laws, applying them fiercely to those who post malign or unsupported missives on the Net. But this is just another example of trying to solve problems by *reduc-ing* information flow. After all, a flamer isn't really different from the motorist who cut you off last week, nearly causing an accident, flipping an obscene gesture and laughing at your frustration, safe behind a mask of anonymity. Driven by rancorous behavior he witnessed in the Net's early days, Stewart Brand, cofounder of the *Whole Earth Catalog* and *Whole Earth Review* magazine, realized there would be no peace as long as nas-

tiness could find shelter behind false identities. Brand lobbied successfully to have anonymity strictly forbidden on the pioneering Internet service the Well.

> True, there are disadvantages to this rule, and I do feel there
> should remain places where anonymous postings are possible,
> especially for whistle-blowers reporting crimes. But anonymity
> just doesn't foster the kind of mature behavior you want among
> your neighbors. Not on our network, at least.

We already know how to scale in our minds the believability of any spoken gossip that we hear—by considering the reliability of the source. Going
back to earlier examples, the chief difference between the anti–K Mart
page and the Pat Buchanan smear was the ease of clarifying identities and
motives. If the originator of some textual calumny turns out to be a business competitor or ex-spouse of the person under attack, even an inveterate skimmer may put it in context, or shrug it off.

In the world outside the Internet, we give "news" told to us by a known
snoop or scandalmonger less weight than what we see reported under the
byline of a respected journalist. Likewise, Net citizens will learn to deal
with flamers and purveyors of diatribe by using high-tech versions of the
same technique. We will factor in data on the author's reputation, either by
having our computer automatically sift the "tag commentary" people have
applied to that person's work in the past, or else by joining a club or service
that collates extensive credibility ratings (see chapter 8), or by having sieves
and bozo filters routinely remove postings by those with abysmal scores
before they appear on our monitors.

People who sling mud will learn that they must either back up their
accusations or else face ignominy. Like the proverbial boy who cried wolf,
they will find themselves isolated. Ignored.

Some view the Internet as a sort of anarchist's paradise, a wild frontier
town where you can saunter down Main Street, draw your pistol, and shoot
anything in sight. But in fact we are human beings. Fancy electronics won't
change that. Not right away, at least. We like order in our lives, plus some
degree of common sense and decency. Bringing these things about through
a free market of credibility and earned reputation seems far more desirable
than having them imposed by government regulations or stifling rules.

In fact, civility just might make a comeback, after all. But not as something exhorted, or enforced from on high. Rather, it may return as a natural byproduct as we all learn to live in this new "commons," a near-future
society where wrath seldom becomes habitual, because people who lash
out soon learn that it simply does not pay.

*Modern media is a mind control technique, so better be sure that*
*you're the one controlling your screen.*       TIMOTHY LEARY

## CHOICE ON THE INTERNET: BLOOD FLOW OR GANGRENE

From its inception, the Internet was perceived in terms that might sound familiar to any immunologist—as a distributed array of randomly autonomous elements, capable of swiftly detecting errors and rerouting around obstructions. By analogy, the Net should be resistant to interference. But metaphors are useful only up to a point. A diligent effort at control might have effects that are just as serious as when a tourniquet is applied to a human limb, cutting off the blood supply to healthy tissue. Such efforts are already under way in some countries, as ruling parties seek to preserve their days in power. (See chapter 10, "Global Transparency.")

In fact, such malignant obstructions may happen without interference by corporate or government agencies. Lately, some observers have expressed the fear that we will see a myriad tiny tourniquets applied by private individuals, each of them determined to create their own version of reality, their own subjective world. For instance, some people will program their home computers/entertainment centers to sift the Web for only those news articles, shows, and magazines that agree with opinions they already have, or reduce all opponents to caricatures. We already see this trend in channels devoted to specific ethnic and religious groups, and in the cult followings of pundits like Rush Limbaugh.

According to Paul Steiger, managing editor of the *Wall Street Journal.* "The ability of people with like minds to talk to each other [on the Internet] is wonderful. But if only people of like minds talk to each other, you get the kind of cognitive dissonance that is destructive to a democracy." As individuals use such new tools to tailor privacy guardians and personalized data sieves, choosing which sympathetic voices will be allowed into their home and which dissenting ones will be blocked out, the result may be nearly perfect isolation in walled-off worlds of the mind. David Shaw of the *Los Angeles Times* posed the dilemma thus:

> What will happen to our already fragmented sense of community
> if everyone is reading different stories on different subjects, seeing
> different advertisements for different products and, in essence,
> communicating by e-mail and in online chat rooms only with
> people who share their own interests? These services deprive their
> readers of one of the newspaper's great charms—serendipity, the
> chance to stumble across, and be riveted by, a story on a subject
> the reader had no idea would interest him.

Back in 1987 I fictionally depicted a future variety of hacker whose aim was not to steal secrets, or preach a cause, but to crack countless barriers of self-imposed isolation and let *surprise* jolt the cozy, insulated realities people crafted for themselves. This would be a criminal act, since people have a right to choose their own worlds of discourse. Still, one can imagine a romantic mystique growing around such peculiar hackers, who aim to shake up the stodgy, like jesters of old.

In a related kind of pathology, a time may come when *simulated experiences* burgeon in number and quality to such a degree that people start having trouble distinguishing them from reality. Such brilliantly crafted hallucinations may help vastly expand human experience, carrying prudent "travelers" to remote milieus, enlarging the horizons of those who retain volition and control. Or else, simulations may become irresistibly addictive. As the humorist Scott Adams explained, "Once anyone has a Holodeck, why would they ever leave?"

Glenn F. Cartwright, professor of educational psychology at McGill University in Montreal, put it more darkly. "What happens to the normal mind when it loses contact with reality . . . when we enter an alternate reality and cannot tell it from the real world . . . [or] if we find we cannot, or do not want to, return to the real world?" Cartwright worries that such illusions might be foisted on unwilling or unsuspecting participants, "who might think they were experiencing mental illness."

Naturally, some in society will apply these technologies in service of one of the oldest and most innately human of all creative enterprises: lying.

Alas, we can only mention a few of these possible yin and yang consequences of new media technology. Further details would stray too far from the main topic. But these few examples should be enough to help pose a basic question: will so-called connecting technologies wind up merely dividing us in the end, fragmenting citizens into acrimoniously bickering tribes, till they forget everything they have in common? All that binds them as fellow members of a great civilization?

Could it be that those working on the Tower of Babel were *thus* cast into confusion? Cursed to speak countless indecipherable tongues by means of something as useful, connecting, and promising as the Net?

*Dissent on the Net does not lead to consensus: it creates a profusion of different views. . . . The conditions that encourage compromise, the hallmark of the democratic process, are lacking online.*

MARK POSTER

## ARENAS FOR FAIR DEBATE

Putting aside the issue of civility for now, let's go back to the much more important business of error correction through criticism.

It isn't only leaders who habitually evade appraisal or censure. Each of us, no matter how honest or humble, shares this trait. It takes courage to face our flaws. But even more than courage, it requires perspective. Immersed in our own personal assumptions and beliefs, we find it well-nigh impossible to question them with anything like true intellectual honesty. Descartes tried to do so, but all he wound up achieving with all his brilliance was to use circular logic and "prove" everything he had started out believing in the first place.

And yet, we *do* change our minds, now and then. Sometimes the world shows us all too clearly, through pain and hard knocks, that we were mistaken. On occasion we even let ourselves be persuaded to see things in a truly new way, heeding the cogent or passionate arguments of people around us. In other words, while I may not be trustworthy to hold myself fully accountable, outsiders will gladly do that job for me. They will be quick to point out my errors. I, in turn, can be efficient at shining light on the mistakes of others.

When expressed that way, it sounds like an equable exchange of favors. Constructive criticism can feel that way, when gracious adults do it in a spirit of mutual helpfulness. So it is with well-motivated teams, when their goals are clear, when the members trust each other, and when there is a shared passion for success, as in times of war. Mutual criticism doesn't hurt as much when people have no time to spare for ego.

At another level, I am talking about the adversarial process, in which two or more opponents attack each other's evidence and arguments, probing for weaknesses, forcing the other side to account for every discrepancy. We are all familiar with this system in countless noisy, unruly forms. When attorneys get involved, their prim attention to every dotted *i* and crossed *t* can become fractious and wearisome to a degree that seems to defy all common sense. So if it appears that my argument supports the necessity of lawyers, please accept that I say it with reluctant awareness that things would be worse without them. Indeed, the adversarial process can be wasteful, disgusting, even puerile in the behavior that it provokes from antagonistic rivals, evoking reproval, disdain, and even dirty tricks.

Unfortunately, no one has come up with a better system to effectively promote accountability. Just as competition generates wealth in a fair market, opposition over policy appears to have resulted in a society that is, on the whole, better run and fairer than most other mass cultures. Faced with the penchant of humans to suppress criticism, it seems that the adversarial solution is the best cantankerous *Homo sapiens* can come up with for the time being.

That doesn't mean the system cannot be improved! In a transparent society, there may be ways to make adversarial accountability more efficient, more civil, more mature—and especially more adept at discovering mistakes before they do great harm.

The Internet already aids countless social and political factions, from environmentalists to neo-Nazis. Through e-mail and discussion groups, they can organize with unprecedented agility, rallying supporters in hours. Both pro- and anti-abortion forces monitor each others' open forums, seeking clues to their foes' next strategic moves. Through colorful Web pages, both gun control advocates and the National Rifle Association (NRA) refine their messages with slick imagery. The EFF shares its cherished cyberspace with the Christian Coalition, even as they battle each other over whether to purge the Internet of disapproved content.

You might expect that I approve of all this rambunctious activity, since it heightens the effectiveness of rival groups, hastening the pace of political opposition. In fact, the trend frightens the hell out of me.

You see, an adversarial system works best if both sides of an issue assail each other's positions in a fair and open manner, and if one result is some coalescence of public opinion about the right thing to do. Not compromise, exactly, but something more like consensus.

Correspondent Mark Poster suggests that the Net's current incarnation offers only some of the ingredients needed to achieve this. "Traditionally, a person's identity forced some stability and accountability, and allowed trust to develop. Since the Internet allows people to redefine and shift identity, dissent is encouraged." This, Poster contends, allows people to talk as equals. And yet, rational argument rarely prevails. Achieving consensus is nearly impossible.

In fact, by encouraging factions to fly off in a myriad centrifugal directions, growing ever fiercer in their radicalism and purity of vision, the Net's present version does little to advance the pragmatic goal of error avoidance and problem solving. When each side uses the Internet to form massively effective pep rallies, the result doesn't help refine their arguments or eliminate flaws in their proposals. Rather, it takes us down an old road, toward the quasi-religious fervor of the Nuremberg rallies in 1936, when in-group solidarity was also reinforced by new technologies—radio and loudspeakers.

There are countless other historical examples, occasions when purified information flows led to catastrophic results. Before the U.S. Civil War, nearly every newspaper in the Southern states depicted abolitionism as the equivalent of devil worship. Other than a few isolated venues, such as the famed Lincoln-Douglas debates, there were seldom ways to read or hear the position of the other side. Similar disparities existed in the North. Might U.S. history have changed if honest argument had been part of the volatile political climate before 1861?

Clearly, something more is needed. Something tomorrow's Internet might easily provide.

Picture an arena where adversaries can no longer scream past each other, but must actively answer each other's accusations, criticisms, and complaints. A place where one group's vision, or model of the world, can be tested, dented by criticism, and possibly improved under the watchful gaze of an interested public.

Until recently, this role was performed (albeit shallowly) by the press, whose code of professionalism dictated that news articles should present fair capsule summaries of any issue. For all the flaws and lapses we have seen during the last half century, journalists fulfilled this function pretty well overall. But lately, things seem to be wearing thin. Are decayed professional standards responsible for this, as James Fallows and some others contend? Or have the increasing complexity of modern life and countless alternative competing outlets led to a decline in the effectiveness of newspapers and television at midwifing national or international consensus? Nick Arnett, author of *Net and Anti-Net*, blames "television-style rhetoric that insists on creating two sides to every issue, demanding that citizens choose one or the other" on a take it or leave it basis. (See chapter 7, "The Devil's Dichotomies.")

A long-range answer to these problems may be found in the twenty-first century's tool kit. If the Internet has proved helpful to advocacy groups bent on marshaling their forces, there might also be hope for it to act as a forum for bringing factions together for argument, comparison, negotiation, and even accord.

In the European Middle Ages, there was a tradition of holding occasional *disputations*, sometimes between Catholic and Jewish theologians. Although these events were seldom fair, and often had been rigged in advance, they nevertheless shed a little light in a dark era. Since then, the art of debate has gone through many changes; for instance, we've come to expect that presidential candidates will have face-to-face encounters, and we complain when candidates for other offices won't agree to do the same. Yet the art of direct and open confrontation seems only to have been refined in the one place where decent folk loathe ever finding themselves: the courtroom. For the most part, we live awash in opinions, savoring caricatures of our opponents, and seldom use the truth-telling power of adversarial accountability to cut through the stubborn clichés.

Now, some philanthropist might endow a series of televised debates concerning major issues of the day. Abortion, say, or gun control, or the war against drugs. Speakers would be chosen not for passionate radicalism but for their ability to paraphrase accurately their opponents' positions, showing that they listen at least well enough to comprehend the other side's deeply felt concerns. Each party would then pose questions, with the answers judged by an expert panel for specificity, not polemical appeal.

That would be an improvement. In fact, a few related efforts have taken place. In Europe, "citizens' juries" have attracted some attention. In the United States, there have been widely televised "town meetings" of thirty or more respected sages, journalists, and intellectuals who mull over an issue together, guided by a roving moderator with a microphone. John Gardner's National Civic League brings urban opponents together to negotiate past entrenched positions. But these attempts have all suffered from the same old problems: limited time, rambling discourse, and comments left hanging in the air that never get the follow-up attention they deserve. Similar drawbacks dog Internet-based discussions, such as Hotwired's "Brain Tennis" program and Slate's "Committee of Enquiry."

The Internet can do much better. In fact, it seems well suited to promote a new style of debating, by establishing *disputation arenas* for truly extended and meticulous appraisal of a topic, moderated by volunteers whose own passionate avocation is for neutral intellectual rigor. The more interesting the arguments, the more attention each arena would receive, and the less the chance that adversaries could afford to turn down invitations to take part.

How to prevent artful evasions, of the sort we see so often in political debates? Superficial and brief, they reward charismatic prevarication more than argument, while evidence plays almost no role at all.

This is where the true beauty of the Internet comes in. For one of its greatest virtues may be its potential for *relentlessness*. A tenacity that, when applied by gifted experts, would enable each side doggedly to pursue its opponents until they finally relent and give a real answer (while offering the same treatment in return). Unlike debates in the world outside, there would be no two-hour time limits. Extended confrontations might last for weeks or months, shepherded by proctors whose picky personalities (we all know the type) won't let go of a logical inconsistency on this side of frozen hell.

In fact, the most important enforcement tool in any such arena will be credibility. If people in the world at large were ever to gain confidence in such a system of well-mediated confrontations, the events might acquire the kind of moral force that men used to invest in duels of honor, incurring shame upon those who do not show up or fight by the rules.

Moreover, the Net can also provide many of the implements of science, analytical projection software and statistical tools drawing on vast databases, enabling advocates to create detailed models of their proposals—and their opponents'—for presentation in the arena. This will be crucial because, as University of California at San Diego Professor Phil Agre has pointed out, much of the "data" being bandied about on the Net these days is of incredibly poor quality, often lacking provenance or any trace of error bars, sensitivity, dependency, or semantics. These problems can only be solved the way they are handled in science, by unleashing people with the personalities of bull terriers—critics who could be counted on to pull apart every flaw until they are forced to admit (with reluctance) that they can't find any more. Discrepancies might be minimized if arena managers developed standard kits of modeling subroutines, improving them under strict scrutiny, so that both sides in the debate must compare apples with apples, not oranges.

It may all sound rather dry. But if, as polls show, large numbers of people actually *enjoy* watching the dry charts and graphs of U.S. Senate Budget Committee hearings every year on C-Span, then there will surely be an audience when more passionate participants display vivid graphics and feisty style in the debate arenas of tomorrow. The important point to remember is that this process will not need *majority* participation in order to work, only the involvement of enough nitpickers from all political persuasions. The rest of us will thrill over the fireworks in plenary sessions, when the distilled results are presented.

Early versions will inevitably seem self-serving and tendentious. (No mere gimmick, however clever or nobly intended, can change human nature overnight!) But if the popularity of games like Sim City is indicative, over time disputation arenas might become fashionable attractions among the demographic segment that loves to watch a good fight.

In any event, let me pause now and venture one firm forecast for the predictions registry: We *will* see arena experiments tried, before this century is out. With so much riding on our decisions in the years ahead, what is there to lose?

## WHAT'S IN IT FOR US?

Under the dogma of otherness, we've been brought up to be fiercely loyal to free speech. But free speech owes us something in return. In the long run, it should be about more than just unleashing everyone to scream at the top of their lungs (though screaming deserves protection, too). Ideally, out of all the yelling and ferment, there should also arise good ideas. Opinions and vehement posturing ought to drift toward argument and analysis. Although self-righteousness is effective at causing inflamed adherents to secrete powerful, druglike endorphins in their brains, motivating them to pounce on perceived errors like good T-cells, persuasion is a more mature and useful goal for any advocacy group.

Not only to feel right but to *be* right, and persuade others to agree.

So far, the new media have served mostly to enhance centrifugal forces in society, tearing us further apart and encouraging an age of heightened radicalism. But new techniques wait in the wings, techniques for "guarding the guardians," encouraging the best kinds of T-cell hackers, and bringing fierce advocates together for honest debate. Methods that society will use for its own pragmatic benefit to solve problems that face our new commons, a territory to be shared by all denizens for their private and mutual benefit.

This commons won't be ideal. At best, it will be intriguing, rambunctious, sassy, noisy, and sometimes rather noisome as well. Human nature will see to that.

But it will be ours.

# ALL THE WORLD IS
# A (DIGITAL) MARKETPLACE

"Numbers can be a better form of cash than paper," said David Chaum of the DigiCash Corporation, who defined *ecash* as "the digital equivalent of cash. You can withdraw digital coins from your Internet bank account and store them on your hard disk. Whenever you want to make a payment, you use these coins. The payment is fast and anonymous, and the payer can always prove that he made a certain payment."

Former Citibank chairman Walter Wriston shares the same vision but moves the electronic locus to something more portable. "The revolution that's waiting in the woods is smart cards," Wriston said in late 1996, referring to chip-bearing cards that would contain a person's account information and handle secure transactions for its owner instantly, any time he or she wants to buy something, from a yacht to a stick of gum. Few visions of the information age are as widely held as the one presented by Chaum and Wriston, which extrapolates present-day trends into a near future when all the dollars, marks, yen—as well as some proposed new monetary units that you would mint yourself—flow through the world economy as pure and incorruptible electronic bits.

From the beginning of this book, I have tacitly accepted this popular wisdom—that one form of secrecy and encryption will be essential for the dynamic world economy to come. And yet, even in this area where everybody seems to be in agreement, we may be rushing ahead without adequately pondering all the dangers, or considering a possible alternative—a transparency alternative.

*Conventional* monetary systems certainly have problems! For one thing, they are slow, entailing the costly and cumbersome exchange of crumpled bills, or hastily scrawled checks, or smudged credit card slips. All this inefficient paper-shuffling puts common folk at a major disadvantage, since the rich can already move their money about with supple, electronic ease. Anyway, don't most of our funds already exist as mere digits in the computer files of our local bank?

Moreover, the old ways seem to attract predators, fostering countless varieties of crime—from bad checks to fraud, currency forgery, and stolen credit cards—creating a huge burden of hidden costs to society. Enthusiasts for the electronic economy vow that new techniques will offer a more secure system, with rapid authentication of every transaction. One promised effect would be to allow a downsizing of law enforcement, when we can finally dispense with battalions of armed authority figures assigned to guard mountains of cash or to hunt down counterfeiters and floaters of bad checks. It all sounds perfectly delightful. A clean, efficient, and better tomorrow.

In fairness, however, one might recall that similar promises were made over a decade ago, when many of the same enthusiasts predicted that word processors and spreadsheets would soon lead to a "paperless office" environment. After all, why should anyone print on sheets of pressed and bleached pulp when onscreen documents are more vivid and can be copied indefinitely, at zero cost? Alas, while the new text and information technologies are helpful, they have also resulted in vastly *more* paper versions pouring from laser printers and copying machines, slaying greater numbers of trees than ever before. The lesson? Unintended consequences are always lurking, preparing to pounce on those who grow too smug in their predictions.

Still, who knows? We might be in an awkward transition phase. The paperless office may yet come to pass. Nevertheless, a warning is in order: Beware transition phases. They can sting.

•   •   •

Today innumerable digital seers and pundits proclaim that paperless *commerce* will banish the flaws of old-fashioned checks and cash, offering individuals and corporations perfect security from both thieves and tax authorities, perhaps even leading to the demise of oppressive national governments. (See "A Withering Away," after chapter 9.) But so far, this has proved difficult to put into general practice. Early means of Internet-based payment have been explored by pioneers such as First Virtual, Cybercash, and Open Market, whose systems were still anchored to a user-supplied credit card number as the basis for ultimate payment. A consortium headed by VISA, MasterCard, IBM, and Microsoft has lately been attempting to bring purchase transactions to the next level with a system called SET, for Secure Electronic Transaction, to allow safe transmission of credit card information over the Net. But even these efforts are still a far cry from Chaum's vision of *ecash,* which would be true electronic money, independent of the centralized accounting systems of VISA and its ilk. For a brave new world of digital currency and instantaneous, globe-girdling electronic transactions to come about, several important innovations must prove reliable.

First, powerful types of encrypted passwords called *digital signatures* must be developed that efficiently confirm either the identities of those involved or their masked right to shift resources and wealth about.

Second, use of encrypted passwords will not remove the need, especially in commerce, for confirmation that a party to a transaction is trustworthy, or otherwise capable of living up to his or her obligations. In traditional marketplaces, this was achieved either through personal reputation or by having someone vouch for you. In a world of secret identities, "vouching" will grow increasingly important. "Many cryptographic protocols for secure electronic transactions require at least one trusted third party to the transaction, such as a bank or a *certification authority* (CA)," writes A. Michael Froomkin, professor of law at the University of Miami, who has analyzed some of the difficulties involved in replacing reputation with ciphered identities. According to Froomkin, these new roles and protocols, partly cryptographic and partly social, "require new entities, or new relationships with existing entities, but the duties and liabilities of those entities are uncertain. Until these uncertainties are resolved, they risk inhibiting the spread of the most interesting forms of electronic commerce and causing unnecessary litigation."

In other words, it is far too early to be certain that any of the most highly touted techniques will work as planned.

CAs might arise out of corporate commerce—perhaps by extending the role of today's banks—or else they might be licensed by state legislation. The latter approach was pioneered by the Utah Digital Signature Act of 1996, which attempted to foster the same role for encrypted passwords in cyberspace that *notaries* have long performed in the age of paper documents. Other such agencies already exist, using cipher codes to confirm transactions for major banks and brokerage houses. But that is a far cry from generalizing the same approach, as some now envision, to an economy where every purchase now handled by cash or credit card would be carried out by strings of bytes and bits, and where every paper receipt would be transformed into a set of secret codes, exchanged at the speed of light.

Predictably, many libertarian-leaning netizens dislike the idea of state regulation, or the licensing of certification authorities. They sniff a malodorous similarity to the Clipper chip notion of "key escrow" (see chapter 7) in the very idea that some specially sanctioned agency—or collection of agencies—may keep registries of identities and ecash key codes.

Moreover, there are problems of liability. In case of fraud, should responsibility for false charges fall on the certifying authority (as in credit card theft, when the customer pays just a basic $50 charge)? That would boost the cost of purchasing each digital signature. So maybe the risk should be borne instead by the person owning the keys—the customer. (Ah, but then should Grandma lose her house, just because she chose a poor password?)

Under the Utah law, there is a legal *presumption* that the person who uses a particular digital signature is the owner. Digitally signed transactions are given the same evidentiary weight as handwritten ones that were physically witnessed by a notary public—a legal step that may be premature, given that the technology is untested.

In fact, as we see throughout this book, there are a myriad potential ways that electronic encryption systems might be broken, compromised, or bypassed. (How will you establish ownership of your ecash if someone else uses a hidden camera to steal your passwords even as you type them?) This new, computerized realm does not eliminate all opportunities for predators. It just changes the type of jungle we must warily pass through, shifting all the landmarks, taking us into strange new territory.

In chapter 10, we will discuss the possibilities of *cyberwar*—in which a frail and complex society may fall victim to deliberately or accidentally triggered breakdowns of essential systems, including power networks, transportation, or emergency services. Above all, no target is more tempting than the luscious flow of billions of dollars through slender electronic conduits.

Electronic cash enthusiasts promise utter security, and seem willing to bet our civilization on it. Should the rest of us make the same wager?

•   •   •

Again, many smart people tell me this is the way of the future, and I cannot say they are wrong. The aim of this book is not to demolish "opponents" or to prove that candor is always superior. (There are no Platonic *essences,* and even a good idea is wrong some of the time.) My aim all along has been to suggest that the promoters of anonymity and secrecy are basing their zeal on untested assumptions and bear a burden of proof before we consign our destiny to their transcendental vision of salvation through encryption. Moreover, this book tries to offer alternative approaches that may be worth considering, approaches that make use of openness.

Consider the markets that human beings have used for millennia—the bazaar, the trading post, the shops on Main Street. In those primitive days, no digital record kept track of each transaction. Yet there was memory, and some degree of accountability.

Reputations were involved, and not only on the part of merchants. Customers belonged to communities and went unmasked. Even when clerk and customer were strangers to each other, there was the implicit right of a victim to make a scene, complaining to the manager, to other customers, or to the police. If either party tried to "pull a fast one," word might get out. True, this was an imperfect recourse. In any single case, a slick-talking clerk might prevail over the customer he shortchanged. But how many times could this happen before management saw a trend and realized that they must eliminate a threat to the store's precious reputation?

Encryption enthusiasts keep claiming that anonymity is the "default condition" in a cash economy, where untallied and untraced bills are exchanged between participants who are mutually unknown. But this is simply untrue when it comes to the thing that matters most—overall accountability between merchants and their customers! Normal people are kept reasonably honest, in part by the values that our parents instilled and in part by the likely damage our reputations would suffer if we betray the trust of others too often.

In fact, almost all of the villainy that afflicts today's cash economy occurs *because* it is partly anonymous! The new electronic age could help to eliminate this source of unaccountability. But instead, encryption aficionados want to go the other way and make the *whole thing* anonymous, eliminating what little certain accountability we already have—the link between normal people and the consequences of their actions. The new world of electronic commerce should not blithely abandon this connection between cause and effect.

In fact there is a way that it might be carried forward into the age of ecash, a way that is so simple—yet so counterintuitive—that nobody I know of has suggested it until now.

*Why not have most transactions take place in the open?*

Consider this possibility. Let us define an "open transaction" between two parties as an exchange that is immediately "announced" or broadcast across the Internet. In particular, a notification streaks *toward* both of the parties involved—a form of electronic receipt that is sent to the official home base that each person or group maintains for accountability purposes. This electronic address cannot be hacked because it stands in open view at all times, checked—routinely, randomly, and redundantly—as often as anyone wishes. It is permanent, a name.

The announcement also goes to as many other individuals or groups as either party might choose, so that it is common knowledge. This message— an attestation *that* a bargain has been struck—requires no secret codes, no potentially fragile ciphers, since it is not the same thing as the transaction itself. When each participant in the deal gets such a message, he or she can do one of three things:

- *Confirm* the transaction. (In most cases, the message-blip will be received just an instant after you strike an agreement, simply restating its terms.)

- *Repudiate* it. If the announcement comes as a surprise, it means someone is trying to spend your money! Repudiation automatically forbids the transfer and unleashes electronic sleuths to begin tracing the source of the bogus deal.

- *Do nothing*—in which case the transaction is either confirmed or repudiated automatically, depending on the user's default choice.

Notice how this system differs from encrypted security, while achieving the same aims. Unscrupulous parties are thwarted because they will accomplish nothing by attempting to forge a false transaction. It will be canceled anyway, and nothing will be gained except to attract attention from the authorities. Because the confirmation request was *broadcast,* the thieves cannot prevent you from receiving it, or deny you an opportunity at repudiation.

Transactions can be verified or rejected swiftly, or else each person can set his or her personal banking system to digest mode, allowing confirmation or repudiation of accumulated deals to take place on a once-a-day basis, or even once a week—just as nowadays you might set a special time aside to balance your checkbook. No money officially changes hands until your scheduled "clearing" time arrives. Companies that want your business will have to accustom themselves to such measures, adapting to a human pace.

(Professor Froomkin describes an old-fashioned encryption-based approach to achieving the same end. According to Froomkin, "a transactional certificate attests to some fact about a transaction. Unlike an identifying certificate or an authorizing certificate, a transactional certificate is not designed to be reused or to bind a fact to a key. Instead, the certificate attests that some face or formality was witnessed by the observer." In other words, Froomkin would use an encrypted certificate to confirm *that* a transaction took place. The problem with his approach is that it relies on the same ornate and unproved technology as all other forms of encrypted certification. In contrast, the open-broadcast approach provides a workable backup that is both simple and redundant, in case *all* forms of encryption prove less reliable than expected.)

Now I am fully aware that the open method will not do for some kinds of transactions. We aren't talking about perfection here. Small daily purchases with your pocket smart card could be set to "automatic-confirm." Moreover, even a believer in openness will have some arrangements that he or she prefers to handle with notarized seals and security envelopes. Certain deals will be better handled by encrypted ecash methods, even if those methods turn out to have flaws and potential drawbacks.

But consider how much better ecash will work if 95% of commercial transactions were openly announced, as just described. Insurance and liability problems would lessen. Authorities or commercial agents could concentrate on protecting the smaller number of cipher-secured trades, while the rest are safeguarded by openness. Villains who do succeed in stealing ecash would not be quite as seamlessly invisible as they might like when they try to spend it in a mostly open economy. Moreover, by reducing the total number of potential "prey" transactions in the marketplace, we will also decrease the overall number of predators. When there aren't many shadows, there will be fewer places for knaves to lurk, or to practice their skills by victimizing others.

The second advantage to a transparency option would be that it is *robust* (a theme we will reiterate later). If only a small fraction of commercial deals are encrypted, no undiscovered flaw in the ciphering software can be used to steal the whole bank or to topple an entire economy. Suppose some virus, or logic bomb, or a nuke in downtown Manhattan, temporarily cripples the financial networks. If 95% of exchanges were already open and recorded on countless durable disk memories around the world, the total economy could be reconstructed almost instantly.

Those who had chosen the romantic habit of using secret codes for every purchase could then spend years suing each other, while the rest of us went back to business with nary a pause.

Finally, this approach might actually give people what they want. While supporters of encrypted and anonymous ecash claim that secrecy is a vital concern, their passion may not be widely shared. In August 1995, Roy Weiller, a New York business consultant from the Management School of Imperial College in England, surveyed attitudes about money and the Net and found that typical respondents rated "security" only fourth in their list of concerns. Foremost, people wanted a form of electronic payment that was "widely accepted;" second, easy to use; and, third, portable.

Anonymity scored dead last out of eight desiderata.

•  •  •

Again, I do not claim this solution is perfect, only that it merits discussion alongside the one that is so cheerfully assumed to be "obvious." Given that secrecy's glaring flaws are evident in both history and human nature, perhaps a second option should also be on the table. We might develop it in parallel, just in case cypherphilia lets us down, like so many utopian schemes that came before it.

Millions of expert-worker-hours have already gone into perfecting the encryption-anonymity option, without coming anywhere near perfection so far. It might be interesting to see what the transparency option would look like, if even 1% of the same skilled effort went into designing systems based on openness and frank accountability.

## CHAPTER SEVEN

# THE WAR OVER SECRECY

*We, the people, have not granted each other total freedom: one person's freedom could be another's oppression were it not for laws against such crimes as murder, rape, discrimination, extortion and robbery. . . . We expect our government to use its authority to uphold our laws and serve justice. We hold it accountable when it misuses that authority.*

DOROTHY DENNING

*When encryption is outlawed, figmujjo icy hwxish.*

A LEGENDARY (ANONYMOUS)
INSCRIPTION ON THE NET

In 1995 and 1997 I attended the Computers, Freedom and Privacy (CFP) conferences held at a hotel near San Francisco International Airport. CFP conventions feature panelists and speakers from around the world who share technical, legal, and political knowledge about aspects of electronic privacy, anonymity, and data security. The meetings also serve as rallying points for those who oppose certain government initiatives, such as the Clipper chip proposal, that might seek to limit the use of cryptography ("crypto") in daily life.

Members of the Electronic Frontier Foundation (EFF) make an appearance at every CFP conference. This activist society was founded in 1990, partly in response to the infamous Steve Jackson Games fiasco, when overzealous federal agents, following a dubious trail of guilt by association, raided and nearly destroyed an innocuous manufacturer of role-playing games, in part because one of its titles, *Cyberpunk*, happened to depict fictitious hackers at work and play. EFF activists rallied with well-justified anger over this flagrant abuse of power, forcing accountability and reparations from those responsible, and setting the tone for later clashes with the federal government. (In chapter 4 we encountered EFF as part of a coalition opposing the National Information Infrastructure Copyright Act [NIICA], which it sees as a threat to unfettered flow of information.)

Also in attendance at each CFP are certain colorful and irrepressible Net aficionados who call themselves "cypherpunks," partly from *cipher*, a class of secret coding techniques, and in part as a tribute to *cyber*punk authors of vivid, hard-boiled science fiction stories—William Gibson, Bruce Sterling, Neal Stephenson, and others—whose tales are often filled with glossy images of computerized gadgetry, set in near-future worlds more dour and forbidding than *Blade Runner*. Cypherpunks enthusiastically promote the notion that widespread use of encryption will help ensure freedom in the coming electronic age.

Among the invited attendees at both CFP 95 and CFP 97 were envoys of major corporations, including many involved in the credit and banking industries. Others came from companies that specialize in gathering, collating, and selling data about average Americans. One might have expected these representatives to tread lightly at such a gathering. But in fact, several firms were listed as corporate sponsors. Moreover, their representatives were as brashly indignant as anyone there, crying out that corporate America needs crypto, not just for the security of electronic cash transactions, but in order to keep their meetings, deliberations, documents, and records secret from rivals, snoops, their employees, and especially the government.

It was fascinating to observe some of the most vociferously anti-authority cypherpunks heaping lavish praise on these corporate speakers, and then turning to denounce officials from the National Research Council, who had flown in to hear testimony at a special evening hearing. As I watched the bleary-eyed bureaucrats endure a five-hour session of relentless lambasting in which speaker after irate speaker denounced Big Brother officials in ringing tones worthy of Thomas Paine, it dawned on me that (1) these cypherpunks were among the most brilliant, articulate, knowledgeable, and boisterous T-cells our society could brag about producing so far; and (2) they had little sense of irony.

Recall chapter 5, when we discussed how suspicion of authority runs through nearly all modern American myths. Among those imbued with this belief, the difference between the political left and right often boils down to *where* you perceive would-be authoritarians trying to accumulate dangerous amounts of power. This tendency was evident during the late-night hearing at CFP, as crypto supporters joined slickly dressed corporation consultants berating those rumpled officials until wee hours of the morning. In decrying grievous federal power grabs, Eric Hughes, Tim May, and their colleagues kept citing *cyber*punk novels that warn about dark dystopias to come.

Yet, in fact, a closer look at those novels reveals that they nearly always portray future societies in which governments have become wimpy and pathetic! Popular science fiction tales penned by Gibson, Williams, Cadigan, and others *do* depict Orwellian accumulations of power in the next century, but nearly always clutched in the secretive hands of a wealthy or corporate elite.

Both the authors and the activists—"cyberpunks" and "cypherpunks"—worry that freedom may someday be lost to dark, conspiratorial forces. Yet the writers tend to veer somewhat left in their fear of oligarchs, while crypto supporters target their ire at nefarious state agencies, a distinction none of them seemed to note.

Now at first this may seem an academic contradiction between writers of an obscure literary genre and their fans in a fringe techno-political movement. But that superficial reading misses several points. First, although both groups choose to call themselves "punks" in stylish rebellion against social structures they perceive as straitlaced or repressive, they are actually mainstream opinion shapers among the hundreds of thousands of technologically informed netizens who are designing and implementing the information age. Almost every high official or member of Congress has one or more vital staff members who care far more about William Gibson and Phil Zimmermann than about Milton Friedman or Paula Jones. The resident techies who maintain Web pages and crucial network access for every major politician, corporate head, academic department, and news outlet are fast becoming indispensable and influential out of all proportion to their numbers. To an ever-increasing degree, they govern what their employers read and see, helping sway the way they view the world.

Moreover, this example illustrates both yin and yang aspects of the social immune system we explored earlier. Exercised to a peak of fighting mettle, cypherpunks practice their well-trained suspicion-of-authority instincts in the most gut-satisfying way, by attacking a single, demonized concentration of power, losing sight of the need to apply accountability in all directions, especially the ignored shadows.

None of this disparages the warnings that they raise. With articulate passion, these social T-cells swarm around some of the right dangers. They diagnose perilous trends. But their chosen prescription should be examined before we swallow it whole.

*One of the things that makes some people reluctant to negotiate is a combination of hard technical determinism with a belief in the efficacy of strong crypto. The coming of small, cheap, and mobile sensor/video camera technologies would seem to undermine this belief system, but so far, a large number of people still think 1s and 0s will save them from bad politics.* JEFF UBOIS

## CLIPPER CHIP AND PASCAL'S CHOICE

In chapters 8 and 9 we will discuss many of the technical and social ramifications raised by innovations like the Clipper chip, harkening to the subtitle of this book: *Will Technology Force Us to Choose Between Privacy and Freedom?* For the remainder of chapter 7, however, we will concentrate on just one aspect—the modern obsession with *secrecy* that appears to have transfixed an alliance of pundits, intellectuals, and activists all across the political spectrum, leading to the widespread acceptance of a bizarre consensus: that liberty can best be protected with masks and secret codes.

First, a little background.

*Encryption* is the art of disguising meaning within a message, so that only the intended recipient will understand its significance. The origins of encryption go back almost to the start of writing itself. Codes, ciphers, and cryptograms have been used for diplomatic and military purposes since at least Babylonian times. Meanwhile, nations have desperately sought ways to *unscramble* the codes of their rivals. During World War I, a clumsy attempt by the German Foreign Ministry to stir up an anti-American, recidivist conspiracy in Mexico was uncovered with the deciphering of the infamous "Zimmerman telegram." This message had the unintended result of pushing U.S. public opinion closer toward siding with Britain and France. A quarter of a century later, ingenious skill at decryption proved even more decisive in human affairs when a team of eccentrics and émigrés succeeded in cracking the Nazi *Enigma* encryption system, giving the British a crucial advantage in the Battle of the Atlantic. Similar success by U.S. officers at

breaking Japanese naval codes helped turn the tide of combat in that theater, perhaps a year earlier than might have happened otherwise.

Throughout the Cold War, an expensive, top-secret campaign of electronic espionage and surveillance was run out of the mysterious so-called
Puzzle Palace of the NSA, where sophisticated spy satellites reported nearly
every whisper carried over Soviet airwaves and telephone cables. America's
top cipher designers pursued mathematical games in deadly earnest. Techniques were developed to scramble data swiftly and efficiently. Meanwhile,
down the hall, others worked just as hard developing methods to *decipher*
the messages of foreign powers.

Even before the Cold War waned, there was also a small but vigorous
research community studying cryptography beyond government circles.
For instance, *public key* encryption emerged from the efforts of a few creative outsiders to come up with a system that would be simple, secure, and
easy to use by a wide variety of groups or individuals. In a public key crypto
system, all the receiving party requires for deciphering a message is a pair
of prime numbers. The product of these two numbers is a public key that
can be used for enciphering, but only knowledge of the secret prime factors allows the message to be decrypted. In order to prevent an opponent's
high-speed computers from penetrating the code by brute force, the keys
have to be quite large, up to hundreds of binary digits long. (We will
describe some of the technical possibilities, and drawbacks, in chapter 9.)

Today many citizens encounter encryption when they try tuning television signals sent by satellite or cable. In most local systems, a paying sub-
scriber receives a "key" electronically, via a cable box sitting atop the television, after which premium channels are supposed to come through with
clarity. Until recently, these scrambling schemes used comparatively simple analog techniques that a gifted electronics engineer might bypass,
resulting in a thriving "cable piracy" black market. But digital technologies
may give the advantage back to mainstream cable and satellite companies—for a while.

Cable television is just the start of encryption entering our lives. Many
telephone sets are now sold with simple, built-in scrambling systems. Impressive hardware/software packages promise both corporations and individuals
ways to conceal their private data from competitors or other prying eyes.

This trend did not escape notice by the law enforcement community.
As early as 1993, speaking to the Executives Club of Chicago, FBI director-
designate Louis Freeh described how his agency perceived a looming
danger and predicted, "The country will be unable to protect itself against
terrorism, violent crime, foreign threats, drug trafficking, espionage, kidnapping, and other grave crimes." Freeh conceded that the age of old-fashioned

analog telephony, carried on easily tapped copper wires, is rapidly coming to an end. As ever more telephone and data traffic goes digital, especially via fiber optics and multi-branched switching systems, the technology of disguising communications under a static haze of encryption has Freeh and his colleagues worried. In the government's view, technology promises to change the rules of daily life, making electronic privacy so secure that even the FBI won't be able to listen in.

Still, the official response of the Clinton administration was not to try to *prevent* private or commercial encryption, but instead to propose a standardization of coding technology that would still (the FBI hoped) meet the needs of justice professionals. Like other methods for scrambling private messages, the Clipper chip would let users encrypt their voice or digital communications so that almost any outsider would have a hard time listening in. Unlike competing methods, however, there would be an exception built in, since the *keys*, or mathematical factors for decoding all "clipped" messages, would be held in escrow, deposited in a pair of separate, secure databases. Armed with a court order, the FBI might then retrieve both keys to a given scrambler and listen in, just as they do today on about one thousand unscrambled telephone lines per year. In Freeh's words, "Advanced technology will make it possible for the FBI to carry out court-approved surveillance in the life-and-death cases."

In addition to the inevitable firestorm of political and ideological objections that followed Freeh's initiative, the Clipper faced many kinks and problems of a technological nature. For instance, in June 1994 a computer scientist at AT&T Bell Laboratories, Matthew Blaze, announced a basic flaw in the proposed technology that would let clever users convert even the supposedly tame Clipper so that it provided relatively "unbreakable" encryption. No doubt later redesigns would have closed Blaze's loophole, even as other ingenious minds applied themselves to finding new ones. (As Marc Rotenberg of the Electronic Privacy Information Center [EPIC] pointed out, any central bank of key codes would become the ultimate target of computer hackers.)

There were other drawbacks, such as standardization on a specific hardware format, nearly always a bad idea during times of rapidly changing technology. If the system were ever compromised at a later date, upgrading would be an expensive, nationwide headache.

No law would have actually banished methods of encoding and decoding data different from Clipper (though such legislation was being discussed as this book went to press). Such alternatives are widely available within the United States and abroad. So far, the federal government has promoted its favored technology with the power of the purse, by requiring its own suppliers to include the Clipper in new designs, and by using Cold War technology transfer laws to restrict the export of competing technologies. The government hoped thereby to create momentum for the Clipper's adoption as an industrywide encryption standard. But anyone serious about evading a wiretap would still be able to use something else, such as the widely distributed public key coding protocol called PGP, or Pretty Good Privacy, written by Philip Zimmermann.

None of this softened the storm of outraged protests by those who perceived this as despotism on the march. Tom Maddox, a columnist for *Locus* magazine, put it this way: "The response from organizations such as EFF and the Computer Professionals for Social Responsibility and a number of corporations was immediate and almost uniformly negative. Seeing Big Brother embodied in the hardware, they balked."

The objections presented by these groups had much to do with their members' collective sense of threatened rights. As PGP author Philip Zimmermann observes, "I think I ought to be able to go up and whisper in your ear, even if your ear is 1,000 miles away. If we install Clipper, then we can't do that, because the government will have a back door into our encrypted communications."

In a world of black and white ideologies, Zimmermann is actually more pragmatic and open-minded than many of his staunch defenders. "I think that the government does have some reasonable points to make. Criminals *can* use this technology to hide their activities," he says. "I think the debate on cryptography is not an open-and-shut case." Nevertheless, Zimmermann sees his role as promoting the crypto side of the argument, and leaving the opposition to others. "I am a cryptographer," he explains. "It's what I do."

Ironically, while the Clipper chip controversy was often couched as an effort to *increase* government power of surveillance over individuals, that is an overstatement. Government wiretapping is going to be hampered by encryption, whether or not something like Clipper finally becomes standard. Instead of the current situation, in which most wiretaps are placed by local cops, needing only a local judge's hand-scrawled (and possibly postdated) "court order" plus a pair of rusty alligator clips, there would be straitlaced procedures required to access the keys for any single Clipper chip, with officials having to present formal documents at two separate escrow agencies. True, one can imagine scenarios under which a corrupt administrator, or invading hacker, or a worker at the Clipper factory might access and sell some keys, but that is possible under any encryption scheme, not just Clipper.

Might opponents in principle have negotiated concessions from the government in the form of rigorously worked out verification procedures?

Certain measures could have made Clipper's key escrow system arguably more resistant to tampering or abuse. For instance, public key encryption can be performed with *more* than two keys. Any arbitrary number may be established, so that a particular message can be decrypted only if all five, ten, or perhaps even a hundred keys are used at the same time. A mathematical technique called "secret sharing" extends this principle to a degree that should satisfy all but the most paranoid. In a five-key system, the "back door" would be accessible to government agents only if they presented highly credible probable-cause evidence of criminality to separate oversight committees in five separate cities — committees that might be set up from the start to include substantial citizen membership, perhaps with a chair reserved for the Electronic Frontier Foundation. (Anything can be negotiated.) Refusal of permission by just one cache authority would thwart the proposed eavesdropping. This measure would also help defend against illicit key collection by invading hackers.

Another possible alternative to the FBI's concept of twin government escrow sites would be a free enterprise solution. Under this plan, which was vaguely and tentatively floated under the unpromising name, Clipper II, individuals or corporations would purchase (or deposit) their encryption keys from a trusted commercial agent of their own choice. These repository institutions would presumably have strong economic incentives to protect their customers' keys, demanding triple verification of court orders and scrutinizing every step of the transaction, because a slipup, letting the government gain access too easily, might ruin the company's reputation and lose it customers. (These repositories would be far easier to hold accountable than the faceless operators of "anonymous remailers," which we will discuss a little later.)

Alas, consensus-oriented ideas such as these were hardly discussed in most public statements about the Clipper initiative, especially by advocates of strong privacy, who almost universally dismissed the possibility of compromise. Nor was this entirely because of their ideological myopia or fixation on a single threat. Indeed, federal officials did little to engender an atmosphere that could lead to negotiation and trust.

### The Government's Fault

On a technical level, bureaucrats contributed to the general wariness by refusing to publish openly the mathematical algorithm on which Clipper was based. Now at first sight this might seem a reasonable security precaution, to protect against future code breakers, but in fact there is a world of difference between the *method* that is used to generate and apply encryption keys and the keys themselves. A computational technique, like any other fine-looking plan, can look excellent on paper, yet be in fact riddled with hidden flaws that will only be exposed after assault by relentless and varied criticism. Corporations and private individuals had a perfect right to examine (and hammer away at) the software underlying Clipper, in order to be sure in advance that *only* the cached keys would decipher any encrypted messages. Refusal to expose the algorithm to scrutiny struck many crypto advocates as suspicious. So did the fact that officials were so slow to suggest more than two cache sites, or the commercial repository alternative.

Even had these problems been overcome, a serious cultural gap yawned between the U.S. government and its critics. Hasty or witless abuses, such as the Steve Jackson Games episode, provided grist for a well-tuned mill of distrust toward bullying authority figures. Many cypherpunks and others were already primed to believe the worst about public scandals, like the calamity that occurred at the Branch Davidian compound in 1993, attributing such fatal episodes to deliberate malevolence rather than bad luck or official incompetence. Bureaucrats exacerbate this reflex by perpetuating high levels of Cold War secrecy and habitually thwarting document requests under the Freedom of Information Act. In this atmosphere, many activists give credence to the worst rumors, for example, that the FBI plans to tap one in every hundred phones, or that the NSA already routinely spies on U.S. domestic telephone traffic (using sophisticated word-sampling techniques to screen a myriad conversations, seeking those worth further investigation).

Although I tend to think that the stupidity of such outrages would far exceed any conceivable benefit (the risk of exposure by whistleblowers could lead to towering scandals), I will not dismiss such concerns out of hand. The fact that a scheme is doomed from the start to become a disastrous embarrassment and put its instigators in prison does not mean that some isolated clique of egotists in power won't convince themselves that it is, in the immortal words of Oliver North, "a neat idea."

Dartmouth Professor Arthur Kantrowitz explains this self-destructive pattern, one that is followed by too many aloof officials. "In a classified project, the vested interests which grow around a decision can frequently prevent the questioning of authority necessary for the elimination of error. Peacetime classified projects have a very bad record of rejecting imaginative suggestions which frequently are very threatening to the existing political power structure."

Whether conspiracy fans are right in their direst suspicions, or paranoid, or somewhere in between, the important point is that in the long run, transparency offers the best hope of preventing such behavior by government agencies. It will do this in three ways:

1. Creating an atmosphere in which whistleblowers are feted and protected.

2. Eliminating the bureaucrats' rationalizations for such activities, by exposing terrorist and other threats in the normal course of events.

3. Distributing the expertise that will enable citizens and amateur or media sleuths to catch official power abusers "in the act."

Although this scenario is hardly perfect, the transparency solution is assuredly less far-fetched than believing that a Web-advertised "underground" encryption package, bought by mail order from some unknown bunch of programmers in Delhi or St. Petersburg, will guarantee protection against both hackers and the finest tools the NSA can bring to bear.

### The Cryptos' Error

While many people took passionate and worried interest in the Clipper chip fiasco, others considered the outcome a foregone conclusion. I was in the latter category, taking bets back in 1994 that the "Davids" would handily defeat "Goliath" (the big bad government). In fact, the Clipper proposal was always ill fated, because a third force, the media, came down with almost total unanimity on the side of the apparent underdogs—the romantic, freedom-loving crypto advocates. For many social reasons discussed in chapter 5, any top-down, hierarchically imposed solution was doomed from the start. As we shall see in chapter 10, this overall trend is good for the survival of civilization in the risky years ahead.

Then why focus a chapter of this book on the Clipper episode? Because it illustrates the type of self-righteous tunnel vision that might keep us from finding useful answers to some of the perils we will face in coming decades. As we have seen in the past, indignant idealism is a paramount force preventing opponents (each self-perceived as "in the right") from working together toward pragmatic goals, such as ensuring *both* liberty and safety, *both* freedom and privacy, an optimization that we will come back to before the end of this chapter.

This inflexible idealism, as powerful a force as government intransigence, was distilled by Eric Hughes in the *Cypherpunk Manifesto*.

> [Strong] privacy is necessary for an open society in the electronic age. Privacy is not secrecy. A private matter is something that one doesn't want the whole world to know, but a secret matter is something one doesn't want anybody to know. Privacy is the power to

selectively reveal one's self to the world. We must defend our own privacy if we expect to have any. We must come together and create systems which allow anonymous transactions to take place. People have been defending their own privacy for centuries with whispers, darkness, envelopes, closed doors, secret handshakes, and couriers. The technologies of the past did not allow for a strong privacy, but electronic technologies do. Let's extend all those other things, the whispers, the darkness, the envelopes. We the Cypherpunks are dedicated to building anonymous systems.

A more reflective and comprehendible case was made by Michael Godwin, legal adviser to the Electronic Frontier Foundation, who eloquently presented a philosophical basis for Clipper enmity in the July 1994 issue of *Internet World* magazine.

> . . . [T]he government subscribes to the reasoning of Pascal's wager. Pascal, you may recall, argued that the rational man is a Christian, even if the chances that Christianity is true are small, [since] the consequences of choosing not to be a Christian are, if that choice is incorrect, infinitely terrible. . . .
>
> This is precisely the way the government talks about nuclear terrorism and murder-kidnappings. When asked what the probability is of a nuclear terrorist [using] encryption and managing to otherwise thwart counter-terrorist efforts, they'll answer, "What does it matter what the probability is? Even one case is too much to risk!"
>
> But we cannot live in a society that defines its approach to civil liberties in terms of infinitely bad but low-probability events. Open societies are risky. Individual freedom and privacy are risky. If we are to make a mature commitment to an open society, we have to acknowledge those risks up front and reaffirm our willingness to endure them.

This well-spoken appeal tugs at the idealist within. It also has strong historical underpinnings, which we will now discuss, before later focusing on the core issue raised by "Pascal's wager," that of *trade-offs*.

Early in the Cold War, faced with dire competition from a ruthless totalitarian adversary, the United States rang with calls to clamp down in the name of national security—to restrict press coverage, conceal the defense budget, restrict citizen movements, intern dissidents, and generally take on a policy of "better safe than sorry."

To the surprise of many, one of the fiercest cold warriors, physicist and H-bomb coinventor Edward Teller, helped lead a persuasive campaign against this strategy of safety through obscurity. Joining Karl Popper and other civil libertarians—many of them diametrically opposed to him on other issues—Teller pressed the point that an open society only *seems*, at first sight, to be disadvantaged against a closed one. True, Soviet spies would learn a lot just by roaming our cities and countryside, paying dimes for magazines containing details about our production and technology, the kinds of details we could only hope to learn vis-à-vis the Soviet Union at great risk and cost. And yet, Teller maintained, this would not matter in the long run.

It would not matter because, over time, the benefits of an open society—cross-fertilization of ideas and error avoidance through criticism—would pay off so well that it was immaterial how many mere facts the other side managed to steal. Facts don't advance creativity, or productivity, or competence. Rather, those traits arise from the interaction of self-motivated, mature adults, free to think and argue among themselves.

True, we are learning that all too many blunders and betrayals *were* perpetrated in secret by U.S. officials during the Cold War, from deceptive nuclear tests and careless waste disposal to obscene contagion experiments on unknowing subjects. As we have seen, such concealed schemes are natural products of ego and human nature whenever men and women experience the drug of power. But one has only to compare these crimes and gaffes with far worse outrages that took place in the shadowy Soviet Union, to see proof of Teller's postulate: the greater the secrecy, the more terrible the resulting cascade of horrific blunders.

In fact, those American exceptions help prove the point! To a large degree, the worst U.S. government scandals of our lifetime—from the Tuskegee syphilis study to Watergate, from the Bay of Pigs fiasco to the Iran-Contra debacle—took place in circumstances where secrecy prevailed over accountability. In other words, they happened when our leaders betrayed the basic rules of transparency and criticism. Indeed, this insight offers perspective on the relentless litany of wretched mistakes that make up much of human history. If one accepts that a curse of human nature makes every leader want to keep secret plans and sweep errors under a rug, then the most surprising thing about an open society is not that bad things still happen. It is that such a society manages to stay open at all.

Teller's role in this (relatively) happy outcome was mixed, to be sure. Much of his activity took place against the backdrop of the infamous McCarthy era in which Teller's record was spotty. Moreover, many idealistic civil libertarians fought for the same goals—openness and free speech—that Teller preached. But it is worth noting that, while those others did it largely for idealistic reasons, the pragmatic Teller appreciated transparency for its *utilitarian* value. The chaotic brilliance of a free people was simply a more effective war-fighting tool, in the long run, than the tempting strategy of suppression. He saw openness as a vital weapon to help his side achieve victory, and convincingly passed on this belief to some key elements of the American establishment. In the end, Teller's case was proved. The society that chose to embrace the risks of openness prevailed.

### Reality Check

Now at first sight this lesson from the recent past seems to support the crypto-advocates' position. Regarding the Clipper chip and related proposals, we appear to face on the one hand, a temptation to let government take on authoritarian powers "for our own good" and, on the other, a courageous decision to accept risk in exchange for the benefits of freedom. Unfortunately, this analogy fails on several levels.

First, reflex anti-authoritarian slogans about Big Brother paint over the fact that this time it is the *government* arguing for a little more accountability (albeit tepidly, ineffectually, selectively, and only in their own favor) by letting the FBI see through a few designated masks. Meanwhile, it is the purported civil libertarians who seem to be proclaiming a universal moral right to conceal and deceive, extolling a world filled with veils, facades, and subterfuges. In other words, although it was dangerous and wrong for the government during the Cold War to obscure its schemes from criticism and sweep mistakes under a blanket of secrecy, it is apparently just fine for megacorporations, criminals, and individual connivers to do so in the 1990s and beyond.

The preceding paragraph may be difficult to grasp, at first reading. That is because we tend to focus habitually, perhaps reflexively, on the *players* in a drama, rather than on their behavior, which can swing rapidly from pro-openness to pro-secrecy whenever the perceived advantage seems to shift. (Recall the "accountability matrix" on page 86.) The trick is to consider who, in a given situation, wants more information and accountability to flow, and who wants less. During the Cold War there was a constant danger of government maintaining too much secrecy. In the Clipper debates, it is government officials who have sought a net *lessening* of shadows where schemes can hide. Their proposals, while self-serving and sometimes even hypocritical, favor a narrow kind of increased visibility. Meanwhile, their opponents find themselves arguing in favor of secrecy! Because it is government asking for more openness, they assume that openness must automatically be dangerous or bad.

And so we return to one of this book's central dilemmas: whether we have retained our freedom till now by weakening government, or by assuring ourselves the power to hold government accountable. The first view—that keeping official authority weak and blind means it cannot harm us—sounds logical. Alas, the logic has three basic flaws:

1. Weak governments can reverse this situation in a flash, whenever an emergency gives some charismatic leader an excuse to claim new powers. From Caesar to Napoleon to Lenin to Mussolini to Hitler, this has been one of the classic methods of creating an instant dictatorship out of a formerly feeble central authority. Few modern governments were ever as weak or "blind" as 1788 France, 1917 Russia, 1926 Italy, or 1933 Germany. Yet, governmental blindness is what strong privacy fans recommend.

2. It assumes that government is the only major threat to freedom, when in fact the government's tools may be needed to stave off other dangers. (Recall "An Open Society's Enemies" after chapter 4.)

3. Logical or not, it bears almost no correlation to the practical way we have actually pulled off the feat of retaining freedom all these years, a point we will reinforce throughout this book.

The accountability approach suffers from none of these flaws. It enables the people to retain control over their officials, even during a crisis. It deals with all threats, not just the one that some activists choose to fixate on. And, above all, it is what works.

Is government the only potential nest of oppressors we should be worrying about? Beyond the examples discussed so far in this book, of corporate data abuse or secretive cheating, consider the way organized crime is turning high-tech. For instance, when Colombian police and U.S. drug enforcement agents recently raided the Cali headquarters of one narco-mob, they discovered sophisticated signal-scanning equipment capable of intercepting telephone calls throughout the region. An IBM mainframe stored the telephone records of millions of Cali residents and routinely sought potential government collaborators by correlating numbers dialed with those of the Ministry of Defense or the U.S. Embassy. Widespread use of personal voice encryption would have done nothing to thwart this devilishly simple technique, which is an example of *traffic analysis*, that is, drawing conclusions from patterns of communication flow without actually having to read the messages themselves.

Drug kingpins now fly jets equipped with signal interceptors that monitor the routes of patrol craft. Gambling emporiums combine computers with overhead cameras to correlate the betting patterns of private wagerers and adjust conditions to the house's advantage. Whether or not you agree with today's drug or gambling laws, that question is orthogonal to the problem of amoral men creating empires of power based on unaccountability, manipulative cheating, violence, secrecy, and the creation of multitudinous victims—a process made no more palatable because it is done outside official government.

Most people by now know about the existence of overseas banking havens. At first glance, they seem quaint institutions that help a few eccentric millionaires evade the widely reviled IRS. It all sounds a bit romantic and harmless—until you start tallying up the numbers, and realize that the shortfall in taxes evaded by some billionaire cheater is then made up by increasing rates on middle-class citizens. Earlier estimates of secretly sheltered funds used to range in the hundreds of billions of dollars, but now such modest numbers seem naïve. Poor nations have been especially victimized by their own elites, who squirreled away close to *half a trillion* dollars since the 1960s—more than the total economic aid that the U.S. gave to the Third World in all that time, possibly making all the difference between potential advancement and the reality of grinding poverty.

And yet, that could be just the beginning. It seems that "haven" banks are now forging alliances with members of the new techno-elite. For instance, self-proclaimed libertarian Vincent Cate moved to tax-free Anguilla not long ago to start Offshore Information Services Ltd., a company aimed at helping companies set up Internet business accounts in a secrecy-friendly country. "I believe that if there is widespread use of encryption, the Internet is going to drastically change society," said Cate, who subsequently hosted a conference of eighty fellow aficionados in Anguilla, where they schmoozed with bankers and discussed how financial cryptography would help protect secret transactions for the world's mightiest financial power brokers, masking them from the glaring light of inspection by society at large.

When the tiny island nation of Seychelles passed a law allowing anyone with $10 million to buy extradition-free citizenship, several of these radical techno-anarchists expressed both approval and blithe amusement, preferring to forge shields made of bits and bytes, rather than mere miles. "Encryption is to the Information Revolution what the Atlantic Ocean was to the American Revolution," commented one enthusiast. "It will render tax authorities as impotent in projecting their power as the ocean crossing did to King George."

Are some advocates of strong privacy selling out? Or are they really unaware that dangerous evil can fester and grow outside government? If they are unworried about drug kings and plutocrat tax cheats, what will they say when kidnappers begin using unbreakable codes to make untraceable demands, taking ransom payments in perfect, encrypted security? (See "The Problem of Extortion," after chapter 7.)

True, the greatest villains of the twentieth century, such as Hitler and Stalin, used state agencies as their chief tools for committing terror across the globe. But the vast majority of other human cultures were ruled by the arbitrary whims of conspiratorial cliques that scarcely resembled government as we know it.

Do crypto-advocates actually believe this ancient threat is over?

## MORE "ESSENCES"—MORE ERRORS

In almost any language it is possible to make simple statements that seem true all by themselves but can lead to huge mistakes when they are strung together, one after another. Plato illustrated this in his *Dialogues,* using the assumed voice of Socrates to construct chains of "logic" that lead the reader to so-called inevitable conclusions. In many cases these inferences were later decisively disproved by science. Yet Plato's heirs continue to erect ideologies based on chains of "if . . . therefore" statements and specious comparisons.

When it comes to the debate over strong privacy, we often see cavalier assumptions of equivalence between properties that are actually quite distinct. For instance, there is a presumption that "privacy" and "anonymity" are close relatives, sometimes treated almost as equivalence twins. The same unquestioning acceptance goes to conflating *privacy* with *freedom,* as if they were two sides of the same coin (for example, in the phrase we saw earlier, "Individual freedom and privacy are risky").

Let us take a series of these pairings, with ~ standing for a rough equivalence between two concepts, and string them in a row to get an interesting Platonic chain.

OPENNESS ~ FREEDOM ~ PRIVACY ~ ANONYMITY ~ SECRECY

What? Taken as a whole, the chain makes no sense! It is an oxymoron. A classic case of Orwellian Newspeak. The incongruity gets even better if we add two more "obvious" equivalences, one at each end.

ACCOUNTABILITY ~ OPENNESS ~ FREEDOM ~ PRIVACY ~
ANONYMITY ~ SECRECY ~ UNACCOUNTABILITY

This paradox is one of an infinite number that can be generated with old-fashioned logical reasoning. Ever since Bacon and Galileo, pragmatic science has been hobbled or blocked by such rhythmic mantras, the hypnotic tools of people who believe they can "prove" something by laying indisputable statements in a row. Of course, the trap always lies in the term "indisputable." In this case, something is clearly wrong with some (or all) of the equivalence signs shown. Even when two ideas have some overlap, or a lot in common, that is a far cry from concluding that they are the same thing.

Later, we shall discuss flaws in the equivalence between "privacy" and "anonymity." But for now, let's return to another ill-matched pairing—the all-too-common, all-too-automatic equating of *freedom* with *privacy*. This equivalence is accepted widely, at all ends of the political landscape. Yet as we saw in chapter 3, there is no intellectual or functional justification for an identity-postulate between two such fundamentally different concepts, no matter how often they are uttered in the same breath.

## WE CAN PRESERVE PRIVACY

At this point I am resigned to having to reiterate an important point. Although freedom and privacy are logically separate subjects, there is no dichotomy between those two highly desirable virtues (despite the provocative subtitle of this book). Rather, it is clear that one *results from* the other. A free people may be able to claim and enforce some privacy—the kinds of vital solitude and intimacy we examined in chapter 3—even in an age of proliferating cameras. But first, in order to achieve this, they must have secured the underpinnings of their liberty.

Personal sovereignty—the power to control your own thoughts, ambitions, resources, and lawful actions—surely does require safety from physical interference, especially by the government or other puissant powers. (Recall how Justice Brandeis emphasized that the most crucial form of privacy is not secrecy but "the right to be let alone.")

And yes, those powers might coerce you by uncovering your secrets, when secrecy is the norm, and above all when *their own* cryptic veils remain secure.

But in an environment of transparency, where officials and CEOs must reveal everything down to their tax returns and billing records, the average citizen's freedom will not be enhanced by maintaining a private right to secrete, plot, and ultimately conspire against his or her neighbors. Such a right will not enhance the average person's freedom for one simple reason: *the rich and powerful are sure to be far, far better at exploiting that right than little people ever will be, any time, any place.*

Ultimately, the average person's secrets will be like open books to the mighty, no matter how many mattresses they are stuffed beneath, or which off-the-shelf encryption program shrouds them. Meanwhile, the castle walls of the aristocrat will remain as opaque as stone, guarded by the very same "privacy laws" that were supposed to protect the rest of us.

Alas, the perception of same-breath equivalence between freedom and privacy leads some strong privacy advocates to the bizarre conclusion we saw earlier—that *only* government is untrustworthy. By implication, only our public officials (already answerable to aggressive media and regular elections), need to be watched lest they lie, cheat, or cover up crimes and mistakes. EFF cofounder John Gilmore expressed this implicit assumption in discussing the Clipper controversy: "The ultimate goal of key escrow is to place the rights of the state over the rights of the individual. The ultimate goal of strong encryption (on the other hand) is to place the rights of the individual over the rights of the state."

Gilmore is an articulate spokesman for liberty, but here he neglects to consider the *ideal* role of the state: an agent that serves, and is controlled by, a vigorous, diverse, and skeptical citizenry. True, we may still be a long way from perfecting that esteemed goal, but reflex anti-authoritarianism should not blind us to the great progress that has already been made in the right direction. Anyway, we can only increase our skill at working such a synergy through practice, by acting *as if* we are all owners, sharing the same useful tool.

Moreover, in articulating a well-tuned contempt for one center of authority, Gilmore neglects to consider the reason states exist in the first place. To paraphrase Alexander Hamilton's aphorism (see "An Open Society's Enemies"), we use government to constrain each other, because each of us has very good reason to fear injustice at the hands of a great many other individuals. Injustices that would become instantly and painfully palpable if those democratically defined constraints ever vanished.

What if it is the *cyber*punks, rather than the *cypher*punks, who have it right? In the long run, William Gibson and other visionary novelists may be correct in forecasting wimpy governments during the coming age, an era when those with the cash will make the rules. As Janet Rae-Dupree of the *San Jose Mercury News* recently put it, "Orwell's vision of a Big Brother government was off in one major respect: Corporate America is insinuating itself into our lives even more than government has." Making a similar analogy, Representative Edward Markey said, "Big Brother has simply subcontracted out to corporate America."

Despite widespread evidence of nongovernment abuses, some strong privacy proponents seem to notice just one threat to liberty. They believe that the principles of open access that underpin the Freedom of Information Act should apply just to civic institutions, and not those whose sole declared ambition is acquiring wealth at any cost.

*Though I lean toward a libertarian view on the free availability of information, I cannot simply brush aside the concerns of the FBI or Interpol that the inability to control the spread of certain information can lead to the mass murder of innocent people. The stakes are larger than they have ever been. It is one thing to say we don't like big government and we don't want Big Brother looking over our shoulder. But do we like the alternative of a world where the most ruthless and most depraved can gain access to the means of mass destruction, apply them and get away with it?*

ALVIN TOFFLER

*We're not ultimately more safe if we're absolutely safe from the government, but not safe from private violence.*

AKIL AMAR, YALE LAW SCHOOL

## THE SINGAPORE QUESTION

Another champion of strong privacy, Tom Maddox, makes an argument emphasizing a different equivalence sign, but reaching similar conclusions. Maddox contrasts contemporary America with the island republic of Singapore, where $500 fines for spitting, or failure to flush a public urinal, have reduced the incidence of certain unappealing behaviors, but at the cost of dramatic restrictions on personal freedom. The situation in Singapore received widespread attention in 1994, when a young American, Michael Fay, was sentenced to several strokes across the buttocks with a rattan cane in punishment for vandalizing cars. Talk shows in the United States roiled with clashing opinions, from those calling Fay's punishment uncivilized to others who, according to Maddox, envy Singapore as

a society virtually free of the kinds of routine semi-barbarism that often characterize life in American cities: littering, graffiti, muggings, robbery, theft, and so on. [Supporters of corporal punishment] ask how can the people of the United States presume to condemn practices in Singapore when the fruits of liberty in this country have become so noxious, perhaps even poisonous.

Maddox goes on to present a quandary he calls "The Singapore Question."

> **"How much chaos are you willing to endure in the name of liberty? Or how much liberty are you willing to forfeit in order to secure a more orderly society?"**

Maddox presents us with a vivid and attractive dichotomy. Attractive, because it poses a challenge that we are invited to answer in just one way — by proudly and courageously choosing freedom over order. By proclaiming our fidelity to personal sovereignty, even if some will abuse that sovereignty to become obnoxious or dangerous to their neighbors. John Gilmore put the idea dramatically when he said, "We favor law 'n' chaos . . . we'd rather have more drug dealers and fewer bureaucrats." But the same deep assumption is also shared by many establishment figures, such as international columnist William Safire, who often cites Singapore when explaining the "price" we must pay for freedom.

Is that our sole and obligate choice, chaos versus tyranny? If so, I would be among the first to join Gilmore, Safire, and an impromptu army of outraged anarchists, righteously clamoring for freedom, even at the heavy cost of turmoil and crime. As with the updated Pascal's wager, I'll choose dangerous liberty over coddled despotism any day. It seems a worthwhile trade-off.

But the "Singapore Question" is a false dichotomy! It arises more out of sour romanticism than any reasonable argument. Worse, in proclaiming that we must either be slaves or barbarians, this tendentious posture speaks ill of human nature at its deepest level. It is a view more dour, pessimistic, and patronizing than the darkest cyberpunk dystopia, implying that we have no hope of escaping two opposite but equally hellish destinies.

Fortunately, one can easily show that there is *no* one-dimensional spectrum, ranging neatly from prim totalitarianism to crime-ridden anarchy. Many cultures have won the label "civilized" through generally enlightened behavior by their citizenry, without constantly being policed by hall monitors in jackboots. As in the case of Denmark during World War II, some societies earned the title *despite* jackbooted despots, whom they resisted fiercely while retaining profound traits of civility and decency.

On the other hand, each of us can name examples of nations that mixed oppression with violent tumult, such as the Zaire of Mobutu Sese Seko and the later-renamed Congo, or contemporary Peru, racked by ruthless civil war. In fact, chaos appears to mix quite well with many kinds of tyranny. Even Singapore has trouble living up to its vaunted reputation for order, as attested by observant visitors who see numerous gated and guarded compounds, innumerable homes and apartments with bars covering the windows, and multiple locks on countless front doors.

The deep premise underlying Maddox's contrived dilemma is as insidious as it is patently untrue. For instance, it is not *freedom* that empowers vandals, thieves, muggers, and rapists in late twentieth-century America. These malefactors *have no such lawful right*, no sanction or protected liberty to pillage and terrorize. Those behaviors are already proscribed by laws now on the books. Steep punishment only awaits their being arraigned and proved guilty under law.

Just one thing stands between those miscreants and justice. That one paramount requirement is that they must first be *caught*. It seems such a simple notion. And yet, amid all the acrimonious debate and recriminations over crime in America, this point appears to be missed by both right and left. Consider the most recent general statistics:

- Out of every 100 felonies committed in the United States, criminologists estimate that roughly 33 are reported.

- Out of the 33 reported, 6 are "cleared" by arrest and filing of charges.

- Out of the 6 thus cleared, 3 are prosecuted and convicted, while the others are found innocent or dismissed for lack of evidence.

- Out of the 3 people convicted, 1 person gets prison and 2 get probation.

- The convict has about a 50 percent chance of receiving a sentence of 5 years or more.

Now consider which of these phases receive attention from our politicians. Conservatives keep demanding a spiral of increasingly severe criminal penalties, despite evidence that any sentence greater than ten years is perceived as pretty much the same by most culprits. Beyond that, malefactors have just one desperate priority: to avoid apprehension, whatever the cost. When the state of Florida tried to crack down on armed robberies by raising the penalty for crimes committed with a firearm, the murder rate of convenience store clerks apparently *increased*. Robbers are said to have reasoned that if they killed the witness-victim, they stood a better chance of eluding capture. Against this benefit, the added *potential* penalty for murder seemed inconsequential.

Liberals, on the other hand, tend to concentrate on the social causes of crime. But while this emphasis may be laudable for other reasons, it will never have much pragmatic effect on felony rates as long as impunity reigns, down on the street. If crime pays well, it will be useless preaching to children that criminals should not be role models.

In fact, the statistics we just looked at clearly indicate where the criminal justice system is least effective. Of all the stages listed, it is the miserable 18 percent "clearing" rate—discovering and arresting perpetrators—that bears the greatest responsibility for crime going unpunished. This failure of swift apprehension is what many criminologists see as tipping the "deterrence equation" toward ineffectiveness. In comparison, severity of punishment is a much smaller factor.

Just one indispensable ingredient enables sociopaths to wreak havoc, and it is not freedom. Rather, it is a pervasive cloak of anonymity that lets villains commit acts of barbarism, careless of any real likelihood that they may be held accountable by their neighbors or the law. If protected by darkness, or by masking their identities in a crowd, miscreants will prosper no matter how many fierce, Singapore-style laws a panicked citizenry frantically passes.

*Without* that shielding cloak, lacking that shroud of hidden identity, criminals would shudder under the light. Crime could not thrive. Fear would ebb. And with lessened anxiety, the public might even be persuaded that we need fewer intricate laws, not more. This is not wishful thinking. Historical precedents support exactly this direct, rather than inverse, trade-off between security and freedom, cases where fear has risen in lockstep with repression, or when both liberty and a sense of safety prospered together. (Recall the earlier examples showing that the worst tyrannies almost always followed chaotic episodes under weak governments.)

We could take advantage of this trade-off, but only if we are not hobbled in advance by absurd assumptions about human nature.

### A Need for Pragmatism

Assume for a moment that believers in the Singapore Question are right. Suppose we face an either-or choice between stifling paternalism and liberated anarchy. Let us also posit that the "right" decision is anarchy.

Ah, but just because it is right, will that necessarily be the selection made by the public, especially if they are ever afraid during a time of dire stress?

As a mental experiment, let's go along with FBI director Freeh and try to envisage what might have happened if those bombers had actually succeeded in toppling both towers of New York's World Trade Center, killing tens of thousands. Or imagine that nuclear or bio-plague terrorists someday devastate a city. Now picture the public reaction if the FBI ever managed to show real (or exaggerated) evidence that they were impeded in preventing the disaster by an inability to tap coded transmissions sent by the conspirators. They would follow this proof with a petition for new powers, to prevent the same thing from happening again.

Such requests might be refused nine times in a row, before finally being granted on the tenth occasion. The important point is that once the bureaucracy gets a new prerogative of surveillance, it is unlikely ever to give it up again. The effect is like a ratchet that will creep relentlessly toward one kind of transparency, the kind that is unidirectional. A one-way mirror, under which we are all watched by officials, from on high. The place that we called *city number one* at the beginning of this book.

Even many of those who express distrust of government admit the trend is unstoppable. Following the disaster that destroyed TWA flight 800 near New York City in July 1996, Speaker of the House Newt Gingrich said, "I believe the more there is terrorism, the more pressure we're under to find systematic ways to solve it." Other government officials have made pronouncements that should serve as weather warnings.

- Vice President Gore: "World wars have been won by advantages in cryptography and we are not entitled, having taken the oath that President Clinton and I have taken to protect and defend the United States of America, we are not entitled to throw caution to the wind and say, 'Well, commerce is the only thing that matters here.' We have to respect the need of our law enforcement officers and national security agencies to be able to protect our national security and so we have been in vigorous negotiation with the industry."

- The Justice Department wants to be able to determine the location of a cell phone caller within a half second and determine whether the user has sent or received voice mail or made conference calls. All these capabilities lie within technological reach (and some have already been used in Switzerland). The deputy director in charge of the FBI's New York City office said, "The privacy people say we shouldn't have this information, but the notion that we in law enforcement should not be able to take advantage of the technology is a crazy notion."

- Upon learning that a complete tutorial on bomb making is available online, including diagrams and tips for passing though airport security, Senator Dianne Feinstein declared, "When technology allows for bomb-making material over computers to millions of people in a matter of seconds, I believe that some restrictions on free speech are appropriate."

- Or take this comment made by former FBI deputy director for investigations, Oliver "Buck" Revel: "If we are unsuccessful in preventing significant acts of terrorism because of a failure to take prudent precautions, the ensuing public demand for action could result in Draconian measures."

These sample statements range from prudent and reasonable to some-what chilling. What they share is a general outlook that seems at first sight to be diametrically opposed to that held by many crypto-advocates—a view of government as an appropriate and necessary defense against those who might bring civilization crashing down around our heads.

And yet, there is a commonality of spirit that neither the hackers nor the bureaucrats would ever willingly acknowledge. Each of the officials quoted here sees the tribe they are part of (government) in a virtuous light, while exhibiting suspicion that some "others" (foreign nations or terrorists) will accumulate the power to do harm. Their natural urge is to use enhanced vision to control that perceived threat, just as the cypherpunks would rein in the menace *they* worry about—government itself. Both sides say, "You can trust *me*. The real danger is over yonder."

The consistency of this pattern amply demonstrates the chief point made in chapter 5: no individuals can be relied upon to hold *themselves* accountable.

That is something we must all do for each other.

But let's get back to the question at hand, which is, can we prevent some future panic or security crisis from alarming the public so much that it willingly surrenders some or all of its freedom, in hope of escaping mor-tal danger?

Now it happens that I agree with the rebuttal of Pascal's wager. Hypo-thetical events, even potentially dire ones, should concern us far less than defending liberty. On the other hand, we should also contemplate whether our pious philosophical positions are *robust* enough to withstand even one disastrous event. (And we will surely experience many disasters, over the years ahead.) Will the public want to hear Platonists prattle ornate rumi-nations about dead French philosophers, while watching some horrific scene of urban destruction on their television screens?

One thing is certain: panic won't be quelled by exhortation alone. I believe a free people *can* be persuaded to accept risk, provided the balance strikes them as sensible and reasonable. (See the discussion of risk analysis in chapter 6.) But grand moralistic statements will seem like droplets in a whirlwind of recriminations if the public ever feels naked, frightened, and betrayed. Politically, it will be impossible to resist an avalanche of legisla-tion granting authorities sweeping new powers, going vastly beyond the scope of pathetic little Clipper.

By then it will be too late to establish a working relationship of negotiated trust between the Justice Department and groups such as the Electronic Frontier Foundation, or to protect freedom by instituting safeguarding systems of reciprocal transparency so that the government's new powers of vision are matched by equally fierce measures for oversight.

Someday we may look back on this era as a time when rational compromises might have enhanced both security and liberty, but those compromises were refused because each side was so busy self-righteously being *right*.

Unless the negotiations to which Vice President Gore referred are undertaken with goodwill by all sides, that tragedy could very well loom on our horizon.

Or else . . .

Or else, maybe not.

Ironically, all of this may matter very little in the long run. The whole argument could become moot for basic technical reasons. As we shall see in chapter 9, some very smart people have begun suggesting that there is simply no such thing as a reliably unbreakable code. Given enough resources, and new innovations on the horizon, any encryption scheme might be threatened, at least enough to deny its users the carefree sense of inviolability promised by crypto-proselytes. Moreover, even the strongest encryption method might be bypassed by a variety of techniques *outside* the computers, in the physical world.

If even a small part of this proves true, anyone relying with total confidence on a favorite downloaded or store-bought scrambling routine—counting on shuffled bits to resist the skeleton keys of great and powerful institutions—might as well supplement that reliance with prayer, a flannel blanket, and a well-sucked thumb.

> *Anonymity on the Internet has an important benefit. It can enable those who fear political or social reprisal to speak out.*
>
> JAMAIS CASCIO

> *Cypherpunks don't want real confrontations or discussions, or they would reveal their identities and make it possible to respond, as most flamers do. . . . Anonymous communication makes verbal violence easy.*
>
> JON KATZ

## THE ALLURE OF SECRECY

Let me start this section with a disclaimer. *Not all secrecy is harmful.* As we saw in chapter 3, there are many times and places when each of us needs to withdraw into a private world, or share specific information or personal musings with a friend, or engage in some private endeavor unobserved and unbothered by others. In fact there is a very real danger, for reasons that we shall cover later in this book, that the coming technologies of pervasive vision may push us too far toward transparency. So, for the record, let me say that a wide variety of secret transactions will be worth trying to safeguard in the next century. For example:

- The relationship confidentiality presently enjoyed by patient and therapist, or attorney and client, or pastoral worker and parishioner should be protected if possible.

- In a dangerous world, states will continue striving to conceal vital technical, tactical, and strategic information from potential foes (see chapter 10, "Global Transparency").

- Professionals need some space to work in without feeling a glare of relentless scrutiny. If all meetings must be open and recorded, participants will feel less free to offer original or impulsive suggestions—"to see if an idea flies"—out of fear that they will forever be branded for some offhand remark. Already, many officials of the U.S. government will not take written notes, lest they later be subpoenaed.

- Sometimes information must be kept secret from the public temporarily, such as when a sunken Revolutionary War gunboat was discovered underwater in Lake Champlain in June 1997. To keep the wreck from being raided by souvenir hunters, the exact location was withheld until a formal expedition could explore the site first.

- It has been pointed out that secrecy is currently the default condition when it comes to communication by mail, or telephone, or in conversing with someone at a restaurant. Most of the time, we engage in such activities with a fair degree of certainty that the information exchanged was not snooped by hidden eavesdroppers or busybodies.

In all such cases, pragmatic solutions may be worked out during the coming years, because the secrecy involved does not necessarily lead to *unaccountability*. For instance, therapists in some states and countries must override confidentiality if they have strong reason to believe that a violent crime is about to be committed. Most Western nations put time limits on the secrecy of important documents, opening them for scrutiny by historians after the set period (often far too generous) has expired. Even many crypto-advocates do not deny the lawful right of justice officers to snoop the mail and telephone traffic of criminal suspects, after fulfilling all the requirements of due process. (As one cypherpunk blithely put it, "They are welcome to try.")

Unfortunately, as we have seen all too often, the natural drives of self-interest and human nature tend to cause those involved to push, or drift, toward ever-increasing amounts of secrecy. People can be counted on to use some genuine need as an excuse for greater concealment than is really necessary for the accomplishment of their beneficial task. While individuals and groups would err toward granting themselves *more* shelter from accountability, it is in society's interest to counter this trend by pressing for less.

What must any pragmatist (or person with compassion) conclude from all of this? Many innocuous kinds of secrecy may find a place in a decent civilization of tomorrow. But since the natural drift will always be to justify too much, we are well advised to be wary of such trends and lean the other way for safety's sake.

Nowhere is this more true that when it comes to the most dangerous form of secrecy. The one kind that is all too often aimed directly at eluding responsibility or accountability.

### Anonymity

Radio essayist Garrison Keillor once described the pleasure he felt, coming to New York as a young man, to find that he could move along the streets and avenues unknown and unnoted by the crowds. It was strangely liberating after life in a small town, where everybody knew everything about everybody else. Such experiences were common in this century. For generations, Americans left village gossips and busybodies behind to dwell among countless strangers, picking and choosing whom to know, while everyone else remained as nameless as clouds, or trees, or blades of grass.

This experience is directly related to the topic of encryption. Indeed, the spread of pervasive anonymity in coming decades will rely heavily on new technologies for creating ever more cryptic secret codes. There is great overlap between those who favor unrestricted private and commercial use of encryption and those who advocate anonymity as a sovereign right, or even a great benefit to society at large.

Lately, pundits and commentators have been telling us that the information superhighway will expand and enhance this power to wear masks and veils. People can sign on to Internet discussion groups using pseudonyms, much like the "handles" that became popular back when CB radios were all the rage. There are many highly publicized ways to send messages or retrieve data anonymously—either for legitimate purposes or in order to make a nuisance of yourself on the Net—and, supposedly, with complete impunity.

And yet, anybody with enough technical background knows better. Nobody can guarantee that a pseudonym will hide your true Internet identity from a truly first-rate hacker who is adamant about finding it out.

An analogy might be made to caller ID, which lets a person, on hearing her telephone ring, consult a little screen to check the number of the person who is calling. So informed, she may choose to ignore the call, or program her modern answering machine to reject a specific party, or to identify someone making harassing phone calls. Caller ID has proved a boon to those wanting some degree of control over whose voice can barge into their home at any hour of the day or night, though it was delayed in California and some other locales because of fears that the technology violated the privacy of *callers*, another example of how privacy is subjective and contingent on each person's point of view at a given moment.

Callers can pay for a service that will deny the recipient this information, that is, they can opt out of caller ID. Recipients can, in turn, refuse to accept "blocked" or anonymous calls. In fact however, the digital identifier tag is never actually removed, even by the blocking service. It is still there in the ring signal, masked by a single "privacy bit" informing the recipient's telephone company that the outgoing number is blocked. It is up to the local company how diligently that blocking request is honored. Consequently, related services such as call trace and call return may still work. This makes it likely that somebody with enough electronic savvy can rig up his or her own illegally souped-up caller ID unit to pluck the information. So-called protection for callers can be pierced by a technical elite, or anyone wealthy enough to hire that kind of professional help.

The story of caller ID is just one example of the murkiness that accompanies attempts at anonymity. We saw earlier how some of the most important Internet communities have been forced to forbid anonymous postings, in order to foster an atmosphere of adult discourse. But the implications range far beyond just propriety and failings of mutual respect. Many thinkers and commentators have explored the pros and cons of concealed identity. Some see great promise in a future when people will feel free to interact with others behind masks. For instance, Marc Rotenberg, executive director of the Electronic Privacy Information Center hopes to see "technologies of anonymity" that liberate citizens to act with truly liberated autonomy. "We need systems of commerce that allow people to buy things without being identified and that allow people to travel in cyberspace without saying who they are. And we need [the] law to keep pace with the technology."

We already touched briefly on anonymous remailers, which enable users to dispatch messages without leaving an electronic trace that others might follow to the source. Several years ago, Johan Helsingius pioneered this kind of communication by running the largest anonymous remailer service in the world, anon.penet.fi, based in Helsinki, Finland. His service rerouted close to ten thousand messages a day, concealing as many as a quarter of a million identities, stripping messages of their originating name and address before forwarding them. Users of his service included suicide counseling groups, and human rights organizations, as well as posters of illicit and obscene information, software thieves, and people eager to speak out without their true names being known. Ultimately, the Church of Scientology persuaded Finnish authorities to force out of Helsingius the identity of an individual who was posting CoS-copyrighted material on the Internet through his remailer, an event that led him ultimately to shut down his system.

There are two interesting lessons to be drawn from the "Helsinki incident."

1. Tens—and perhaps hundreds—of thousands of people who thought their secret identities were secure later found out that they were not. Their faith in one "anonymizer" proved misplaced. Will others turn out any better?

2. As events like this become more commonplace, and larger nations place restrictions on wholesale anonymity, little countries (for example, banking havens) will step up to provide Internet secrecy for a fee.

Combine these two facts and one can picture a dark possibility. Regular people will use anonymizing services that are wholly owned and controlled by elites whose own secrets are secure, but who can use their hidden influence to pluck out the name of any little guy, any time.

Anonymity also pervades the vast and popular realm of chat rooms, discussion groups, and "multi-user worlds" on the Net. Author Dorian Sagan describes how, while researching a range of Internet experiences for an article, he felt liberated by portraying various personae online, including a thirteen-year-old girl.

On the Net, you can work your personality like a novelist imagining a character. The only caveat is that, like the novelist, you must be consistent in your lies if you want to be taken seriously . . . the longer you talk to people lying about their identities, the greater the chances that you will cross them up in their lies: while electronic transvestitism is admittedly easier than its real-life counterpart, it still takes effort, motivation, and skill to put up a convincing false front for any length of time. . . . To make the most of my new identity I had to do what other fly-by-nights and pathological liars do—I had to escape from the limited audience of those who were getting to know me all too well.

Sagan appreciated "cyber-reality's ability to reproduce the erotic atmosphere of a Renaissance masquerade, since behind our masks we are no longer as inhibited as we would have been had our real selves been on the line."

If this sounds just a bit effete and abstract, that does not make it any less a form of "self-expression," to be defended according to our already existing social compact, which protects eccentric behaviors that do not harm others. Moreover, there is also a serious and pragmatic side offered by those arguing in favor of anonymity: it frees individuals to exercise personal sovereignty by performing legal actions for their own benefit, actions that might be thwarted by embarrassment or social sanctions, if true identities were known.

While some champion the advantages of anonymity, others cite its downside. Professor Trotter Hardy, at the College of William and Mary, says, "Anonymity is power and I think it will be abused on the Net." The White House computer network has received anonymous death threats against the president. Electronic "mail bombs" (Trojan horse programs and viruses) can now be sent anonymously, and individuals can pirate software without being traced. There is concern that digital cash, a form of electronic money that allows for untraceable financial transactions, will usher in new forms of racketeering and money laundering. An Internet site called Fakemail let people write mail from an imaginary e-mailbox, using an alias. Commonly used names included Bill Gates, Bill Clinton, Elvis, and God. The service shut down when numerous people traced harassing mail back to its source, but others have taken its place.

Anonymity also has a long-standing role in demagoguery, as when Senator Joe McCarthy claimed to have scores of independent sources to verify his wild accusations of Communist infiltration into the U.S. government. Sources that he "could not reveal"; nevertheless, the claim lent him credibility with some citizens. We have seen anonymity at work in countless fabrications and calumnies, from the *Protocols of the Elders of Zion* to the *Turner Diaries*, but it also plays a subtly powerful role in some of the most respected modern media journals. Speaking about unsigned newspaper editorials, E. M. Forster wrote that "anonymous statements have . . . a universal air about them. Absolute truth, the collected wisdom of the universe, seems to be speaking, not the feeble voice of a man." In other words, they have the flavor of *ex cathedra* statements, pronounced from the throne of impersonal expertise. On the Internet, this same effect can be seen at Internet Oracle, where people e-mail questions, and others anonymously answer, leading to a kind of collective wisdom, almost like the composite voice of Teilhard de Chardin's parousic deity, but without any real omniscience to back up the illusion.

According to Esther Dyson, publisher of *Release 1.0* newsletter and a prominent EFF board member, "The damage that can be done by anonymity [on the Internet] is far bigger than in any other medium. In the end, you need to be able to get at somebody's identity to enforce account-ability, and the question is how do you also enforce freedom of speech and freedom from prosecution for unpopular opinions."

Although conceding that anonymity has some drawbacks, Michael Godwin explained his reasons for supporting far-reaching levels of protec-tion for the widespread use of concealed identities, calling it ". . . well-established that anonymity can be used to serve social, as well as anti-social ends." He went on to cite examples such as twelve-step addiction recovery programs, which use anonymity to help sufferers talk about troubling issues, or participants in various alt.sex. discussion groups, who may be try-ing to work out their confusion about matters of sexual identity. Whistle-blowers can feel a need for anonymous cover before reporting secret abuses by corporations or state agencies. Foreign nationals may wish to discuss controversial issues on the Net without fear of retribution by violent oppos-ing factions, or by a repressive government back home. Even the U.S. Supreme Court has ruled that anonymity can be somewhat justified if it seems needed to let individuals step forward and assert other, more explic-itly protected rights such as free speech, especially in an environment where fear of retribution may be well founded. In deciding the case *Talley v. California* in 1960, the Court stated, "It is plain that anonymity has some-times been assumed for the most constructive purposes."

Let me stress that I understand and sympathize with all of the above-mentioned positive uses of concealed identity. Especially when it comes to whistleblowers, society's interests absolutely require that we provide means and venues for individuals to drop anonymous "tips," leading investigators toward hidden malfeasance, a case where anonymity is the direct servant of accountability.

Chapter 8 discusses practical ways to safeguard most beneficial types of anonymous transactions.

And yet, as we saw in earlier chapters, anonymity's dark side is more than merely troubling. Almost by definition, anonymity is the darkness behind which most miscreants—from mere troublemakers all the way to mass mur-derers and would-be tyrants—shelter in order to wreak harm, safe against dis-covery or redress by those they abuse. In fact, it might be hard to name any famous villains—even those standing atop a pinnacle of state power, like Hitler—who did not rely at least in part upon anonymity to enhance their own (or their henchmen's) power to destroy. The glare of light can be irri-tating to the honest, but it is devastating to knaves and despots.

Moreover, the lack of any clear consensus about anonymity is particularly telling. While some think we already have too much, others claim that anonymity's drawbacks are simply the price that must be paid in order to protect civilization's unconventional or downtrodden members. Meanwhile, purists extol anonymity as a fundamental right, to be safeguarded no matter how many disadvantages may accrue.

Does a purist approach ever make any sense?

Sometimes. When it comes to free speech, the beneficial outcomes— adversarial accountability, plus the empowerment of individuals to enforce their own sovereignty—are overwhelmingly evident. Meanwhile, the liabilities of open expression—shrillness, plus some pornography—are merely irksome, and easy enough for a great commonwealth to endure for the sake of a broad principle. In other words, free speech is protected at least as much by a commonsense tabulation of pluses and minuses as by preaching its quasi-mystical attributes. Even a pragmatist can see that some things must be defended with the ferocity of a zealot.

But when it comes to anonymity, even most proponents can envision worst-case scenarios of "too much" sheltering villains so effectively that it tears civilization apart. In other words, anonymity is not a chaste essence, but a tool that can prove useful in service of specific desired ends.

> *While a man remains in a country village his conduct may be attended to, and he may be obliged to attend to it himself. . . . But as soon as he comes to a great city, he is sunk in obscurity and darkness. His conduct is observed and attended to by nobody, and he is therefore likely to neglect it himself, and to abandon himself to every low profligacy and vice.*  ADAM SMITH, REPUTATION

### The Place of Secrecy in Human Life

Back in chapters 2 and 5, I talked about what appears to be the deep-seated motive driving many strong privacy advocates, a motive that I share down to my core. To all of us, it is a matter of ultimate self-interest that we defend society's tolerance of eccentricity, the power of individuals to explore corners of the human experience without undue interference, so long as they do not impede or harm others. Where my friends and I part company is over which commodity will best defend this tolerance—shadows or light.

I have made this point before, but while we are specifically discussing anonymity, let me reiterate with an analogy.

If you see a person engaged in some bizarre activity in your neighbor-hood—perhaps performing a strange dance, or erecting a mysterious device, or just mumbling to himself—which of the following two scenar-ios is more likely to arouse feelings of unease, and possibly a temptation to oppose or suppress that person's behavior?

1. The person is wearing a ski mask and heavy overcoat. It is a total stranger who refuses to explain anything about his background, motives, or reasons for being there.

2. It is someone you know. A person whose life history is familiar, who readily answers questions, and whose past quirky episodes turned out to be at worst irritating, and sometimes even amusing.

Which of the above is likely to provoke tolerant shrugs, as people smile about "our harmless local crackpot"?

Which one will provoke mothers to call in their children, and fathers to gather in a wary, murmuring crowd?

Which "eccentric" is more likely to be let alone?

This provokes a final, rather basic question. Where does anonymity rank in the pantheon of "natural" human qualities?

Consider the ancient Cro-Magnon tribes of our ancestors, engaged in a life of hunting and gathering back in the late Pleistocene. These tribes were probably varied and sophisticated, each with its own complex internal culture. For instance, one can envisage a range of attitudes toward self-expression, with some clans holding open campfire discussions while oth-ers bowed to the whim of priests, or a charismatic chief. All of these are well-recorded and typical human behaviors that anyone can mentally picture.

What is hard to imagine is *anonymity* playing much of a role in those days! Among the human beings that a cave dweller encountered during that long epoch of sparse populations, only total strangers would be anonymous—and then largely in the role of enemies. (I cannot prove this, of course. It is a mere thought experiment, worth contemplating for a while.)

In our evolutionary background, there was probably a lot of give-and-take that prepared our brains to deal with issues of persuasion, cooperation, com-petition, friendship, coercion, deception, and many varied kinds of account-ability. But when would we have had much practice using *anonymity*, except as a way to dehumanize enemies, making it easier to justify doing them harm?

Many of today's anonymous practices do precisely that. They help peo-ple dehumanize others, thus making it easier to dismiss their concerns or harm them.

The point is especially significant because some of anonymity's strongest promoters talk as if their recommended path is a natural and obvious one. But in fact it is unexplored territory. No other culture ever encouraged a daily use of hidden or false identities to the extent that we may see in the coming century.

Even if this new kingdom of masks and shrouds eventually turns out to have all of the advantages that its boosters extol—and none of the disadvantages that worry me—it remains a daunting territory, without clear trail markings, or any prior history of human habitation. It might be reassuring if our guides showed a little humility and caution while urging us down such a road. After all, only time will tell if they are right.

> *My second fantasy is to make encryption ubiquitous, common-place, and therefore unthreatening.*    MICHAEL GODWIN

## DEFEATING THE TRICKS OF TYRANTS

Most of the strong privacy advocates I have cited so far, though profuse in their accusations against state authority, would willingly concede that they are members of a civilization worth defending, and that our debate should be over *how* to defend it. There are others, however, who would make no such admission—who believe they already suffer under a foul and oppressive totalitarianism. Several of this type were profiled in a gushing article that *Fortune* magazine ran, in September 1997. Among these self-described "cyberlibertarians," Walter Wriston, former Citibank chairman and author of *The Twilight of Sovereignty*, foresees a decline of national governments through the power of technology, especially encryption, which will be key to transferring social and economic power from nation states to the PC-packing populace. "The government can't do much about it. It's another thing slipping through their fingers," Wriston said.

Others featured in the article—some involved in setting up Internet secrecy services for the rich through banking havens such as Anguilla—have emphatically called for an end to overbearing governments. Making cypherpunks seem like tepid compromisers, these neo-anarchists alternate between fiery denunciations against villainous bureaucrats and expressions of serene confidence in their own inevitable triumph.

Earlier, we discussed the allure of the underground, a proud, romantic righteousness that lets some people have the best of both worlds—living as coddled Brahmins in a gentle, fun society, while at the same time ranting against the culture that subsidized and spoon-fed them lessons of indignant individualism in every movie they saw or novel they read. Although such attitudes may seem churlishly ungrateful, let me emphasize again:

ingratitude is largely *irrelevant*. Society's anti-error immune system requires that some individuals be doped on irate pique. Alas, outrage endorphins can also foster profoundly inaccurate mental impressions of the world. T-cells become useless if their subjective visions are detached from objective fact.

In this case, it all boils down to a two-part question.

1. Are we presently living in a tyranny? If so, what methods will best combat it and offer hope for eventual freedom?

2. If we are not presently living in a tyranny, what methods will best prevent one from coming about?

Now I'm not going to get into a raging argument over whether the current situation in the neo-West, or America in particular, is already one of wretched despotism as some contend, or if instead it is an awkward-but-promising adolescent phase along the way from a wretched past to a better, more liberated tomorrow. What matters here is whether encryption truly does offer the liberating power proclaimed by its most radical promoters, or if that technomystical belief is just more hogwash, distracting them (and us) from the grownup work that will make oppression forever impossible.

*Suppose, for the sake of argument, that we are already living in a tyranny.* Or that the basic institutional tools are already in place, simply awaiting a coup, tomorrow or the next day, that will put us under some dictator's thumb. What are the methods of control used by despots, and will encryption help against them? At first sight it seems obvious that an ability to mask our electronic exchanges in static will demolish a despot's ability to govern. But first impressions aren't always accurate, nor will simply saying something over and over again make it so.

Turning our gaze to the past, we see that nearly all forms of tyranny have counted on the same ultimate methods of control: indoctrination, subornation, terror, surveillance, and informers.

By controlling state institutions of *indoctrination*—media, religion, and education—dictators and kings would cast propaganda spells to instill loyalty in the populace. This did not have to be perfect in order to create a situation in which the resentful would have to be careful and keep their voices low, lest an indoctrinated neighbor overhear and report them.

*Subornation* involves using secret police methods to trick individuals into situations where they suddenly find they are already working for the Master, with no choice but to continue. A good example would be several United States Marine Corps guards at the American embassy in Moscow, during the 1980s who, having broken regulations by having affairs with Russian women, gradually found themselves drawn into a web of blackmail and forced to engage in ever more serious levels of espionage against their own country. East German spymaster Markus Wolf was expert at using this technique, sending eighty or more "Romeos" to West Germany in the 1960s, targeting lonely divorcees who worked for sensitive agencies.

*Terror* is the use of state power to torment individuals and make them crack. Torture is one method. Another uses threats against family members. There is a long history of underground cells being discovered and cauterized because the police broke just one individual and began unraveling an ornate skein of intrigue.

Encryption offers no relief whatsoever against these first three methods.

As for *surveillance*, Wriston and his compatriots claim to have a magic shield against being spied on, just because their data and telephone conversations *might* be safely encrypted into undecipherable noise. Of course, this is pure cybertranscendentalism—that syndrome where technophiles mistake a machine (or code) for the real world. As we shall see in chapter 9, encryption would have stymied hardly any of the surveillance techniques used by the Gestapo, or Beria's NKVD, let alone the far more advanced abilities that will be available in an age of gnat cameras, data ferrets, and spy satellites. The sole exception is the power to scramble telephone conversations—and how long do you think the masters of an overt dictatorship will let *that* continue before they make it a capital offense?

The final method used by tyrants, *informers,* is by far the most important and effective. The long history of human despotism has refined a system of carrots and sticks—lavish rewards for those who turn in their friends, combined with insidious methods to make people fear they are about to be informed upon and conclude, "I'd better do it first." Saddam Hussein is a master of this art. A typical Iraqi officer—call him Captain Ali—will be approached, perhaps once a year, by a close friend offering to bring him into an anti-Saddam conspiracy! Nine times out of ten, this will be a deception, arranged by the secret police. Ali had better report the contact at once, or be arrested as a traitor. Even his best friend, who hates Saddam, will do this to Ali, because it is a routine duty of Iraqi officers to take part in such ruses. (When Ali's turn comes, he will be wired for sound, and sent to try and lure a comrade into treason. Failure to act convincing is punished.) This means real enemies of Saddam can scarcely get organized. Even if you know your friend shares your anti-Saddam attitudes, you cannot be sure this particular overture is not a trap. You must hand him over!

Such techniques are the result of many centuries of development by "leaders," applying human ingenuity to support a long tradition of domination. In their appalling ignorance about these details, cyberanarchists demonstrate that theirs is a doctrine of faith, not knowledge or pragmatism.

Will encryption avail at all against such dire techniques of enslavement and repression? I am going to surprise some readers by answering *yes*. Even under the gaze of the efficient Gestapo, Angelos Evert, who served as police chief of Athens during its World War II German occupation, saved many Jews from arrest and deportation by issuing them identity cards with Christian affiliation. Many other heroes of that time performed similar miracles using tricks of deception and false identity. Even in the United States, this practice has sometimes served the greater interests of justice, as during the blacklisting era in Hollywood, when some film writers used noms de plume to evade McCarthy-era witch hunts.

Positing for the moment that we may face some hypothetical future era of high-tech repression, I have no doubt that secret codes would be valuable to any underground movement. There are clever tricks, for example, "steganography" (see chapter 9), that could help conspirators contact each other without it being easily known that encryption is used. Such techniques would allow extremely savvy hacker-rebels to communicate without knowing each other's identities. In fact, I hope and pray that if we ever do face a true tyranny, the most brilliant hackers will go to work. Operating with subtlety, patience, and utter practicality, they may save us all.

But in order for these insurrectionary techniques to be effective, they will have to be executed by true geniuses. You aren't going to defeat a major state security apparatus by using an off-the-shelf package of Pretty Good Privacy (whose designers will be tortured into revealing any weaknesses in the program). Nearly all of the "anonymizers" will be police fronts. In fact, the brilliant methods used against such an Orwellian state will have to be original, innovative—exactly the sort of tricks that truly splendid hackers will be toying with throughout the coming age of amateurs, exploring the techniques just for the fun of it.

But this will not be a job for impatient or self-righteous zealots. Those who today proudly extol the "ghost shirt" armor of ciphered communications will not be part of any future underground movement, because they will be the first targets of any new secret police. Subornation, terror, and the use of informers will shatter the cells of romantic transcendentalists— those who fool themselves into thinking that encryption is anything more than a tool, one of many that must be used sparingly and delicately during the long struggle, if we ever find ourselves oppressed by ruthless tyrants.

In fact, though, we do *not* presently live in a dictatorship. No proof of this could be more decisive than the existence and popular-hero status of cypherpunks! Moreover, a strong state that is carefully watched by a confident and diverse citizenry is far less likely to become despotic than a weak one that is unable to serve as a flexible tool for delivering justice and a fair competitive playing field. As we discussed earlier, Weimar Germany, Romanov Russia, and China in 1948 are just a few examples of weak states that transformed, almost overnight, into systems of overwhelming control.

The job we face is far more complex and grown-up than the cyber-romantics' cozy fantasy of a brave resistance movement. We must take a culture that is already moderately free, and ensure that liberty increases, at a steady rate.

*Now, assuming we are not presently living in a tyranny, what methods will best prevent one from coming about?*

Here is where arguments for accountability become paramount. This entire book is based foremost on one premise, that government is only a *method* of using power, a tool that can be seized and abused by any number of self-justifying cabals. Despite simplistic slogans cherished by those who say utopia will emerge if we all start babbling in indecipherable tongues, the future is going to be a lot more complicated than that.

> *First they came for the hackers. But I never did anything illegal with my computer, so I didn't speak up. Then they came for the pornographers. But I thought there was too much smut on the Internet anyway, so I didn't speak up. Then they came for the anonymous remailers. But a lot of nasty stuff gets sent from anon.penet.fi, so I didn't speak up. Then they came for the encryption users. But I could never figure out how to work PGP anyway, so I didn't speak up. Then they came for me. And by that time there was no one left to speak up.*
>
> WIDELY COPIED INTERNET APHORISM, A PARAPHRASE
> OF PROTESTANT MINISTER MARTIN NIEMÖLLER'S
> STATEMENT ABOUT LIFE IN NAZI GERMANY

## THE DEVIL'S OWN DICHOTOMIES

Just one more point to raise, before moving on to the next chapter. In our foregoing discussions, we've seen a lot of people talking about trade-offs. While some take ideological positions of starkly righteous purity, most others, from FBI agents to EFF activists, have based their arguments on a single shared notion. This common belief is that we must skirt our way along a knife blade, delicately and cautiously seeking just the right balance between the needs of society and what is good for individual citizens.

Not long ago, Professor Dorothy Denning of Georgetown University argued that the government's need for potent investigative tools weighed heavily enough in an age of terrorism to justify the Clipper initiative. Michael Godwin was fierce in rejecting this position, propounding this interpretation of the U.S. Constitution: "The framers recognized, as we all must recognize, that every guarantee of individual rights has a price: Governments have to sacrifice some efficiency to preserve those rights." He went on to assail people like Denning for talking earnestly about a social contract that strikes an equilibrium between individual rights and government necessity: "But the whole point of the Bill of Rights was to *remove* some rights from any balancing act. The framers knew that, without some kinds of strong guarantees, it is invariably easy to justify a small diminution of individual rights when one is concerned about public safety."

While this righteous statement contains some wisdom, especially in warning about the potential for a slow diminution of rights, it should come as no shock to the reader that I also find much to disagree with.

First, and most awkwardly, the word *efficiency* was never used, or even implied, by the framers in the context described. Moreover, here we see again, as in the "Singapore Question," a pernicious underlying assumption that there exists a direct link between tyranny and efficiency! A relationship that cannot be proved, and probably does not exist outside the minds of its believers. Open societies may seem inefficient because they are raucous and noisy, but by almost any measure of actual wealth creation, problem solving, error avoidance, or overall productivity, those nations that follow a strategy of transparent accountability have been dramatically more successful than closed ones, such as the former Soviet Union.

In fact, any careful reading of the *Federalist Papers* shows that the framers knew all about the advantages of accountability, seeing it as a virtue that would simultaneously benefit both the individual *and* the state. Vigorous protection of particular liberties in the Bill of Rights would benefit all citizens, as well as the republic that was their chattel and tool.

Someone would have to pay for all this, and the Constitution ensured that it would be *leaders*. The state's high officials, not to be confused with the state itself, had to sacrifice something. Not "efficiency" (which is actually enhanced by some kinds of accountability). Rather, they had to give up the smooth pleasure of unencumbered, unsupervised command that had always been the temptation and privilege of rulers in times past. A privilege that often led them down spirals of self-deception and eventual ruin for the states they governed.

Moreover, anonymity, secrecy, and privacy are never mentioned anywhere in the U.S. Constitution or the Bill of Rights. These were not rights set aside for pure protection. They are given only a weaker, implicit shield deriving from the Fourth Amendment's ban against state thugs barging into people's homes. In an earlier chapter we asked why such values were virtually ignored, while freedom of speech got precisely the sort of fierce, uncompromising guarantee that protects against diminution. Strong privacy aficionados sometimes explain this apparent lapse by claiming that privacy is now under greater *threat* than it was two hundred years ago, when people simply took it for granted. But that is mistaken, as anyone who ever lived in a small village can swiftly attest. In countless ways, today we have more genuine privacy, and more power to enforce it, than people of the rustic 1780s. Yet, instead of now taking it for granted, we talk about privacy so much more than our ancestors did.

The real reason that free speech was (and still is) defended so fiercely is simple. As long as open debate is protected, people may vote about other things—like privacy law—and change their minds later on. As long as we retain free speech and citizen sovereignty, there is a chance to back out of mistakes. We can experiment and fine-tune other matters, debate consequences, criticize the present situation, and then maybe shift course yet again. But there are some things we can never dare to fiddle with. If free speech itself is compromised for any reason, we might lose that precious power to argue and reevaluate—to discover that we made an error, and correct it. For that reason above all, both citizens and the courts have defended speech rights with fierce ardor. It is the one trait of our society that enables us to leave our options open.

All right, then, anonymity is like privacy, a contingent desideratum. Does this mean Professor Denning is right, that hard and unpleasant choices have to be made? Should we simply ignore the ideologues and concentrate instead on working our way through an endless quagmire of hard, practical trade-offs? Shall we render unto the government certain powers that we know will erode particular freedoms, while staking other liberties with DO NOT TRESPASS signs?

I respect Dr. Denning. She and I are pragmatists who agree on the desirability of negotiation and consensus. And yet, I must demur this time, because once we start saying that we can buy some security over here in exchange for a little freedom over there, the path to ruin lies open before us.

*Say what?*
The reader may be understandably confused.
*I thought Brin favored compromise . . . and now he's talking like a purist!*
Let me explain. I *am* a pragmatist, and as such, I refuse to get trapped into either-or choices that are flawed and dangerous in their very essence.

Do you remember our earlier discussion of memes? Those were ideas that (according to Richard Dawkins's fascinating theory) may have certain traits enabling them to act like infectious or parasitic organisms, taking root in host creatures (human minds) and then spreading out from there (through persuasion) to infect others. I have referred to several possible memes in the course of this book, such as the cyber libertarian insurrection fantasy discussed in the previous section. Some of these contagious notions manifest as simplistic but widely held ideologies—such as the models of Marx, or Freud, or Ayn Rand—that describe humans as far less sapient than we are clearly capable of being.

An entire class of these pesky notions are what I call the *devil's own dichotomies*. These insidiously simple social models basically assert the same thing: that people are forever constrained by pairs of polar (and often equally vile) opposites, forcing humanity always to sail between some dreadful Scylla and its equally loathsome Charybdis.

The "Singapore Question," which proclaims that we must either be protected slaves or else liberated savages, is one example of such a dichotomy. So is the atrocious concept that freedom is somehow at odds with competent government, or that eccentrics can survive only if protected by antisocial masks, or that liberty and efficiency must each suffer in order for both to eke along.

It is the odious worldview of those who believe in zero sum games, the dour theory that each win must be balanced by a loss, and therefore the best one can hope for in life is a tenuous, break-even.

Well, I do not accept it, and neither should you. This conviction that we are all engaged in an endless, tense balancing act, a dangerous dance down a narrow knife edge between chaos and dictatorship, is enticingly melodramatic. But it is also an exhausting and ultimately futile image. One that says, "Sooner or later, you will all take one wrong step and tumble off the tightrope, left or right. Then, zap! It will be over. Chaos or dictatorship will follow, for you and all of your posterity."

It is a ridiculous notion, unfitting for a civilization filled with ambitious, proud, and compassionate people who have spent most of their lives *having* their cake, *eating* it, and *sharing* it, too! People who have dined at a fine table, grown up with liberty, seen the dawn of both science and ecological sensitivity, filled their minds with ripening knowledge that took millennia to germinate, and yet now find themselves coaxed to accept awful, pessimistic models of human nature that bear no relation whatsoever to the wondrous civilization that surrounds them.

Excuse me for being greedy, but I want freedom *and* good government. Both a flourishing economy *and* a well-cared-for earth.

A society that is diverse *and* communal . . .

. . . that offers *both* privacy and accountability.

One that can afford a big conscience, along with lots of neat toys.

In fact, despite the relentless propaganda about "trade-offs," it should be evident by now that all five of these pairs will either prosper together or wither on the same vine. They are linked. They share the same blood supply.

What evidence can I offer for such a strong and iconoclastic statement?

The same evidence I have used several times before.

Us.

*We* are all the evidence anyone should need. If you write down all ten of the desiderata that I just listed, our present civilization clearly has more freedom, wealth, diversity, privacy, accountability, and neat toys than any other large society across the ages. People might argue heatedly over whether we are more communal, or if our moral conscience is adequate, but I see little evidence that other cultures, ancient or recent, did much better. Moreover, the millions who nowadays complain that we should care more are in themselves strong evidence that we are trying. Even when it comes to tending the earth, our marks may be better than you at first expect.

The point is that we score high on so many scales at once because these factors are synergistic with each other. And even if they weren't, our best course would be to act as if they were.

As a parent and a citizen, I must demand both liberty and safety. More-over, I refuse to *choose* between prim tyranny for my children, on the one hand, and a world of violent anarchy on the other.

Shrugging aside such cruel dichotomies, why don't we just move on? Getting practical, let us set about doing what our civilization is best at— solving problems.

# THE PROBLEM OF EXTORTION

As we have seen, there are two branches to the strong privacy movement. Both seek to solve worries about freedom and privacy by reducing information flows—in effect by enabling some people to prevent other people from knowing things—but they would do this in strikingly different ways. One faction would pass new laws, establish European-style privacy commissions, and unleash bureaucratic organizations to enforce ornate rules controlling the use of personal data. The other wing expresses an abiding libertarian distaste for anything resembling government involvement. They would empower private parties to create masks, false identities, and secret messages via technological means, especially encryption.

In this book we discuss many real and potential flaws inherent to both kinds of strong privacy. But one fault in particular is so glaring that it has received worried attention from the cypherpunks themselves. That problem is *extortion*. In the early-to-mid-1990s, several extended e-mail discussions took place among key figures in the crypto community concerning the following scenario:

· · ·

*You are a blackmailer or kidnapper. You have in your possession something that is precious to someone else—either an important piece of information or an abducted loved one—and you want to extort payment. Do the new tools of encryption offer you a chance to commit the perfect crime?*

· · ·

Nowadays, kidnapping and blackmail are extremely hazardous to attempt in a peaceful Western society. They are dependent on secrecy, which can be broken at several stages: when making the threat by letter or telephone, when physically collecting the ransom, or when cashing the payment (spending potentially marked or bogus currency). Police experts have acquired many sophisticated techniques to expose a perpetrator's identity at any of these phases.

But these are exactly the steps that some believe could be made foolproof through new methods of ciphering. By allowing both messages and money to be transformed into untraceable strings of electronic bits, secret codes can assist an extortionist in several ways.

1. The demand or ransom note can be transmitted in such a way that only the victim will be able to access or read it, thus preventing inadvertent discovery by outsiders or agents of the law.

2. By taking advantage of multiple anonymous remailers, the sender can conceal perfectly his or her location and identity.

3. Replies by the victim can be posted (in code) at open bulletin boards, so that the extortionist could read them without giving himself or herself away.

4. Finally, payment, in the form of ecash [see "All the World Is a (Digital) Marketplace," after chapter 6] can be sent encrypted so that the extortionist is able to pick it up, decrypt it, and spend it without a trace.

Encryption also enables the criminal to create a "calling card"—like the trademark glove left behind by the jewel thief in *The Pink Panther*. Such a unique identifier would be useful for many kinds of extortion, for instance, transmitting arson or death threats ("Pay up or I'll burn your factory"). Those warnings that are backed up by a credible track record will be taken most seriously. Only this calling card will be untraceable by even the most meticulous forensics expert. The technique also enables foolproof corruption of public officials, such as fire inspectors, since the bribing party remains perfectly concealed and immune to sting operations.

It is a tribute to the intellectual honesty of some cypherpunks that they raised this issue themselves, not waiting for their opponents to bring it up. Alas, their deliberations produced only a slim set of recommendations:

A. Don't read unsolicited mail. If nobody gets the extortionist's threats, no one will pay him, and the racket doesn't work.

B. Never pay. Arrange things so that some third party must approve all your transactions (and you, in turn, do this for some stranger). Each "guardian" will prevent payment of extortion threats, even if the victim pleads for the money to be sent. If extortion never pays, it will stop being tried.

C. Assume the worst. If it is a kidnapping, assume the loved one is dead. If it is blackmail, tell everything before the blackmailer can.

D. Make your life so secretive and shrouded that no enemy or predator will ever know that you are rich enough to pay anything or know how to reach you with an extortion threat.

E. Rely on police competence in finding other kinds of clues.

These solutions swing back and forth from extravagant versions of spasmodic "openness" to desperate measures of extreme secrecy. The principal problem with suggestions A, B, and C is that they benefit only society in the long run. They do little for the individual victim of a particular kidnapping or blackmailing, and so there is no incentive for a victim to cooperate. A clever extortionist will set a price that the prey is willing to pay rather than risk a far greater harm.

Solution D appeals to those radicals who are unabashed solipsists and would resign from civilization if they could. Their ultimate aim is to be not only "extortion-proof" but also "judgment-proof"—immune to accountability to taxing authorities, civil courts, or their neighbors. In fairness, most crypto enthusiasts consider this position both antisocial and wildly unfeasible.

The intractability of the extortion problem vexes the most thoughtful members of their community. In the words of Hal Finney: "My worry is that 'crypto-anarchy,' rather than being the somewhat 'tamed' anarchy we usually discuss in the context of privatized law and such, may come to resemble the more prevalent public conception of anarchy, a constant tooth-and-nail fight of all against all. Cryptography will provide a nearly perfect shield behind which all but the lowest-rung criminals can hide, and in such a system justice is impossible."

Finally, when the discussion settled down, they were left with suggestion E, which seems rather strange coming from a faction whose chief agenda is to blind government and deny police powers to the state. Yet, in an irony that we will explore in chapter 9, solution E is exactly what may work in the years to come. Advancing technologies and improvements in professional skill may either bypass encrypted masks or render them far less effective than today's boosters envision, eliminating the extortion threat by shining light wherever perpetrators try to hide.

In fact, Finney and others point out the hand holding the flashlight need not belong to an officer of the state. Illumination may be cast by private services or even the amateur sleuths we described in chapter 2. Or indeed by countless citizen-neighbors. Solving the problem of extortion does not have to entail reckless flight in the opposite direction, surrendering vast powers to bureaucrats.

Throughout this book the principal question has not been whether accountability will flow—it will, no matter what cyber-transcendentalists say—but whether it can be cast in all directions, pinning down the police at least as much as the rest of us. There is still time to negotiate such a covenant, though the opportunity to work out a deal may pass by if we wait until a wave of masked extortion threats and unsolvable terrorist violence drives citizens into a panic, seeking refuge as the people of Weimar Germany did, in the arms of the nearest demagogue.

# PART III
# ROAD MAPS

*How extraordinary! The richest, longest lived, best protected, most resourceful civilization, with the highest degree of insight into its own technology, is on its way to becoming the most frightened.*

A. WILDAVSKY

# PRAGMATISM IN AN UNCERTAIN WORLD

*Numerous mechanical devices threaten
to make good the prediction that "what is
whispered in the closet shall be
proclaimed from the housetops."*

SAMUEL D. WARREN AND
LOUIS D. BRANDEIS, 1890

*Any high-integrity identifier represents a
threat to civil liberties, because it
represents the basis for a ubiquitous
identification scheme, and such a scheme
provides enormous power over the
populace. All human behavior would
become transparent to the State, and the
scope for non-conformism and dissent
would be muted to the point envisaged
by the anti-utopian novelists.*

ROGER CLARKE

Might society use practical ingenuity to sidestep those outrageous dichotomies we discussed in chapter 7? When it comes to identity, for instance, is it possible to safeguard *beneficial* uses of secrecy without sheltering harmful acts and evil men?

In fact, some creative combinations of accountability with limited anonymity have been around for a long time. For example, the venerable secret ballot merges substantial transparency where it is needed— through poll watchers, open inspection of voter rolls, and extensive citizen involvement—with a narrow zone of sacrosanct privacy, the ballot itself, where the voter's conscience may be expressed without fear of betrayal or retribution. In other words, the fact that a transaction (voting) has taken place, and by whom, is openly verifiable, but the details of personal choice are not. Even where arguments rage, for instance, concerning improper registration by noncitizens, the debate concerns some local enforcement laxity, not the overall approach of mixing fierce accountability with narrowly focused privacy.

Lately, fear of jury tampering has led some U.S. jurisdictions to institute "juror anonymity," disguising panelist identities through numbered ID badges, partial visual barriers, and legal rulings ascertaining that jurors are not "public figures." Yet the names are on record so that both defense and prosecution teams can investigate and rule out potential bias. Neutral outsiders may also view the records under regulated conditions. Similar mixtures of confidentiality and assigned responsibility are seen in other areas, such as scientific peer review and witness protection programs.

We shall explore later this principle of considering the legitimate needs of groups and individuals to keep either narrowly defined or temporary secrets. Also in this chapter we will discuss a range of pragmatic tools that might help us achieve a more open society in the next century. But first, let us examine the problem of identity, and a misconception that is causing far more aggravation than it should.

## NAMES, PASSWORDS, AND SOCIAL SECURITY NUMBERS: THE PROBLEM OF IDENTIFICATION

At times a storm of controversy can arise, provoking irate calls for urgent action, only for people to realize much later that the whole situation arose out of a simple mistake of definition. Take the public angst now raging in America concerning Social Security numbers (SSN). Most legal U.S. residents carry one of these nine-digit figures around for life. Yet the Social Security card is not officially a national identification document. While citizens of other lands take such things for granted, many Americans share a traditional hostility toward the notion of a universal ID card.

In theory, the SSN has a single purpose: to track benefits under a retirement and disability insurance system that does not even encompass the whole population. Still, for many Americans, who shift home addresses—

and sometimes names—like changes of clothes, their SSN is the one unique tag that will accompany them through vagabond lives. And universality came a step closer when the IRS began requiring that toddlers get an SSN in order for their parents to claim a dependent deduction at tax time. Some civil libertarians foresee a hated national ID certificate, ending the cherished American fantasy that a citizen might conceivably live and thrive within the boundaries of the United States while somehow remaining invisible and uncounted by any government.

Of course, only a zealous fringe believes such invisibility will remain possible during the next century. Still, the SSN has become *the* symbolic threat to modern privacy in the United States. Corporations want it for quick, efficient correlation of facts from many sources. State governments now use SSNs to find absconded parents and extract delinquent child support, and some use the SSN as a driver's license number. Credit agencies say they need it to foil defaulters because, while it is legal to change your name without filing documents, you cannot do likewise with your SSN. All sorts of quasi-official agencies—from your college, to your bank, to your HMO— prefer this number for tracking purposes. In fact, hardly a week goes by without someone finding a new application for the handy, nine-digit figure.

If it is so useful, why do people get livid when they learn that some data clearinghouse is storing and selling the SSNs of millions of people? The Lexis-Nexis Corporation was caught doing this in 1996, until protesters sent enough e-mail to shut down its Internet server for a while. So outraged were consumers and privacy advocates that bills were introduced in Congress, banning use of the SSN to identify records in any commercial database. Other laws already restrict use of the number by federal agencies.

The reason for all this heated reaction involves a lot more than some quirky American mythology about free-spirited autonomy, inherited from the wild frontier. It is pragmatic and worrisome. A stranger who knows your SSN can *harm* you.

When a customer telephones his or her bank to transfer funds between two accounts, or perhaps to order a new credit card, an SSN will be required to validate the transaction. So a criminal who learns your SSN might fraudulently check your bank balance, or have a "replacement" credit card sent to his hotel room. Access to your SSN can also be the starting point for that irksome modern nightmare, identity theft. In other words, some privacy paranoia is soundly based!

And yet, this whole controversy is rooted in misconception, a failure to note the distinction between a *password* and a *name*.

•   •   •

It seems that people living in Korea have a problem. A large majority are born into just five patronymic family lines. If a Korean's surname isn't Kim, or Park, just three more guesses will likely nail it down. The same winnowing of family names happened in China, only on a vastly larger scale. Within the Peoples' Republic dwell more than 80 million people with the surname "Li" or "Lee." Together, the five most frequently used Chinese appellations cover at least 300 *million* human beings, the equivalent of nearly everyone in the United States and Canada being named Smith, Jones, Williams, Cohen, and Diaz. Moreover, the *personal* names given to Chinese boys and girls are restricted by tradition and numerological beliefs. This results in considerable confusion. In one recent Chinese case, the victim of a crime, the trial judge, and the perpetrator all had the same full name, as well as some poor fellow who spent weeks in jail before he could prove he was a different guy.

Things are a bit better in the West, but that is no guarantee against error. Newspapers frequently report instances where the wrong man was arrested with the same name as some fugitive. (Some years ago a bank put a lock on my funds while a credit agency pursued another David Brin, whom I never met.) This is why companies want to use SSNs. As an identifier, each SSN is supposedly unique for each resident or citizen of the United States. That makes it a nearly perfect, unambiguous *name*, supplementing the one your parents gave you. A separate way of professing, "This is the unique and only me."

Unfortunately, through laziness or lack of imagination, many American institutions long ago began using the SSN for an entirely different purpose, with obnoxious consequences.

Look at it this way. When you approach a stranger and introduce yourself, you are *asserting* a certain identity. The other person has a choice. She can say, "I'll take your word for it." Or else, she can reply, "Prove it to me!"

In daily life we take such assertions at face value. Why should people lie? But matters are different for financial institutions. It is incumbent on banks and fiduciary agents to be skeptical. The assertion of identity must be followed by verification. A driver's license or photo ID may be visually compared to your face, if you are present. In telephone transactions, or on the Net, a skeptical party demands that you state or transmit some datum that only you should know. Whether a single word or a hundred-digit number, this datum serves as a *password*.

Names and passwords have distinct qualities. Your name lets someone else call up specific records, or personal memories. A password or verifier proves that you have a right to make decisions on the named person's behalf. A name never (or rarely) changes. You want it to be stable, so that the chronicle of your activities can be cohesive—like your life. Even if you try to leave all your mistakes behind, it is in society's interest that some continuity be maintained, so that basic obligations are met, and others won't be blamed for things you do.

Most of the time, there are few dire repercussions if others know your name. Even strangers who overhear it at a party or look it up in a phone book can be irksome, but seldom harmful. In fact, many people yearn to achieve "name recognition," to be known for virtues or accomplishments (or infamy) and even become a household word. Often, humans take pride in imagining that their names may continue to be spoken after death.

A password is different in many ways. A predator who acquires it can swiftly do harm—snoop, change essential records, bill phone calls to your account, or even steal your life savings. Lots of people know your home address (a name), but the metal key to your front door is a kind of password whose loss might conceivably endanger your life. If you suspect it has been copied, you don't change addresses; you change the locks. If you fear a password is violated, you throw it away and get a new one.

Clearly, the SSN is a *name*. Unique, permanent, and difficult to change, its aims are specificity and constancy, distinguishing one "Mary Q. Smith" from another. The SSN lacks a single trait of a password!

Then why is it used that way?

Because in earlier times, people knew their own SSN, but almost no one knew anybody else's. To banks, it seemed a convenient test for use during telephone transactions—like your birth date, or another quaint verifier, your mother's maiden name.

Nowadays, birth dates and mothers' names are routinely published in *Who's Who*-style bibliographic reference works, which have expanded their scope in recent years far beyond the ranks of the rich and famous to cover almost all people of modest prominence in their field of endeavor. More important, the number of remote transactions has grown exponentially. How many times can you tell your birthday to strangers before the datum becomes useless as a password? Whenever you purchase by credit card, either in person or by phone, there is a chance that someone will copy the number and use it for fraud.

But at least you can change credit card numbers! With your birth date or SSN, all it takes is a single lapse for the whole world to know it the next day, and forever after.

A daunting prospect, to which the logical answer is . . .

". . . so what!"

Okay, in the short term, it *is* a serious matter. But only because of that lazy misunderstanding by major institutions. As a name, your SSN cannot harm you, even if a million thieves know all nine digits. Only the archaic practice of using it as a verifier-password makes its discovery dangerous.

So long as that practice continues, no American's savings are truly secure.

Perhaps ancient peoples understood this distinction between names and passwords better than we sophisticated moderns do. Under some religious or mystical systems, individuals possessed two names: one for daily use, plus a secret designation known only to intimate relations. According to these beliefs, an enemy who learned your hidden or "true" name could use it to inflict grievous harm. The means in those days were subjective and magical, and today they are technological, yet eerie similarities remain. You can get in trouble if some enemy learns your password!

To deal with this problem, we must do three things.

1. Get used to a world in which passwords will be routinely changed.

2. Experiment with new technologies, including certain types of encryption such as digital signatures, to make the use of password-based transactions both reliable and convenient.

3. Ensure that predators, and abusers of the system face a high certainty of getting caught, resulting in a world where passwords merely verify what we already know—that we are safe.

The contrast between a name and a password goes to the core of many modern privacy problems, and their potential solutions. Names are what help keep people accountable. They should not enable others to harm you. Names verify the fact that a transaction is taking place, which is a completely separate matter from giving *permission* for the transaction to proceed. Names are inherently open things. We base countless decisions on having fair knowledge about the reputations of others—whether they are skillful, credible, or reliable, for instance. On the other hand, passwords set transactions in motion. They require secrecy, even in a transparent society.

Alas, SSNs aren't the only case where both functions have been mixed, creating confusion and danger. Take the de facto national ID card, your driver's license. Many people have their license number printed on bank checks, alongside their home address, as both a time-saver and a convenience for retail clerks. When simply written down, the license number serves as a supplementary name, to help the store find you if the check bounces. The number by itself *verifies* nothing. Only when your face is compared with the picture on the license does an act of confirmation take place, though high-tech criminals keep getting better at counterfeiting, while states strive to upgrade the cards in order to thwart them.

When you choose to give strangers your telephone number, it becomes a password, offering them the power to intrude on you at home. But what about when you call out for a pizza? Often nowadays (in California) the restaurant begins by asking your phone number, to check their computer records. If your household ordered from them before, you won't have to repeat lengthy delivery instructions. Now your phone number serves as a *name*, much easier for the restaurant to type in without error than having you carefully spell out "Thomasina Lumumba Chang-Jones" each time you call out for triple-cheese on a thin crust. Instead, the clerk obligingly asks, "Do you want pineapple and anchovies, like last time?"

If I order from a gift catalog, do they want my phone number because their filing system needs it to find me? Or because they want to have their autodialer robot call and breathlessly explain their latest sale, every week, during dinnertime, for the rest of my life? (A clear case for legal restraint of information flow!)

Visionaries speak of a time when each of us may need only a single telephone number through our entire lives. Already some telecom companies offer to bounce calls from your office to home to car, and then to your portable unit, depending on where you are (and whether you choose to be "in"). It will be ridiculous to keep secret a number that is equivalent to your name. Whether this second name is liberating, or feels like an indelible tattoo on your arm, will depend on how the system works. The devil lies in the details.

Let me reiterate. If a datum is permanent, like the SSN, it has no business playing the role of verifier. In fact, the clever men and women designing new "electronic cash" systems have decided that the ideal password will be used just once! Applying methods of public key coding, each "e-transaction," from a dollar to a major shift in the national debt, will be enciphered by pairs of prime numbers more than a hundred digits long. Numbers the user will never glimpse, because all the fancy encrypting and decrypting take place *behind* the transaction, in an exchange of "locks" and "keys" that should be seamless and foolproof.

Am I dubious that this will actually work as planned? Well, yes and no. Although this book expresses skepticism toward most forms of secrecy, it seems clear that encryption will have a major role in the coming world economy. At least, a great many smart people say so.

There is no conflict. My point has always been that encryption and electronic secrecy, like all fruits of science, have potential for both good and ill. No inherent threat to openness or liberty lurks in using codes to verify a purchaser's identity, just as we will see that it is reasonable to encrypt an occasional sensitive document, so long as doing so does not lead to a pervasive and pernicious *habit* of secrecy, blinding us all in a fog of bitter static.

Ideally, we will learn how to distinguish open accountability of names (the fact that a transaction is taking place) from the prim confidentiality of passwords (giving permission for the transaction to go forward). When those passwords become both huge and ephemeral, perhaps banks will finally stop asking anachronistic, sexist questions about maternal "maiden names."

Some other traditional verifiers may be on their way out, for example, using handwritten signatures to prove identity. For one thing, many children are no longer taught the art of cursive writing. Anyway, a handwritten scrawl can be fabricated, not just by photocopying but by taking several samples of a person's signature, then having a computer randomly morph between those data points, generating a result that is different each time, and yet stylistically a good semblance. Companies like United Parcel Service have been collecting digital images of signatures for years on handy little portable units. Their security measures have held so far; still, it is only a matter of time before your scribble becomes too widely known to rely on as a password anymore.

Fingerprints are another old standby that should remain useful for catching run-of-the-mill crooks. (In some states, thumb imprints are now routinely required of people applying for mortgages, or welfare.) But their effectiveness, too, may not endure against a technological elite. Well-financed criminals will almost certainly develop those artifices long seen in spy thrillers: an artificial fingertip covering, crafted by adroit machines to fool some of the new print readers that are coming on the market. It will work . . . until countermeasures regain the lead. A similar arms race between ingenious felons and legitimacy verifiers will complicate every other proposed ID system, perhaps all the way to on-the-spot DNA appraisal.

A new field of *biometric identification* uses the body itself as a password. Retina scans, facial contouring (your face is your PIN), electronic fingerprinting, hand geometry measurement, voiceprint verification, body odor parsing, wrist-vein recognition, and keystroke dynamics are among the techniques being examined; the hope is to build an array of traits so unique to each individual that the combination cannot be thwarted by even the most diabolical spy. In 1997 the Intrust Bank of Wichita, Kansas, began using *voice biometrics* to identify telephone customers by unique characteristics of speech. England's Nationwide Bank is testing ATMs outfitted with scanners that verify the iris patterns of a customer's eye. Eastman Kodak has discovered a way to compress the image of a human face two-hundred-fold, so that a recognizable visage can take up a mere 50 bytes. This will allow a credit-card bearer's image to be stored on the unused portion of the card's magnetic strip and be displayed on a smart cash register whenever a purchase is made.

Biologists have long used electronic tags to track wildlife specimens, studying migratory paths and living habits. Earlier we saw how miniaturized transponders are available to have implanted under your pet's skin. Data about the animal's health can be downloaded at close range, and chips may be detectable at ranges up to a mile. NASA and the military have looked into applying this technology for astronauts, soldiers, and others heading into danger. Many nursing home residents with dementia wear bracelets that trigger an alarm if they wander outside. Tags can identify a stolen motorcycle, or shoplifted retail items, as well as bales of wool, ski lift tickets, parking passes, meal cards, and club ID cards. We already mentioned dashboard transponders providing quick access to toll roads and bridges, which may let others monitor your car's precise location on the road. In late 1997, a bill was given preliminary approval by the Republic of Korea National Assembly, mandating that an electronic ID card, containing personal information on a chip, be issued soon to all citizens over age seventeen. These cards would be required in all dealings with public offices, banks, police, and other official agencies, creating an efficient and pervasive electronic record that would follow citizens everywhere.

Some techno-buffs envision all of the above being combined in a single capsule inserted subcutaneously at the birth of each new citizen. As journalist Simson Garfinkel put it, "what a pain carrying all those cards around. Wouldn't it be far simpler to implant a chip into your shoulder and be done with it? Stay tuned."

All of this gives some people the willies. Televangelist Pat Robertson sees evidence of approaching Armageddon. "The Bible says the time is going to come that you cannot buy or sell except with a mark placed on your hand or on your forehead. . . . It is happening, ladies and gentlemen, exactly according to the Book of Revelation."

In the United States, such fears have been cynically manipulated by groups trying to delay even small-scale plausibility studies of using SSNs to enforce immigration laws. When the U.S. Senate considered authorizing a pilot investigation to test methods of verifying employment eligibility—a long way from establishing a national ID card or worker database—Grover Norquist, a conservative lobbyist, led a campaign using that "666 scenario" to stir opposition. Said Norquist, "It was great. We had our guys walking around with [barcode] tattoos on their arms. It drove [Senator] Simpson nuts because . . . the implication was he's a Nazi."

And yet, these delaying tactics will not prevent the coming of a new century and millennium. The ID verifiers will arrive—if not mandated by government, then seized upon eagerly by industry and private persons who have no other way of corroborating the identity and reputation of a myriad strangers. If they are outlawed, new tools of encryption will mask their use, as corporations employ them anyway.

You don't have to be a fundamentalist or Luddite to be troubled. Some are concerned whether these new technologies, and their supporting software, will be robust or reliable. Even if the front end interface is perfect, system managers will still wake up nights sweating that their futuristic sensors may be suborned by a clever hacker, or by some disgruntled employee using a "back door" to change records at a basic level. We are entering an age when innumerable science fiction scenarios may come true, in whole or in part, creating decade after decade of interesting times. Technological fixes will come with fanfare, disappoint with unexpected flaws, and be replaced with others that are advanced with equal amounts of ecstatic hype. And when a method finally *does* work reliably, some will proclaim it as the onset of some wretched Big Brother tyranny.

Or, as novelist Thomas Pynchon put it, "Once the technical means of control have reached a certain size, a certain degree of being connected to one another, the chances for freedom are over for good."

Must this happen?

Obviously, any group that is allowed to monopolize such techniques will gain profound, possibly permanent, advantages. Yet trying to impede their arrival will be futile, like stopping the ocean tide with fortifications made of beach sand. Hence, for the sake of both survival and freedom, we may have to apply these tools universally—*especially* on the mighty. If the tycoon and bureaucrat have it in their power to tap a key and get my location or my dossier, then I want to be able at least to find out that they are looking, and possibly to look right back at them. Already this principle is starting to take shape, in regulations that let consumers know who examines their credit records, and allow them to track which files IRS employees access. Only if this process of reciprocal accountability advances further will we stand a chance of having a little real privacy. The mighty won't dare look too often, if their only prayer of being left alone lies in helping to create an ambience of courtesy and restraint.

In the long run, our best defense may be to avoid relying overmuch on nifty tools. This can be achieved in a society where the overall daily habits of life are above board. Where accountability shines into so many corners that the occasional lapse won't matter. Errors and malfunctions in such a society won't cause economic collapse, because the fact *that* most transactions took place will be open knowledge, observed and recorded in many diverse ways, allowing their reconstruction after the dust settles. (See "The End of Photography as Proof of Anything at All" at the end of chapter 1.)

As for ingenious criminals who steal successfully via secret trapdoors, they will languish over the long run, if they cannot spend their ill-gotten gains in a world of light.


All abstract ponderings aside, we must still make some practical decisions about countless murky areas of modern life. For instance, once the distinction between names and passwords grows clear, there should emerge greater awareness of how pointless it is to pass laws against corporations or government agencies using the SSN to identify individuals in databases. True, a universal nine-digit code would let big-time data users exchange and correlate information about citizens in a swift and unambiguous manner. But banishing the SSN won't prevent such activities, because computers are now so fast and sophisticated that they don't have to be efficient anymore!

Suppose a typical person—Mary Smith—has entries in several dozen databases gathered by her supermarket, video store, credit union, HMO, and so on. Ostensibly, each company keeps no more information than it needs for that specific line of business. Yet, should they choose, the corporations would have little trouble sifting and comparing information about Mary, even without an SSN, simply by using her given name plus profiling statistics to separate this "Mary Q. Smith" from all others with the same zip code who are *not* thirty-six years old with three children and no moving violations but two outstanding parking tickets. . . . Passing laws to forbid a uniform nationwide ID system would make such activity more cumbersome and secretive, but rules won't prevent it for long. In fact, banning the SSN from use in database correlation will only ensure that errors do occur. Ludicrous errors. Or tragic ones, as when a computer "guesses" wrong and mixes up crucial medical records.

It makes more sense to allow universal use of the SSN as a safe *name*, but then to separate databases with unique password codes for each *type* of information. Such methods are under active study. It is a better idea, yet I doubt that even such improved measures will remain effective for long.

The truth of the matter is that we will never succeed in preventing pow-erful institutions or individuals from collecting as much information about others as they can. Nor will we stop folks from constantly sifting, correlat-ing, and drawing conclusions about their neighbors—even things that are "none of their business." That is because the underlying impulse goes beyond issues of power or profit. It is deeply rooted in human nature.

### Gathering and sorting data is what we do!

From gossip to sport statistics to obscure facts about the O. J. Simpson case, we are habitual, incurable information junkies. Whatever a person's education level, chances are you'll find some area of knowledge that each individual claims to be "expert" in. At times, the pleasure people derive from this kind of mental activity can get heady, and for those with access to the most information, the high can be intoxicating. The scruffiest com-puter hacker, operating out of his parents' basement as he explores far-off crevices of cyberspace, is no different from the chief of database systems for Experian Credit, Inc. One can easily picture both of them, late at night, chortling softly while rubbing their hands, "More data! Ooh, give me more!"

Seriously, hasn't our common experience with the failed "drug war" taught us a lesson? When dealing with deeply rooted human desires, we are better off trying to regulate and moderate, rather than standing obsti-nately in the path of a juggernaut, crying out, "Stop!" Driving a seductive activity underground is no way to ensure that it won't be abused. Especially if corporations start setting up their databases in banking havens free of reg-ulation or moderating influences, using the SSN without any supervision or accountability to the individuals involved. Just as drug prohibition cre-ated a vast illicit economy run by remorseless criminals, so will an under-ground information network develop if we legislate bans and sanctions against groups of people "knowing things."

Anyway, as we already discussed, common sense shows that it matters less what a person knows than what she or he does with the knowledge. It is our actions that determine both moral and legal culpability. Knowledge may be power. But it is action that determines true good and evil.

*A right of anonymity is a troubling legal concept, especially when it comes to information that may cause damage, and the person or institution originating the message may need to be held responsible.*

ANNE WELLS BRANSCOMB

## ANONYMITY VERSUS PSEUDONYMITY

As we saw in the last chapter, defenders of anonymity often put the dilemma in stark terms. Citizens must have the power to conceal themselves at will behind encrypted messages and shrouded identities, or tyranny will almost surely ensue. If crime, spiraling rudeness, and a general breakdown of accountability are the price we must pay, then so be it, because some kinds of free speech can take place only when people can wear masks.

Although I have only contempt for foolish dichotomies, it *is* true that veiled identity can sometimes make the difference between candor and muzzled silence. We cited some examples in the last chapter. Others might include a telephone information line for teens seeking to avoid contracting sexually transmitted diseases, or a forum for battered spouses, or an honest engineer blowing the whistle on his company's defective parts. In each case, the glare of instant identification might deter those hesitant first steps from the shadows. Moreover, one of the great, unsung benefits of the Internet has been to welcome so-called wallflowers, people whose shyness often cripples them in a physical world filled with handsome, articulate strangers. Many claim to have at last learned to open up online, growing confident and outspoken while clothed in the protective attire of an assumed name.

Despite the central thesis of this book, that transparency is beneficial to all levels of society, we must surely protect the power of private individuals to do certain things under cover of feigned identities. And yet, to repeat Esther Dyson's remark earlier about the damage that can be done by anonymity: "In the end, you need to be able to get at somebody's identity to enforce accountability, and the question is how do you also enforce freedom of speech and freedom from prosecution for unpopular opinions."

Is this a true trade-off, as the encryption aficionados would have us believe? Or another false dichotomy? Might it be possible to answer Dyson's question by encouraging beneficial uses of concealed identity, while discouraging those that threaten a breakdown of civil society? One suggestion that offers promise is called *pseudonymity*.

Imagine that you feel impelled to assume a false identity for some limited purpose that is legal, yet fraught with potentially unpleasant repercussions (either embarrassment or fear of reprisal) dire enough to deter you from coming forward openly. Is there some way to get the shelter you need without wrapping yourself in a blanket of complete immunity from the consequences of your actions? Can people be offered masks that conceal innocuous behaviors yet allow them to be held accountable if they break laws or harm others?

In my 1989 novel *Earth,* I suggested just such a system, now rumored to be under development, in which any individual or corporation could purchase a pseudonym from a licensed outlet, such as a bank or perhaps even the Electronic Frontier Foundation. Multiple sites could be used, as with key escrow, in which no single cache holds the key to connecting a real person with the pseudonym. Once registered, this false name might be used for a wide variety of endeavors on the Internet, even some commercial transactions. For all normal purposes it would provide anonymity, since the bank or issuing authority would be prohibited, under threat of severe sanctions, from revealing any primary information about the original purchaser, except by court-ordered warrant or other due process of law. Only strong probable cause of criminality or a major civil judgment could force disclosure—and then under strict conditions and safeguards.

This scenario is closely related to the "trusted third party" approach to the escrow storage of encryption keys discussed in the last chapter. And again, competitive pressures would make commercial registration services fiercely defensive of their clients' rights, since those with a reputation for tenacity would attract the most customers and do a profitable business selling pseudonyms. For their own prestige and self-interest, cache services would force the police and courts to follow every procedure to the letter.

The obvious benefit of pseudonymity is that these false identities are intrinsically limited. If used to commit crimes, they can be traced. If used to fling slander, the mask will not avail against rightful redress in civil courts. And yet, they would remain useful in many financial transactions, and they should protect any eccentric whose sole aim is to express unpopular opinions, or to associate with whomever he or she pleases without opprobrium.

Moreover, there would be a secondary benefit. Every pseudonym could come with a parity check, or tag, to let it be known that this name *is* a pseudonym.

Again, I know that my strong privacy friends will object. But look again at the legitimate users of assumed names that I listed above, and in the previous chapter. Would any of them be appreciably harmed by this admission? By having it be known that a person was participating behind a John or Jane Doe disguise? No more than any of the people who write to newspaper advice columnists, like Ann Landers, under assumed names. In fact, whole realms of the Internet already swarm with pseudonymical personae engaged in swapping opinions, confidences, and outrageous lies. Anyone entering such a domain should be forewarned that extravagance is its great resource, not necessarily truth. Anything gleaned in those areas should be taken with several cups of salt.

Meanwhile, other territories of cyberspace will copy the example of The Well, requiring that participants stand forth openly, wearing their own names. Even pseudonyms are insufficiently accountable in such territories. With all anonymity disallowed, the virtues of civility and credibility come to the fore. In such "adult" venues, there is less extravagant bombast or posturing, and higher reliance on the veracity of what other people tell you.

In other words, while there should be sanctuaries on the Net for unrestrained and even outrageous speech, there must also be realms for grownups, where the unit of exchange is fact or supported argument, backed by reputation, not rumor or innuendo. Anyone attempting to enter under a pseudonym would be told, politely, that this is a territory ruled by light. No "tagged" personae are allowed inside.


There is another, even more controversial, way in which some transparency radicals would consider limiting pseudonymity, that is by setting time limits. Each pseudonym would come with an expiration date—perhaps five, ten, or twenty years. After that period elapsed, the link between a mask and its owner's true identity would be released. Why add this measure? To retain some residual coupling between a person's deeds and the consequences of those actions, even if they were legal at the time. In this way, we would model real life, in which cruel gossips can eventually be forced to own up to the hurtful things they said. There has always been a connection between our actions, the effects they have on others, and the repercussions that occur later, when we reap what we have sown.

There is precedent for this in the laws granting U.S. government agencies authority to maintain secrets. These already operate under time limits, which have been reduced in recent years. After expiration, only the most severe threats to national security are supposed to justify continued concealment of facts. Again, government must be held to a much higher standard, but might the same overall principle apply, especially to other potentially dangerous centers of power?

On the other hand, do you really want your great-grandchildren to read what you posted to alt.abuse.recovery—or alt.sex.bondage—back in your days as a confused teenager? Perhaps some kinds of transparency should be put on the table for discussion—and then left alone.

In fact, an argument can be made for the opposite measure: forgetfulness! For letting the past swallow up uncountable little mistakes that weren't criminal, but nevertheless can pile up in memory as great, simmering heaps of remorse and/or resentment. There is already a tradition in many library systems to purge borrowing records automatically as soon as each book is returned. This is not done primarily to stave off tyranny, but to give clients and readers a little more peace of mind. Perhaps the same principle might apply to other records in the future. If, after twenty years or so, nobody has come up with an accountability-related need to look at a given file, then it might be consigned to dust, and the electrons freed to participate in different bits and bytes.

Earlier we saw that cameras are becoming more like us—more numerous, more "curious," and capable of lying. Maybe the computers and capacious databases will join this trend, learning how to both forget and forgive.

If it seems at times that I am fence straddling, that is because I do not claim to have all the answers. While this book makes strong contrarian points about general principles of freedom and accountability, the details have been left somewhat murky, because that's the way life is. Despite the simplifying rhetoric of idealists and ideologues, the process of finding pragmatic solutions will always be a messy one. In the previous example, where we discussed time limits versus forgetfulness, I can see arguments for both sides and would not want either proposal put into universal effect without a lot more discussion, criticism, and plenty of pilot studies. That is how "neat ideas" get tested and the foolish majority of them eliminated. So it is with encryption.

The reader will note that I got all the way through chapter 7 without once elucidating how I would solve the problem typified by the Clipper chip, key escrow, and anonymous remailers. I chided government arrogance and crypto-advocates' myopia, as well as the dangerous logic of cruel dichotomies, but made no specific suggestion to break the deadlock.

The primary reason is that I feel the situation, for the next few years at least, is a foregone conclusion. Governments will keep floating proposals, pushing legislation, promoting treaties, and accomplishing very little that is not superficial or cosmetic. Social forces within the neo-West will ensure that technological momentum carries us forward, into a world of chaotic diversity, with a thousand innovative crypto-packages being offered by as many individuals and fly-by-night companies. Ciphering has already moved into the field of voice communication by telephone. Increasing numbers of e-mail messages arrive accompanied by "signatures" in PGP, or some other encryption package. A variety of cybercash systems are emerging to code and verify financial dealings, masking them from the scrutiny of outsiders. Anonymizer services thrive, and banking havens offer new ways for money to be not only laundered but dry-cleaned, pressed, and starched. Governments and citizenries will have to be pushed a lot harder against the wall before they make truly significant moves against such a tidal surge. For now, at least, the trend seems unstoppable.

Then why present this book at all? Because fundamentally, it is not about encryption, or the Clipper wars, or the Communications Decency Act, or any of those details. It is about the overall range of choices that face us during the coming decades, and some widely held assumptions that badly need contrarian discussion. If the reader comes away with more questions than answers, that is just fine.

And yet, if pressed to make a suggestion — what to do about encryption — I might put something on the table.

*The worst thing is to rush into action before the consequences have been properly debated.*                    PERICLES OF ATHENS

### A Modest Proposal

The government appears to say, "We don't mind everybody using encryption at will. We just want a back door, in case we need to eavesdrop for the greater good." To this, one "godfather of encryption," Whitfield Diffie, responded for the cypherpunks: "Electronic communication will be the fabric of tomorrow's society. . . . By codifying the Government's power to spy invisibly on these contacts, we take a giant step toward a world in which privacy belongs only to the wealthy, the powerful, and perhaps, the criminals."

Those are the "official" entrenched positions, and their flaws were discussed in chapter 7. But now suppose that, against all odds, a majority consensus starts to coalesce around a third approach, the idea that openness is better, and that accountability is an essential ingredient of liberty to be applied against government and other power centers alike. Imagine that some accord is reached in principle that secrecy should be reserved (with some wary skepticism) for only those situations where authentic and compelling personal needs outweigh a general priority for transparency.

My outrageous third proposal? Leaving cybercash out of the discussion, should we banish nonfinancial encryption from public dataways?

Such an idea would probably be unenforceable, given the cleverness of programmers at concealing bits among other bits (see chapter 9). Anyway, let us concede that encryption's attractions will be irresistible to many, especially at the beginning, while it has a fashionable techno-allure. Given what we know about human nature, a transcendentalist love affair with secret codes appears to be unavoidable. Any attempt to repress or prevent this would be impossibly quixotic, and would quite possibly spark a revolution led by society's smartest. Long experience has taught us better ways of dealing with *inevitable vices*.

One approach is exhortation—and yes, asking people to start thinking of the greater long-term good can be effective in certain cases.

Another approach is to make the disapproved practice slightly unpleasant. Taxes on alcohol and tobacco products, for instance, are designed only in part to raise revenue (aimed at compensating for the damage they cause). A larger function is to make those products more costly and thus less desirable. Raising the price of cigarettes in this manner has been found to have dramatic effects on teen smoking. The trick is to avoid applying taxes so onerous that customers turn to an underground economy of smuggling or illicit manufacture. While libertarians may not like this concept in theory, it has proved to be an effective pragmatic way for societies to sway mass behavior gently away from noxious or harmful habits, without banning those habits altogether.

Suppose there were a small but real cost or penalty to encryption—perhaps an encryption tax or tariff—mere pennies on the megabyte, with a large allowance weighted in favor of small-time users, aimed at discouraging corporations or government officials from being secretive out of pure routine. It might be looked at as an environmental fine, like the recent practice of allocating "pollution credits," harnessing free-market forces to keep a necessary evil constrained. As long as encryption carries enough probable cost to be slightly more irksome than openness, the common instinct will *not* be automatically to obscure. Instead, people may ask themselves, "Do I really have a good reason to conceal this?" Or, more to the point:

> **"Why should I care if someone sees this?**
> **I have nothing to hide."**

In fairness, and to foster openness where it is needed most, the same principle should be vigorously applied to government agencies, in order to put omnipotent institutions on a secrecy diet. Otherwise, they will surely conceal everything.

Either a slap on the wrist or a tiny tax, repeated often enough, may suffice to keep the Net mostly open and transparent, rather than a turbid cloud of reflexive secrets and paranoia. And that, in turn, would affect the whole atmosphere, the culture that people carry with them into business and discourse in this new world. A world where masks, trench coats, and sneakiness are at best seen as occasional necessary evils, perhaps a bit childish, or in somewhat bad taste—things we'll eventually outgrow. A world where open, honest trade is the norm, and we are therefore free.

So much for my radically simple suggestion. It hasn't a prayer of coming true, at least not in the near term. But there it is, on the table.

*Government is not reason; it is not eloquence; it is force! It is a dangerous servant and a terrible master.*   GEORGE WASHINGTON

## PRAGMATIC TRANSPARENCY

A lot has changed since Washington's day, but there is timeless truth to his warning. I have emphasized that I hold government in no less suspicion than civil libertarians and crypto-advocates do, just because I also see threats looming from many other directions. It is the unproven supposition that government can be controlled by *blinding* it that I find dubious. Those who love quoting Washington's epigraph above seldom go on to present his complete views on the matter: "*No man is a warmer advocate for proper restraints and wholesome checks in every department of government than I am; but I have never yet been able to discover the propriety of placing it absolutely out of the power of men to render essential services, because a possibility remains of their doing ill.*"

I cannot repeat too often what history shows, that the worst modern tyrannies arose in states whose regimes were weak and blind. In France (1789), Russia (1917), Italy (1926), Germany (1933), Spain (1936), and China (1949), outsiders conspired unchecked to seize power and converted formerly impotent governments into instruments of savage repression. Despite frequent claims to the contrary, there is no evidence that freedom can be preserved by hobbling a democratic, constitutional government and preventing officials from doing their jobs.

Accountability through transparency is the tool that has worked so far, but it needs constant reinforcing and fine-tuning. Countless public officials have tried to obstruct this glare of skeptical observation, covering their tracks, thwarting independent audits, or classifying everything in sight "top secret." That is only human nature, and we should not take it personally. Nor should we permit them to succeed.

Transparency can be forced on government through law, by coercing (through voter pressure) legislators to pass codes like FOIA. Although there are official channels devoted to accountability *within* government, such as investigative committees, special prosecutors, and so on, the most effective technique has been to unleash interest groups (such as the ACLU, class action attorneys, the news media, or advocacy organizations) to file lawsuits and force FOIA compliance from reluctant bureaucrats. It doesn't always work, but relentless T-cell attacks can wear down resistance like corundum. Many new tools of the Internet will surely help this wholesome process.

One chief point of this book has been to demonstrate that a similar immunological response should apply against any new or traditional center of power consolidation, wherever clusters of egotists might rationalize making secret decisions that affect us all, whether for personal aggrandizement or "for our own good." Among these alternative hubs of influence, corporations represent a special class. In a codicil to the social contract that is still much debated, corporations have long been granted most of the rights of living citizens, even though a corporation's financial muscle and potential immortality might better be compared to the traits of Olympian gods.

How is accountability forced upon corporate titans? The standard bureaucratic solution—some huge government agency, staffed by battalions of inspectors carrying edict-filled binders—will almost certainly continue to be necessary here and there. Yet, that whole approach seems rather "un-hip" for the agile twenty-first century. We have been down that road, learning that maximalist meddling can take a free market to the brink of stifling ruin. Besides, in the long run we don't enhance freedom by shackling one giant and giving another the keys. New methods should be found to supplement, and even supplant, centralized bureaucratic solutions to social problems.

### Public Feedback Regulation

Fortunately, society has already begun exploring ways to hold corporations accountable without fostering vast bureaucracies. One of these techniques is called *public feedback regulation*, a trend recently analyzed by Ohio State University law professor Peter P. Swire.

For some years now, U.S. airlines have been required to publish on-time arrival records and statistics on lost baggage. This data goes to a government agency, which collates the figures and then does absolutely nothing about them *except* publish them in newspapers and on the Internet.

That turns out to be plenty! The effects of these twin regulations were dramatic within a few months of their enactment. Airlines scoring near the top of the lists brayed their status in advertisements, triggering frantic efforts at improvement by their competitors. Consumers were the winners.

Ironically, nothing like this exercise in openness has occurred in the area of airline *safety* records, which might presumably matter to the public even more. Indeed, this new kind of oversight has been applied in an apparently random, patchwork fashion elsewhere. Auto makers must give the Department of Transportation accident rates for each car model. Telephone carriers have to inform the Federal Communications Commission of service outages affecting over three thousand customers. Corporations must disclose the compensation rates of their top officers. In all of these cases, the most effective recipients of the correlated data are not bureaucrats but interested members of the public.

Under a 1975 act that was strengthened in the 1980s, lenders have been forced to disclose denial rates for home mortgages—broken down by race, sex, income, and census tract. These reports swiftly and dramatically highlighted long-standing patterns of discrimination, such as the fact that blacks were being turned down for loans a startling 2.7 times as often as whites with the same income and creditworthiness. As a result, nearly every national mortgage institution established fair lending policies, and a majority instituted outreach programs that have so far roughly halved the embarrassing discrepancies. Companies face a cynical but effective market incentive to at least try to stay out of the bottom third of this list.

Many chemical companies were in the habit of allowing routine release of toxic materials just up to the ceilings allowed under Environmental Protection Agency (EPA) rules, until the 1986 Toxics Release Inventory law started requiring publication of meaningful exposure levels, even legal ones. (Some states like California enacted even tougher disclosure rules.) This created competitive pressure to become *cleaner* than limits enforced by the EPA.

Regulations like these have been familiar in the stock market for years. Issuers of stock must disclose copious information to the Securities and Exchange Commission, especially when it comes to potential insider trading, exposing the data to scrutiny by both the general public and the "expert public" (brokerage houses).

These examples show how government, instead of distorting markets, can instead act, in the words of cyber-futurist Jaron Lanier, as a benign "vessel within which the fluid of the marketplace sloshes about, seeking the most efficient resting place." Notably, public feedback regulation does not generally need coercive bureaucratic meddling, or even lawsuits, to change the behavior of the regulated entity. Rather, the aim is to end asymmetries or inequities in the flow of information, and then let market forces drive the results.

So when universities were told to disclose graduation rates for college athletes, public ridicule forced many of them to revamp their standards. Likewise, candidates for federal office have to disclose information about their contributors, enabling voters to judge by their associations (a partial measure that still has far too many loopholes). Moreover, we have seen the same process of narrowly defined accountability applied against private citizens, for example, Megan's Law, under which convicted sex offenders must register their addresses for local parents to peruse. Other examples include states that publish the names of parents who have defaulted on child support payments, or of scofflaws who write bad checks or fail to pay parking tickets, or of "johns" picked up in prostitution raids.

Clearly, there comes a point where this kind of regulation can transform from a profound public good (helping consumers act as smarter agents in a free market) into a kind of vigilantism. It takes no leap of imagination to picture some majority using the technique to impose its own priggish standards on those who prefer a different lifestyle, by posting registers of people caught doing things that a homogenized mass of conformists don't like. For example, at an Ivy League university, a conservative hacker collated and published the names of all those on campus who had subscribed to the Usenet group alt.sex.stories.

In other words, public feedback regulation is a *partial* solution, like so many others. Although a powerful tool that will likely be expanded beneficially, the method has intrinsic limits to its usefulness and legitimacy.

How can we prevent abuses, or a kind of tyranny by busybodies and prudes? The knee-jerk response is predictable. Forbid some types of list making! Tell people they can't collect or publish certain kinds of information! Protect privacy by setting up legal barriers to knowing things!

Needless to say, there is a different approach.

*Those who have the greatest case for guilt and shame*
*Are quickest to besmirch their neighbour's name.*
*When there's a chance for libel, they never miss it;*
*When something can be made to seem illicit*
*They're off at once to spread the joyous news,*
*Adding to fact what fantasies they choose.*

MOLIÈRE

### Mutually Assured Surveillance

Sometimes the wisdom of a policy can be known only in retrospect. A strategy of *reciprocal deterrence* seemed extremely dangerous during the Cold War, forcing us all to live in fear of a nuclear apocalypse. But it worked. Although direct warfare between large nations had been routine for many thousands of years, this persistent nasty habit was abruptly broken when two mighty empires faced MAD—or *mutually assured destruction*— a threat of total annihilation if either of them initiated head-on conflict. Despite a litany of shameful and costly surrogate wars, this fifty-year experiment had one valuable outcome: it proved that people and nations may sometimes behave more soberly when they face inescapable accountability for their actions.

This notion of reciprocal accountability as a balance of power can be seen elsewhere in many forms. Take, for instance, the uniquely American romance with personal firearms. One favorite myth of the Wild West, depicted in countless films, has been the power of a humble man, armed with an "equalizing" six-shooter, to resist thugs or corrupt officials. This notion was generalized into a forceful ideology during the 1940s, when John W. Campbell, editor of *Astounding* magazine, propounded, "An armed society is a polite society."

Campbell posited that even a mighty gunslinger will be foolish to abuse other people, if everyone around him is also armed! Under such circumstances, no swaggering bully, even one with a quick draw, will last very long. The "inevitable" result, promoted by Campbell (illustrated in novels by Robert Heinlein and others), must be a society of great manners and courtly caution, where weapons wind up being used rarely just *because* they are ubiquitous.

This ideology underlies many of today's arguments against gun control legislation. Alas, as with the "just so" tales of Karl Marx and so many other ideologues, Campbell's fabulous leap of logic does not survive the test of evidence. (Like communism, it might apply to some other species of sapient beings, but not to humans.) The definitive experimental test is currently under way on the streets of countless North American cities, where a plethora of handguns has brought about anything *but* a renaissance of civility. The problem with Campbell's notion is that many human beings, especially young males, have intensely wrathful emotional reflexes, often blinding them to abstract long-term consequences. In former times, when fists were the chief schoolyard weapon, lashing out caused no more than a black eye. But with firearms, one angry spasm can lead to at least a pair of tragedies: a dead victim, and an assailant whose life is effectively ruined. There are no "take backs" if you lose your temper with a gun. No saying, "I'm sorry" or "I didn't mean it."

And yet, one wonders. What if some way were found to remove the major drawbacks from Campbell's idea? Suppose that instead of *pistolas*, we all carried something nonlethal, that would nevertheless be profoundly effective in enforcing accountability for vicious actions?

A stun gun? No, that's still too literal.

How about cameras? The kind with a live remote feed to some distant recording device, as described in chapters 1 and 2.

Ponder an image of everyone sauntering down the street with one of these "weapons" on their hips. Naturally, one result is a near absence of street crime—that is a given. But what about the price? To many folks, the first picture that leaps to mind will be of a *nosy* place, snooty and provocative, with everyone shoving lenses toward one another at the slightest cause, real or imagined.

But would that actually happen? Recall the *restaurant analogy* discussed in chapter 1. People already have the power to stare at strangers! Yet blatant gawking doesn't happen very often, because most folks just don't like Peeping Toms. It is generally more embarrassing to be caught staring than to be observed with crumbs in your beard, or soup on your tie. True, it is one of life's hazards that someone you know may "make a scene," attracting unwanted attention in public, and the famous or beautiful will always lure the eye. But these are bearable life hazards—or else restaurants would be empty. For the most part, the deterrence of two-way visibility already works in daily life, helping to keep things generally cordial.

So why not extrapolate the same overall sensibility to a future world of enhanced vision? Aren't cameras just extensions of our eyes? What holds for a restaurant should apply when we have tomorrow's amplified senses, assuming that such powers are distributed evenly. If it is considered boorish to brandish your camera too openly, people will "shoot back" at those with itchy trigger fingers, retaliating by spreading reputation-damaging evidence of their voyeurism on the Net. However, most of us will leave courteous neighbors alone, not because of some utopian civility, but out of general self-interest—the same muted balance of power that today lets us have an islet of privacy amid a crowded diner.

Perhaps, after a while, Campbell's aphorism might come true after all. A photographically "armed" society *could* turn out to be more polite. Only there is one paramount difference from his scenario that used lethal firearms. With cameras, one can aim and fire without ruining lives. The first to shoot does not always win. And it is possible to apologize after a flash of temper. In a world of cameras, in other words, there can be "take backs."

This metaphor is applicable to the problem we saw earlier, in discussing public feedback regulation.

Strong privacy advocates often assert, when objecting to transparency, that a homogenizing rabble may assail eccentrics with conformist harassment, pursuing any idiosyncrasy with braying cries for blood. Only through *concealment*, say the advocates of anonymity, can nonconformists find hope of safety from the mob.

Their supposition is not baseless. Without any doubt, this was true at other times. Most societies punished nonconformity. Even slight deviations from the norm might bring on waves of devastating gossip. Take anthropologist Sally Engle Merry's description of life in an isolated Spanish village: "Every event is regarded as common property and is commented on endlessly. . . . People are virtuous out of fear of what will be said."

But that was there. That was then. Evidence from our own society refutes the image of relentless conformism, especially amid the waves of pro-eccentricity propaganda discussed in chapters 2 and 5. By coming boldly *out* of the closet, homosexuals are winning vastly greater acceptance than they ever had while cowering within. The same trend applies to the slow weathering away of racial stereotypes, as modern media expose us to admirable, or normal, or idiosyncratic figures wearing many shades of skin. All sorts of quirky eccentrics achieve their fifteen minutes of fame through shows like *Strange Universe* that celebrate the outrageous and unorthodox. This is one of the chief drivers bringing on a "century of amateurs."

Even if that weren't true, the case for reciprocal transparency would still stand, because there is no greater weapon against the intolerant than exposing *their* peccadilloes.

The reader may remember a song that was popular some decades ago called "Harper Valley PTA." It tells the story of a single parent who is targeted as an unfit mother by vicious gossip in a small community. One night she shows up at the local parent-teacher association meeting, steps forward, and proceeds to "sock it to" the local busybodies, reciting every secret skeleton that her persecutors had so long and so carefully concealed in their attics. "You're all Harper Valley hypocrites," Jeannie C. Riley sang.

Great art? Not exactly. Decisive evidence? Well, no.

But the spirit of ornery independence showed by the song's heroine, plus a determination to use *light* in her own defense, makes her almost an icon for reciprocal accountability. It demonstrates an essential point: if enough people are eccentric or individualistic in the coming age, they will almost certainly rally together on one issue, in a single cause uniting all the cypherpunks, amateur scientists, loners, polygamists, librarians, celibates, skateboarders, llama breeders, volunteer firefighters, paraplegics, UFO-maniacs, libertarians, agoraphobes, street jugglers, college professors, hobos, members of every ethnic minority or small religious denomination, and millions of others who just happen to like tolerance and diversity. Despite all their myriad differences, they may fight for a general policy of live and let live.

This air of tolerance won't happen because of admonitions to be nice, but out of cantankerous self-interest. In fact, via this strange irony, we may thus find that a little privacy *can* be secured in the coming age of universal sight, when a democratic balance of power makes it society's worst sin to judge others too harshly.

**Cast not stones, ye who live in glass houses.**

*When I began my career as a futurist I believed a free society required promises and dreams—not just by experts, but by everyone. . . . But now I see uncertainty as the necessary handmaiden of freedom. . . . Instead of being confident in our plans, we can be confident in ourselves.*     PETER SCHWARTZ, *THE ART OF THE LONG VIEW*

## A TOOL KIT FOR THE TWENTY-FIRST CENTURY

Up to this point, readers might have formed an impression that the new technologies are inherently friendly to secretiveness and the subverting of accountability. So, before continuing with the overarching discussion of transparency in chapter 9, the next few pages will explore how some plausible technical innovations may have the opposite effect. We will see that openness, credibility, and responsibility might be enhanced as entrenched systems of hierarchical control loosen, enabling citizens increasingly to dispense with intermediaries and participate directly in the running of their civilization. In each case, it will happen by *increasing* the flow of information to those who can best make use of it.

Take an example recently proposed by science fiction author Neal Stephenson, a hybrid between openness and privacy, wherein people around the world would band together in ad hoc teams to keep an eye on each other's safety and property, allowing (or forcing) the police to draw back to a lesser role in everyone's lives. Under this "global neighborhood watch," homeowners would set up their own cameras to monitor nearby streets and surroundings, feeding those images across the Net to friends on the other side of the world. While you sleep, a camera takes enhanced, real-time images of the gloom outside your house—images that then appear in a corner of the computer monitor of a distant acquaintance—say a software engineer at work in New Delhi. That engineer notes if anything suspicious is going on near your house, and calls you or your local constable directly if things seem serious enough. Conversely, when he goes to bed it will be your turn to keep an eye over your distant partner's home and goods, glancing at a little window in the corner of your screen, while the moon shines down on India.

Another notion of autonomous accountability is as old as a skit from the 1970s television series, *Love, American Style,* which depicted a young woman whose blind date has just appeared at her door. Politely, she asks for some ID, and feeds his driver's license into a computer (then depicted with rows of flashing lights). Soon a printout appears from a database containing reports by all the women that the young man previously dated! While this skit was done for humor, who can doubt that such databases will appear in future years, if enough women choose to take part? (On several Ivy League campuses there are already underground feminist booklets containing the names of alleged "date rapists," sometimes published anonymously on the Internet.) And yes, coteries of impolite boys will maintain dark versions, unsavory listings of women and their attributes, equivalent to the older habit of scribbling names on bathroom walls. Nevertheless, on balance, the harm avoided through the first example may far outweigh the harm caused by the latter. In any event, the issue is not whether something like this should happen, but merely when it will.

*If self-replicating chemicals had as hard a time reaching maturity as good ideas, this planet would still be lifeless.*

ROBERT QUALKINBUSH

### "Percolation," or Bypassing the Know-Alls

Nearly every large-scale human society up till now has been pyramidal in its social structure, with a few at the top lording it over masses below. Only recently have we arguably shifted to a new geometry, one that is wider in the middle than either at the top or at the bottom. In another venue I discuss this historically unprecedented phenomenon, a diamond-shaped society, where the well-off actually outnumber the poor. A progressive stage that is still far from complete, yet a worthy step toward a better world.

Despite this shift to a diamond pattern within neo-Western society as a whole, the classic pyramid still represents the social order in one modern realm: the arts.

There is talk about how the Internet will free creative people from dominion by an elite—the studio producers, gallery operators, record executives, and impresarios who decide which artists become stars while others, equally talented, languish in obscurity. "Alternative artistic zones," like *Kaleidospace* and *IUMA*, offer ways for musicians and others to exhibit their works on the World Wide Web, selling copies by direct order. In theory, wide-band multimedia should help creative individuals bypass rigid corporations.

Some have mixed feelings about this prospect, among them James Burke, the author of *Connections.*

> Whether it be music, or three-dimensional architecture, or sculpture, or three-dimensional art, or literature—when everybody can publish, what are the standards? . . . Michelangelo happened because Julius II happened. Mozart happened because the Bishop of Salzburg happened. Wagner happened because Ludwig of Bavaria happened. Almost every artist you look at—up until recently—has been supported by patronage.

Perhaps it reflects the different memes we were brought up under, but I feel less daunted than Burke by the prospect of artists striking forth in a free market, peddling their creativity like buskers putting on a show at a sidewalk bazaar. We are already seeing a breakup of monolithic culture. Teens no longer listen to all the same bands at the same time, but participate in several dozen tribes of musical interest. Those who predicted a homogenization of Western culture could not have been more wrong. Ideally, this should lead to ever greater diversity and creativity.

But let's not exaggerate. The "suits" at Time Warner, Paramount, and Disney still seem confident with good reason. While there are more gifted amateur film makers than ever, equipped with inexpensive video and other equipment, we won't see a sudden flood of lucrative independent cinema pushing aside the old dinosaurs soon, for two reasons.

1. Systems of distribution and publicity are still so concentrated and expensive that only the largest companies can participate in them.

2. Production standards keep going up, remaining beyond the reach of private newcomers. There *are* more independent movies, just as there are fresh alternative ways to get news, but not enough to make Michael Eisner or Rupert Murdoch lose sleep.

The role of producer or critic won't vanish. Nor will the pyramid magically flatten because new media enhance the infobit flow rate. Yet the "century of amateurs" will never be complete so long as some grand culture know-all must reach from Olympian heights in order for genius to be plucked from a sea of wannabees. We need alternative ways for talent to flourish. One I expect to see is *percolation*. Its repercussions will spread beyond the arts.

> *Good ideas are not adopted automatically. They must be driven into practice with courageous impatience.*
>
> ADMIRAL HYMAN G. RICKOVER

In his 1967 essay "Towards a Semiological Guerrilla Warfare," philosopher and novelist Umberto Eco said that if you give people tools that help them criticize the messages they are receiving, these messages lose their potency as subliminal political levers. One means to achieve this might be through *tag commentary*, consisting of a few parasitic bytes affixed to any data stream — or simply a Web link — where each reader or recipient may add a brief comment, perhaps a succinct plus or minus, signifying "thumbs up" or "thumbs down." These blips will be ephemera, not formally part of the data packet they comment on. Their sole aim would be to sample reactions to a particular document, program, or posting. As the system grows more sophisticated, a user might send software agents to read the tags of most extant copies of the same document, taking a "poll" of reader responses. An ad hoc merit system could judge documents, proposals, or works of art. The more people give favorable nods, the more widely the item will spread.

Does this sound like "word of mouth"? Informal systems of commendation could learn your tastes and start giving greater credibility to the tag comments made by some people (presumably, those who are right a lot), and less to others.

A pertinent parallel to "tag commentary" might be the way academic citations already track most papers in science and scholarship. Checking how often (and by whom) an article has been cited, busy researchers get a rough idea which articles are "must reads" in their field. Though some complain that the process fosters a herd mentality, most participate anyway, because citations-tracking proves so damned useful.

Jaron Lanier, sometimes called the "father of virtual reality," expressed the need for some such process in an essay written for the Global Business Network, where he observed, "New democratic institution[s], expressed in a combination of technical design and law, can and should be created that tend to [foster] quality and truth without creating a privileged editorial position."

Such semi-anarchic systems might elevate an artwork, or a particularly insightful essay, even one that was first posted by some unknown person to a dim corner of the Net. In time, the piece could percolate out of obscurity—via reprinting, reposting, and perusal by ever greater numbers—on a path uncontrolled by the moguls who own vast media empires. This second route to renown will be crucial to a transparent society. For as long as good ideas, unusual art, and biting criticism have alternative routes, powerful "opinion shapers" will never be able to keep a mortal lock on what we see or think.

Some might claim that this alternative route already exists. An almost random caroming of ideas already takes place on the Internet, with the best postings receiving more attention because enthusiasts remail copies to their friends, and so on. Many Web sites proudly proclaim the number of "hits" they receive from interested parties who drop by for a perusal after receiving a personal recommendation. But few would claim that this chaos currently rewards quality in any proportionate way, except by accident.

Early attempts at systematic percolation are under way, however. Pascal Chesnais's *FishWrap* is an electronic newspaper that mixes the editor's personal choice of stories with encouragement for readers to hook on additional items they think may be of interest. Articles are then ranked according to the number of people who read each one. The process of collaborative attention moves according to a complex mixture of quality and passing enthusiasm, without subjecting the *FishWrap* community to strict homogenization of viewpoint. An element of serendipity and surprise remains.

There are potential drawbacks to such methods of ranking merit. Percolation may resemble a "free market" of creativity, but in any market some cheat, for example, by logrolling with friends, reviewing their own works, or "hacking" to raise their scores artificially. Some scandals we'll see in future decades may make "payola" seem quaint and rather innocent.

Finally, what if the new era becomes too amorphous for any general sense of direction to coalesce out of several billion cantankerous individuals? If every person who says "right" is balanced by another who says "wrong," the result may not be a rich amalgam, but a world where every meaning is canceled by its opposite. In other words, the great big stew of future culture may have no sense of up or down. No direction for the "best" to percolate toward. James Burke mulled over this possibility, worrying about an age when "it's up to the new leaders of taste—that is, the entire population—to decide what the standards are. And I believe what will happen is the standards—that's the old historical term—will disappear."

Even those with a hankering for diversity might find such a world disorienting, and possibly lonely as well. So let's consider how to avoid it.

Percolation may have drawbacks. Nevertheless, we are better off trying some innovative new ways for art and ideas to shift and rise by their own merit, allowing eclectic trends in our new renaissance to sort themselves out. A simple, semianarchic system of popular value could powerfully supplement hierarchies of media pundits and producers.

*We are entering the age of mirages, illusions and make-believe. While some people are blinded by all-pervading noise, others acquire X-ray eyes, letting them see beyond all the old, traditional walls.*

*For a while, this will create a golden time of opportunity for swindlers, blackmailers, and all kinds of cheaters.*

*Then we will adapt.* M. N. PLANO

### Credibility Ratings

Some years ago, writer-director Buck Henry illustrated "credibility ratings" through a skit on *Saturday Night Live*. Ostensibly, all the seats in the audience had been equipped with "attention monitors" that would make Henry's television image diminish when viewers got bored, and grow when they were interested. As he droned on about the advantages of this technology, Henry's face shrank and a worried expression took over . . . until he shouted, "Sex!"

Abruptly, his image filled the screen. Thereafter, it stayed large so long as he pandered to the audience, telling them all the salacious, low-brow things he did *not* plan on talking about.

Of course there were no monitors in the seats. It was a spoof, and the audience guffawed appreciatively. But that may change. Picture a typical twenty-first-century television reporter coming on screen. Under his talking head, you see a numerical score. (Or several competing scores: one compiled by *Consumer Reports,* one by Nielsen, and others gathered directly from viewers, reacting in real time.) These little numbers show how trustworthy or believable customers find the product the video personality is trying to "sell," whether merchandise, commentary, or news. Imagine these credibility ratings changing in real time. Envision perspiration popping on our ace authority's brow as his score rapidly plummets before his eyes. Now picture the same thing happening to a politician, having such a figure flashing away at the bottom of her TelePrompter screen!

The downside is obvious. Although it *could* serve to elevate the level of debate, it could also debase it terribly. One can imagine some popular figure asking followers to downgrade a competitor's ratings, all at once. Or some senator playing to the mob, reciting whatever words the numbers say they want to hear. Later, it might lead to *demarchy,* a chilling form of democracy, in which television viewers watch shallow five-minute arguments on the tube and then vote yes or no with a button on their remote control, no longer delegating their authority to elected deliberators, but instead exercising sovereign power each night, deciding issues of the day after the most superficial forms of "debate."

Will we find Buck Henry's *Saturday Night Live* skit about slavery to instant audience reactions dismally prophetic? Does it illustrate the decadent, homogenized future awaiting us as soon as the low-class masses gain total control of content through high-speed feedback mechanisms?

Or did Henry's satirical little play demonstrate something else? Perhaps that people already have a sense of humor and perspective about this very topic, and are willing to laugh at such tendencies in themselves?

It is the latter possibility that offers hope. No one said a transparent society would come without drawbacks, or challenges to the good judgment of twenty-first-century citizens.

*The classic Mayan civilization (now long extinct) had a superbly pampered class of brilliant astrological futurists.*

BRUCE STERLING

*I never make predictions, especially about the future.*

YOGI BERRA

### A Predictions Registry

"The secrets of flight will not be mastered within our lifetime . . . not within a thousand years."

This prognostication, singularly famous for its irony, was reportedly uttered in 1901 by none other than Wilbur Wright. We can presume he said it during a foul mood, after some temporary setback. Smiling with the benefit of hindsight, we know Wilbur and his brother would prove the forecast wrong in just two years. Indeed, most attempts to divine the future seem so ineffective that it is a wonder we humans keep trying.

But there's the rub. We *do* keep attempting to look ahead. In fact, it may be one of our species' most salient features.

Oversimplifying a bit, many neuroscientists picture the human brain having evolved through a process of layering. It still uses nearly all the same suborgans as the nervous system of a reptile, from cerebellum to hypothalamus. But atop those ancient circuits for action and emotion there later spread the sophisticated mammalian cortex, talented at visual and manipulative imagery. Upon this layer, primates laid down further strata in the frontal zones for more advanced styles of contemplation, such as planning sets of imminent actions some steps ahead. Finally, in humans, the prefrontal lobes appear to be the latest additions, perhaps just a few hundred thousand years old. When these tiny organs fail, following a lobotomy, for example, patients experience deficits that include lessened ability to meditate on the future. They no longer exhibit much curiosity, or worry, about tomorrow. In other words, they have lost something that makes us uniquely human.

For the unimpaired, no topic so captivates as the vista that lies ahead, in the future's undiscovered country. One of our favorite pastimes is the thought experiment (Einstein and Mach called it *Gedankenexperiment*) — dwelling on some planned or imagined action, considering possible consequences. By exploring potential outcomes in the tentative world of our thoughts, we hope to cull the most obviously flawed of our schemes, perhaps improving our chances of success.

*No conceivable power entices humans more than improving their accuracy at forecasting the future.*

Now, in its pure form, prophecy is just a lot of hooey. If any psychic could do true divination, she would not be hawking her wares on late-night television, but would be a megabillionaire taking part in running the world. Yet the fact remains that we do spend a lot of time and money trying to improve our odds of being right about future events. Economists keep struggling to improve their conjectures about markets, shooting at an ever-moving target as those markets adjust rapidly to each new model. Stockbrokers, politicians, and diplomats all seem eager to project "what might happen next." The intelligence community devotes immense efforts to forecasting the behavior of nations and other international players, to satisfy the demands of policymakers. Pollsters claim insight into the next wave of opinions and trends among common citizens. Commodities traders are called geniuses as long as their luck holds, until statistical chance catches up, and they lose the bank. It can be fascinating to realize how much of our economy is dedicated to variants of the same theme—people buying and selling predictions. When you get right down to it, almost any advice or decision made in a human context is a kind of bet, based on some guess about future outcomes.

Nowhere is this more true than in science. Philosopher Karl Popper held that prediction is the one true test of any theory. It is not enough to offer a hypothesis that explains past observations. To gain respect, your model must explore unknown territory, calculating, estimating, or otherwise foretelling observations not yet made! Only by exposure to potential falsification can a theory prove its worth and become accepted as a useful "working model" of the world. For instance, despite wishful yearnings, cold fusion was tested and disproved in the late 1980s by open-minded investigators who held fast to objective procedures—the same procedures that *vindicated* other "rebel" theories about black holes, punctuated evolution, and new treatments for AIDS. Some pragmatic forecasting tools, for example, probability theory and weather modeling, save countless lives and billions of dollars, while the hot new field of risk analysis is helping researchers understand how real humans act to preserve their own safety.

Two of the highest human virtues, honesty and skill, are routinely tested by making open, accountable assertions, then observing the effects of time. Few statements enhance credibility with a spouse, subordinates, adversaries, or colleagues more than the cheerful proposal, "Let's check out your objections, and find out if I'm wrong."

Alas, it's one thing to predict a mass for the Top quark, and test your theory by experiment. It is quite another to claim that you can divine future trends in culture, commerce, or politics, especially when the thing at stake is not a single reputation (like mine, in writing this book) but the future of a project, a company, or an army in the field. How will the Russian electorate react to the next expansion of NATO? Might the unstable North Korean regime ignite a desperate war? Should your consortium launch a communication satellite system, or will the falling price of fiber optics make such a venture untenable? Will more customers buy personal computers next year? Can harsh penalties deter crime? Will more people be lifted out of poverty via racial preferences, or by exposing them to the harsh discipline of the marketplace?

Each era seems to have its own fads regarding how best to do forecasts. In the 1960s and 1970s there was passionate interest in "Delphi polling," which involved asking a large number of knowledgable people about the likelihood of certain future events. The average of their opinions was thought for a while to have some unbiased validity, when in fact it simply reflected the notions that were most fashionable at the time. In one infamous example, the renowned Rand Corporation released a set of predictions that included reliable long-range weather forecasting and mind control by 1975; manipulation of weather, controlled fusion, and electronic organs for humans by 1985; and sea floor mines, gene correction, and intelligent robots by 1990.

Modern institutions of government and private capital are deeply concerned over the murkiness of their projections. Each summer many hold workshops, encouraging top-level managers to consult with experts, futurists, and even science fiction authors in pondering the long view. Yet the management of great enterprises ultimately comes down to the judgment (and guesswork) of directors, generals, and public officials.

Things may be worse than most leaders believe. Earlier in this book we referred to modern observers who think we have entered an era of unpredictability. In *Out of Control*, Kevin Kelly described how chaos theory and new notions of emergent properties mean that complex systems will tend to behave in unpredictable ways as tiny perturbations propagate through time, almost as if they are taking on a life of their own. Elsewhere we discuss how open criticism can ameliorate such problems. But can it solve the basic dilemma of unpredictability? Jeff Cooper, director of the Center for Information Strategy and Policy for Science Applications International Corp., contends that the very notion of prediction may become untenable in the years ahead, forcing us to rely on developing new skills of rapid evaluation and response in real time.

All of that may be true. Any effort at basing our forecasts on a firm foundation may be doomed to fracture as the ground keeps shifting underfoot. Yet we won't stop trying, because that is one of the things humans *do*. We try to predict events and potential consequences of our actions. The desire to peer into the future is hard-wired in our brains. Even if chaos rends our best projections, we'll keep trying.

In fact, new electronic tools may offer an alternative. Not a better way, but maybe a chance to improve the ways we already have.

●　　●　　●

Once, a junior State Department officer caused a ruckus by predicting that Saddam Hussein was planning to invade Kuwait. The fellow grew irritated with his bosses, and they with him, until they parted company.

A while later, Saddam invaded.

Was the young prophet vindicated? Did he get his old job back, with a promotion?

In real life, social skills count for a lot—almost as much as whom you know, or where you went to school. Why would any normal person choose to hire back a fellow whose presence each day would be a living reminder of how wrong you once were? It is easier to rationalize. (Maybe he was just lucky that time.) Besides, nobody keeps records of who was right, how often, or when.

Until now, that is.

Lately, modern media have begun (crudely) to keep track of predictive successes and failures, by making available to journalists the complete records of statements made by public figures. All through the late 1980s, for instance, the Board of Supervisors of Orange County, California, largely ignored John M. W. Moorlach when he criticized their risky strategy for investing public funds. Later, when the county went bankrupt in one of America's biggest financial scandals, Moorlach's earlier jeremiads appeared on journalists' computer screens. He subsequently was hailed as a visionary.

The idea of a predictions registry may have originated when Sir Francis Galton (1822–1911) attempted to perform experiments statistically measuring the efficacy of prayer. (He discovered what skeptics now call the "placebo effect.") In the 1970s, efforts were made to catalog predictions using the crude technique of mailing postcards to a post office box in New York City, but sorting through shoe boxes did not prove an efficient or comprehensive method of correlating results, and the effort collapsed.

The Internet has changed all that. For example, a "predictions market" has been set up by Robin Hanson, a researcher at the University of California at Berkeley. In his Web space, visitors bet against each other about future trends in science, much like Vegas odds makers, or gamblers on the Chicago commodities exchange. Winners are those whose guesses (or sage insights) prove correct most often. The step to a more general registry would be simple. Anyone claiming to have special foresight should be judged by a simple standard: success or failure.

The first use of such a registry might be to debunk psychics and social vampires who now prey on the gullible, by having skeptical volunteers score *all* their predictions, not just those they later choose to remember. Each forecast would get a specificity multiplier, if it gives names, places, and exact dates. By this standard, Jean Dixon's warnings that a youngish Democrat would be elected president in 1960 and die in office, and that Robert Kennedy would later be assassinated in California, would receive major credit—perhaps compensating for countless failures she swept under the rug. In contrast, all the vague arm wavings of Nostradamus would score near zero, no matter how often adherents claim success, since obscurity lets them be applied almost anywhere, any time.

This is transparency in action. Just as citizens now rely on laws requiring truth in advertising and accurate product labeling, a time may come when we expect all would-be prophets to show accuracy scores before demanding our attention. Only there will be no need for government involvement, since predictions registries will be established privately, starting as amateur endeavors.

It could go beyond debunking scam artists to revealing anomalous *positive* scores by individuals who have a knack for being right noticeably more often than chance. However they achieve this—whether via clever models or unexamined intuition—society should take notice, for whatever insight their methods offer.

The most important predictions are warnings. Earlier we talked about one of the key ironies of human nature, that criticism is the best-known antidote to error, yet individuals and cultures find it painful. Leaders are naturally inclined to snub critics. Where are those who heroically warned about the dangers of Chernobyl-style nuclear reactors? Brezhnev sent them to gulags. Now that Brezhnev is gone, are the heroes in positions of influence?

Life has no guarantees. The more complex our undertakings become, the more we'll face unexpected repercussions. Edward Tenner's book *Why Things Bite Back: Technology and the Revenge of Unintended Consequences* lists many well-meant endeavors that had disagreeable side effects.

Disagreeable, yes. But wholly unanticipated? In how many cases did *someone* warn against the very unpleasantness that eventually happened? Someone who might have seemed irritating at the time, and was pushed aside? Would it serve a useful purpose to grant high prediction scores after the fact, as consolation prizes to Cassandras whose original dire warnings were ignored?

The answer is, it couldn't hurt. There might even come a time when prediction becomes a captivating spectator sport, as fans suspensefully follow champion seers competing for prizes and honor, staking their vaunted reputations on one of the most valued human skills, being right.

All kidding aside, the point is that predictions registries *will* happen—perhaps scores of them, maintained by both august institutions and private aficionados. In the awkward beginning they may be objects of fun or ridicule. Then we'll wonder how we lived without them. Such forums represent another tool for accountability in a world that can no longer afford vague murkiness, or leaders who blithely dismiss their mistakes with arm wavings and eloquent nonexplanations.

As society becomes more transparent, we may learn to be more forgiving of each other's flaws, for nobody is perfect, or on target all the time. On the other hand, when someone makes bold assertions to having special insight, it seems fair to arm people with the means to verify such claims.

*Everybody wants everything. History moves in some of these directions.* BORIS STRUGATSKY

### Preserving "Basic" Privacy

Some people believe we will be able to preserve privacy neither through exhortation nor through a reciprocal balance of power, but only because the mighty will not bother spying on innocuous little guys like you and me. In other words, we know about the Prince of Wales's mistress's underwear because his cell phone conversations were intrinsically interesting (to a few million "celebrity watchers"). Prince Charles *could* listen in on you or me, but why would he care? (Also, since he is so closely watched, he'd fear getting caught.)

EFF cofounder John Gilmore has pointed out that there is a big difference between individual and mass surveillance. Acknowledging that specific encryption regimes might be broken by top government computers in a concerted effort one at a time, he nevertheless maintains that applying the same approach to millions will prove impossible. But there are flaws in the argument that the mighty will find it too onerous and tedious to spy on small folk, if each of us takes pains to fade back into the crowd.

First, who wants to fade into a crowd? Not outspoken citizens in a civilization of aficionados and individualists—and certainly not John Gilmore! Anyway, technology keeps enlarging the power of big shots to stare at the teeming masses. We cannot count on sheltering our privacy in a throng of peasants, hoping predators won't notice us amid the "practical obscurity" of other sheep. Whether through software agents, or keyword scans, or some closely held breakthrough in decryption technology, there may at any time come a sudden, many-orders improvement in the power of government agencies (or oligarchs) to *see*. If this happened, obscurity among the masses would be a frail refuge.

Which is a shame, since a way truly must be found to protect "bedroom privacy." As we discussed in chapter 3, there is a realm that each of us calls deeply personal, wherein we seek either solitude or intimacy. A place to hold things we want kept private, from love letters to facts about embarrassing physical limitations (incontinence, infertility, psychiatric disorders, or the tragedy of a miscarriage). There is a long-standing legal concept called "curtilage," which stands for the protected area of a person's home and its immediate surroundings. In the coming era, when camera-bearing robots may swarm the skies, we will all need something like this, some zone of sanctuary where we can feel unobserved. Some corner where our hearts can remain forever just our own.

As we'll see in future chapters, basic personal privacy may yet thrive in a relatively transparent world, but only if we apply the right tools, combining principle and practicality with the ability of each citizen to enforce the Golden Rule.

In this chapter, we sampled just a few items from the transparency tool kit of tomorrow. These and other innovations share one essential trait. No authorities must be assuaged—no priests, kings, or Senate committees propitiated—in order for them to come to pass. In a century of amateurs, it won't occur to citizens to ask permission. The resources required to start a predictions registry, for instance, or percolation, are so small that some experiments will doubtless be initiated by readers of this very book.

As for "watching the watchers," this trend is already under way. In the neo-West, it will be stopped only if all cameras are banned. This won't eliminate the cameras, just make them smaller, restricting their use to the mighty and influential. (For a much darker set of scenarios, describing how the camera-filled world of tomorrow could go sour, see the section "How Things Might Go Wrong" in chapter 9.)

The important point is what these examples say about openness and candor in the world to come. Without tools for encouraging accountability, all the fancy toys and high-speed dataways will do little for our lives in the area that counts most, fostering a confident civilization of free individuals. A culture with the courage to strike out along new paths, and the wisdom to look out for errors and pitfalls along the way.

In a transparent society, citizens must have the habit of knowing.

They will refuse *not* to know.

# THE PLAUSIBILITY MATRIX

*Show me the assumptions on which you base your facts.*

ANDREW CUTLER

*In history there is no such thing as the sum of many vectors.*

LEO TOLSTOY

The debate between transparency and strong privacy involves underlying suppositions about what will be technically possible in the twenty-first century. If certain social trends or scientific accomplishments come to pass, openness will fail to deliver real accountability. In that case, secrecy may wind up being the little guy's only hope.

Does that sound like a strange admission on my part?

Perhaps it does, after so many pages spent vigorously opposing a world of masks. But this book is an exploration, not an ideological polemic. An honest person should willingly consider the possibility of being wrong. So chapter 9 will examine a number of ways in which transparency might bring truly unpleasant consequences.

But first, let's discuss whether transparency can happen *at all*.

Recall the accountability matrix at the end of chapter 3. There we saw how our individual desires may clash with our own long-range interests. Now let's consider a different kind of chart, shown on the following page, dealing with what may be plausible in the coming century.

*BOX ONE*
Feasible technologies
*enable* citizens to enforce
accountability on the
mighty.

Feasible technologies
*enable* the mighty to
enforce accountability on
citizens.

*BOX TWO*
Feasible technologies
*enable* citizens to enforce
accountability on the
mighty.

Feasible technologies
*thwart* the mighty from
enforcing accountability
on citizens.

*BOX THREE*
Feasible technologies
*thwart* citizens from
enforcing accountability on
the mighty.

Feasible technologies
*enable* the mighty to
enforce accountability on
citizens.

*BOX FOUR*
Feasible technologies
*thwart* citizens from
enforcing accountability on
the mighty.

Feasible technologies
*thwart* the mighty from
enforcing accountability
on citizens.

Just as in the accountability matrix, it is quite possible for more than one of these boxes to be true at the same time! Two sets of technologies may exist, one that helps shine light on centers of power (such as government or potential oligarchs) and another that helps guard their secret conspiracies. If two boxes are both plausible, then a debate over *policy* becomes relevant. As a civilization, we could then use law, research, and social persuasion to decide which technology to emphasize, and thus sway the direction in which things go.

What we *cannot* do is use policy to cram our way into a situation that is technologically unfeasible. The most eloquent argument in the world will be impotent if its aim proves impossible.

Suppose box number 1 became totally dominant, making the other three improbable. For instance, if "gnat cameras" became utterly pervasive, cheap, and universally accessible, a world of obligate openness might be inevitable. Transparency would happen automatically, no matter whether or not openness aficionados like me succeed in convincing a single person. Strong privacy could win every debate, and still become an ideological relic within a few decades.

Contrariwise, we may see that powerful trends drive us toward the situation described in box 3, where the mighty can look at those below them, while thwarting vision or accountability directed their way. This is the classic predicament that occurred in almost every major human civilization to this date. If technology offers a range of powers, then the rich or those in authority will surely gain access to the very best tools. It will be only natural for them to enhance and take advantage of this difference. A cynic, influenced by history, might predict that only box 3 is a credible long-term prospect. We may be fated to be drawn into its unyielding grasp, no matter how hard we thrash and squirm.

But suppose it *is* a matter of choice. If several boxes are plausible at once, then both the strong privacy advocates and I share a common goal. All of us will fight like hell to escape the world of obligate tyranny arising out of box 3!

That still leaves a lot of space between me and the cypherpunks. For instance, I see countless threats to freedom, looming in all directions, while they tend to fixate primarily or solely on government. But an even more important difference has to do with which heading we would take, in fleeing from box 3.

*I* would aim "upward" across the plausibility matrix, heading toward box 1, whereas the strong privacy advocates' belief is that we can best preserve liberty by moving to the "right," toward box 4.

This latter point of view was expressed by a prominent cypherpunk, Hal Finney.

> I'd say that encryption offers for the first time a chance to put the little guy more on an even footing with the big powers of the world. There is an asymmetry between what big governments and big companies know about me and what I know about them. With encryption there is for the first time a chance that I can draw a shield of privacy around my activities. This will put us on more even ground.

Keep this passage in mind for later, when we consider the "garden of Akademos." I very much favor the concept of even ground, but can it be accomplished with shields?

In effect, we are carrying out a debate on two levels. First, what is *plausible*, and second, what is *desirable*.

Let us assume for a moment that boxes 1, 3, and 4 are all realistic. Each one might seed a culture, depending on which technologies are emphasized, encouraged, supported, and socially sanctioned. This implies, among other things, that publicly available encryption schemes might truly conceal the little guy's secrets as advertised, even from the NSA or a Mafia clan.

In that case, our decision about which way to go should depend on three issues:

A. Where do we want to end up?

B. Who has the ultimate advantage in each situation?

C. Which situation is robust or stable?

I won't go deeply into question A right now. Throughout this book I have painted the world of box 4, filled with widespread and habitual secrecy, as a dour place, massively paranoid and rather inhuman. But I am no prophet or seer. I can only argue my case and let time prove it right or wrong.

Where logic does shed some light is on questions B and C.

Who has an ultimate advantage in each world? In a transparent society (arising from box 1), the rich and mighty do have an edge, but only in direct proportion to their legitimate wealth or exertion of lawfully supervised authority. Moreover, their boons are counterbalanced by the fact that average people will look at such individuals a lot more.

At the opposite extreme, in a world of shadows and masks (arising from box 4), perhaps the mighty know nothing about you, and you know nothing about them. Each of you is free to conceal whatever you like, any machination or scheme. In that case, the reader may contemplate who will be better equipped to take advantage of this sovereign darkness. Obviously, I believe the mighty will use such pervasive secrecy far more effectively to advance their own unchecked designs.

Regarding our third question—issue C—we must ask which is sturdier, a transparent society or a masked society? Which one is robust against the buffets and upsets that will inevitably occur with the passage of time?

One strong privacy advocate accused me of basing my arguments on "pure speculation," because I cite the possibility that a gnat camera may someday plant itself in your ceiling to stare down at your keystrokes as you type at your computer, bypassing and neutralizing all your fancy encryption software.

"We can't make decisions based on speculative possibilities," my critic said.

Well, yes we can and should—*if* those speculations are relatively plausible, and if they point out a potentially devastating failure mode for the opposing plan!

In fact, the world arising out of box 4 is a frail one. Suppose that some-day a new technology comes along, one that promises to shred the veils, blow through the encryption haze, or send light piercing past all the cherished opaque walls. As we shall see in chapter 9, such possibilities are quite credible. They range from new decryption algorithms, quantum computers, and gnat cameras, all the way to noninvasive mapping of another person's cerebral activity down to the neuron level (a field where immense strides have recently been made). Who can say what tomorrow will bring? The point is that in a world where secrecy already reigns, such advances will likely be snatched up by some nexus of power accumulation—a government agency, or some cabal of the rich, or a band of merry techies in the cyberelite. The rest of us probably won't even hear of the breakthrough. Moreover, *it will be in the interest of the mighty to make sure that we never do.* To our eyes, the haze will continue. We won't even be aware that new gods have been born. A race of supermen with X-ray eyes, who can see through our beloved veils.

Italian novelist and philosopher Umberto Eco expressed this concern eloquently.

> *There is a risk that we might be heading toward an online 1984, in which Orwell's "proles" are represented by the passive, television-fed masses that have no access to this new tool [the Net]. . . . Above them there'll be a petite bourgeoisie of passive users, office work-ers, airline clerks. And finally we'll see the masters of the game, the nomenklatura—in the Soviet sense. This has nothing to do with class in the traditional sense—the nomenklatura are just as likely to be inner city hackers as rich executives. But they will have one thing in common: the knowledge that brings control.*

The same cannot be said for the world emerging from box 1. If every technological advance is instantly revealed and discussed by a feisty, argumentative society, each potential misapplication or failure mode will be loudly assailed by innumerable T-cells. Use of any new technique by power centers will receive especially close scrutiny. Moreover, a conspiracy to evade such supervision will be risky, to say the least. In a society where whistleblowers are popular heroes, it will be hard to trust your henchmen. This is not to suggest that something truly staggering won't happen, a breakthrough so unexpected and earth-shaking that it fractures even a transparent society. But when it comes to robustness against surprise and change, there can simply be no comparison with the fragile, masked world of box 4.

•  •  •

*But what if box number 1 is not feasible?*

In fact, the entire discussion in this book is based on a single, and possibly flawed, premise: that *all* of the boxes are possible. That we actually have a choice about what will happen.

It might not be so.

Indeed, one can imagine technical and social trends that make box 1 entirely untenable. In that case, historians of the obscure will look back on this book as a weird piece of semiutopian literature by a forgotten astronomer turned science fiction author. A tract with as little long-term relevance as the ravings of Savonarola, Lysenko, or Rand. If this turns out to be the case (and we'll discuss some possibilities in chapter 9), there may be no choice but to take the cypherpunks' advice and strive as hard as we can for the sanctuary of box 4.

The haze may be blinding, and the air in your mask may grow stale. You will worry all the time about what is going on in the dark, mysterious towers of the rich. But the world of anonymous strangers and secret codes may offer a kind of safety. For a little while.

•  •  •

Before we move on, the reader may be wondering about box 2! It represents a quirky, inverted situation in which those on top are held accountable, while those below have genuine privacy.

Hey, it sounds like the best deal of all, eh?

In fact, this is the very world that many strong privacy advocates *claim* they are aiming for! After all, the policies they promote seem to demand openness from the great enemy, government, while protecting the little guy's right to keep secrets.

The flaw in this claim bears repeating over and over again. Government is not the sole source of peril. Any potential power center can be dangerous, and none of them, not even cypherpunks, can claim exemption just by saying, "Oh, don't worry about me, because *I'm* harmless!"

I can see the validity of box 2, in principle. Certainly, a sliding scale of scrutiny may apply, from relatively little needed for some middle-class schoolteacher all the way up to a relentless light that must shine on the dealings of billionaires and attorneys general. In fact, this commonsense approach is already the de facto situation in America and several other countries when it comes to the privacy tort protections. Public figures are deemed to enjoy less shelter against observation by news media, for instance, than average citizens. Moreover, a general sense of fairness and decency makes people tend to stare less at quiet neighbors than at the famous, or those who deliberately seek wealth and power.

Perhaps we who stand at the extremes, both strong privacy advocates *and* believers in transparency, underestimate how smart folks really are. Over the long haul, people may work their way toward a clear-headed mixture of our purist positions, finding pragmatic ways to aim heaps of light toward governments *and* corporations *and* criminals *and* the techno-elite, while at the same time securing an enviable curtilage of privacy for average citizens and their families.

In that case, I hope my cypherpunk and hacker and strong privacy chums will join me partaking in a pleasant meal of crow. For it is often the punishment of ideologues that the people prove much smarter than we ever imagined.

# CHAPTER NINE

# HUMILITY AND LIMITS

*For decades now there have been privacy-busting technologies to which I have no easy and convenient countermeasures (long-range cameras, tiny audio recorders and radio transmitters, etc.), but I don't feel threatened by them. I feel (rightly or wrongly) that my privacy is adequately protected by a combination of other people's sheer lack of interest in my life—I'm a fairly ordinary person—and by social constraints. When such respect is widespread, snooping into other people's lives is disapproved of. I think this will go on providing protection which, while not perfect, is enough for most ordinary people to feel comfortable, and that new snooping technologies will not fundamentally change the picture.*

RICHARD TREITEL

*As long as we live and breathe we'll be paranoid. We always have to be careful, but it isn't going to stop the movement of this technology.*

DAVID BARRAM

## THE JUDGMENT OF MATHEMATICS: IS SECRECY POSSIBLE?

Way back in chapter 2 we discussed technologies that transformed past ages. Both chemistry in the nineteenth century and physics in the twentieth opened doors to new powers while posing ever greater challenges to our good judgment. Many now predict that biology will be the next generation's transfiguring science, altering our farms, medicine, pets, and even our children. But to a few visionaries even these changes are small potatoes. To them, *mathematics* is perceived as the ultimate revolutionizing field, with groundbreaking potential that may force strong choices on humanity, for good or ill.

Will encryption, like the atom bomb, serve as the vehicle by which a formerly innocent field comes to "know sin"? According to Lawrence Lessig, a Harvard law professor: *"Law is becoming irrelevant. The real locus of regulation is going to be [computer] code."*

Recall the plausibility matrix at the end of the last chapter. Of all the factors affecting which box may dominate the world to come, mathematics may be crucial, since it could determine whether the encryption schemes so widely touted by some strong privacy advocates can ever keep their promise to protect users from prying electronic eyes.

Now I will admit that I am ill prepared to deal with this issue. Perhaps a journalist would feel less intimidated, but with a background in physics I am just barely competent enough at math to blink in wonder at the work being done in this field by some very brainy guys. Matthew Blaze, Whitfield Diffie, Philip Zimmermann, their colleagues, and competitors work in an intellectual hothouse that is both steamy and exciting. Their community of mind could be compared with that of the whiz kids who worked on the Manhattan Project more than five decades ago, but this time the talent is widely distributed around the world. Only a small fraction of today's cryptographic wizards work for the NSA and its famed Puzzle Palace. Naturally, there are research groups in other countries (and even allies have few compunctions about cracking each other's codes). Some of the best are employed by corporations, universities, or small entrepreneurial companies. At their gatherings, one can't help but notice crypto-sorcerers exchanging wry smiles and knowing looks in the halls. These are their glory days.

There seems little point in trying to explicate the ins and outs of cryptography here. The interested reader is encouraged to pick up works that cover the subject in detail, such as Bruce Schneier's *Applied Cryptography* (which also contains a thorough "reference list from hell"). Nevertheless, a little coverage is called for in this book, if only to fathom whether math has already rendered its judgment, or if the jury of algorithms is still out, deliberating on our destiny.

As we discussed earlier, cryptography is concerned with the use of mathematical functions, called ciphers, which separate the security of a message's content from the security of the media over which it is transmitted. In other words, if a letter is opened, or a telephone line is tapped, that intrusion will reveal nothing about the actual meaning that is being carried if the message has been scrambled in advance by a clever coding technique.

There are several types of ciphers. The most familiar make it difficult to understand the content of a message without prior knowledge of a secret "key." A related type of function can ensure that information has not been altered in transit from sender to recipient. Applications include securing wired and wireless voice and data traffic against eavesdropping, protecting computer files from unauthorized access, and enabling secure electronic business transactions.

In 1976 Whitfield Diffie, Ralph Merkle, and Martin Hellman invented "public key" cryptography, which splits the scrambling-and-descrambling key into two components (a widely distributed public module and a closely held private one) so that users may communicate in secrecy with people they never met. "Digital signatures" can verify that an e-mail message really was generated by the person claiming responsibility for it. Among other problems, Diffie is now looking into how to evaluate systems to see if they have a "trapdoor" built in by their creators. Commenting on the encryption wars, Diffie maintains "It has been thoughtlessly said . . . that cryptography brings the unprecedented promise of absolute privacy. In fact, it only goes a short way to make up for the loss of an assurance of privacy that can never be regained."

Another "demigod" of cryptography is Leonard Adelman, a mathematician who recently helped demonstrate that DNA molecules can be used to compute complex problems. Adelman's work in the past focused on algebraic number theory and the higher mathematics of secrecy. He was also one of the inventors of a patented electronic encryption system called RSA, so powerful that governments and businesses worldwide have adopted it. But the DNA computer has drawn special attention because it could apparently outperform (in theory) the most advanced digital electronic calculating engines by many orders of magnitude, at least when it comes to certain kinds of well-defined problems. It would accomplish this by using the massively parallel approach of assigning quadrillions of molecules the random task of checking out countless different mathematical avenues at the same time. Only those that came close to success would "survive" and then continue "evolving" toward a correct answer.

Even more startling potential breakthroughs have been claimed for "quantum computing," which seems to offer a means to bypass the strict logic of cause and effect, using quirky aspects of the Heisenberg uncertainty principle. Among other things, this approach implies that no eavesdropper could tap a message without being noticed, since eavesdropping requires observation, which inevitably disrupts a quantum system in detectable ways.

Then there is *steganography*, or the art of "covered writing," encrypting a message by "burying" it in something else. A simple example might be a text where the third letter of each sentence can be strung together to reveal a memorandum, or the "acrostic" messages that some claim they can find in works of Shakespeare, which were supposedly hidden there by the "real" author, Francis Bacon. (Similar assertions have recently been made for messages encrypted in passages of the Bible.) A modern steganographic technique is taking an image, represented as an array of color pixel elements, then weaving a message (a stream of bits) in the low-order bits of the colors. (A difference between green level 233 and green level 236 would not be detectable to the naked eye.) One can use this technique in any medium where the precision of the medium is greater than the "noise level" of typical contents (such as images or audio). One early use of steganography that has been widely publicized is the encrypting of "watermark" verifiers by *Playboy* magazine into many of its published photographs, in order to track copyright violations. Using steganography, a coded message can be hidden in any image, so an opponent would be hard pressed to guess it was even there.

After a recitation like this one, anybody might imagine that the pro-encryption lobby has proved its case, at least on a technological level. But there *have* been rude surprises for this side, such as the incident described earlier in which a famous encryption standard was broken by an ad hoc nationwide network of personal computers "about a trillion years earlier" than previous estimates predicted it could be done. And yet, each time such an episode is announced, crypto-enthusiasts greet the news with smiles and blithe shrugs. After all, it is a simple matter to make their favorite codes much, much harder to break. For instance, instead of using an RSA public key that is 768 or 1,024 binary digits long, try one with 1,536 or 2,048 bits! Instead of using DES with 56 bits, use Triple DES with 168, or Blowfish with 448! Each additional bit increases the intended recipient's difficulty of translation at only arithmetic rates, while the job of code cracking by an opponent seems to rise exponentially.

At a CFP conference in 1995, I asked Whitfield Diffie if he felt this meant that the outcome of the numerical arms race was a foregone conclusion. Had the advantage been permanently settled in favor of the encryptor, over some team of well-equipped math wizards trying to break another person's code? Diffie's answer surprised me: "No, I can't say any such thing. I don't think that's been decided at all."

A puzzling, if honest admission on the part of one of the fathers of modern cryptography. It has subsequently grown clear that, for a number of compelling reasons, the jury will be out for quite some time.

1. So much attention has been paid to the *length* of encryption keys that only a few experts seem to recall that keys are only as good as the algorithmic "locks" they are designed to open. These are the software routines that a computer program uses to unshuffle a message. Several once-vaunted algorithms have met their downfall over the years since Alan Turing inspired the breaking of the German Enigma code, during World War II. For example, the random number generator you use may be flawed in some way that your opponent can predict. "Smart" credit cards were recently shown to have an inherent and potentially fatal mathematical fault that was completely unanticipated by the designers. No one has yet announced any serious chinks in the armor of the present-day Cadillac, RSA Public Key, but that doesn't guarantee that nobody will—or indeed that the masters of the Puzzle Palace haven't already done so. As Bruce Schneier put it: "Security is a chain, and a single weak link can break the system."

2. All right, so your message can't be cracked by an opponent immediately, here and now. That may be all the surety a corporation needs, since many commercial messages lose their worrisome significance after a few days or months. But then, what about the other coded missives that you hoped to bury *forever* in encrypted Gehenna? Your enemy may have intercepted and recorded them on great spools of tape. Sure, the recordings may seem like impenetrable static right now, but what about next year? Or the year after? (After all, the DES standard seemed impregnable for a while.)

In the cypherpunks' world, people could all too easily mislead themselves. We may get into the bad habit of counting on our codes remaining unbreakable, envisioning that they are safe through eternity. But nothing lasts forever. Next year there may be DNA computers, or quantum processors, or newly powerful algorithms. And with each breakthrough those tapes of static could come off the shelves to be sifted, clarified, and read. In other words, *time-delayed transparency* may occur without being created by deliberate policy, a worst possible scenario for those who fall into the unwise custom of assuming that today's solution will always last.

3. One crypto expert recently conceded, "Even a system which is perfect in theory may have weaknesses when put into practice by fallible human beings . . . especially when the original designers are still out there, knowing more." Many of today's computer security experts wring their hands in despair over the twin banes of their existence: first, lazy customers who routinely write their passwords in easy-to-find places, or who use obvious mnemonics (like their birthdays), or practice sloppy procedures; and second, the lurking danger that an entire system may be infested with "back doors" or other Halloween tricks, left behind by the techno-mavens who originally wrote the million-line controlling program. Regarding the latter danger, many of today's sysops and software designers admit admiring the novel *My Name Is Legion*, by the late Roger Zelazny, a tale about a twenty-first-century software designer who helps set up a worldwide personnel records database, lacing it with secret paths enabling him to manipulate information at will, creating new identities for himself at the drop of a hat. Of course, being a Zelazny fan does not automatically mean you will follow the protagonist's example. But few doubt that there are lots of secret access points out there, designed and left in place by otherwise well-meaning fellows who rationalize, "If you can't trust a nerd, who *can* you trust?"

4. Then there is the problem of uneven access to technology that we referred to earlier. Let us assume that steady progress is made with "teraflop processors," then "petaflop" machines, and even DNA or quantum computers. In theory these advances can be compensated for. By constantly ratcheting up the number of bits in their keys, encryptors should retain the advantage at any particular point in time.

Assuming both sides *truly* have the same level of power available.

But what if one side quietly gets its mitts on a petaflop machine, or a potent quantum unit, years ahead of its competitors? Then the inherent advantage shifts dramatically. As Steven Levy of *Newsweek* put it, "The strength of cryptography determines who's going to try to break in. . . . if it's the Mafia or a national government, they'll have plenty of resources." (Recall box 3 of the "plausibility matrix" on page 272.)

The important thing to realize is that you can never know if this is not already the case. At least, you cannot know except in a fiercely open society, where enough light shines that even the NSA would find it hard to hide a technological breakthrough for very long.

• • •

Can anyone say for sure what the answer is? One former strong privacy advocate recently told me that he was finally turned off by the prospect of an endless encryption-decryption arms race. "Whoever wins, wins all! Money, power, etc. Lives in a clear world, while all others live in fog."

This dismal scenario was illustrated in the movie *Sneakers*, starring Robert Redford, Sidney Poitier, and Dan Aykroyd, in which the heroes steal an all-powerful code-cracking chip from the bad old government. But then, instead of sharing it with everyone (creating transparency), they proceed to impose their will omnipotently upon the world, rewarding causes they (or the movie's producers) think "good" and punishing those they consider "bad," thus demonstrating the danger we'll face when some group of bright, well-meaning T-cells acquires a secret advantage, assuming heaps of power with no one to hold them accountable.

And yet, despite all of the above, I am forced by my respect for the cryptographers to admit that they may very well be right. The new math techniques for shuffling messages, and transmitting them enciphered so that only the intended recipient can read them, may be flawless. As I have said repeatedly, some types of secure coding may be essential if the new electronic economy is to flourish.

Does it really matter, though? What we are actually seeing here is yet another round in the long struggle between idealists and pragmatists that has been going on ever since that "father of philosophy," Plato, attacked poor Archytus for daring to build a mechanical calculating device—the world's first practical computer—betraying the "essence" of pure numbers with his defiling bits of wood and metal. Like all transcendentalists, Plato didn't much care for the real world. But the real world is where we live.

In the long run, transparency will not thrive or fail because of the metamagical games played by encryption enthusiasts. The wizards do not control our fate, after all. There are just too many ways to go *around* the math.

> So, Nat'ralists observe,
> a Flea Hath smaller Fleas that on him prey,
> And these have smaller Fleas to bite 'em,
> And so proceed ad infinitum.        JONATHAN SWIFT

## THE JUDGMENT OF TECHNOLOGY

Theory and practice are two very different things. For instance, the most crack-proof encryption system known, the onetime pad, has an Achilles heel. The intended recipient has to already possess the lengthy deciphering code, which must have been transmitted earlier (and possibly snooped) or else delivered in person by a potentially fallible courier. Public key encryption was designed to get around that flaw, but as we discussed, it has weak links of its own. Even if the keys are never cracked by brute force, the deciphering algorithm may be flawed, or compromised by some intentional or unforeseen "back door."

Computer hardware isn't any better. Viruses and Trojan horse programs might lurk in your hard disk, waiting to copy your password and later e-mail it to your adversary. Many people use passwords that are based on mnemonics an enemy can guess, or work out by trial and error, or find scribbled in a coworker's desk. I mentioned earlier the old-fashioned method of sending a sexy spy to seduce and then blackmail the loneliest member of your staff into simply handing over the passwords in a paper envelope. Until humans have some automatonlike ability to adhere rigidly to procedure, and until the procedures themselves can handle all circumstances, there will be no lack of chinks in the armor that can be used by well-heeled skulkers, able to afford skilled and amoral help.

Some of these chinks will be widened into gaping holes by new technologies. For instance, this book has alluded several times to wasp-sized, or even gnat-scale, mobile cameras, sent flitting into an opponent's office or bedroom to spy from the ceiling, observing a password as it is being typed, or just relaying every keystroke before encryption software can conceal it. Are such things really possible?

- Sony already sells a digital color camcorder the size of a passport, weighing just over a pound. A miniature video camera developed by ORNL has a pinhole opening and is small enough (the size of a microcassette case, $1 \times 2 \times 0.5$ inches) to be hidden behind badges or other small objects. The camera has a built-in transmitter.

- Sandia National Labs are developing robots the size of large cockroaches, called MARVs (miniature autonomous robotic vehicles). These could be used to inspect nuclear power plants or enemy lines on a battlefield.

- In 1995, an Advanced Research Projects Agency (ARPA) study group proposed the idea of "surveillance dust," where each particle would contain tiny sensors with a miniature parachute, microphone, and infrared detector. Sprinkled over a battlefield or disaster zone, this dust—or micro-electro-mechanical system (MEMS)—would float for four or five hours to transmit information on enemy locations. In a separate endeavor, ARPA suggested developing a hand-sized micro-unmanned-aerial-vehicle (UAV) which could fly for an hour and for distances of up to 16 kilometers, using microturbine engines which have already been developed.

• Researchers at Tokyo University and Tsukuba University plan to implant microprocessors and microcameras into living cockroaches, to help search for victims in earthquake rubble.

• At the Institute for Microtech in Mainz, Germany, researchers developed a 1-inch microhelicopter, which weighs one-hundredth of an ounce. Alan Epstein of MIT fabricated a jet engine the size of a shirt button for the U.S. Navy.

So if gnat cameras are not yet a proved technology, they certainly seem plausible at this point. Should we try to limit such developments? Remember, keeping such tools out of the hands of your neighbors will not prevent the military and other influential power centers from using them.

Such developments may prompt the free market to develop antignats, designed to seek and destroy those little flying (or crawling) interlopers. Antignats would have a simpler mission—homing in on gnat cam traces such as sound vibrations or radio emissions—but they will have to patrol relentlessly. Therefore, they must be cheap and far more numerous. Another defensive technique will be to sweep rooms with electromagnetic pulses, aimed at disabling any unshielded trespassers, until the gnats are made pulse-proof, that is. A captured gnat cam might also be hacked (electronically dissected) to learn its programming and/or point of origin, and possibly even be turned against its former masters. (There is an old saying in spy circles: "He who goes into enemy territory is forever tainted for having been there.")

Similarly, in the software world, *watcher agents* will be dispatched to spy on opposing companies, nations, or individuals; but there will be danger that *other* software entities might hack into the watchers and control what they take back to their masters. In effect, watchers must contain their own encrypted "genetic code" to check and make sure they have not been tampered with.

At first sight, this ebb and flow of spying and counterspying resembles war, but on another level it begins to sound like the world of parasitism in nature! In the long run, might the result be more like an ecosystem, mimicking the biological world as time goes on? Gnats, preyed upon by mites, which are attacked by amorphously programmed amoebae, which are plagued by viruses. . . . How long before such a rapidly evolving world sloshes out of the narrowly programmed confines that we designed, spreading in ways that we never intended, or imagined?

Perhaps it would be best to tread along this brave new path slowly and cautiously. To accomplish this, we might pass laws against gnat cams. That approach will fail. Alternatively, we might try to limit this micro-arms race by encouraging people to feel less paranoid in the first place. That can happen only if each person feels he or she already knows most of what is going on.

Stepping back from far-out speculation, we have already seen some transparency-related tools coming of age. Take the Witness Program that we mentioned back in chapter 1—a project of the Lawyers Committee for Human Rights, conceived by rock star Peter Gabriel and funded by Reebok Foundation. Its aim, you will recall, is to improve the documentation and communication of human rights conditions around the world. The program offers private rights groups the tools of mass communication, such as hand-held video cameras and fax machines. Other organizations have begun supplying cameras to groups within the United States, so they might form neighborhood crime watch teams, or else hold the police accountable within their communities. Even if the cameras don't shrink to gnat size, we might as well face the fact that they are here, in droves, in swarms, and here to stay.

Cameras aren't the only kind of surveillance technology to loom ominously. In addition to developments cited in chapters 1, 2, and 3, consider:

- A computer can be tapped by tracing the electro-magnetic radiation given off by its video monitor, using the building's water pipes as an antenna. ("Tempest" is the terminology used for such techniques a spy can use to eavesdrop on electronic activities inside a building, even through walls, even when the system is not linked to the outside world.) Future computers are supposed to be "tempest safe." But only a fool would declare this arms race over.

- A "micropower impulse radar," developed at Lawrence Livermore National Laboratories (to measure fusion reactions caused by the lab's powerful Nova laser), may soon retail for as little as $25, finding applications in burglar alarms; automobile obstacle detectors; automobile air-bag deployment; and pipe wire, or sewer line detection through walls or soil. It will also add to the list of "eyes" that can peer at us, even through fog or gloom of night.

- So you use anonymous remailers to reconvey all your messages, so that nobody (except the remailer owner) can trace your identity? Better be careful. Experts at linguistic analysis are developing effective ways to appraise and detect spelling and grammar patterns that are unique to each individual. According to one prominent cypherpunk, "even today, where people use anonymous e-mail, analysis of style and word usage could probably identify many of the authors, if people cared enough to look."

Here is another thought-provoking piece of news. A new kind of *artificial nose* has been developed by MIT professor Nathan S. Lewis, tracking electrical resistance across an array of polymer sponges—each one absorbant to a different range of molecular types—to detect, recognize, or classify an almost infinite variety of odors, each with its own unique spectral response. Such devices will cheaply and tirelessly monitor home or office for air quality or watch out for the telltale scent of drugs, perfumes, or possibly even a person's characteristic aroma. Tools like these, if monopolized by some government agency, corporation, or secretive clique, would make ludicrous any chance of walking about anonymously or unrecognized.

Recall that some strong privacy advocates want to apply controls on companies that collect information on vast numbers of people for commercial purposes. They suggest this may be achieved by establishing "ownership" rights for information of, by, and about each individual. I have already predicted failure for this effort, because it flies in the face of the basic human drive to gather as much knowledge as we possibly can. And now technical means seem to be coalescing that will allow information collection and dispersal free of interference by any law. There are reports of "floater" information sets, semiamorphous data clusters that drift among many different memory loci at any given time, allowing each system operator to deny local responsibility or ownership. These techniques are still tentative, but if they achieve full potential, it may become impossible to outlaw the "possession" of contraband information, since anyone will be able to read (or add to) such databases without accepting liability or responsibility for them. In a sense, the knowledge will have a life of its own, in cyberspace.

Whether or not this dodge ultimately proves practical, there will always be a fallback position for "data impresarios." They can turn to the banking (and now information) havens—countries that specialize in selling confidentiality to anyone who can afford the price. All that a data-hungry consortium would have to do is hire some consultants under the table, to do the actual fact collecting, while the corporation itself preserves deniability. Cypher-enthusiast Eric Hughes calls this "crypto arbitrage"—moving secret transactions to sites with the fewest regulatory impediments. Hughes depicts the phenomenon as intrinsically liberating for individuals who want to whisper to each other at great distance without being overheard. But the real winners will be massive institutions. Once a computer in the Cayman Islands has everybody's SSN, or bankruptcy records stretching back more than seven years, or copies of "protected" medical records, how will the strong privacy crowd hope to get such information back? What is to stop government agencies from using the same dodge as corporations: hiding their darkest secrets overseas, out of reach of inspection by society's agents of accountability?

If encryption becomes a universal norm, how will we know if the databases are there *at all?*

How ironic that many strong privacy advocates *support* the national money-laundering cartels as refuges against government tyranny. Yet, until transparency floods through Berne and Vaduz, the concept of data privacy is guaranteed to be a pathetic joke. You can shout that "personal information is personal property" until the Moon spirals away toward the Milky Way, but that won't change a thing as long as big shots can shelter their databases beyond reach of all civilized norms.

Every technological advance we have talked about so far in this section is fairly mundane and predictable. (Yes, including gnat-sized cameras.) But now let's ponder some that are more speculative and potentially disturbing. For instance, what conceivable breakthrough might turn out to be the ultimate transparency tool of all time?

How about a truly effective *lie detector?*

I'm not talking about the ill-famed "polygraph." In 1997 the U.S. Supreme Court began hearing yet another round of arguments that this venerable device was at last ready to take its place among respectable tools of jurisprudence, despite a spotty record giving the whole concept an aura of crackpot magicianship, a reputation that deterred many futurists from considering what might happen if a truly effective technique were ever found, allowing people reliably to separate fact from fabulation.

Clearly, this is one of the most tantalizingly difficult problems faced by humanity. Trying to distinguish truth from deceit may be one mental activity to which we devote even more gray matter than making guesses about the future! Each of us can recall many painful episodes in life when we pondered worriedly about another person's veracity, or else sweated it out while someone else paid us the same acute scrutiny.

I would never underplay the difficulty of inventing a truly effective lie detector. Scientists have found that human beings are especially talented prevaricators. I mentioned earlier how Robert Wright's book *The Moral Animal* lays out the current theory that deception became a crucial skill in the human mental inventory as we evolved. Moreover, it has been demonstrated that an important part of this skill is deftness at fooling ourselves! In other words, we can lie much more convincingly if we somehow manage to create a vivid set of realistic supporting images and feelings in our minds, almost as if the whopper we just told were actually true. Making up tales—and believing in them, at least temporarily—is a favorite human pastime.

This makes the task of designing an effective lie detector challenging, to say the least. And yet, there appears to be some growing enthusiasm for the idea. As researchers sift and parse the brain's workings down to neuron-by-neuron analysis, who can guarantee that they won't discover some "verity locus" that we all share, or some set of telltale autonomic signs that might even be detected and read from afar?

If such a device is ever developed, there will certainly be a variety of reactions. The late columnist Mike Royko once wrote an essay titled "Let's Give Lying the Respect It Deserves," claiming that without lies we would have chaos, rioting, and a collapsed economy. If our leaders told the truth, they would most likely all be out of jobs, and we would all be nervous wrecks. Stressing the diametrically opposite perspective in *Radical Honesty: How to Transform Your Life by Telling the Truth*, Brad Blanton says, "Lying is the major source of all human stress." Blanton recommends eliminating even the "little white lies" that seem to smooth life's daily encounters at work, on the street, or at the breakfast table. For most of us, a less radical midway opinion may be more typical. We want to catch evil, but to leave enough slack for the little prevarications that ease life along.

In any event, the point here is not that a foolproof lie detector is desirable, or even that it is likely, only that it may be plausible. If a truth machine ever did appear, it would have tremendous potential, either for beneficial use or wretched abuse.

If restricted to the hands of just a few, it could be a tyrant's dream come true.

If distributed instead to the world's billions, it would surely be a bloody damned nuisance, one that we'd all need time to adjust to.

But we would adapt. And the machine would then be any despot's worst nightmare.

Related to lie detection, but even more disturbing, is the concept of *proclivities profiling*. Suppose it became possible to combine a suite of factors, from both nature and nurture, and from them draw a statistically valid inference regarding which individuals in society are likely, or predisposed, to commit crimes?

If the very idea of this question scrapes a raw nerve, good! It ought to. History shows that people have an ancient and pervasive habit of judging others by whatever standards are fashionable at a given moment, quickly pigeonholing them into categories, then shunting their destinies toward peasantry, isolation, persecution, or even death. Most of us will admit falling all too often for this nasty temptation to stereotype those around us in daily life. And yet, some progress can be seen in the fact that our official morality at last rails against it. According to modern sensibilities in the neo-West, it is sinful to prejudge a person merely for being a member of some group, even if there is a statistical correlation suggesting he or she may be somewhat likely to commit transgressions in the future.

But think about it. Whether you believe that behavior is influenced most by genes or by upbringing, or whether (like most of us) you figure both play a complex, synergistic role in the mystery of individualization, who would be willing to bet their life savings that researchers *won't* find sets of highly significant correlations in the near future?

It could be a combination of blood type with an inherited allergy, a history of beatings in the home, plus having watched too many Chuck Norris movies while eating a particular brand of cheese puffs. . . . The important point is that, in a world filled with curious and inventive sleuths, equipped with fantastic laboratory and computational tools, any such correlations that do exist will be ferreted out during the next few decades. Even if some connections later prove spurious—lacking true underlying causality—they will draw lots of attention, so we had better be ready for the howling storm of public opinion when the announcements come.

How should we react, when some group of researchers announce that they can profile people according to their proclivities toward violence, or other unsavory behavior? One supposes that this analysis would not be the same as the *Love, American Style* dating skit, in which boys were judged according to their actual past behavior. Rather, these profiles may stick to people who have, as yet, done nothing wrong!

An automatic (and in many ways admirable) response would be to forbid proclivities profiling from the very start. But that opens up a real can of worms, including issues of free speech and squelching open scientific enquiry. Any high moral position that rests on suppressing knowledge stands on shaky ground.

Moreover, if violence is sickness, might we somehow help the predisposed in advance, offering special training to control their inner drives? What happens when a set of profiles results in the actual avoidance of a certain number of crimes, sparing some potential victims from injury or death? In fact, let's take another look at Megan's Law, and related codes that require the registration of sex offenders' histories and addresses, warning neighbors if a former sexual predator starts living in their midst. Surely such laws fall into the category we are talking about, branding people because they manifest a higher likelihood of committing *future* crimes. In this case, the increased danger is demonstrable, based on past transgressions, and potentially severe enough to merit strong measures. But isn't that exactly what you'd expect to see, the first time such profiling procedures work their way into law? Once the basic principle is established, we are only arguing over details.

This issue used to lurk at the fringes of science, promoted by enthusiasts with marginal credentials, whose agendas were sometimes redolent of racism. But the field has progressed considerably to the extent that *Psychiatric Annals* devoted an entire volume to "Psychiatric Aspects of Wickedness."

Let me emphasize that my feelings about this are just as mixed and muddled as any reader's. The potential for abuse is horrifying, yet it is tempting to imagine how many of the harmful people one sees in the news—from spouse abusers to serial killers—might have led better lives if they had been offered a choice of eclectic and caring medical helpers, long before they proceeded to wreak havoc around them. On the one hand, proclivities testing could be used as a powerful tool for the suppression of diversity. And yet, the most harmful possible outcome isn't always what happens when we stumble into a new and unavoidable branch of science.

Again, I find this prospect unnerving, even terrifying. Nevertheless, it's clear that such tools will only be made far worse if held closely by a secretive cabal. If proclivities profiling is inevitable, we may be better off sharing responsibility for it, arguing passionately over what the techniques imply, and reflecting on how best to minimize the harm they may do.

Might a "glass houses" effect preserve us against the worst abuses? Could it be that our main hope for tolerance will be found in the imperfections that we all carry around? In the fact that each of us has flaws and shortcomings that need empathy or forgiveness from others? What if *self-righteousness* were ranked right up there as one of those potentially harmful tendencies, measured as a proclivity to injure others by stereotyping them too harshly or too quickly? What if kids were routinely taught to recognize this potentiality in themselves, and to compensate for the impulse with a little self-control? Might that cancel out the potential for abuse?

If so, this extraordinarily searing kind of light may not do quite as much harm as envisioned in our worst fears. Especially if it teaches us to mix pragmatism with hope, pity, and a whole lot of humility.

From physical gnat-sized spy cameras, to creepy software "agents" that might invade and rifle your files, to untraceable databases, to possible lie detectors and proclivities profiles, the future seems to offer a plethora of plausible ways for others to peer at you. Interestingly, almost none of the examples mentioned in this section would be hampered in the slightest by that utopian panacea, encryption. (Recall that encryption also fails to address most of the classic techniques used by old-fashioned tyrants.)

Some people will inevitably suggest eliminating threats such as these by passing laws, assailing the *knowing* of certain things. But in yet another irony, those people will be reaching in supplication toward the one power center that they claim to fear most, government, pleading that we should grant the authorities whole new avenues of regulation and control. New bureaucracies to direct and confine how much or what types of knowledge people should have. Of course, the mighty will flout those laws, as surely as Napoleon made himself emperor. Information will be sought and paid for, even if the market is driven underground to create an economy of smuggled contraband, controlled by unscrupulous people.

Before moving on, however, let me say that all is not lost! Perhaps some new technology, even more far-out than the ones I've just described, will come along to rescue us from ourselves, providing a way to shield you and me against being peered at, poked, analyzed, and parsed right down to our genetic code. This new gimmick may arrive in time to be our salvation.

I wouldn't count on it, though.

A better answer may be found elsewhere. To paraphrase the futurist Peter Schwartz, if it is not possible to be confident in our tools, or our predictions, perhaps we should try having confidence in ourselves.

> *Most people are cowed by the power of large institutions, and resent at least some aspects of the surveillance society. The imposition of social control mechanisms, including the enforced use of intrusive identification, could stimulate an increased degree of conscious non-acceptance of authority. This could in turn bring on the collapse of . . . the nation-state, and with it the disappearance of regional enforcement of law and order. The cyberpunk genre of science fiction works on the assumption that the social surveillance and control movement contains the seeds of its own self-destruction.*
>
> ROGER CLARKE

*Science Explores: Technology Executes: Man Conforms*
SIGN ABOVE THE PORTALS OF THE 1933 CHICAGO WORLD'S FAIR

## HOW THINGS MIGHT GO WRONG

In addition to being called an "enemy of privacy," I have also been labeled a "wild-eyed optimist" because I believe that cantankerous, self-deceiving human beings can learn to behave like creatively eccentric but cooperative citizens of a free and open society.

I refuse to cop a plea to either of these accusations, especially to being a Pollyanna. After all, my entire premise is based on the fact that people *are* often rotten to each other, especially when they think they can get away with it. Admittedly, I consider accountability to be strong medicine, perhaps potent enough to accomplish what all the past exhorting philosophers never managed—getting most of us to act like decent grown-ups. But that, at best, represents a guarded type of optimism.

If I'm not a starry-eyed idealist about human nature, perhaps a more accurate appraisal was made by one friend, a member of the Electronic Frontier Foundation, whose unswerving demand for privacy laws, encryption, and anonymity more closely fits the tenor of these times. "You're a damned *contrarian*, Brin," he accused. "If everyone was talking about openness, you'd be the one screaming for masks and secret codes. If everybody else said the world was okay, you'd shout the sky was falling. You're just taking the other side because you know it'll bug people."

Am I? It doesn't feel that way. At least not at the surface, though I admit that my friend's thumbnail psychoanalysis fits the profile of a modern T-cell, as described in chapter 5. If so, this ornery contrariness is exactly what society trained me (and millions of others) for, so it's hardly my fault.

Anyway, I *may* turn out to be right!

On the other hand, I might not.

A learned person once told me about her favorite sentence, one that she said comes closer to defining human maturity than any other. When spoken, either aloud or in the recesses of the heart, it can mark a person's first steps toward wisdom.

### *"I could be mistaken."*

Well, then, in the name of maturity, let us swing away from optimism about a positive transparent society and explore some possible downsides. What if I'm completely off base about the likely consequences, as cameras and databases pervade our civilization in the years ahead?

How might things go terribly wrong?

In 1991, White House aide Vincent Foster drove to a Washington, D.C., park, pulled out a pistol, and took his own life. Despite endless investigations, rumors, and tirades by radio "hate jockeys," nobody has come up with a credible reason for Foster's action other than the one that seemed apparent at the time. Evidently, Foster was mortified over having given his friends the Clintons poor legal advice during the "Travelgate" affair. In a state of shame and despair, he reeled before the ensuing glare of klieg lights and reporters' hammering questions, until finally concluding that he could take no more. At least, that seems to be what happened.

One reason for the various wild conspiracy theories that followed Foster's death was incredulity by many hard-nosed Beltway insiders that anyone would commit suicide over something so "trivial." True, administration opponents tried to inflate the dismissal of a few members of the White House travel office into a major scandal, and the media cooperated for a while, sniffing after a spoor of blood. But polls showed that the public viewed the affair as picayune. It would have blown over, if not for the suicide.

Those accustomed to the D.C. pressure cooker found it hard to conceive that remorse and embarrassment might roil a decent man's gut over a matter most Washingtonians would take in stride, shrugging and moving on to the next gambit, the next crisis. But Foster wasn't a Washingtonian. Though power and fame can lure almost any man, he hated the hot scowl of relentless scrutiny. Criticism *hurt*. When people were unfair, he did not see it as just another move in "the game" but as a personal blow. Perhaps it was all too much to bear.

This story illustrates a crucial issue that may have been overlooked in previous chapters that concentrated on high-falutin' abstractions such as law, rights, privacy, and accountability. Even assuming that transparency will be a necessary pragmatic tool for securing freedom into the twenty-first century, the cost may be bitter if it also brings alienation and pain to the shy, the reserved, the reticent. Some people don't care to have a harsh, cleansing glare shine on them, even if society puts a light-saber in their hands and says, "You're free! You're safe! Aim bright light right back at them!"

Oh, transparency could have a downside, all right.

> *. . . some people foresee a "dystopian" future in which the top third of the population takes care of itself by hiring the middle third to protect it against the bottom third.* STEVEN E. MILLER

According to one dour vision, penned by Gary T. Marx, we may be heading for a *security society*, composed of five interrelated subsocieties.

- A *dossier* society. Computer records follow each individual as inescapably as a shadow. Bill Gates's "documented life" mutates into an unfailing tally system tracking every mistake you ever made, offering a permanent, unforgiving list for all to see.

• An *actuarial* or *predictive* society. Decisions are increasingly based on predictions of our future actions, through statistical analysis of the groups and categories you belong to. (See the discussion of proclivities profiling.)

• An *engineered* society. Your choices are constrained by physical and social adaptations required for living in a deteriorating world.

• A *porous* or *transparent* society. All the boundaries that used to protect privacy are weak or vanishing.

• A *self-monitored* society. Auto-surveillance (self-scrutiny) becomes useful, necessary, and then a compulsive part of daily life.

In this vision, we will be under constant observation, with everything going on immutable record, known to a myriad others. No more border between public and private. Control will be embedded in a universal network of dossiers, informers, and classification. In other words, we'll see Orwell's world, or that of Terry Gilliam's dystopia, *Brazil*, brought to life with a vengeance. According to Gary Marx,

> Such a society is transparent and porous. Information leakage is rampant. Barriers and boundaries—distance, darkness, time, walls, windows, and even skin, which have been fundamental to our conceptions of privacy, liberty, and individuality —give way. Actions, as well as feelings, thoughts, pasts, and even futures, are increasingly visible. The line between the public and the private is weakened; observations seem constant; more and more information goes on a permanent record, whether we will this or not, and even whether we know about it or not.

There are ironies in comparing Marx's scenario with mine, besides the fact that both use the phrase "transparent society." Note, for instance, that he also foresees the importance of something like "predictions registries." Only in this case their function is not to provide a free market of accountability, as I envision, but rather to serve as tools of regulation and control.

Professor Marx presents a familiar view of the future, seen in countless novels and movies, the one dark dread that most of us in the neo-West have been alerted against over and over again. Yet things *could* still happen this way, despite all the warnings. It depends on who gets to watch, who controls the flow of information, and how they act on that knowledge. In fact, I can extrapolate four different scenarios for how transparency might go wrong, starting with the most obvious version offered by Professor Marx.

## 1. Surveillance Elites

In the world we all fear most, the answer to that question, "Who watches and controls?" will be hierarchical power structures. Some form of oligarchic tyranny. (See box 3 in the Plausibility Matrix on page 272.) It hardly counts whether the elite is based on inherited wealth, personal connections, public office, ideological purity, fighting prowess, demagoguery or several other standard methods by which groups organized themselves to dominate others in the past. What matters is that this despotism will be like none other, because it will know all and see all.

In 1990, Marx illustrated this chilling scenario by creating a composite corporation to serve as an example, combining a spectrum of already current surveillance techniques under one roof. Job applicants underwent extensive medical and psychological screening, including detailed background questions about their parents' health. The company searched databases, credit, and police records. Employees were checked weekly by an automated health analysis of urine, blood pressure, etc. Workplace chiefs monitored more than two hundred criteria to assess productivity—including keystroke speed, errors, and time away from the job. Computer screens sent periodic productivity messages. In addition to audio and video surveillance, all telephone numbers dialed were recorded. In Marx's composite scenario, "transparency of human behavior for the purposes of total control" became habitual, addictive. Unseen managers monitored people down to the smallest detail, recording and detecting all variances in a process called "accountability through visibility."

We needn't go into the towering hypocrisy of managers refusing to let the same degree of all-penetrating scrutiny apply to them. That is simply what people in power will do, if they are allowed to get away with it—the very outcome that *reciprocal* transparency might prevent. Certainly, if left unchecked, this tendency could inexorably bring about Marx's maximum security society. A world not of glass houses, but of one-way mirrors.

In such a world, we would have just one hope—that eventually a generation of rulers might feel less frantic and driven than their fathers. Perhaps, eventually, these sons and daughters of the mighty will grow bored with watching and controlling everybody else. But this is only a slim reed to clutch if we ever find ourselves living in such an awful world. Anyway, I doubt this particular dismal future will come to pass, simply because we are already so wary of it from a relentless drumbeat in countless works of culture and fiction. Surely, the worst danger must lurk in other directions.

## 2. Surveillance Obsession

A second dark vision also fits Marx's overall scenario of a maximum security society. In this rendition of tomorrow, privacy has vanished, as in example 1. We live harried, supervised lives. Only now those doing the watching are not an elite, but *everybody*.

Remember city number two back in chapter 1? That's the metropolis where the people control the cameras. Everyone enjoys the same high level of access. As a result, citizens have more freedom. The police are supervised. Everyone is held accountable.

But this vision could go desperately wrong if folks grow *obsessed* with watching.

Here, my restaurant analogy has broken down. Instead of being deterred from staring, people become addicted to it. In their rising paranoia, the natives of city number two might get stuck in a viciously competitive cycle. Believing that any lapse in vigilance could cause them to lose out, they band together in groups of common interest, peering at their foes relentlessly, pursuing them across the cityscape and through corridors of cyberspace, suspecting that any shadow may conceal a conspiracy. And they, in turn, are just as vigorously pursued. Encryptions and illusions spread, along with tailored viruses sent to corrupt opponents' precious data stores in a war of attrition that only accentuates the desperate race to see more with gnat drone cameras, which are countered by antignats, and so on. In such a society, you might officially have plenty of freedom, and yet be so frightened and lost that life as a sovereign individual becomes impossible.

Utterly dependent on the protection of your "tribe," you will conform to every social ritual and constraint the group demands of you. Recall from chapter 6 how Philip Agre and Christine Harbs described a similar scenario: "Shorn of the ability to enter into relationships of responsibility and trust, individuals will tend to gravitate towards a safe average, suppressing their individuality and creativity in favour of a thoroughgoing orientation to the demands of an omniscient observer."

In effect, such a world is ruled not by monarchs, nobility, or captains of industry, but by a new class of witch doctors, cyberpunk-style hackers whose sophisticated software hexes may offer just a little shelter against the endless swarm of eyes that fill an awful night. It is a world of accountability gone mad, reminiscent of Dr. Seuss's children's story about the land of Hawtch-Hawtch, where citizens were so frenetically busy keeping an eye on each other ("watching") that "today all the Hawtchers who live in Hawtch-Hawtch are watching on Watch-Watcher-Watchering-Watch."

Frankly, I can think of better ways our descendants might choose to spend their time.

### 3. Surveillance Acceptance

There is another possible "chilling" outcome to a world of universal surveillance, one that is very different from those we just looked at.

Suppose the cameras do eventually pervade everywhere, creating a society where not a single nook or cranny is left unobserved. And let us venture further that everyone has access to all the cameras (hence no overt tyranny). Now, let's add one more supposition.

The first generation to be surrounded by lenses may feel nervous under the pervasive gaze.

The next is mildly irked, though used to it.

And later generations?

Growing up with this situation, they take it completely for granted. From infancy, they have looked at a myriad strangers all over the globe, and have been looked at by just as many. Their fear levels are low, since nothing can happen to such children—either by accident or deliberate harm—without it being instantly known by those who love them. Watched over in this way, eight-year-olds feel free to wander both city and countryside, exploring as most children could not possibly be allowed to do nowadays.

The author Damon Knight described such a world in his short story "I See You," a fascinating tale about a future when all people own machines that can look through any wall. Defying the hackneyed plot of abuse by some dictator, Knight instead posited an era when everything has eerily changed. Lies and injustice have vanished, and privacy is considered a quaint, archaic concept, like phlogiston. In Knight's spooky world there are no mysteries. Moreover, people find, at first to their surprise, that they do not miss them.

Elsewhere we have envisioned transparency being all about accountability and freedom, while preserving a curtilage of decent reserve and genuine privacy for individuals and families to retreat within, whenever they choose. In fact, I see transparency as a principal tool for *preserving* some privacy. But in Damon Knight's alternative scenario, a flood of light has effectively transmuted humanity into something new. A people as much unlike us as . . .

. . . as *we* are unlike our Cro-Magnon ancestors, who likewise saw and knew everything about one another, almost all the time.

Of course, Knight's tale is just a vivid fabulation, the sort of "what if?" that makes a reader go "huh!" and mull silently for a while, as the best science fiction is supposed to do. Personally, I doubt human nature would provide for such happy attitudes in a world so utterly transformed. In any event, I am not ready to live in a society anywhere near that transparent.

### 4. Surveillance Overload

A final dystopic vision of transparency is called *data smog*. It tells of a time, a few years or decades from now, when the sheer volume of information does to us what all the secret codes and ciphers never could—deafening us in a cacophony of noise, blinding us in a bitter fog of our own profligacy.

This scenario is disturbingly realistic in one way. Every time humans discovered a new resource, or technique for using mass and energy, one side effect has always been *pollution*. Why should the information age be any different from those of coal, petroleum, or the atom?

Already, those who manage the Internet have to contend with a rising fraction of bits and bytes that can only be defined as "garbage": old postings that keep reappearing after they have been erased and go on multiplying for no apparent reason; stored drafts of documents, minutely different from one another, that no one dares to throw away; "spammed" messages that take on a life of their own, reproducing endlessly; acres of bandwidth taken up by funky Web pages that feature live video images of a goldfish bowl or coffee pot. Updating an old lawyer's trick, some corporations and government agencies nowadays respond to reporters' freedom-of-information demands by spewing back more raw data than any journalist could possibly sift through in a dozen lifetimes. This "fire hose" defense often proves an effective way to stymie investigators, holding accountability safely at bay and neutralizing some of society's best T-cells.

Even if encryption proves overrated—or if we somehow evade the seductive trap of secrecy fetishism—there remains a danger that the proud promise of this new age may drown in an effluvium of openness. We may lose all the advantages of candor in an acrid data smog of our own making.

Each of these four scenarios depicts a world of transparency taken to some logical extreme. Naturally, I have a reply to all four extrapolations. The answer is that *human nature rebels against oversimplification,* such as drastic social systems that limit the breadth of our ability to experiment and experience. This response will be especially true in a society whose most popular myths sermonize from the pulpit of eccentricity. For instance, our best hope against unhappy worlds 1 and 3 above may lie in the power of boredom to make the act of watching start to pall. A quid pro quo, a polite averting of eyes, could reduce the oppressiveness, if each person chose to see self-interest beyond the nose on his or her face.

In our hypothetical society plagued by data smog, there is a good chance that the problem would be solved by the development of new software agents, sophisticated autonomous servant programs designed to cull and search through the morass, adroitly sifting the information byways with our needs foremost in mind, clearing away dross and eventually restoring clarity to cyberspace, the way the air of Los Angeles is gradually becoming breathable once again.

As for the benighted denizens of dystopia number 2 (Surveillance Obsession), their self-made suffering will inevitably end in a way that they deserve, either when some clique or dictator finally takes over, or else when a computer, program, or virus finally evolves out of that fetid "darwinnowing" ferment, rising up to achieve artificial intelligence. Such a sapient program might then take over the world—a laudable situation, since the citizens of that wretched commonwealth have already exchanged sovereign judgment for paranoia. Fools forsake any right of mastery over their creations, a truth that has always held for parents, and may apply to humanity as a whole.


These four scenarios were radical extrapolations of what might happen if we are stupid and let some malign trend reach its ultimate conclusion. In fact, though, I have faith that citizens of the neo-West will notice and correct such dismal tendencies before they get that far.

Can future Vince Fosters—and all the others who find in-your-face confrontation painful—feel at home in a transparent society? While extroverted "T-cells" go careening about, challenging errors and battling threats to freedom, will there be serenity for the reticent and the shy? Throughout this book I have maintained that a culture of openness will sustain some privacy, if that is what free citizens want, and if Peeping Toms have reason to fear getting caught. Courtesy may return as an important moderating force, for the simple reason that it will make life among the cameras more bearable—and because those who don't practice it will be found out, losing their neighbors' good will.

I believe this balance of technology with common sense may result in a world where we are observed only about 80 percent of the time, and still have that personal curtilage, a sanctuary where we can relax unwatched, share intimacy, or simply be solitary for a while. Those havens may not offer enough space for a mad scientist's lab. Only a very small conspiracy will be able to meet in your sanctum or bedroom. But that's okay. People won't have much use for conspiracies in a civilization filled with well-educated amateurs and dedicated eccentrics.

Above all, citizens will be much too busy to spend time peering at one another. They'll have better things to do.

• • •

In contrast to these five views of a transparent society (four of them chilling and one guardedly optimistic), the chief alternative is a world filled with a different kind of blinding fog. An encrypted haze that will nonetheless completely fail to thwart the sophisticated surveillance tools of the rich and powerful, who will simply work *around* the mathematics. Most of us will live in houses with glass roofs. Our neighbors may not be able to peer at us through the surrounding murk of anonymous masks and secret codes, but those dwelling higher on the restored social pyramid will look down and know everything about our lives, even the smallest detail, while we happily imagine that the mighty are still somehow our equals.

They won't be. They never have been. Among all the human cultures yet devised, only one came close to applying the tools of accountability evenly in all directions. But if we choose secrecy as our course, we will abandon the only reliable weapon that freedom ever had.

# A WITHERING AWAY?

*Governments of the Industrial World, you weary giants of flesh and steel, I come from Cyberspace, the new home of Mind. On behalf of the future, I ask you of the past to leave us alone. You are not welcome among us. You have no sovereignty where we gather.*

• • •

This quotation from John Perry Barlow's "A Declaration of Independence of Cyberspace" illustrates one of the essential issues that will confront us in the coming decades: a realignment of the relationship between individuals and nations. We can see signs of this process all around us: in the breakup of the old Soviet Union; in a devolution of power from the British Parliament to regional assemblies; in rising influence by nongovernmental organizations (NGOs) on the international stage; and in a reborn American "states' rights movement," whose fringe elements now eagerly spurn a flag they were brought up to revere.

"Just as during the Enlightenment the nation-state took over from 'the church' to become the dominant seat of action, so the nation-state is now receding, yielding center stage to the marketplace," says Lawrence Wilkinson, cofounder of the net-wise Global Business Network, who goes on to suggest that national patriotism may fade to the level of affection people now give sports teams, or even "brand loyalty" to their favorite companies.

Amid a spate of recent books extrapolating this trend to a stateless future, financier Walter Wriston's *The Twilight of Sovereignty* contends that, whereas geography once made history, the information revolution will make geography history. "How does a national government measure capital formation when much new capital is intellectual?" Wriston asks. "How does it track or control the money supply when financial markets create new financial instruments faster than regulators can keep track of them?" *The Sovereign Individual*, by James Dale Davidson and William Rees-Mogg, makes the same argument by pointing out that technology is reducing the ability of government to enforce its power and control. The overhead cost of the modern industrial state will no longer be supported when people find ways to escape it. Wriston has supported efforts to transform offshore banking havens into high-tech sanctuaries, masking cybercommerce from national taxing authorities. Taking a slightly different approach to the same notion, David Post and David Johnson, codirectors of the Cyberspace Law Institute, have proposed that cyberspace should be a separate legal jurisdiction with its own laws and regulations, created and enforced by the online community.

This is not a new dream. A thread of resentment toward hierarchical power structures has always gained strength from time to time, aided by some promising (usually informational) technology; for example, the printing press encouraged dissemination of vernacular bibles, breaking the rigid hold of church officials on religious thought and encouraging the rise of "individualist" Protestant alternatives. But the decline of church influence turned out to be only partial, as it adapted to changing times. Moreover, we should note that nation-states soon took advantage of the same technological innovations, replacing church authority and gaining strength from the increased information flow, rather than losing ground to it. Stephen Kern's *The Culture of Time and Space: 1880–1918* describes how the telegraph, telephone, and airplane helped prompt "a general cultural challenge to all outmoded hierarchies." But other kinds of hierarchies soon emerged, from the totalitarianism of Hitler and Stalin to the business empires of Ford and Du Pont. The tendency of humans in leadership to leverage permanent positions atop pyramids of power should never be underrated.

Despite all the transcendentalist proclamations we have heard that the Internet and new media will inevitably level social differences and empower individuals, most of the cash (and accompanying influence) seems to be passing through major corporations.

In an article in the December 1997 *Atlantic Monthly* titled "Was Democracy Just a Moment?," Robert D. Kaplan paid respect to the resiliency of authoritarians in adapting to fresh styles of technology and control, including the corporate boardroom. Picking and choosing in order to cite a few tyrannical success stories, and largely ignoring the error-prone, war-loving, and self-delusional nature of most dismal autarchies, Kaplan nevertheless did strike home by pointing out how nearly universal has been the tendency for cliques to take over during times of chaos, transition, or unaccountability. Extending this into the future, Kaplan's view is that "Corporations are like the feudal domains that evolved into nation states; they are nothing less than the vanguard of a new Darwinian organization of politics."

• • •

What can we conclude from these seemingly contradictory predictions? We seem to be surrounded by bright fellows who think they have road maps for tomorrow. Kaplan, at least, has some history he can cite to support his dour view of natural trends. The cyberanarchists have nothing but a vivid dream.

Still, the revolutionizing power of the information age *is* impressive, fostering reinvigorated utopian hopes. As discussed in the section "An Open Society's Enemies" at the end of chapter 4, many libertarians have long called for dismantling those state structures they believe hobble and corrupt a natural free market—after which poverty and oppression would presumably vanish, dissolving in a cornucopia of unleashed creativity and enterprise. While some libertarians, such as those at the prestigious Cato Institute, would define this dismantling process in cautious or moderate terms, negotiating an evolving consensus with society at large, a radical or "anarchist" wing sees nothing about the word *government* worth preserving.

The Internet's arrival has stoked this quixotic aspiration to new levels, provoking proclamations of a coming age when tyrants and bureaucrats will smolder away in a soot of their own irrelevance. While the U.S. Libertarian Party polls only single digits in most elections, informal surveys indicate that up to 40 percent of the most technologically sophisticated netizens sympathize with libertarian agendas and goals.

It can be interesting to compare the vision of radical libertarian utopianism with another one that was penned more than a century ago, by Karl Marx. Both look forward to a natural and supposedly inevitable *withering away of the state*, and a resulting civilization without coercion or authority figures, where free adults deal with each other under conditions of perfect independence, gravitating to any work they desire. The chief difference between these two transcendentalist world views, one "extreme left" and the other "far right," has to do with *how* this result will be achieved.

Marx believed that it would occur once industrial societies finish constructing the means of production. After the needed capital—factories, infrastructure, and all that—is completed, there will be no further need for the specialized skills of "capitalists." Their services can then be dispensed with, along with the governments that protect their privileges.

Anarcho-libertarians project a somewhat different path to the same goal. Their ideal society of free and rich individualism awaits one prime task: assertively demolishing the oppressive and inefficient state apparatus.

In retrospect, the progression described by Marx sounds incredibly naïve. For instance, there is never a point in time when society finishes "forming capital." In the modern era, factory equipment becomes obsolete with ever-increasing speed, requiring rapid and agile retooling that will leave us needing innovatively competitive "capitalist" managers for any foreseeable future.

Alas, the anarcho-libertarian vision is no more realistic. Believers can cite no historical cases when following a prescription of unbridled individualism caused productivity and freedom to skyrocket in the manner they predict.

We do know that markets often respond well to a moderate and continuing easing of onerous government supervision, a self-correcting process of gradual deregulation that many nation-states are currently performing through their own political processes, even as we speak, and one that we have discussed several times in this book. As Jaron Lanier put it, "Of course government intervention screws up a market, but at the same time it is the existence of government that creates markets in the first place. Otherwise, people would resort to violence instead of money to get things." A position that is perfectly compatible with moderate libertarian thought.

Without a doubt, many areas of public policy merit further attention for possible deregulation, for example, numerous cases of "corporate welfare." In fact, mainstream economists believe that enhanced openness of information flows will result in gradual easing or replacement of many bureaucratic structures, as cheating is eliminated and all market players can participate with full knowledge. In other words, transparency.

Unfortunately, libertarians in general (even the moderates) have little voice in this ongoing process, because a large fraction have politically marginalized themselves through blanket contempt for gradualism. By publicly ridiculing the current consensus, worked out by a free and educated citizenry over the course of many decades, enthusiasts like Wriston emulate the followers of Marx in dismissing their fellow citizens as puppets and dupes. Hardly an effective way to elicit support.

. . .

Ironically, the dream that anarcho-libertarians and Marxists share may yet come about, though not in the manner that either group ordains. Instead of happening through some transcendent revolutionary transformation—a semiviolent or semimystical upheaval—their ideal world of true individual sovereignty might appear through a gradual combination of the pragmatic tools and skills that have been described in this book.

1. Rising wealth and education levels may extend people's horizons, encouraging them to consider alternatives to traditional tribes and empires. New affections won't necessarily banish the old.

2. The propaganda campaigns described earlier—a tsunami of films, books, and images promoting individualism and suspicion of authority—will accelerate a desire by billions to find ways of perceiving themselves as somehow unique and special. Millions will actually succeed in achieving truly creative eccentricity.

3. Where this results in a proliferation of avocations, or "hobbies," many private individuals and groups will take on tasks that formerly only state bureaucrats were thought capable of performing, such as nosing around for inefficiency and error. As shown by the example of public feedback regulation discussed in chapter 8, many paternalistic protections may prove less necessary, and even fade away, once consumers have ready access to the correlated information they need for making truly informed choices.

4. Human nature will not change (though both Marxists and anarcho-libertarians seem to expect it to). Cliques and groups of would-be oligarchs will always conspire to improve their position through cheating rather than fair competition. But in a world of free-flowing information, these efforts may prove futile. Infections of nascent tyranny will heal under liberal applications of light. Government will be an essential tool for preventing coups and criminality in the short term. But transparency may eventually reduce or eliminate the need for armies and police to safeguard our lives and property.

5. Poverty will not go away all by itself, or through some idealized magic of free markets. But when all the world seems "next door," it will be impossible for the well off to escape hearing, seeing, and ultimately feeling the pain of their neighbors. They will help. The detailed methods may range all the way from person-to-person charity to collective (tax-supported) efforts, but *we* will help. Or else we will not deserve a better world.

Again, this scenario is perfectly compatible with the views of many reasonable and mature "libertarians," who see no harm in gradualism, as long as real progress is being made. But to those we saw at the beginning of this section, gleefully rubbing hands over the imminent demise of nations, this particular sketch for a "withering away of the state" lacks one vital feature that both anarchists and Marxists adore about their ideologies—a "them versus us" resentment so well illustrated by Barlow's wonderfully vivid "Declaration of Independence."

In contrast, an empirical-gradualist approach, using transparency to slowly replace government with free will, suggests that we are already far along the path. Moreover the neo-Western liberal democracies that got us to this point will be essential tools for helping us travel the rest of the way. They have (so far) provided a benign environment in which we can stretch and explore unprecedented realms of freedom. These are balmy parks compared to the fear-drenched chiefdoms of our ancestors—peaceful commonwealths where we've been fed, clothed, and tutored, even as we dream about outgrowing them.

Centuries ago, the inventor of modern democratic theory, John Locke, replaced mystical-Platonic justifications of power with a new model: a "social contract" in which rulers were ultimately answerable to the people. Under Locke's *implicit* contract, the sole recourse of an afflicted populace was to rebel against oppressors and replace those at the top of the pyramid, a crude model, but one appropriate to an age when few could read.

Now we may be headed for an era when the social contract will become *explicit*. When each of our supereducated grandchildren may negotiate fresh trade-offs of liberty and responsibility with individuals and remnant institutions in a world of sophisticated, sovereign human beings.

If so, this utopian vision will come about only because we passed successfully through *this* complicated, irritating, noisy, indignant-but-hopeful era of transition. A pragmatic, gritty progression that was fostered and enabled by some of the world's states. By governments that are occasionally oppressive, but are far more often our possessions and tools.

In other words, our nations, which still deserve our rambunctious citizenship, some loyalty, and perhaps even our wary love.

## CHAPTER TEN

# GLOBAL TRANSPARENCY

*Spreading corruption, robbing youths of moral values, decadent clothes and sexual problems are all deviations bred by satellite television.*

LOTFALLAH ZAREI QANAVATI, MEMBER OF
THE IRANIAN PARLIAMENT, MARCH 1995

*If you criticize, I learn, and I don't mind how much you criticize. Feel free and do your best. This is the policy of the government. Hopefully it will be very helpful for the successful operation of the government.*

KAMAL KHARRAZI, FOREIGN MINISTER
IN THE RECENTLY ELECTED IRANIAN
GOVERNMENT, SEPTEMBER 1997

During the summer of 1997, a pair of aircraft took off on simultaneous transcontinental flights, one from a Russian air force field and one from an American base. Crammed with cameras and "spy devices," each plane crossed international boundaries to begin a long tour, photographing and probing the territory of its former enemy. Once almost unimaginable, this mission was first in a series of verification overflights, mandated under arms control agreements between the United States and inheritor states of the former Soviet Union.

These missions are the fruition of a dream almost fifty years old, a missed opportunity for wholesome transparency that seems to be coming true at last. At the dawn of the atomic age, as the United States and the Soviet Union prepared to launch into a long era of nuclear brinkmanship, several attempts were made to avoid the looming Cold War. First came the "Baruch Plan" (named for statesman Bernard Baruch), proposing that all nations place their nuclear reactors and explosives under the supervision of a single global agency. The concept was supported (tepidly) by the U.S. government but roundly vetoed by Stalin.

The same fate greeted an initiative made by President Eisenhower, the "open skies" proposal, an offer to exchange overflight privileges so that potential adversaries might photograph each other's military and industrial facilities, calmly evaluating the extent of any perceived threat and forestalling cycles of escalation. Eisenhower knew that professional intelligence services routinely exaggerate any foreign menace, partly through institutional self-interest or habitual paranoia, but also as a legitimate reaction when confronting some bellicose power notoriously inclined to both secrecy and violence. Under those conditions, "better safe than sorry" always seemed a prudent policy.

Eisenhower reasoned that full knowledge about each other's capabilities would be better—potentially denying hawks on both sides the excuse for an expensive and hazardous arms race. Now, at the century's close, Eisenhower's vision seems to have revived from the grave. In addition to overflights, sophisticated satellites detect any major shift in forces, while on-site inspectors track weapons stored or destroyed. Communication among scientific and legal professionals fosters trust, interdependency, and a mutual grasp of the other side's competence. Nuclear power plant inspections and nonproliferation agreements help delay the inevitable spread of weapons of mass destruction.

What does all of this *transparency* tell us about the interconnected world to come?

In 1983, Michael W. Doyle commented on the common observation that democracies almost never wage war on one another. Understanding the reasons for this phenomenon may be crucial to our hopes for preventing devastating conflict in the next generation. Which attributes of democracy foster this essential trait of mutual nonaggression?

One thesis has been that peoples with more than a certain level of wealth have too much stake in the status quo to willingly risk their comforts in military strife. This contemptuous postulate has been popular among aggressive despots, from Hitler to Saddam Hussein, but the assumption proved delusional each time the citizens of democracies turned to shoulder sacrifices in defense against hostile tyrannies, just as Athenian citizen soldiers dealt capably with macho-fanatic Spartan professionals for more than a hundred years.

Putting forth a related notion in the *Atlantic Monthly*, Robert D. Kaplan supported the "assertion that prosperous middle classes arise under authoritarian regimes before gaining the confidence to dislodge their benefactors." In other words, dictatorships create the economic well-being that later leads to democracy. While there certainly are examples of this phenomenon, Kaplan's argument ignores the fact that some great democracies, especially the United States, lifted themselves out of initial primitiveness and poverty by their own bootstraps, while simultaneously working out the kinks in a deeply flawed but steadily improving democratic system. It is facile to pick and choose examples, giving tyrants credit for fostering the roots of freedom, just because a few egomaniacal overlords were a little less malignant than the rest.

In contrast, mainstream economists (as we saw in chapter 1) often attribute war to faulty information flows, that is, one side being unable to estimate properly the other's capabilities and resolve. Since democracies are far richer in information, and have a diversity of contrasting opinions to point out glaring policy errors, it is believed that the basic logic of markets enables such nations to hammer out their differences through negotiation long before they reach an obstinate breakdown or the recourse of war.

The same idea manifests in social-psychological terms, since it is difficult to demonize and dehumanize an adversary population enough to justify slaughter, if they appear frequently on your streets as tourists, exchange cultural symbols and memes, and are defended by their friends in the local open media. Such exchanges also help to clarify the other side's *intent*, which can be even more important than mere strength of military forces. (For instance, the United States never worried about nuclear weapons held by Britain, whose designs toward America were verified, on a myriad levels, to be benign.) According to political scientist Michael Byron, accumulated evidence suggests that the dispersed availability of information and communications technologies can be far more relevant than levels of income for predicting a nation's degree of democratization. Hence there are strong reasons to make the fostering of open-knowledge systems a matter of paramount international policy.

Of course it is no longer a bipolar world. Non-Western nuclear-capable states refuse to enter the new era of transparency, perhaps because they feel it unwise to let potential adversaries see their unreadiness for war.

National pride propels prickly Third World leaders to defend secrecy staunchly in the name of "national sovereignty," while some national elites may also fear that releasing budgetary details would reveal skimming and graft.

Yet another logic underlies the imperative toward secrecy, one that was adhered to for many years by Soviet planners: *As open societies, America and Western Europe cannot prevent our spies from crossing their territory, reading their free press, learning almost anything about them. But the West must expend great effort and expense to learn just a fraction of our vast store of secrets. Knowledge is power, so we will eventually win.*

As we discussed in chapter 1, this reasoning was fallacious, but overwhelmingly tempting. Many factors helped America and the West evade the "pitfall of security." All political wings can claim some credit, from civil libertarians to cold warriors such as Edward Teller, who understood that openness promotes creativity, eventually outclassing secrecy every time. Henry Kissinger wrote that the existence of nuclear weapons called for a reversal of the standard role of diplomacy; instead of concealing the national strategy, it was now necessary to make sure that potential adversaries were absolutely clear as to your nation's intent. Hence, while intelligence remained vital, openness became equally important.

Two essential points are worth reiterating here.

1. Strong privacy advocates appear to accept the same fallacy of security. They believe not only that masks, shrouds, and shields confer advantages on those that use them but also that those advantages can benefit the little guy, if only he imitates the maestros of secrecy.

2. This alluring belief is also held tenaciously by many elites around the world, who pursue it as a fierce national policy. A policy that fundamentally endangers citizens of the neo-West, because it allows those foreign elites to engage in adventurous miscalculations without benefit of error-correcting criticism.

Can such policies succeed in the coming decades? While the Soviets spent huge sums on radio jamming, and while China and Cuba continue doing so (China also allows internal distribution of only 10 carefully selected foreign films per year), no similar effort is made by Western nations to block outside propaganda. Nor would citizens in Europe, Australia, or North America put up with such an effort. Western attitudes about the relative toxicity of ideas (see chapter 5) assume that external propaganda or memes won't threaten our populace, or society's overall cohesion. Few listen to China Radio, but millions would scream if we were denied the choice.

This contrast is dramatically demonstrated by the way dictators react to the Internet. If power elites find foreign radio broadcasts threatening, imagine how they see a new medium where data flows are greater, more flexible, and more difficult to monitor. We have seen how some nations seek strict control over service providers. Net idealists in the West sometimes predict that such efforts are pathetically doomed to fail, but tyranny is an old, well-developed form of governance that takes advantage of basic human drives. There is no guarantee that despots won't come up with a different type of network—one that enhances, rather than diminishes, their power.

Such efforts must be opposed. But how?

Earlier we suggested that it may be a mistake to promote human rights around the world strictly in terms of Platonic essences, the sanctimonious contention that free speech and other liberties are "fundamental, sacred, and inalienable." First, none of these statements is supportable in the context of human history. Such rights have been rare anomalies, all too easily taken away by domineering despots. They seem far from innate to cantankerous human nature. (Recall the "Paradox of the Peacock.")

Secondly, elites in other nations have learned how to fight back in terms of the very values the neo-West espouses. Citing the virtue of diversity, they insist that human rights campaigns are efforts at cultural imperialism, treading callously on other ethnic or national styles that merit as much respect as democracy, for example, Confucian paternalistic hierarchicalism.

When it comes to arguments over human rights, another arrow must be added to the quiver of liberty—the pragmatic arrow of enlightened self-interest. Reiterating a point covered in chapter 1, it is essential for both governments and activists in the neo-West to explain, forcefully, that we are pushing human rights for all the world's citizens *for our own safety's sake.* Indeed, nations ruled by narrow oligarchies who ignore criticism from their own masses have a miserable record of making devastating mistakes and strategic blunders, such as adventurous wars. Wars that they *will* lose . . . but perhaps only after wreaking havoc on the world.

This link between human rights and legitimate self-interest is too seldom mentioned. But in fact, it is arguably the most bitter and dangerous conceptual issue separating antagonistic blocs of nations at this time, exacerbating every East-West or North-South disagreement and preventing many ancient problems from being solved the way the Cold War was.

Of course, it is ironic to hear dictators defend their practice of sealing borders and clamping down with official secrecy, using justifications that are semantically almost identical to the irate communiqués issued by encryption and strong privacy advocates. ("We have a right to control information about ourselves, to act anonymously or secretly, to put our own house in order without meddling criticism, and to resist outsiders' definitions of accountability!")

If we look once again at the accountability matrix, on page 86, the reasons for this similarity become sadly apparent. They go much deeper than the superficial individualism and devotion to freedom expressed by leading privacy advocates. The grown-up world of Woodrow Wilson's "open agreements, openly arrived at" can be viscerally far less satisfying than indignation. It takes aplomb to lay all your cards on the table, and demand that others do the same, for the sake of an abstract common good.

As illustrated by the opening epigraphs of this chapter, our old dispute over the inherent toxicity of ideas rages on, through every nation and society across the globe. Please recall that in chapter 5 I did *not* claim either side of the ancient argument could prove its case yet, nor that the "maturity thesis" would inevitably win out over a frailty-based model of human nature. The jury is still out, even though I know which side of the contest will have my loyalty during the struggle ahead.

Those leaders who feel that they and their people will be harmed by influxes of alien knowledge are no different from ideologues who want to squirrel away troves of personal or national secrets, lest they be injured by what others know about them. Ultimately, what we are talking about is a struggle between confidence and fear.

> The best weapon of a dictatorship is secrecy, but the best weapon of a democracy should be the weapon of openness.    NIELS BOHR

## NETWAR

Unfortunately, fear can be extremely dangerous.

Each time another "age" began to exploit a new kind of technology or resource base (such as coal or petroleum), nations and other groups began struggling to wrest control over the critical resource. Few expect the information age to be any different. Although a major case of transnational aggression via computers has not been announced yet, numerous studies have already described plausible scenarios for future strife, creating a vocabulary of terms we may see much more of in the decades ahead.

•　　•　　•

The term *cyberwar* refers to knowledge-related conflict at the military level. Outcomes in future clashes may depend less on armed mass or mobility than on which side knows more. As we saw earlier, enhanced powers of sight range from spy satellites to tiny, camera-bearing robots that an infantry squad can deploy to inspect the next hedge or street. Piercing an opponent's shrouded communications can be as important as fielding divisions. The specialists who broke Japanese and German ciphers during World War II arguably hastened victory by as much as a year, but today such breakthroughs could decide the issue in days, even hours. All the better if you can hamstring the enemy's internal communications.

And yes, secrets play an important role in military matters. Even openness advocate Arthur Kantrowitz endorses the benefits of *temporary* secrecy, as long as highly motivated teams classify information for strictly practical reasons, not as part of a creeping culture of self-justification and control. When such groups know that the secrets will eventually be scrutinized for accountability purposes, there is little reason to deny our forces the advantage of keeping enemies in the dark.

It is also worthwhile to send selected information *toward* your foes. Deceptions and false leads used to make up much of this flow. They will remain important on the battlefield, as the side with better technical abilities may choose to conceal some forces, while creating "ghost" units to present a credible threat elsewhere. In recent generations, however, a new approach has been to assail your opponent aggressively with truth. During the Cold War, individuals throughout Eastern Europe came to rely on Voice of America, and especially the BBC World Service, for news and interpretation, because of their reputation for relative veracity in an age of lies. During future conflicts, this reputation may undermine an enemy's attempts to picture Western powers as malign aggressors, thus degrading the dedicated prowess of opposing forces.

Yet the West has its own weaknesses. The U.S. General Accounting Office reported that in 1995 alone, the Defense Department may have experienced as many as 250,000 hacker attacks (attempts to penetrate confidential computer systems via the Internet), of which an estimated 64 percent were successful. In order to safeguard against this security problem, in-house computer systems at many agencies are deliberately severed from all contact with outside computers, separated by "firewalls" of varied effectiveness. Numerous U.S. officials, including State Department officers posted overseas, have no Internet access at their desks or workstations, and are thus handicapped by having to do modern jobs in old-fashioned ways. At the opposite extreme, some worry that our forces may become too reliant on fancy portable computers in the field, which may be vulnerable to cyberwar attacks just as the bombs and missiles begin to fly.

It is a frightening new era. Military analysts cannot even agree what they are talking about. According to Jeffrey Cooper: "Some propose information itself as the target in warfare; others treat information as the weapon; some see information as a critical resource; and still others see information as a realm (like space) or an environment (the 'infosphere'), as a medium for military operations (like air power). Information could also be considered a catalyst or as a control parameter in a process; and in both of these cases, information is neither transformed nor spent." What some analysts fear, and others relish, is the possibility that cyber war may bring the realization of Sun Tzu's two-thousand-year-old dream — "vanquishing the enemy without fighting."

*Netwar*, a related topic, is the use of information-based means to threaten or damage an enemy's homeland, citizenry, or infrastructure base. This use of information technology has become a hot issue during the late 1990s, at summer workshops and gatherings of think tank experts. *If our economy and national health are increasingly dependent on information systems, how can we ensure their safety against sabotage or infiltration by those who wish us harm?*

Because at present the military capabilities of NATO partners appear unassailable by conventional means, there is increasing concern about potential vulnerability on the home front, where complex societies rely on nested webs of intermeshed computers, communication grids, and intricate software to keep functioning. Unlike past (and ongoing) terrorist threats, the fear in netwar has little to do with direct physical attack against one site or another. The Net's inherent resistance to damage, as originally designed by Paul Baran to survive nuclear war, still means that a blown cable or data node here and there may have little overall effect. What worries experts far more than old-fashioned explosives is the prospect that some enemy may develop software-based systems capable of ruining their military networks, or bringing the economy to its knees.

In October 1997, the U.S. Commission on Critical Infrastructure Protection reported that the danger was very real. They reviewed security in eight areas: electrical power distribution, telecommunications, banking and finance, water, transportation, oil and gas, emergency services, and government services. They concluded that the yearly budget assigned to infrastructure defense, about $250 million, should rise fourfold over the next six years. According to the commission's executive summary, "Today, the right command sent over the Internet to a power station's control computer could be just as effective as a backpack full of explosives and the perpetrator would be harder to identify and apprehend."

The Computer Emergency Response Team (CERT), a Defense Department group at Carnegie Mellon University, handled over 2,400 reports of cyber attacks in 1995 alone, as a growing sense of siege developed, along with an expectation of worse to come. Some experts believe netwar may be to the twenty-first century what *blitzkrieg* was to the twentieth. Winn Schwartau, author of *Information Warfare: Chaos on the Electronic Superhighway*, suggests that the United States could need a fourth military service, a cyberforce, to control this theater of battle. "Net war may be the dominant mode of societal conflict in the 21st century."

Some early capabilities were demonstrated during the Gulf War of 1991, when electromagnetic pulse bombs were apparently used by coalition forces to disable the Iraqi power grid without having to completely wreck the civilian infrastructure. Homing beacons were included on the circuit boards of military-related products the Iraqis had bought on the open market, and then turned on by remote control when coalition forces were ready to attack. But now planners worry that systems in North America and Europe may be even more vulnerable in their vast intricacy, perhaps to "militia programs" such as worms or logic bombs that might undermine controlling software, wreaking economic damage out of all proportion to some foe's expenditures. Antagonists need not be hostile nations. Terrorists, drug cartels, black market profiteers, weapons smugglers, extreme ethnonationalists, or grumpy homegrown ideologues might have the resources to mount such a strike. Peter Neumann of Computer Science Laboratory warns of an "electronic Pearl Harbor" unless government and businesses prepare for the threat. Along similar lines, former CIA director John Deutch told Congress that a number of countries around the world are developing strategies and tools to conduct attacks on U.S. information infrastructure. (He did not name countries.)

In his novel *The Cool War*, Frederik Pohl portrayed a disturbingly credible near future in which tit-for-tat acts of covert sabotage become the rule in international affairs. Citizens are barely aware of combat in the traditional sense—there are few battles or casualty reports—but they endure a spiraling decay in quality of life as ships collide, cities suffer blackouts, bridges collapse, databases dissolve, and commutes snarl in hellish traffic jams. Pohl depicts a world that might have been wealthy, dissolving instead into chaos because of a secret war that few know about and nobody can stop.

•　　•　　•

At first sight, defending against such threats may appear hopeless. How can nations guard a "front" that is as porous and hyperdimensional as the Internet? Nevertheless, suggestions have been offered.

1. Pursue research to create "mapping programs" that can accurately describe even the complex and convoluted Internet, locating critical points of vulnerability that should receive special attention, then building security systems and firewalls to defend those crucial nexi.

2. Develop systems of validation and verification, many of them encryption-based, that may prevent false or forged authorizations.

3. Encourage the design of new systems that are "fail-safe," that is, operate at least minimally, even when severely degraded or damaged.

4. Encourage all organizations that keep vital records, including banks, hospitals, and so on, to maintain and update nonvolatile memory storage backups at secure locations, so that important services and parts of the economy can be reconstructed in case information systems are corrupted.

5. Unleash vigorous "tiger teams" of imaginative and well-trained hackers to test important systems by launching attacks under controlled conditions. (Recent experience in the military with such teams shows that they succeed in their mock assaults over 80 percent of the time, often with trivial ease. The best way to solve such lapses would be to keep hammering away until most flaws and errors are found.)

6. Then, within the limits of realistic security, invite *outsiders* to test a variety of systems, by establishing a series of challenge awards to any clever hackers who succeed in uncovering hidden failure modes. (An added condition for the prize would be to suggest solutions.)

7. Keep as few secrets as possible. The remaining ones will be easier to protect. And the trust engendered will help demolish many of the paranoic fantasies that are eroding faith in Western institutions.

8. Encourage a society whose distributed nodes of power, services, and expertise are capable of operating both in unison with remote locales and in isolation, in much the same way that the Internet can absorb damage and route around it. These nodes must include nongovernmental and noncorporate units that are capable of supplementing, and even standing in for, more formal institutions in the event of an emergency or breakdown. In other words, take advantage of the century of amateurs.

9. Undertake strong measures to ensure that aggressors will be identified and punished, so that impunity does not encourage more of the same. (See further discussion later in this chapter.)

10. Recognize that doing all these things properly will involve letting go of hierarchical power, without necessarily giving up the advantages of a clearly defined modern state. This is hard to do, but the neo-West already has a myriad precedents, as well as an educated population that is more than willing to turn the devolution of skill and authority into a national resource.

This final theme arises in a recent book about netwar and cyberwar, edited by Rand Corporation researchers John Arquilla and David Ronfeldt: *In Athena's Camp: Preparing for Conflict in the Information Age*, a collection of papers that explores many of the new and perilous types of confrontation that we touched upon briefly here. Most of the contributing authors appear to agree on one conclusion: the information revolution favors and strengthens networked forms of organization, while making life difficult for hierarchical forms. Those nations that take advantage of networks and minimize the vulnerabilities of hierarchical control will stand a better chance in the years ahead.

Ultimately, the secret to surviving attacks against our infrastructure's vulnerable keystones will be to have none. When the cathedral is transformed into a living forest of semiautonomous trees, an enemy may topple pillar after pillar, yet never succeed in bringing down the roof.

> *Repression is not defensible whether the tradition from which it springs is Confucian, Judaeo-Christian, or Zoroastrian. The repressed individual still suffers, as does society, and there are consequences for the global community. Real costs accrue in terms of constrained human creativity, delayed market development, the diversion of assets to enforce repression, the failure of repressive societies to adapt well to the rapidly changing global environment, and the dislocations, struggles and instability that result from these and other factors.*
> DAVID ROTHKOPF

## CAN NETWARS BE WON?

At present, the overall advantage in information warfare still seems to lie with the neo-West, which can aim torrents of alluring, individualist-oriented media toward any center of totalitarianism. In a conflict between world *Zeitgeists*, one benefit of openness is an ability to unleash autonomous groups to challenge the opposition. The activities of these groups need not be centrally coordinated and can even be disavowed, as was the case when activists Dan Haig and Richard Schneider set up full Internet capabilities for the Tibetan government in exile in 1997, enabling it to contact and coordinate the dispersed refugee community. Such activities are in harmony with overall Western goals, while public officials can claim total detachment, which is just as well, because no government could interefere in any event.

There are also potential drawbacks to openness. Free movement and lack of internal passport controls may frustrate the FBI and other agencies charged with public safety, and we just saw that a complex modern infrastructure provides a wealth of tempting targets. When sabotage efforts finally succeed (and some will), one effect may be to deflect the national agenda. By engendering a sense of fear, adversaries may hope to change neo-Western society, provoking panicky laws that shut down some freedoms, "for safety's sake."

Worse, our citizens may come to accept the vile concept of "trade-offs," attempting to walk the knife edge of some devil's dichotomy, with both freedom and safety offered on a sacrificial altar. If such a plan succeeded, it would be a greater defeat than any the West endured during the Cold War.

There is a transparency option. Terrorists operate under cloaks of anonymity and secrecy, their movements, supply routes, and sources of funding carefully hidden. This is especially true of their concealed finances, which are often funneled through those so-called banking havens we discussed earlier. Recent scandals over accounts hidden from Holocaust victims after World War II may have begun eroding the benign mask of smiling neutrality worn by such institutions, but the real impulse to force them open may only come after some band of terrorists manages to kill thousands with a gas attack, or blow up a skyscraper, or poison a reservoir, or "dust" a city with radionuclides. When this happens, many will call for draconian solutions, granting the state new police powers. But there may be an alternative, deflecting citizen ire toward a true center of culpability.

The transparency option would demand that the world's cash flow finally become open and accountable, thus denying criminals, terrorists, and conspiratorial elites the power to hide away—and hide behind—mountains of untallied cash.

I am well aware of many difficulties blocking such a reform. It would have to come by some degree of consensus, with plenty of sympathetic help for tiny, independent countries that have few resources other than their banking laws. Above all, it would require reciprocity from the U.S. and other governments—an opening of secret ledgers in Washington, New

York, and elsewhere—a win-win scenario from the perspective of those who worry about *all* potential threats to freedom. Without substantial and verifiable reciprocity, the enhanced financial transparency would be unbalanced and potentially destructive.

Economists would be thrilled to have the flow of dollars, yen, and marks openly observable by all, freeing markets from many unnatural biases and handicaps. Honest agents of the law would appreciate the way it helps them make the world safer, though the price they pay in nosy citizen oversight panels and open budgets might feel irksome at first. Middle-class taxpayers could see their burden ease a little as wealthy tax cheaters pay their share or at least explain in an open political process why their interests merit special treatment. And poor nations might find out where present and former dictators stashed the loot from decades of graft. In contrast, the reader is invited to write a list of those in the world today who would suffer *actual*, rather than ideological, harm by such a "radical" move. Decide for yourself if protecting a right of anonymity for a short catalog of unsavory characters justifies maintaining the status quo.

Again, it is probably too drastic a move to happen overnight. But the discussion has to begin somewhere.

Global transparency is much too involved a topic to be covered here in any detail. For instance, it is quite clear that Western corporations will need to use sophisticated tools of encryption in many foreign lands for some time to come, because transparency works best when it is truly reciprocal. The open society may ultimately be a far better game for humanity, but it can be difficult to manage when the other side insists on playing by older rules. Clearly, common sense is essential during a time of transition.

In the long run, our best strategy may be to overwhelm others with puppydog-style friendliness, an eager torrent of information and generosity that may at first seem like cultural imperialism.

Only it won't be, because we will also listen, now and then.

At least that would be the right—and the smart—thing to do.

# A LITTLE LOYALTY

*The dilemma of today is not that human values cannot
control a mechanical science. It is the other way about:
the scientific spirit is more human than the machinery of
governments. We have not let either the tolerance or the
empiricism of science enter into the parochial rules by
which we still try to prescribe the behavior of nations.*

JACOB BRONOWSKI

Whenever I have given public talks about transparency, I found that certain kinds of audiences react differently. For example, some angry young men on college campuses understandably react sharply to being called "T-cells," whose rebelliousness was programmed by relentless propaganda .

But my most difficult audiences by far are scientists.

When I speak in praise of criticism as an antidote to error, they shrug. When I observe how easily human beings fool themselves, and discuss the ever-lurking temptation to conceal our mistakes, they respond with looks of strained patience, as if I were stating the obvious. In describing transparent accountability and the productive synergy between cooperation and competition, I am preaching to the choir.

"So?" they respond. "Tell us something we don't already know."

Some critics will surely say that my emphasis on mutual accountability comes from my background as a physicist. Transparency is the fundamental mode of interaction in science, where hypotheses and evidence are posed openly. Scientists are trained to invite, and sometimes even relish, the eager criticism of other sharp minds.

This does not make them saints—far from it! Preening and egotism are as rife in science as any other realm of human endeavor. But it does show that openness has a good track record of achieving its chief goals—fairness, error correction, and rapid creativity—in at least one vast and highly profitable arena. A track record that merits close attention from the rest of society.

I say this not only from my experience as a scientist, but as one who has worked in many other walks of life, including the arts. I've witnessed examples of wit, inventiveness, generosity, humor, and even genius in all those areas, on a par with scientific experts. Many people have feet planted in two or more worlds, using hobbies and avocations to conquer archaic boundaries of specialization, as we saw in chapter 2. Those who have spent at least some time in the scientific world tend to speak often about the importance of accountability for the achievement of genuine honesty.

This approach is relevant to the issues we've been discussing for one major reason. Strong privacy advocates often talk about how appreciative they are for the glorious Internet. We have seen quotations proclaiming the Net to be a greater advance than Gutenberg's printing press. In sometimes fervid paeans, they describe how electronic media will open up a bright future for all humankind. And yet, they seldom note, or seem to recall, where this wonder came from!

It came from science. Scientists conceived it, built it, improved it, and then shared it with everybody, all according to the principles they live and work by. In its nascent forms, the Internet had little use for encryption or anonymity, because these were alien concepts, anathema to most of its originators. Rather, it burgeoned, thrived, and grew beautiful in an ambience of near-total accountability.

Now I am fully aware that things change. The needs of a vast worldwide user base clearly differ from those of a few thousand technical workers. We may need to make a great number of alterations and pragmatic compromises in order to serve those masses. Some of those compromises will certainly involve confidential pseudonyms and forms of encrypted secrecy. The tool is ours, to modify as we see fit.

And yet, if the Internet is so wonderful, why are strong privacy advocates so eager to rush and change the premise, the most fundamental core belief, that underlay its origins?

The Internet is a gift from science to the rest of humanity. If we admire the Net, should not a burden of proof fall on those who would change the basic assumptions that brought it about in the first place?

In the end, the argument for transparency goes beyond logic and pragmatism, boiling down to plain good manners.

When you've been invited to a really neat party, try to dance with the one who brought you.

## CHAPTER ELEVEN

# THE ROAD OF OPENNESS

*Men's natural abilities are too dull to see through everything at once; but by consulting, listening, and debating, they grow more acute, and while they are trying all means, they at last discover those which they want, which all approve, but no one would have thought of in the first place.*

BARUCH SPINOZA

*It is our nature to strive to explore everything, alive and dead, present and past and future. When once the technology exists to read and write memories, one mind to another, the age of mental exploration will begin in earnest. Instead of admiring the beauties of nature from the outside, we will look at nature through the eyes of the elephant, the eagle, and the whale. We will be able, through the magic of science, to feel in our own minds the pride of the peacock and the wrath of the lion.*

FREEMAN DYSON, *INFINITE IN ALL DIRECTIONS*

## THE GARDEN OF LIBERTY

A Greek myth tells of a farmer, Akademos, who did a favor for the sun god. In return, the mortal was granted a garden wherein he could say anything he wished, even criticism of the mighty Olympians, without retribution.

I have often mulled over that little story, wondering how Akademos could ever really trust Apollo's promise. After all, the storied Greek deities were notoriously mercurial, petty, and vengeful. They could never be relied upon to keep their word, especially if provoked by censuring mortals. In other words, they were a lot like human leaders.

I concluded there were only two ways Akademos could truly be protected. First, Apollo might set up impenetrable walls around the glade, so dense that even keen-eyed Hermes could not peer through or listen. Alas, the garden wouldn't be very pleasant after that, and Akademos would have few visitors to talk to. The alternative was to empower Akademos, somehow to *enforce* the god's promise. For this some equalizing factor was needed to make them keep their word, even when the mortal and his friends started telling bad Zeus jokes.

That equalizing factor could only be knowledge.

The roots of this particular legend permeate Western thought. In the days of Pericles, free citizens of Athens used to gather at the Academy, named after that same garden of Akademos where individuals would freely debate issues of the day—a liberty that lasted while Pericles was around to remind them of the contract they had made. A pact of openness.

Alas, it was a new and difficult concept, far more complex than rule by king or oligarchy. For a variety of reasons, the miracle did not long outlive the great democrat. Outspoken Socrates eventually paid a stiff price for practicing candor in the Academy, whereupon his student, Plato, took paradoxical revenge by writing stern denunciations of openness, calling instead for strict government by an "enlightened" elite (of his own design). Plato's advice, which served to justify countless tyrants during the following two and a half millennia, remained influential almost to this generation.

But now, at last, the vision of Pericles is getting another trial run. Today's "academy" extends far beyond the sacred confines of the world's thousand or so major universities. Throughout the neo-West, and to some extent the rest of the world, people have begun to accept the daring notion that ideas are *not* in themselves toxic. At least not to those (from all social classes) who cultivate brave minds. Free speech is increasingly seen as the best font of criticism, the only practical and effective antidote to error. Moreover, most honorable people have little to fear if others know a great deal about them, so long as it goes both ways.

Let there be no mistake; this is a hard lesson to swallow, especially since each of us would be a tyrant, if we could. (Some with the best of intentions.) Very little in our history has prepared us for the task ahead, namely, living in a tribe of more than six billion equal citizens, each guided by his or her own sovereign will, loosely administered by chiefs we elect and by just rules that we made through hard negotiation among ourselves. Any other generation would have thought it an impossible ambition, though countless ancestors sweated and strove, getting us to the point where we can try.

Even among those who profess allegiance to this new hope, there is a bitter struggle over how best to protect it from the old gods of wrath, bigotry, conspiracy, and oppression—spirits who reside not on some mountain peak, but in the hearts of each man or woman who tries to expand a little secular power, or to profit by suppressing others. Perhaps someday our descendants will all be mature enough to curb these impulses by themselves. But meanwhile, a way is needed to foil the self-justified ambitions of those who would rationalize robbing freedom from the rest of us, saying that it is their right—or that it is for our own good.

According to some vigorous champions of liberty, the best means to protect our worldwide "academy" is obvious—we must build walls to safeguard every private garden, so that freedom may thrive in each secure sanctum of the mind.

To this I can only reply that *it's been tried.* And there is not a single example of a commonwealth based on that principle that thrived.

There is a better way. A method that is primarily responsible for this renaissance we're living in. Accountability is a light that can shine even on the gods of authority. Whether they gather in the Olympian heights of government, amid the spuming currents of commerce, or in the Hadean shadows of criminality, they cannot harm us while pinned by its glare.

Accountability is the only defense that ever adequately protected free speech, in a garden that stands proudly, with no walls.


I am not the first to say this. Pericles, Bruno, Spinoza, and countless others gave openness a voice during their own dark epochs. Nor can I pretend to have offered the scholarly precision and eloquence that Karl Popper poured into *The Open Society and Its Enemies,* at a time when it seemed all too likely that our grand experiment would be destroyed, either from outside or from within. During the dark early days of the Cold War, Popper movingly praised those common folk who manage to transform themselves into *citizens*—independent, cooperative, and indomitable.

Writing about the "longing of uncounted unknown men to free themselves and their minds from the tutelage of authority and prejudice" he posited hope in "their unwillingness to leave the entire responsibility for ruling the world to human or superhuman authority, and their willingness to share the burden of responsibility for avoiding suffering, and to work for its avoidance."

Even when it comes to popularized versions of the same message, I am not alone. Take the following extract from an article that appeared before this book went to press.

> With the coming of a wired, global society, the concept of openness has never been more important. It's the linchpin that will make the new world work. In a nutshell, the key formula for the coming age is this: Open, good. Closed, bad. Tattoo it on your forehead. Apply it to technology standards, to business strategies, to philosophies of life. It's the winning concept for individuals, for nations, for the global community in the years ahead.

In this *Wired* magazine commentary, Peter Schwartz and Peter Leyden went on to contrast what the world may look like if it takes either the "closed" route or an "open" one. In the former case, nations turn inward, fragmenting into blocs. This strengthens rigidity of thought, stagnates the economy, increases poverty, mutual fear, and intolerance, leading to the vicious cycle of an even more closed and fragmented world. If, on the other hand, society adopts the open model, then a *virtuous* circle turns cultures outward, making them receptive to innovation and new ideas. Rising affluence and trust lead to growing tolerance and trade, smaller economic units, a more open society, and a more integrated world.

Synergies like this underlie the movement for openness, in stark contrast to "zero sum" approaches offered by the *devil's dichotomies*, which call for wretched trade-offs between pairs of things we cannot endure without. Those who favor an open society believe we can have both liberty and efficient government, both freedom and safety. In fact, we know that those pairs will thrive or fail in unison, as they have for years in our present culture.

This confidence extends to the way we would envision developing the character and institutions of the information age, which until now have been "deposited like sediment" rather than sapiently planned. Drawing an analogy to the framing of the U.S. Constitution, Jaron Lanier called for a pragmatic mutualism of competition and cooperation as we design, and then redesign, the Internet to come.

> Well-meaning and brilliant people with nasty, conflicting interests somehow created a collective product that was better than any

of them could have understood at the time. . . . [A]s in Philadelphia two hundred years ago, a collective product [the Internet] has to emerge that is better than any of them, or any of us, could achieve singly.

In such negotiations it is perfectly reasonable to "trade off" particular interests and resources, negotiating a give-and-take of concessions from one group to the next. That is adversarial pragmatism, a form of accountability. But it does not have to entail accepting dour dichotomies about matters of fundamental importance.

If we are all doomed to be either courteous slaves or liberated barbarians, what's the point? In the long run, what use is a civilization unless it gently helps us become smart, diverse, creative, and confident enough to choose, of our own free will, to be decent people?

*Teach your children to be politely but firmly skeptical about anything they see or hear [on the Net]. Teach them to have no fear of rejecting images or communications that repel or frighten them. Teach them to have a strong sense of their own personal boundaries, of their right to defend those boundaries physically and socially. Teach them that people aren't always who they present themselves to be [in e-mail], and that predators exist. Teach them to keep personal information private. Teach them to trust you enough to confide in you if something does not seem right.*

HOWARD RHEINGOLD

## A SHOPPING LIST FOR THE FUTURE

If a transparent society *is* in our future, there will be a rough transition before its advantages crystallize around us. A transparency threshold will have to be reached before the odds of getting caught finally make sneakiness and cheating unprofitable. When people feel safer, we will worry less about what others know about us. In the meantime, we may need ways to track society's degree of "sentinelity," or how effectively our myriad "T-cells" are watching the watchers and guarding the guardians.

Many of the practical tools we discussed in this book will help, including free-market means for testing the veracity of would-be prophets (predictions registries), as well as alternative routes for good ideas and surprising art to rise to our attention, uncontrolled by the masters of media (percolation). Ways must be found to solve the problem of intellectual property. If old approaches to copyright are no longer effective, it behooves us to come up with new social compacts to achieve the same basic practical aim of rewarding inventive people for sharing their creative efforts rather than caching them secretively away. This openness will be especially urgent when it comes to double-edged breakthroughs that have potential *either* to foster *or* to undermine freedom, depending on how they are used. Examples might include lie detectors, proclivities testing, new techniques for parsing neural patterns of thought, or countless other plausible discoveries that could serve the purpose of tyrants, unless revealed and openly discussed.

Regarding the Internet, it is interesting to note that this supremely connecting system, which ironically arose out of deadly suspicions dividing the human race during the mid-twentieth century, might not have received funding under any logical peacetime criteria. Its deep sturdiness against physical destruction eventually implies robustness against coercion—or even, in the long run, legal authority. And yet there are worries. Will the new tools empower citizens, or exacerbate a widening gulf between "haves" and "have nots"? Oceans of information are available, but much is not well organized, cataloged, or verified. Data overload looms as a real danger, sometimes making it seem as if we are "sipping" from a fire hose. Controlled anarchy and creative chaos have their charms, but can they last for long before demands ring out for order?

Can anyone agree what kind of order would best serve a world that is so rapidly turning on, tuning in, and downloading?

Right now the Internet serves countless diverse groups, helping them to coalesce and organize. But this "centrifugal" trend should ideally be countered by inward or "centripetal" forces that draw these adversarial groups back together again. One way to help this happen without pushing conformity will be through the establishment of "disputation arenas," managed by persnickety T-cell types whose own peculiar fetish is a passion for fair and meticulous debate. If it becomes an accepted norm for advocacy groups to send their greatest champions into arduous duels that go on for months, watched and heckled by a fascinated populace, the result could be not only superb entertainment but also the demolition of many bad ideas. Even more important, it may help improve some good ones.

Such arenas might also remind us of an essential truth: free speech deserves our devotion, but we have a right to ask for something in return. In the long run, free speech should be the rich stew out of which better models of the world emerge. Surprises that rock our complacency. Better paths into the future. New virtues that we'll share in common.

If transparency is to thrive, it will be especially important that nothing impede the continuing rise of an age of amateurs, in which skill and expertise become so widely dispersed that no cabal of professionals can ever become dominant, or indispensable. Above all, the mysteriously pervasive Western propaganda campaign—the relentless drumbeat of messages extolling individualism, eccentricity, and suspicion of authority—must continue. This "new meme" is essential if rambunctious T-cells are to pervade everywhere, using their expanded powers of sight and free speech to test every assumption, probe every so-called "neat idea," and discover potential errors before they are allowed to shatter this new and profoundly interdependent world.

Would it be so bad if the media would also start leavening these cantankerous themes with a soft murmur of humor and gratitude? A little appreciation for getting to live in such a civilization? That slight modification might help some bright T-cells remain passionate error seekers, instead of transforming into self-righteously paranoic cancers. But it is far more important that this new and vibrant commons have a vigorous "immune system" than none at all.

As Alfred North Whitehead once said, "It is the business of the future to be dangerous." We should not shrink back from that trial. The only proper response is to embrace it.

> *The challenge is not to keep everything secret, but to limit misuse of information. That implies trust, and more information about how the information is used. At the same time we may all become tolerant if everyone's flaws are more visible.* ESTHER DYSON

## NEGOTIATING WITH THE ENEMY

For those who pored through this book expecting prescriptions and were aggrieved only to find tentative suggestions, all I can say is that I never promised a road map to a transparent utopia. Idealized essences and ideologies have caused enough death and suffering during the last few centuries.

My main task was contrarian—to criticize too much attention being paid to an appealing but wrongheaded mythology: that you can enduringly protect freedom, personal safety, and even privacy by preventing other people from knowing things. A fallacy no more true because it is believed all across the political spectrum. And yet, I realize the opposite notion, transparency, could be just as bad, if taken to extremes, or if applied unevenly or too soon. We need to study how it has worked at fostering the three greatest, most successful endeavors of humanity: science, free markets, and democracy. In each case there have been pragmatic compromises . . . while maintaining a basic fealty toward openness and light.

It is still a dangerous world. The forces that crushed every other brief renaissance in history are always at work, those "other enemies" of freedom that so many people seem to forget about. They would return us to a social order shaped like a pyramid, the "natural" structure of human society, that dominated every major culture for thousands of years. Avoiding this fate will depend on our nurturing two apparently contradictory traits, tolerance and boisterous individualism, together with the notion that history does not have to repeat itself.

Children *can* learn from the mistakes of their parents. Or else, why bother?

Above all, we must learn to stop dismissing our fellow citizens as mindless sheep. They can be frustrating, even silly sometimes. But they deserve better than contempt from the members of an elite—including whatever elite *you*, the reader, consider yourself to be a member of. Sometimes the people may even surprise you, as they continue to become more practiced in the arts of citizenship.

> *The old saying "love of money is the root of all evil" was never convincing. There have always been counter-examples. But replace "money" with "secrecy" and you get an interesting aphorism. Though secrecy does not always cause evil, one would be hard put to name any great evil that was not made worse by it.*
>
> M. N. PLANO

There are those who say that they cannot choose openness, because their enemy (usually government) is so horrible and oppressive that skulking secrecy is the only recourse for staying free. To this plaint I can only answer— *We'll miss you at the negotiating table. Your input, insight, and even your dark suspicions, would have been helpful. But go play games with secret decoder rings, if you want. Nobody's going to chase you down and force you to join.*

What negotiating table?

Why, the one where we talk about transparency, of course. You didn't think I would start lowering my own walls and barriers without getting something in return, did you? If the government says it needs new powers of sight in order to protect us, we should not spurn the requests of skilled and dedicated professionals without a hearing. On the other hand, we should make government come begging deferentially, and extract something in return each time. New kinds of supervision. New guarantees of openness. Snap inspections by teams of randomly chosen citizens! A fully numbered inventory of secret documents! New measures to keep us confident that government is still our loyal dog, and not the wolf that all too many others have become.

This is, simply, the method we have been using all along to stay free.

Nor is the principle limited to official authority. Whenever anyone asks for more openness from you, it is perfectly reasonable to demand that it be reciprocal. That is what the tussle of accountability is all about. It is why city number two will always be so much noisier than city number one—and so much freer.

Again, the cameras *are* coming. You can rail against them, shaking your fist in futile rage at all the hovering lenses. Or you can join a committee of six billion neighbors to control the pesky things, making each one an extension of your eyes.

> *Everything on the Web is ultimately about trust.*
>
> NICHOLAS NEGROPONTE

> *We must never forget that the human heart is at the center of the technological maze.*
>
> STEPHEN BARNES

## THE FLOW OF INFORMATION, THE FLOW OF LIFE

All right, let us suppose something truly amazing happens, that we citizens resist the inveigling, siren calls to vote in a myriad so-called privacy laws and instead choose to embrace accountability. In the village, it wasn't fear of retribution, per se, that kept you from behaving callously toward your neighbors; it was the sure knowledge that someone would *tell your mother*, and bring shame to your family. Tomorrow, when any citizen has access to the universal database to come, our "village" will include millions, and nobody's mom will be more than an e-mail away.

Soon, that fellow who laughed on the freeway as he cut you off, nearly causing a chain collision, may not be able to hide behind a shield of anonymity anymore. The kid who swipes an apple from a shouting fruit vendor can expect to get a call on his wrist phone before he runs more than a block away. Would-be burglars will have to be awfully clever, when cheap video cameras in any home automatically alert the police and then track the fleeing intruders down the street. True, a con artist may be able to look up facts about your finances, but that intrusion will be outweighed when *you* call up her rap sheet while she's just getting started with her irresistible sales pitch.

Perhaps the word *reputation* will regain some of its former meaning as one of a person's most precious assets, the way we can tell if some stranger is worthy of our trust.

Will we wind up having to choose between privacy and freedom? This is one of the most vile dichotomies of all. And yet, in struggling to maintain some beloved fantasies about the former, we might willingly, even eagerly, cast the latter away.

It doesn't have to come to that. I think and hope we can have some real privacy, as a benefit and product of liberty. As I've tried to say repeatedly, a free people will be able to demand some—assuming we truly are free.

Transparency is not about eliminating privacy. It is about giving us the power to hold accountable those who would *violate* it. Privacy implies serenity at home and the right to be let alone. It may be irksome how much other people know about me, but I have no right to police their minds. On the other hand I care very deeply about what others *do* to me and to those I love. We all have a right to some place where we can feel safe.

After all these pages playing the contrarian, I actually retain a fair amount of pragmatic skepticism aimed in all directions. Until I see that it really works as advertised, I'd be happy to have transparency move ahead in baby steps.

But I am sure of one thing. People of bad intent will be far more free to do harm in a world of secrets, masks, and shrouds than in a realm where the light is growing all around, bit by steady bit.


It was fun while it lasted, living on these city streets amid countless, nameless fellow beings, not knowing any of them unless you chose to, being able to walk away from any embarrassment or petty discourtesy, just another forgotten face in the crowd.

It was also lonely.

Today, you read about old folks found dead in their apartments months after anyone last saw them alive, and about children who were abused for years without the neighbors suspecting, or doing a thing about it. That won't happen anymore when the village returns. Busybodies will gossip, but you'll know *their* secrets—and you'll be able to leave your doors unlocked. Your bedroom will be protected from snoops by electronic guardians, but most of all by the fact that voyeurs and snoops will fear being caught. Your taxes may be public knowledge, but so will every suspicious deal made by any politician or captain of finance. Anyone will be able to find out how much you paid for your nose job, or what salad dressing you buy; and your reaction will be, "Who cares?" It will be like having people know what color sweater you are wearing.

Courtesy, at first enforced by a mutual deterrence of vision, may become a simple, comfortable habit. One that respects a world of wildly varied eccentrics. One that gives each person a little more space than he or she would have inside a mask.

Meanwhile, you and your kids will have friends in every part of the world, whom you met through shared interests on the Net. And when you travel, those friends will pick you up at the airport with open arms, as familiar as any member of your family, even though you never met in person till that very moment.

Perhaps, after all is said and done, most of us will even decide it's better that way. Better to know our neighbors (in their multitudes) than to live a fiction of splendid, lonely isolation.

Assuming we have the slightest choice in the matter.

# NOTES

## CHAPTER 1

11   ... *neo-Western civilization* ... I use this term throughout the book, while leaving it intentionally vague. By one way of looking at things, the neo-West is a vast region that includes all the world's constitutional democracies, at least those where freedom of expression and information are accepted norms (even if imperfectly practiced). By this standard, the neo-West would encompass most of Europe and the Americas, Australia, New Zealand, Japan, along with much of south and east Asia. In the course of this book, however, we'll see that a stricter definition may be needed. When I speak of a shared cultural outlook based on individualism, eccentricity, and suspicion of authority, it becomes evident that even large portions of the U.S. population exclude themselves from the *neo-West* with attitudes that better align with older human traditions. For that reason, I see the term not as having national boundaries, but rather fluid zones where cultural assumptions about diversity and openness are strong or weak. (See the section on "Toxicity of Ideas.")

13   ... *"Declaration of Independence for Cyberspace"*. . . see http://www.ultranet.com/~kyp/barlow.html.

13   *Will technology force us to choose between privacy and freedom?* In the sardonic words of Chris Peterson of the Foresight Institute, "Freedom will get you through times of no privacy better than privacy will get you through times of no freedom."

14   ... *much of this chapter* ... see David Brin, "The Transparent Society," *Wired*, December 1996.

15   ... *poking tiny holes to penetrate the "protective" curtain* ... But what if it is a *high-tech* curtain, designed to scream when poked? Perhaps the balance would then tip in favor of belief in protection with barriers ... for a while, until new kinds of penetration are discovered. This kind of surveillance arms race will be discussed in chapters 8 and 9.

16   ... *Pericles and his allies were roundly derided by contemporary scholars* ... Opponents of Athenian democracy included not only Socrates (as reported by Plato) but

also the chief historian of the era, Thucydides, who was a member of the oligarchic party of Athenians.

19 . . . *information on a CD-ROM that can be viewed at most police headquarters* . . . Shortly after California's CD-ROM was made available for viewing at police stations, an individual began posting all 65,000 names on his Internet site, claiming that the inconvenience of the official system stymies its effectiveness. (See chapter 3, where we discuss the pros and cons of "practical obscurity.")

20 . . . *Electronic Frontier Foundation (EFF)* . . . See http://www.eff.org/.

20 . . . *Privacy Information Center (EPIC)* . . . is a public interest research center based in Washington, D.C., established in 1994 to focus public attention on emerging civil liberties issues and to protect privacy, the First Amendment, and constitutional values. See http://www.epic.org/ or (202) 544-9240. EPIC also administers Privacy International, based in forty countries, which keeps an eye on government and commercial surveillance worldwide.

21 Beth Givens, *The Privacy Rights Handbook: How to Take Control of Your Personal Information* (New York: Avon Books, 1997). To reach the Privacy Rights Clearinghouse call (619) 298-3396 or e-mail: prc@privacyrights.org., 5384 Linda Vista Road #306, San Diego, CA 92110.

22 . . . *The Great Game of Business* . . . by Jack Stack (New York: Doubleday Books, 1992).

22 . . . *According to cartoonist-humorist Scott Adams* . . . In fairness, it should be noted that Mr. Adams is also on record predicting that we will all soon be enslaved by squirrels and put to work in their nut mines. See Scott Adams, *The Dilbert Future: Thriving on Stupidity in the 21st Century* (New York: HarperCollins, 1997).

23 . . . *Kevin Kelly* . . . *expressed the same idea* . . . Josh Quittner. "Invasion of Privacy," *Time*, 25 August 1997.

23 . . . *I have no secrets myself* . . . John Perry Barlow is quoted in *Netview: The Global Business Network Journal*, summer/fall 1995. The rest of Barlow's paragraph follows: "I am concerned with what happens when you've got a government that has access to very detailed, granular information about people and a lot of people who think they're living lives of secret shame. The answer is to get rid of the secret shame. But that's a leap we're not going to make right away. In fact, we're headed in the other direction."

25 The Witness Program was conceived in 1992 in partnership with the Lawyers Committee for Human Rights, musician Peter Gabriel, and the Reebok Foundation. Transparency International, based in Germany, has national chapters all over the world. See http://www.transparency.de/.

28 . . . *erase "nonpersons" from official history* . . . For a guided tour of Soviet photographic fakery, see David King, *The Commissar Vanishes* (New York: Metropolitan, 1997), which is simultaneously hilarious and chilling as the reader sees what can happen when one clique takes control of a society's "consensual reality." George Orwell's vivid, terrifying "Ministry of Truth" was based in part on this notorious activity. His nightmare regime in *Nineteen Eighty-Four* believed that "falsification of the past . . . is as necessary . . . as the work of repression and espionage."

28 . . . *"pedigree" of their photographic evidence* . . . Several quotations in this section were taken from interviews with James Cameron, Ken Burns, and others on ABC *Nightline*, September 1997.

31   *... members of an empirical civilization ...* Once again we see the influence of Plato in all the hand wringing over the "end of photography as proof." What we are witnessing is the end of photography as *perfect* proof. The Platonic impulse is then to deny that a flawed tool has any further usefulness. But when photographic deceit can be canceled out by *other* cameras, we wind up with a situation pragmatists can cope with.

## CHAPTER 2

34   *... extensive physical rights-of-way ...* Because they already own extensive rights of way, across the country and into most American homes, natural gas companies bid fair to become huge players in the information age, simply by stringing tiny fiber-optic cables alongside already existing lines. The same holds for railroads—one created a subsidiary called MCI. Their chief competitor in the short term will be cable television operators, whose "cable modem" capabilities may dominate the field in the immediate future.

34   *... new era of wireless communication ...* A consortium led by Motorola is creating the "Iridium Project," whose sixty-six low-orbiting satellites will offer worldwide digital telephony service. Another group, Teledesic, involving Microsoft and McCaw Communications, has the more ambitious aim of using hundreds of satellites to transfer data, and even real-time video, between millions of users all over the globe.

37   *... midwifing something that might ultimately distribute authority ...* Part of the reason may lie in long-standing U.S. military doctrine, which has for generations trained junior officers to exercise initiative, if necessary operating for long periods without orders. Another factor we will discuss later may have been a strategic decision to avoid the debilitating "fallacy of security." Warned in advance by some of the best minds in the West, the right people may have understood that stifling the flow of information applies a tourniquet to the limbs of a free society, hampering the virtues that give it strength. If this is true, it runs diametrically counter to everything we are taught to believe about officious and obtrusive bureaucrats.

37   *... the chief "designer" ...* According to John Gilmore, "Paul Baran vastly underestimated the difficulty of routing the messages. Breakthroughs are needed (at each stage) to get a system that is robust and scales to the whole planet. Today's Internet is fragile and maintained by intense human effort." These problems will have to be dealt with in the next generation of networks.

37   *... the post-Darwinian principle of "pre-adaptation" ...* Comparing the Internet to organic life has one further, intriguing implication—that artificial intelligence may be far more likely to evolve out of an ecologically based network than from any specific "drawing board" approach. This is reminiscent of theories proposed by MIT Professor Marvin Minsky in his 1990 book *Society of Mind.*

38   *... system of address designations ...* Outside the United States, computer ISPs are usually denoted with addresses ending in the initials of their country of origin. Some North American computers also use this kind of nomenclature, such as the popular service called "the Well" whose address, well.sf.ca.us, tells network message handlers to zero in first on the United States, then California, then the San Francisco area, and finally a computer called "Well." Most other American access points are grouped into one of six "domains" with the respective trim abbreviations gov, mil, edu, org, com, and net. These abbreviations stand for government, military, educational institution,

organization, commercial entity, or network gateway for other networks. More domains are planned, as the initial niches are filled at a rate many times faster than the originators ever envisioned. The most interesting thing about this system is how little bureaucracy is involved. A small commercial service is allowed to franchise out domain names for a small fee on a first-come, first-served basis.

39 ... *author Vernor Vinge* ...For more on the "singularity" see Vinge's novel, *Across Real Time* (New York: Baen Books, 1986).

42 ... *a long, hard road getting here* ... I have long been amazed that some people seem driven to claim that our varied ancestors (whether European, African, Native American, etc.) were in many or all ways better, wiser, smarter, and more honorable than we are, as if this somehow honors their memory! In fact, that is not a tribute. Nothing would more horrify decent people of any age than to be told that their descendants would turn out worse than they were. It basically means that all their struggles and hopes were in vain. The best and noblest of our predecessors would have wanted us to exceed them—just as we dream fondly that our grandchildren will be better than we are.

42 *Elsewhere I discussed* ... David Brin, *Otherness* (New York: Bantam Books, 1994).

43 ... *higher intratribal homicide rate than* ... *downtown Detroit* ... Regarding the high murder rate among !Kung bushmen of the Kalahari, R. Lee tabulated 22 homicides over 50 years, which in their small population worked out to a per capita rate of 293 per million per year. Fifteen of the murders happened amid blood feuds. (R. B. Lee, *The !Kung San: Men, Women and Work in a Foraging Society* [Cambridge University Press, 1979].)

43 ... *that 20 to 30 percent of males in preindustrial societies died at the hands of other males* ... For further discussion see C. Boehm, "Egalitarian Behavior and Reverse Dominance Hierarchy." *Curr. Anthropol.* 34 (1993): 227–254. Also B. M. Knauft. "Violence and Sociality in Human Evolution." *Curr. Anthropol.* 32 (1991): 391–428. S. Krech III, "Genocide in Tribal Society." *Nature* 371 (1994): 14–15. And R. W. Wrangham and D. Peterson, *Demonic Males: Apes and the Origins of Human Violence* (Boston: Houghton Mifflin, 1996).

43 ... *people who agree on the fundamental desirability of tolerance* ... Regarding society's sometimes uneven march toward acceptance of diversity, see the discussion in *Making All the Difference: Inclusion, Exclusion and American Law,* Martha Minow (Ithaca, N.Y.: Cornell University Press, 1990).

44 ... *cast our thoughts further ahead* ... Hence, perhaps, the modern popularity of films, books, and television shows about aliens?

45 ... *nonconformists are among the* ... *best-paid* ... What matters to an artist nowadays is not how many people hate you, but how much attention you can get. Those who disapprove cannot have you burned at the stake. Merry masters of outrage, like Serrano or Andrew Dice Clay, enjoyed decrying the philistine resistance of the majority—while profiting handsomely from the patronage of a tidy minority of the public. Others, such as Howard Stern, translated such niche positions into cult hero status. The lesson? In a free and diverse society, majority opinion is meaningless to all but politicians. Sell yourself to a select group. Become a cult figure to just 5 percent, and you can reap rich rewards of money and ego from millions, while having the satisfaction of calling the remaining 95 percent idiots. Talk about having your cake and eating it too!

45 ... *no one foresaw the personal computer* ... One classic failure of prediction can be seen in the fact that not a single science fiction story or novel written before 1970

predicted the home computer. Countless tales extrapolated computers as vast, monolithic machines served by hordes of white-coated attendants. The reason for this lapse is rooted in basic storytelling, which is often served by showing the reader or moviegoer some frightful center of power for the protagonist to oppose. The Big Computer fit this role so well that no one pictured the opposite—a distribution of computational power, and accompanying independence, to the citizenry at large.

48  The Society for Amateur Scientists, based in San Diego, California, can be reached at (800) 873-8767.

48  ... *assure us that their favorite encryption system is foolproof* ... For more about the amateur-collective effort to break the DES, see http://www.rsa.com/des/. Also, http://www.frii.com/~rcv/deschall.html.

49  ... *gatherings of enthusiastic eclectics* ... These confabs range from obscure "shirt-sleeve" summer studies, sponsored by government agencies to foster reevaluation of old approaches to famous gatherings, such as the annual "Renaissance" weekends, with invitations more sought after than a spot on the fabled social register. Others, like TED conferences run by polymath Richard Saul Wurman, feature famous and obscure intellectuals from around the globe, but almost any university nowadays hosts cross-disciplinary seminar series, many open to an interested public. For-profit conclaves also cater to this growing demand for confab mental stimulation.

49  ... *almost nothing of recognized value ... will ... be lost* ... Some early readers defied me to find interest groups passionately dedicated to preserving eight-track music systems, or hand-winding iron core computer memories, or sawing ice from frozen rivers to store in root cellars, or collecting movies on Betamax format, or reading 800 bpi magnetic data tape. I could answer by emphasizing the "recognized value" phrase. But in fact, I have already found people pursuing several of these hobbies, and suspect a persistent search would come up with quirky individuals styling themselves "world experts" in the rest of those obscure areas of human knowledge.

53  ... *newsgroups that specialize in debunking legends* ... See Joel Furr, "Chicken Little, Myth, Reality and Absurdity in alt.folklore," *Internet World*, February 1995.

**CHAPTER 3**

57  ... *clicking on a site on the World Wide Web may wind up creating a "biography"* ... Even experienced and techno-savvy denizens of cyberspace sometimes feel helpless before persistent attempts by voracious computer systems to learn everything about everybody. For instance, "cookies" are little text files that a World Wide Web site may drop onto your hard drive—files the site may collect later, when you revisit. Cookies may simply contain data that smooth the process of reconnecting, so that each subsequent visit goes smoothly, perhaps a formatting record of previous purchases at the site, or your password, or past preferences, etc. Such innocuous uses may smooth a lot of transitions, enabling more agile use of the Web. On the other hand, the information can be used to create personalized and individually targeted marketing databases, or even to glean information about the contents of your own hard disk drive.

58  *An industry of "how to" manuals* ... Just a few examples offer simple methods to get around almost any privacy law:
*Privacy for Sale: How Computerization Has Made Everyone's Private Life an Open Secret*, by Jeffrey Rothfeder (Simon & Schuster, 1992) shows how "data cowboys" both legally and illegally gain access and sell private data. The author swiftly

acquires information on Dan Rather, Dan Quayle, and other public figures as a demonstration that anything can be found with relative ease.

*How to Get Anything on Anybody: The Encyclopedia of Personal Surveillance,* by Lee Lapin (Paladin Press, 1991) covers available surveillance hardware and techniques used by private investigators. "Most bugs are planted by people to spy on their spouses, or to get advantage in business."

*Privacy in America: Is Your Life in the Public Eye?* by David Linowess (University of Illinois Press, 1989) describes how privacy laws are regularly flouted by governments and businesses alike, ranging from genetic screening data to electronic fraud.

60 ... *credentials to establish identity ... potential for fraud* ... Gary T. Marx, "Fraudulent Identification and Biography," in D. Altheide et al. *New Directions in the Study of Justice, Law, and Social Control* (New York: Plenum, 1990). Professor Marx goes on to point out that, in our society, skill at playing roles is encouraged in education and acting. More than 4,000 people have been given new identities under the federal witness protection program. Other common fraudulent presentations of self include a student taking a test for another, a traveling businessman claiming to be unmarried, teenagers using fake IDs to purchase liquor. One book, *The Paper Trip,* offers a step-by-step guide to creating a new identity.

Another illustration of identity scenarios, *My Name Is Legion,* a science fiction novel popular among libertarians and cypherpunks, depicts a future hero using his computerized "back door" to alter the worldwide identity database in order to give himself new identities at will, moving like a god among mere mortals who are pinned to society by their universal ID numbers.

64 *Computerized medical databases cross state lines* ... Ann Wells Branscomb, *Who Owns Information?: From Privacy to Public Access* (New York: HarperCollins, 1994).

65 ... *they should know if doctors are HIV-positive* ... The only known cases of doctor-to-patient transmission involve six patients infected with the HIV virus by a dentist. One of them, Kimberly Bergalis, a young woman in her early twenties, subsequently died.

65 ... *assure consumers access to their own records and impose sanctions* ... This problem is not new. In fact, many privacy advocates would be happy just to see enforcement of recommendations by a 1973 task force formed at the U.S. Department of Health, Education, and Welfare to study the impact of computerization on the privacy of medical records. Their resulting Code of Fair Information Practices suggested the following guiding principles:

1. Openness. There must be no record-keeping systems of personal data whose very existence is secret.

2. Disclosure. An individual must be able to find out what information about him is in a record and how it is used.

3. Secondary usage. An individual must be able to prevent information about her gathered for one purpose from being used for other purposes without her consent.

4. Record correction. An individual must be able to correct or amend a record of information about him.

5. Security. Any organization that creates, maintains, uses, or disseminates records of personal data must assure the reliability of their data and take precautions to prevent misuse of the data.

(See Robert Ellis Smith, "Law of Privacy in a Nutshell," *Privacy Journal* (1993): 50–51.)

69 ... *idea that privacy, once plentiful, is only now endangered* ... Janna M. Smith, *Private Matters: In Defense of the Personal Life* (Reading, Mass.: Addison-Wesley, 1997), p. 8.

70 ... *reputation remained as important as ever* ... Jeffrey Obser, "Privacy Is the Problem, Not the Solution," *Salonmagazine*, June 1997.

70 ... *writers and commentators have offered their own learned remarks* ... For a substantial (though not unbiased) reading list, see the recommended books section of the EPIC at http://www.epic.org/.

71 Ellen Alderman and Caroline Kennedy, *The Right to Privacy* (New York; Knopf, 1995), p. 154.

72 *This class of privacy* ... *"right to be let alone"*. ... *personal sovereignty* ... Nowhere is the entanglement of two separate issues—freedom and privacy—greater than in discussions involving abortion and other matters of personal choice. In its decision in *Roe v. Wade*, the Supreme Court upheld a woman's right to choose abortion as a birth control technique, citing an inherent (though largely unwritten) "right to privacy." But in fact, the personal sovereignty issue has much more to do with freedom of action than with any purported right to keep secrets. Though "information privacy" is often vague, impractical, or even partly illusory, the right of individuals to *act* freely for their own benefit without harming others need not be reduced, even in principle. Nevertheless, some individuals may refrain from some actions because they feel that those actions cannot be performed except in secret. Accountability will always be on our minds.

73 ... *A new "right" became widely* ... *defended* ... It should be noted that, although many more invasion-of-privacy suits are *filed* nowadays, people who sue rarely win. A University of Arkansas study found that state and federal courts dismissed over 70 percent of privacy lawsuits filed in 1992.

74 ... *Privacy Law in Allied Nations* ... See Colin Bennet, *Regulating Privacy: Data Protection in Europe and the United States* (Ithaca, N.Y.: Cornell University Press, 1992). A comparative study of privacy protection law.

75 ... *unlikely that American standards will be adequate* ... Ironically, a study of European business practices conducted by a Harvard Business School student found indications that companies there honored the vaunted and centralized EU codes more in the breach than in the observance.

76 ... *no initiative will cut them off* ... "Practical obscurity" seems particularly absurd when one realizes than many of the data in government computer files have been entered by incarcerated felons, who apparently can be trusted with bad-but-open information that the rest of us should have to peruse at glacial speed.

78 Alan F. Westin, *Privacy and Freedom* (New York: Athenaeum, 1968), p. 31.

78 *The virtue of privacy* ... Janna Malamud Smith, *Private Matters: In Defense of the Personal Life* (Reading, MA: Addison-Wesley, 1997).

86 ... *that restricting the amount of information flowing to government* ... Critics of this idea, seeking historical support, have cited the fact that Jews and other minorities in Nazi Germany were harmed by the knowledge that the German government had concerning its people. And yet my statement about history stands. Countless other governments knew the same things and did not kill their citizens. The factor that enabled the Nazis to control the state and use its power to wreak horror was a monopolization of the information flow running *to* people, which explains why they

deemed the Ministry of Propaganda the paramount agency of the Third Reich. Above all, they made certain the public would have no insight into the deliberations, plans, and character of their rulers. In other words, from the perspective of the ruling clique, it was imperative to make sure that boxes 1 and 2 in the accountability matrix were maximized, while boxes 3 and 4 were savagely repressed.

87   *. . . each new heinous act will be followed by government appeals for greater surveillance powers . . .* This happened after the World Trade Center and Oklahoma City bombings. In each case a small but significant "antiterrorism" bill passed the U.S. Congress. While the legal effects were minimal, elected representatives felt impelled to be seen "doing something." As such crimes proliferate in the future, this trend will continue . . . so there had better be a countertrend—one establishing ever higher levels of citizen vigilance and control over the officials enforcing these new laws.

88   *. . . people choosing different boxes depending on point of view . . .* For instance, modern tools to collect and correlate medical records or credit reports might be filed in slot #1 by doctors or accountants; but to somebody with a genetic disorder, or a person who had a minor shoplifting conviction back when she was seventeen, the answer would be #3 . . . accompanied by feelings of violation and outrage. Likewise, caller ID seems a handy idea when you are at home screening out cranks, but not so good if you are a battered wife, trying to conceal your present location from an abusive spouse.

## CHAPTER 4

91   *. . . if carried to its logical conclusions . . .* The most extreme position toward data ownership is held by some followers of Andrew J. Galambos, who cite his teachings that an ideal society would be defined by property rights, and that all individuals should own 100 percent control over not only published works but also their ideas. Thus, Einstein might have denied the state any right to use the formula $E=MC^2$ to make bombs and kill people. Individuals would own any product of their thoughts, and pass those property rights to their descendants in perpetuity. Needless to say, I find this cross between Platonic mysticism and Randian solipsism to be insupportable at any level. (It provokes one to wonder how the Galambos notion jibes with another one we'll look at in chapter 5, that of "memes," or infectious ideas. If a meme takes up residence in your mind, do you own it because your thoughts gave it manifestation? Or does it, after a fashion, own *you?* If memes are proved to be "life forms," could they then sue for royalties on every idea we've ever had? I believe I will end this particular parenthetical aside with ;-)

92   *. . . artisan guilds kept control . . .* Surviving remnants of this practice are seen in the restrictive licenses required for participation in many skilled—and even semi-skilled—occupations. One can certainly see the point of some regulation when it comes to physicians and truck drivers, though a tendency toward self-serving insularity must always be fought. But in the strict certification of hairdressers one can see the influence of medieval guilds still flourishing.

93   *. . . creators were rewarded for sharing. . .* An early example was the generous prize offered by the British admiralty for developing clocks that would help mariners solve the problem of navigating longitude. Under this tradition, the ample prizes for highly esteemed discoveries/inventions made the idea of selling one's idea, rather than the devices resulting therefrom, both acceptable and attractive. Most awards were of sufficient size to allow a commoner who immediately invested his prize to live on the proceeds in comfort for the rest of his life.

94 *During any generation the test* . . . Many developing nations have laws that require mandatory licensing or "working" of patents. If negotiations with the patent owner fail, a hopeful licensee can lease the patent for a set statutory rate. Even in countries, like the United States, that do not have mandatory licensing or working requirements, companies can only repress bought-up technology for the life of the patent. Part of the quid pro quo of patenting is full disclosure. Everyone knows how the invention works and can watch the clock ticking down, preparing to exploit it the day the patent expires.

95 . . . *This can be especially tempting* . . . The willingness of corporations to use patent law to *thwart* innovations, something that individuals seldom do, points out one of many flaws in the traditional legal position that corporations are rightfully individuals under the law. I am not radical enough to reject this principle entirely. The "incorporation" of rights in a limited liability company has been useful for encouraging flexible application of capital through the economy. Nevertheless, it may be proper to rethink those specific aspects of this legal artifice that serve to harm the pragmatic interests of real human citizens.

95 *The publishing industry was shaken* . . . D. T. Max, "THE END of the Book?," *Atlantic Monthly*, September 1994, 61–71.

96 . . . *computer software companies lose a dollar to pirated* . . . These estimates are based on the questionable assumption that purchasers of pirated copies would have gone out and paid retail prices for legitimate copies had pirated versions not been available. It is always hard to get a grip on "might have been" scenarios.

96 . . . *keeps many users willing to stay legal* . . . Nowadays, with relatively cheap recordable CD-R drives, piracy is becoming easier once again. For a while, software companies tried innovations such as formatting floppy disks in unusual formats, or having the user look up a password found on the "7th line of page 145 of the manual," but inconvenience to consumers eventually led to the demise of such practices.

97 . . . *Creative Incentive Coalition* . . . See David Angel and Eli Zelkha, "The Copyright Question: Making the Net Safe and Profitable for Copyrighted Content," *Internet World*, January 1997. For more on the Creative Incentive Coalition, see http://www.cic.org. For more on the Digital Future Coalition, see http://www.ari.net.dfc.

98 . . . *writers are reduced to the honorable penury* . . . Both Mark Twain and Charles Dickens, whose works were routinely pirated in the last century, supplemented their incomes by going on extensive speaking tours, taking gate receipts from fans who flocked to public readings. But this "solution" only helps the top rank; it does nothing for mid-list authors or other journeyman artists trying to get by. Incidentally the Three Stooges did much the same thing in the 1940s, making their fortunes not through movies, but at personal appearances. So perhaps there will be a living to be made by people like me in the future after all, moving agilely back and forth from the sublime to the ridiculous.

99 . . . *"noncreative" information, such as telephone directories* . . . Recent court decisions seem to have preempted this area. Other jurists believe it is wide open for negotiation or modification by Congress. The issue is of real importance. Someone has to invest the time and money to consolidate, organize, and package such information, and there should be a legal construct that values and protects that labor. If copyright (and patent) law grants protection for a limited period of time as an incentive to disclosure of "creative" info-properties, then it seems fair also to offer incentives for open use of information that is not copyrightable.

99    *... CoS attorneys ... forced the owner of the world's most renowned "anonymizer" ...*
      For one perspective on this event, see: http://www2.thecia.net/users/rnewman/
      scientology/anon/penet.html. See also *Net.Wars* by Wendy M. Grossman (New York
      Univ. Press, 1997).

100   *... corporations force executives and other employees to sign nondisclosure ...* In a related,
      disturbing development, the doctrine of "inevitable disclosure" is expanding the ability
      of employers to use laws on trade secrets to prevent ex-employees from going to work for
      competitors. This is precisely the tempting, but stupid, "fallacy of security" that the likes
      of Karl Popper, Edward Teller, Arthur Kantrowitz, and others have been fighting for
      years—a self-defeating program that prevents these companies from hiring valuable
      expertise from *other* companies, stifling the overall flux of useful innovations and skills,
      thus destroying the health of the entity it was meant to protect. (See later discussions of
      how the West barely avoided this trap in the Cold War.) An interesting case in this area
      is *PepsiCo, Inc. v. Redmond*, 54 F.3d 1262 (7th Cir. 1995). Or see Mark Halligan's trade
      secrets home page at http:// www.execpc.com/~mhallign/doctrine.html.

102   *... propose ending the "fiction" of copyright ...* See Lee Daniel Crocker, EXTROPI-
      ANS commentary: http://www.piclab.com/lcrocker.html. Robin Hanson of the Uni-
      versity of California at Berkeley dealt with similar ideas as far back as 1987. See http://
      hanson.berkeley.edu/linktext.html and http://hanson.berkeley.edu/findcritics. html.

102   *... Give it your best shot ...* This is said with a smile ... and acknowledging that
      book reviews are already a simple implementation of "tag commentary."

104   *... look foolish trying to charge for songs played ...* ASCAP and BMI do, in fact, try
      to charge for songs played by local bands, by imposing a facilities license on places
      that typically host weddings. Any restaurant with a banquet room or a piano player
      in the bar is fair game for random monitoring of frequency of songs played. Those
      statistics are used to apportion the nonitemized revenue among songs in the ASCAP
      catalog. At one point, ASCAP sought to establish the same site licensing system for
      nonprofit summer camps. Because those camps do charge for their programs, they
      fall technically under the "public performance for profit" section of the Copyright
      Act, but the resulting public uproar convinced ASCAP that its idea was a bad one.
      The ASCAP/BMI system may be instructive. It shows how suppliers of information
      could band together and set up a system for aggregating and apportioning revenues.
      In fact, both companies are said to be developing high-speed Web browsers to patrol
      the Net looking for music infringements. Well-funded content owners may be
      among the first to have truly sophisticated software agents doing their work of polic-
      ing their own self-interest on the Net around the clock.

108   *... one paramount source of danger ...* Steven Levy, *Newsweek* technology columnist
      and author of *Crypto*, a book about the cryptography revolution, who has been fol-
      lowing the "Clipper chip" controversy and its follow-ons, observed the persistence of
      single-direction ire in the controversy over encryption. "As the years go by, the subject
      gains more attention, almost all of it directed at attacking the government's case. . . ."

109   *... governments that are well grounded in what works ...* This passage from Dorothy
      Denning comes from personal correspondence with the author, as does the follow-
      ing comment by Barry Fulton, a project director for the Center for Strategic and
      International Studies: "I am struck that government as the Great Enemy doesn't
      sufficiently distinguish among types of governments. I would want to make a sharp
      distinction between the government of an authoritarian state and that of a genuine

democracy. There are clearly examples of deceit, malfeasance, and ignorance in the most benign of governments (ranging from the Tonkin Gulf resolution to Watergate, from forced sterilization in the Scandinavian countries to a safe haven for Nazi gold in Switzerland)—but there is no evidence among modern democracies of systematic, sustained campaigns against their citizens. Totalitarian governments, on the other hand, often sustain themselves at the expense of their citizens. That citizens in a democracy maintain their vigilance against the possible abuses of government is healthy; that government comes to be defined as the enemy is either evidence of the failure of government or mass paranoia."

109    *. . . define the terms . . .* Hal Finney is senior software engineer with Pretty Good Privacy, Inc., and was an original developer of the widely used Internet cryptography program PGP. He has been a central figure in the cypherpunks mailing list, developing cryptographic and anonymity software in conjunction with other cypherpunks.

110    *. . . government is ideally a tool . . .* This point of view was charmingly expressed by a nineteenth-century jurist, who described constitutional law as a set of rules made ". . . by Peter when sober, to govern Peter when drunk."

112    *. . . civil service . . . in imperial China . . .* Some people offer the vaunted Chinese civil service system as an example of enduring, merit-based social mobility. I agree it should be appreciated in the context of its time. But in truth, the tests drew candidates from a narrow pool of scholars in the mandarin social order. That still left the vast uneducated majority to fester below in a society whose Confucian ethos justified paternal despotism no less readily than Plato did.

     On another matter, it might have been preferable to choose a company other than Procter & Gamble, when I spoke of corporations (not) having the potential to take over the world. While it seems odd that the same company would manufacture both a line of disposable diapers for adults and a new fat substitute that promotes incontinence, this seems less worrisome than, say, the fact that General Dynamics Corporation, at any given moment, controls more warships, missiles, and war planes than all but a half dozen nations on earth. A thought-provoking concept—even if at present not quite worrisome.

112    *Examples include the takeover . . .* Each of these examples had its own unique aspects, recalling an expression sometimes used by scholars who study the past: "History never exactly repeats itself, but it sure does *rhyme* a lot."

112    *. . . prevent takeover by a true ruling class . . .* Thomas Jefferson, warning about the danger of self-entrenching aristocracies, prescribed a new revolution every twenty years. This is usually read as exaggeration or polemic. But a historian might argue that America has steered its narrow course between despotisms of left and right by sticking close to Jefferson's formula, tweaking and adjusting the rules every generation or so. Some of these evolutions were violent, notably the Civil War. Early twentieth-century Progressive movements, on the other hand, left an enduring legacy of antitrust and other reforms which could also be thought "revolutionary." So might the populist revolt of Andrew Jackson, or, in a cultural sense, the Roaring Twenties. Consider the effects of one well-timed act of Congress, the GI Bill of Rights, which helped a million returning World War II veterans—sons of farmers and factory laborers—get university educations hitherto undreamt of. This piece of social engineering nearly demolished the functioning class system in America for more than a generation—at least for white people. For others, justice and opportunity had to wait twenty more years, for the civil rights movement and other medium-scale social fevers, which, largely nonviolently, inocu-

lated the nation with more renewal and change. Whatever other effects these episodes had, from music and culture to law and leisure, and whatever faults they left unsolved for later, each made American culture more open and equal than before.

## CHAPTER 5

117  *. . . who claim to have been abducted by UFOs . . .* Carl Sagan pointed out that in no known instance has a returning UFO traveller revealed a significant and verifiable new fact that science did not already know.

A more general repudiation of this modern mythology can be found in an essay "What to Say to a UFO," published in my collection, *Otherness* (New York: Bantam Books, 1994). In brief, I am not averse to discussing the possibility, or even the likelihood, of extra-terrestrial life "out there." As a scientist I've written extensively about SETI (the Search for Extra-Terrestrial Intelligence), and as a science fiction author I am well known for depicting interesting, plausible aliens. I am even willing to posit that Earth may have been visited in the past. Yet, most UFO "reports" seem to have a special quality that coats them in the same dreamlike aspect. The key element to note, shared by nearly all such tales, is the purported *behavior* of those little silver guys, (as related by witnesses and/or purported kidnapping victims). Not one report describes the sort of activity that would be engaged in by grownups. From twirling wheatfields to disemboweling cattle, or subjecting humans to rectal and neural probes, or simply buzzing Washington, D.C., in the dead of night, each "incident" instead depicts the same kind of behavior that other cultures once ascribed to fairy beings or elves — capricious, secretive and rather nasty. In fact, the "elf" analogy is deeply thought-provoking.

I'm not asserting as an absolute fact that UFO aliens don't exist. But if they do, they are the sort of noxiously unpleasant visitors who deserve to be snubbed.

119  *. . . what benefits the individual leader nearly always prevails . . .* The example of peacock selection strategy illustrates one of the chief rules of evolution believed by most biologists: that it is *individuals* who are the grist of evolution. In fact, only a few scientists believe that groups or species experience direct Darwinism, and those few concede that it is a weak or secondary effect, compared to the dominant role of individual selection.

120  Robert Wright, end of chapter 9, *The Moral Animal* (New York: Pantheon, 1994).

123  *Plato preached that much art . . .* See *The Republic.* Although his chief paternalistic concern was with the soul-purity of men governing the state, not with the masses, Plato favored universal censorship because there was no way to predict which men would pass the tests for membership in the council of rulers.

123  *. . . legends have preached that knowledge can be dangerous . . .* For a scan of this notion through past literature, see Roger Shattuck, *Forbidden Knowledge: From Prometheus to Pornography.* As for modern fables, it can be interesting to juxtapose what two motion pictures from the same franchise say about the toxicity of ideas. Throughout the film *Star Trek II: The Wrath of Khan*, viewers are shown a side-plot about a daring thirst for knowledge. Characters in that film boldly create an entire solar system, including a planet covered with new life forms. The story ends with them gazing proudly at their beautiful creation. But the sequel, written and directed by others, seemed obsessed with reversing this theme. Step by step, *Search for Spock* checked off every box of the "Frankenstein Syndrome," preaching that humans who arrogate the powers of heaven will be punished, their false creations destroyed, and the individual responsible for this

act of hubris killed by his own monster. In this illustration from popular culture we see how the two conflicting attitudes described in chapter 5 remain at war to this day.

123 For more on the concept of *memes* see Richard Dawkins, *The Selfish Gene*. A more recent and detailed treatment provided by Aaron Lynch in *Thought Contagion* (New York: Basic Books, 1996).

124 . . . *a solid moral grounding and some common sense* . . . Quote by Howard Rheingold, *Whole Earth Review*, Winter 1994, 95.

125 . . . *flip side of living in* tribes *is living in the world* . . . *in the* kosmos . . . Private communication to the author by Stefan Jones, Oracle Corporation computer scientist.

125 . . . *some wise elite should hold sway over what others see* . . . Another idea liked by both intolerant rightists and intolerant leftists is the notion that humanity is meant to live in "tribes," and that attempts to mix or melt cultural and ethnic boundaries are both futile and unfair. Certain leftists appreciate this notion because it offers another excuse to beat up on dead white imperialist males and replace the "melting pot" with a "salad bowl." Certain rightists savor the way it absolves them from having to worry about human rights in foreign lands ("It's just their way. What right do we have to intervene?") and gives fresh legitimacy to the hoary old notion of racial separation. The important point to note is that such alliances cross old-fashioned political boundaries, almost at 90-degree angles. Their shared postulates can be stronger (and scarier) than any normal ideology.

126 . . . *"thinking it is the same as doing it"* . . . A minor note: it has been said that if thoughts are morally the same as actions, few human males will be found in Heaven.

126 . . . *an effort to extend government authority beyond the physical into the mental* . . . John Perry Barlow here refers to his "Declaration of Cyberspace Independence," *Wired*, June 1996 (cited earlier).

128 . . . *cite a popular book or film* . . . *whose professed message is conformity* . . . One that comes to mind is *The Nightmare Before Christmas*, which seems to preach that someone born to one class or profession should not aspire to compete in another realm. Yet, the main character is so joyfully bold and irreverent that the film can hardly be called "conformist" in tone.

129 *Government may not, through the CDA, interrupt that conversation* . . . In the United States District Court for the Eastern District of Pennsylvania—*American Civil Liberties Union, Civil Action et al. v. Janet Reno*, Attorney General of the United States No. 96-963 before Sloviter, Chief Judge, United States Court of Appeals for the Third Circuit; Buckwalter and Dalzell, Judges, United States District Court for the Eastern District of Pennsylvania June 11, 1996.

131 *Project Censor: The News That Didn't Make the News* . . .Contact Peter Philips, Sociology Department, Sonoma State University, 1801 East Cotati Avenue, Rohnert Park, CA 94928, or project.censored@sonoma.edu.

132 . . . *they diagnose why some events may not be not covered* . . . Although they use the word "censorship" liberally, *Project Censor* activists explain that underreporting of news in the United States is less often due to deliberate intimidation than to sociological or structural factors. Examples include (1) a desire not to offend advertisers, (2) overreliance on official PR handouts for story content, and (3) ideological self-censorship, that is, avoiding coverage of positions that lie too far from consensus points of view, either to the left or right.

133   ... *tenable that advertisers and politically connected publishers wield undue influence at various periodicals* ... Of course there are attempts by corporate and government interests to meddle in the reporting of news. Given the nature of conceited alpha males, it would be surprising if bosses did not try to exercise feudal power over journalists, to suppress stories they dislike. The question is rather how frequent, successful, or corrosive of accountability such efforts are nowadays. In a passionate article in *Newsweek* (21 July 1997, 53), Jonathan Alter recently proclaimed, "We can't expect everyone in journalism to be a martyr. Even so, it's important to complain loudly when editorial freedom is trampled on by corporations, just as we would if the government told us what to print." A deeply moving appeal, which I support wholeheartedly. And yet, when it was time for Alter to give an example of heinous interference, he came up with just one, in which an editor friend received a tepid request from on high. His friend refused the intrusive demand and came away unharmed.

Surely worse examples happen. At a local level, perhaps every day. On the other hand, if the only case Alter could cite had a happy and courageous ending, his plaint sounds like praising the present system with faint damns.

And yet, there is a major "catch" in the argument that reporters can always move to greener pastures if they feel their freedom of inquiry is being squelched. In order for this to be true, the law must be fiercely protective of press freedom, a condition that has not yet ripened in many parts of the world, and is unevenly enforced in many parts of the neo-West. Another problem can be press monopolies. For instance, in Australia—a land noted for independent spirits—most cities are served by newspapers that are members of either the Murdoch or the Packer consortia. Under these conditions, a print journalist who wants a steady living might feel obliged to heed the advice of major clients and advertisers.

134   ... *not the way living organisms do it*. ... Recall how the Internet arose out of concern over how best to defend the United States against foreign foes. Overly rigid central command systems were seen as fatally flawed. New concepts of dispersed responsibility led to packet-switching technology, and eventually the Internet's magnificent chaos.

134   *Criticism might be viewed as a civilization's equivalent of an immune system*. ... In fact, mutual criticism in society has the potential of being far more effective in correcting errors than the immune system of a living organism. As John Gilmore points out, "The immune system can't improve on the body's pre-existing design. But criticism can." (Personal communication to the author.)

135   ... *archetype is copied in such endless profusion* ... What protects the "sullen loner" image from becoming clichéd? Perhaps just the simple fact that we were all teenagers once, a stage of life when sometimes the only thing enabling a kid to get through yet another dreary day of adult domination can be the serene emotional sanctuary of disdain. Often it doesn't matter what you are *for*, so long as it serves to offend, or at least somewhat unnerve, those in authority around you. This refuge will remain attractive, even if the drumbeat of resentful propaganda eases.

136   ... *whys and wherefores of this exceptional phenomenon* ... Such consistency can hardly be an accident. And yet, this is one propaganda campaign that cannot be blamed on "the powers that be," since it would hardly interest conspiratorial oppressors to suckle generations of youths on the milk of defiance! Could the relentless propaganda campaign to spread suspicion of authority be evidence of some intentional profreedom design? If the "societal T-cell" exists, it is more likely that we will someday recognize it

as an "emergent property" of a new type of civilization, rather than an intentional innovation we can feel proud of. Grateful for, yes; aware of, certainly. But a deliberate policy? I'm not quite paranoid enough to credit a scenario so convoluted or bizarre.

139     . . . *self-righteousness addicts* . . . Regarding the habit-forming properties of indignation, I am reminded of a hilarious yet wise skit that appeared on television's *Saturday Night Live*. The scene was set in a hospital, where a harried female nurse had to deal with a series of outraged males, each of them storming in to make demands.
    IRATE YOUNG COP: "How DARE you keep me from the patient! She was a witness to a crime! I have a sacred duty to *protect* the public!"
    IRATE YOUNG REPORTER: "How DARE you keep me from the patient! She was a witness to a crime! I have a sacred duty to *inform* the public!"
    IRATE YOUNG PHYSICIAN: "How DARE you people come storming in here! I'm a doctor! I have a sacred duty to *heal!*"
    All the actors then freeze their poses, and the announcer's voice comes on —
"Welcome to another episode of *The Young and the Self-Righteous!*"
    Again, this skit may offer a peek at our future—one filled with incensed people on outrage-doped endorphin highs. Or else it may signify that we already have within us the one truly effective antidote to fevers of excess indignation, a sense of humor.

139     . . . *fortifying some lonesome dissenter . . . shouting, "Wake up!"* . . . University of California at Berkeley's Robin Hanson ponders, "I find it hard to understand the evolutionary advantage of this behavior for the individual." This raises fascinating questions about why a fraction of humans seem driven to behave in extravagant ways, even though it exposes them to danger. One might presume that, in our long past, such behaviors had occasional big payoffs that compensated for the risks. In this chapter, however, I seem to be arguing that "social T-cells" arise to benefit civilization. This, in turn, appears to suggest some sort of group selection, which is anathema to many modern biologists. But such a purist rejection would be unfortunate, for societies clearly *do* evolve, developing new traits through trial and error—and sometimes through actual forethought. The process is not purely Darwinian. We do not understand it, except in crude outlines. But it happens, and we are the beneficiaries.

140     . . . *mask their egomania behind a shield of indignant "professionalism"*. . . Elsewhere we mention the phenomenon of *"microtyrants,"* people who talk themselves into believing that any action can be justified in the name of their craft, e.g., the paparazzi "news" photographers who hounded Princess Diana both before and after her fatal car crash, proclaiming dedicated craftsmanship as an excuse. Overdosing on self-righteousness can push a vigorous and abrasive "T-cell" over the edge, transforming individualism into solipsism.

141     *Even retractions do little good* . . . Since Goddard's confession in November 1997, some conspiracy fans refuse to credit the retraction, claiming that the government "got to him." The notion that truth will always chase down and slay a lie may prove unsupportable unless accountability plays a large role in tomorrow's rumor-drenched society.

141     . . . *other surveys reveal substantial overall confidence* . . . In a *Los Angeles Times* poll (August 1996) citizens were asked, "Would you be willing to give up some civil liberties, if that were necessary to curb terrorism in this country?" 58 percent answered that they were willing, 23 percent were not willing, and 13 percent said it would depend on which liberties. Yet when the question was posed differently, "How con-

cerned are you that fighting terrorism may wind up restricting some civil liberties?,"
68 percent expressed strong concern.

141 ... *After raising several generations* ... How long has this been going on? For how
many decades have media czars been preaching nonconformity as *the* conformist
message (while selling us their goods) and telling us from on high that we should
resent authority? It is an interesting question. A cursory appraisal of national myths
suggests that it's been going on for quite some time. Whether the American War of
Independence was a true revolution or (as some contend) a minor coup by a portion
of the preexisting white male ruling class, the myths and hagiography—from George
Washington's cherry tree, to the legend of Cincinnatus, to the log cabin birthplaces
of William Henry Harrison and Abe Lincoln—all testify that the theme is an old
one, in North America, at least. Indeed, suspicion of authority may be the one ingredient that was missing in nations that freed themselves from Spanish domination in
the early nineteenth century. From Mexico to Chile, they all copied the U.S. Constitution, with its vaunted checks and balances, and yet few remained free of domination by oligarchies. It could be that those constitutional provisions are only effective in thwarting tyranny if they are backed up by an attitude of cantankerous
resentment of constraint that has to be taught from an early age.

If suspicion of authority does have such long-standing provenance, it nevertheless was never like today. Movies from the 1930s and 1940s definitely show the same
basic ingredients, namely, protagonists who prove their mettle by standing up to
some officious or domineering figure. Yet, films such as *Mr. Smith Goes to Washington* or *From Here to Eternity* are moderated by underlying connective themes,
such as patriotism, that are largely missing from those made today. The centrifugal
influences had a centripetal counterpart, so that we flew like moons—only loosely
bound, and yet joined in orbit around a common, uniting theme.

141 ... *protecting the privilege of millions to be wrong* ... It should be noted that the analogy
with a human immune system is inherently limited. For instance, in our own bodies, T-
cells are ruthlessly winnowed by the thymus gland (hence the *T*) in order to ensure that
these vigorous antagonist agents do not attack the self. Should we emulate such a culling
mechanism, in order to prevent the harm done by "cancerous" cells, like Timothy
McVeigh? Of course not! That would undermine the whole notion of error correction
through criticism. And yet, might the same function of a social "thymus" be accomplished somehow through education and mental health? By instilling a loose sense of
participation, community, and humor, while at the same time leaving undampened the
eagerly individualistic drives that make for vigorous social critics? In that case, what
would be winnowed would not be the individual, but the toxic notion of violent rage.

142 Jack Stack, *The Great Game of Business* (New York: Bantam, 1992).

143 Jean François Revel, *Democracy Against Itself: The Future of the Democratic Impulse*
(New York: Macmillan, 1993).

144 ... *pouncing on errors that seemed too "minor" to notice in the past* ... For example,
making political fund-raising calls from an office telephone, a practice that was universal in the past but is now no longer acceptable (although using another telephone, just down the hall, would be).

144 ... *As if aware of this synergy* ... The analogy between free speech criticism and the
immune systems of living beings can be taken even farther. For instance, just as the
brain is mostly unaware of the body's immune system, which functions quite well

without conscious direction, so society's leaders are largely unaware of this "T Cell" synergy—except when the perceived errors being targeted happen to be their own. Individually, leaders nearly always squirm and try to evade this scrutiny. Nevertheless, in a democracy the system forces most of them to accept accountability.

But what of those societies and corporations where leaders *have* successfully insulated themselves from criticism? University of Texas Professor Joseph D. Miller points out that our bodies' T cells normally do not cross the "blood brain barrier." The central nervous system—the "head of government"—is immunologically privileged, though there is a type of brain cell, called *microglia*, that performs certain immune-like functions. Does this mean that our new democratic social systems may *surpass* natural immune systems, since the heads of government in a democracy cannot escape immunological surveillance? Or does it suggest that Singapore-style governance, in which the topmost social layers insulate themselves against criticism, is more inherently "natural" somehow?

These ideas are new. We must explore some more, before leaping to premature conclusions.

**CHAPTER 6**

151     . . . *fewer new words in English, and a lot fewer new ideas* . . . Bruce Sterling, *Magazine of Fantasy and Science Fiction*, February 1993. Note that some languages *are* "owned," in a sense. Take, for example, certain copyrighted computer codes and compilers. Then there is the alleged authority over the French language that is repeatedly asserted by the *Académie française*.

152     " . . . *goofy, Jolt cola–swilling UNIX freaks* . . ." this genuinely affectionate characterization was first coined by author Bruce Sterling.

152     . . . *Internet to be even more wild and free* . . . Administrators faced a critical decision. On the surface, they suffered a continuing drain on resources in the direction of "frivolous" pursuits. They might have clamped down, as Germany, China, and several other countries have done in recent years: reining in the disorderly mob; establishing firm rules and oversight procedures; and enclosing the fields and pastures of cyberspace into tidy, fenced-off, accountable territories. Instead, many of those big shots of the 1970s and 1980s willingly let their institutions "tithe" a steady subsidy for irrelevant, extracurricular, impractical, unprofitable, flippant, and even trivial uses, defying the prosaic image of mean-minded bureaucrats by watering a crop whose emerging properties they could but dimly perceive. (See chapter 2 references to the prescience of Vannevar Bush.)

153     Steven E. Miller, *Civilizing Cyberspace: Policy, Power and the Information Superhighway* (Reading, Mass.: Addison-Wesley, 1996).

153     . . . *individuals will tend to gravitate towards a safe average, suppressing their individuality and creativity in favor of . . . the demands of an omniscient observer* . . . From Philip E. Agre (University of California, San Diego) and Christine A. Harbs (University of San Diego), "Social Choice About Privacy: Intelligent Vehicle-Highway Systems in the United States," *Information, Technology & People*, vol.7, no.4 (1994).

157     Esther Dyson, *Release 2.0: A Design for Living in the Digital Age* (New York: Broadway Books, 1997), p. 216.

159     . . . *such abuses are not confined solely to despotic societies* . . . See Gary T. Marx, *Undercover: Police Surveillance in America* (Berkeley, CA: University of California Press, 1988).

163   *"There is no strength in security through obscurity . . ."* British journalist Oliver Morton points out one implication—that encryption algorithms and procedures should be subject to rigorous peer review, like any other important scientific or technical innovation that nations and economies rely on. According to Morton, "A lot of the hatred of Clipper [chip] came from the fact that the government would not release the algorithm, so that people could assure themselves of its strength."

In fact, peer review may be one way of looking at benign hacker attacks. When Georgetown University Professor Dorothy Denning defended the "Hacker A" types who seek entry to forbidden computers without deriving gain or wreaking harm, she praised their role in testing system failure modes, helping operators improve after receiving the benefit of helpful "criticism." Denning's later role in defending the government's position in the Clipper controversy is therefore not as ironic or inconsistent as some maintain. In both cases, she took a position favoring accountability, whether pursued on an ad hoc basis by benign hackers, or formally, by duly assigned officers of the law.

164   *. . . uncovering flawed security systems . . .* In a recent irony, the National Security Agency (NSA), a secretive government bureaucracy that many hackers see as satanic (due in part to its mandate for code breaking and data surveillance), has announced a technology transfer program with a stated goal to help companies spin off commercial products and processes from the NSA's extraordinary technical expertise. One impetus for this program is apparently the agency's growing concern about the potential vulnerability of government and private industry computer networks to acts of terrorism or sabotage. By opening systems up to criticism, they purportedly hope to expose errors and trapdoors, resulting in more secure systems, even if it means releasing some treasured technologies the NSA had previously been keeping to itself. Some libertarian-leaning netizens, characteristically suspicious of this overture, call it an "obvious farce."

167   *. . . truth will . . . slay any calumny or lie . . .* According to this argument, the Internet may render libel law obsolete and irrelevant because (1) it turns many more people into public figures, and (2) it increases our ability to rebut charges, correct the record, or flame our defamers. "If someone writes one hundred lines of false statements about you, you can file one thousand lines of point-by-point refutation. A cheap day in court," says EFF lawyer Michael Godwin. Mike Godwin, "Libel Law: Let It Die," *Wired*, March 1996.

167   *. . . anyone can construct a "shadow identity," a slanderous characterization, that sticks to your cyberidentity like glue. . . .* See Wright, "The Cybersmear."

I am resigned to a high likelihood that somebody will try doing this to me, probably after taking offense at this book, or at an impulsive misinterpretation of its message. If that happens, I may have to count on the technical skills of friends throughout the computer industry, including some mentioned in this chapter, to help act as my "T-cell" protectors. Alas, many other people don't have such resources to call on when *they* voice opinions different from Net dogma. We shall see if reciprocal transparency solves such problems in the long run. In the short term, however, it can be worrisome to stick your head up and speak.

167   *. . . net culture . . . will change more toward the mainstream as the mainstream joins the net. . . .* Esther Dyson, *Release 1.0*, 23 December 1993.

168   *. . . list of other breaches of Net civility . . .* Roger Clarke's paper, "Net-Ethiquette: Mini Case Studies of Dysfunctional Human Behavior on the Net," can be accessed at http://www.anu.edu.au/people/Roger.Clarke/II/Netethiquettecases.html.

168   ... *pine for the good old days* ... Andrei Simic, professor of social anthropology at the University of Southern California, theorizes that America's incivility is due to the fact that we are "in a period where we have the illusion of the greatest individualism we have ever had." A *U.S. News & World Report* poll of 1,005 adults found that 89 percent of Americans consider incivility to be a serious national problem, fostering violence, dividing community, and eroding values.

170   ... *the cult followings of talk show hosts* ... As a "joke," Rush Limbaugh offered his listeners special radios with their tuners soldered exclusively to the nearest station that carried his broadcasts. Although he regularly teased his "ditto-heads" for their devoted and dutiful agreement with his opinions, Limbaugh seldom brought challengers onto his shows, or let articulate dissenters poke and test his notions before the public eye.

176   ... *Net can also provide many of the implements of science* ... An early example of this kind of extended discussion on the Internet was the Sustainability Hyperforum experiment performed jointly by Caltech and the Rand Corporation, under the leadership of Professor Bruce Murray in 1996. Participants made use of a range of analytical and graphical tools, provided as common resources by the organizers. Some initial endeavors along this line might be viewed at http://www.hf.caltech.edu/hf and at http://crit.org.

176   ... *moral force that men used to invest in duels* ... For one vivid fictional depiction of the disputation arena concept, see Marc Stiegler's 1988 novel *David's Sling* (New York: Baen Books).

178   *Numbers can be a better form of cash* ... To begin leaning more about electronic cash and related technologies, see Web pages by Prof. Michael Froomkin at: http://www.law.miami.edu/~froomkin/articles/cfP97.htm

180   *Many cryptographic protocols* ... A. Michael Froomkin, "It Came from Planet Clipper: The Battle over Key Escrow," from the "Law in Cyberspace" issue of the University of Chicago Legal Forum, 1996, U.Chi.L.Forum, p.15.

**CHAPTER 7**

185   ... *the Computers, Freedom and Privacy (CFP) conference* ... For further information see http://www.cfp.org.

190   ... *Cold War technology transfer laws to restrict the export* ... As of this writing, the United States still maintained an official policy that exporting advanced encryption technology beyond its borders constituted a crime. This was justified by ruling that encryption software was equivalent, under the law, to munitions, an interpretation that caused even the government's harshest critics more whimsy than outrage — especially since national boundaries in cyberspace are as porous as a mesh window screen. Some companies have simply moved their encryption-related operations overseas, for example, to mathematically sophisticated Russia. Moreover, *printed* versions of RSA programs and other software are protected as free speech, and thus safeguarded from interference. At this time, it remains unclear what officials hope to accomplish by the munitions interpretation, except perhaps to make encryption aficionados pause for a few seconds of sober thought before sharing their techniques with foreign dictators.

192   ... *measure would also help defend against illicit key collection by invading hackers* ... Especially if one of the five key escrow sites was forbidden to be in electronic contact with the outside world. Multiple cache sites would also help against the many nonelectronic "bypass" methods of spying discussed in chapter 9.

192    *... officials were slow to propose ...* This alternative, sometimes called "trusted third party encryption," in 1996 became the official approach pushed by the United States for international adoption by leading nations of the OECD. While this step is an improvement in principle, it has not increased the degree of trust between government officials and outside groups. As of this writing, a consensus seemed unlikely.

195    *... Edward Teller, helped lead a persuasive campaign ...* Few could have been more surprised than this author to discover, while researching this book, how influential Teller was during the early Cold War, as he repeatedly campaigned against yielding to the temptation to solve security problems by stifling information flow.

196    *... all too many blunders and betrayals ...* To scale the difference in levels of error that are tolerated in an open versus a closed society, think about taking a sip from almost any river in the United States, and comparing the taste to a sample from any waterway in China or Russia. Yet there is an ironic corollary to this difference between a system of noisy, adversarial accountability and one based on hierarchical "management." Citizens of an open society may worry much *more* about water quality, and perceive it as a greater problem, because error-correcting confrontations appear frequently in the news (but are suppressed in closed societies). In the words of Barry Fulton, "It seems to me that the new technologies can simultaneously ensure that government does not become abusive *and*, through normal revelations of day-to-day incompetency and deceit, create a public opinion of distrust. Is this a paradox of the new technologies? Does shining a light into the corridors of power build or destroy trust?"

196    *... worst U.S. government scandals ... took place in circumstances where secrecy prevailed over accountability ...* In 1953, during the Cold War, the U.S. Army apparently sprayed zinc cadmium sulfide (a mock biological warfare agent) near a school in Minneapolis in order to simulate covert biological attacks. The students in the school were never told about the testing or its possible harmful effects. Several of these students' children have been born with birth defects allegedly resulting from the testing.

     Investigations reviewing the history of government-sponsored atomic experiments have found that because debates over the need for human experimentation and the policies that should govern it were kept secret, many contractors and university researchers were apparently unaware of legal and ethical concerns surrounding the experiments they were paid to conduct. For example, Charles E. Wilson, secretary of defense during the Cold War era, directed that human radiation experiments should be conducted by following the strict code of medical ethics that emerged from the postwar Nuremberg trials, but then marked the file containing this directive "top secret."

     Under the Verona Project, several Soviet codes were said to have been cracked following World War II. President Truman and Secretary of State Dean Acheson were not informed of the project or its results. Data were kept secret by J. Edgar Hoover, giving him power to wrongly accuse many officials of being Communists. (See Joseph Albright and Marcia Kunstel, *Bombshell: The Secret Story of Ted Hall and America's Unknown Atomic Spy Conspiracy* [New York: Times Books, 1997].)

196    *... a curse of human nature makes every leader want to keep secret plans ...* According to a June 1994 report by ABC News, more than 32,000 U.S. government employees were still engaged primarily in keeping secrets, at a direct cost to the taxpayers of $2 to $3 billion annually (not including hidden CIA and NSA expenditures), plus an added $14 billion or so paid to defense contractors for secrecy-related activities.

197    *... passed on this belief to some key elements of the American establishment ...* To those familiar with Teller's checkered history during and after the Manhattan

Project, as well as his reputation as a dogged Cold War friend of right-wing causes, this portrayal may seem strange. Yet so convinced was he of the self-defeating nature of secrecy that he often floated the notion of eliminating *all* document classification within the federal government, even nuclear weapons blueprints! In fairness, we should note that Teller enjoyed provoking a reaction, and exaggeration is a useful rhetorical device for getting your point across. Still, this mind-boggling suggestion will be worth recalling later, when we discuss "dangerous" physical technologies.

In a surprising example of "Tellerite" openness, the NSA's technology transfer program has the purported goal of helping companies spin off commercial products and processes from the agency's extraordinary pool of technical expertise. One impetus for this program was a Clinton administration mandate to find new and more efficient ways of doing business. Another stated motivation was the agency's growing concern about the potential vulnerability of government and private industry computer networks to acts of terrorism or sabotage. Opening systems to criticism is seen as safer, in the long run, than keeping them secret. Naturally, this is seen by the agency's critics as a minuscule step, and possibly no more than a public relations ploy. In light of the NSA's past history, those critics may be right.

198  . . . *traffic analysis, that is, drawing conclusions from patterns of communication flow* . . . Crypto-advocates are quite aware of this chink in the armor of encrypted secrecy-for-all. Fear of traffic analysis by government agencies underlay the original motivation for anonymous remailers, which pass messages back and forth in encrypted form, mixing them thoroughly before sending them on to their destinations. But they are only partly effective. What is lacking so far is a similar technology for stream connections on the Net. One proposal, called PipeNet, would be like a remailer but for direct connections. In conjunction with off-the-shelf technologies like Internet Phone, users could make encrypted telephone calls on the Net, with the data intermixed with other data en route. Technically, it is much more challenging than remailers, but this is the direction in which the cypherpunks want to go. See "The Problem of Extortion" for an appraisal of how this technology might affect a world in which people can harm one another with almost pure anonymity and safety from detection.

200  . . . *paradox is one of an infinite number* . . . Bruce Sterling poses another delicious "false logical chain":

FREE SPEECH ~ LITERACY ~ GOVERNMENT EDUCATION FOR ALL ~
UNIVERSAL INDOCTRINATION ~ TYRANNY.

Cute. Again, the flaws are right there in the equivalence signs. This sort of thing explains why many people are turning away from the seductive ideologies that have spread so much ruin during this century. Logic is just a tool, a first step on the road to learning from the universe. Logic is not an excuse to yammer at the cosmos, telling it the way things ought to be.

205  . . . *Out of every 100 felonies committed in the United States* . . . Crime statistics organized by Bryan Vila of the University of Wyoming, from figures released by the U.S. Department of Justice.

206  . . . *tipping the "deterrence equation"* . . . One reason for relatively low conviction and imprisonment rates is now ascribed to reluctance on the part of many juries and judges to enforce draconian and life-ruining sentences against those who are caught abusing illegal drugs, often harming nobody but themselves.

206  . . . *precedents support exactly this direct, rather than inverse, trade-off between security and freedom* . . . In fact, the best example of low fear levels coinciding with free-

dom happens to be . . . again . . . *us*. This is masked by omnipresent ululations about crime that spill across the media. But in fact, many parts of the United States, Canada, Australasia, and other areas of the neo-West are currently experiencing rates of violent crime that are much lower than our ancestors faced in the towns and villages of Europe, Asia, or Africa. Per capita comparisons are masked by the fact that Americans *hear* about crimes that take place all across a major continent filled with a third of a billion people. And yet, deep inside, we *know* that things are actually pretty good. People mostly walk and drive with a daily confidence reflecting a general atmosphere of tolerance that would surprise people from almost any other era in history. A confidence that allows us to indulge in a national and civilizationwide passion for self-criticism, constantly reminding each other of our faults and measuring not the progress we've made, but how much farther we have yet to go.

207   *. . . public demand for action could result in Draconian measures . . .* Bruce Frankel, "New Sides to Old Debate on Surveillance," *USA Today*, 25 April 1995, A1. After the Oklahoma City and World Trade Center bombings, officials called for an expansion of the government's power to investigate domestic groups. As it happened, the actual scope of new legislation was very minor. This article goes on to discuss how in the 1970s, FBI agents began returning their domestic cases marked "Closed" because of their own personal hostility toward politically motivated intelligence work. It also gives a brief listing of other democracies facing terrorist threats who have given the police much broader powers.

210   *Professionals need space . . .* The National Academy of Sciences, on being told all advisory committees must hold open meetings, responded by threatening not to hold any.

211   *. . . No pseudonym will hide your true Internet identity . . .* Cypherpunks naturally disagree. While they admit that simple pseudonyms can be hacked and traced, there are methods that "will be beyond the reach of even a first-rate hacker." The simplest proposed technique is to send e-mail from throwaway accounts, using a different one each time, going through anonymous remailers, and signing the message with your pseudonym. The disadvantage of this technique is that no one can send a message back to you. If a message can get to you, often a motivated hacker can do so as well. The problem with all of these methods is not their theoretical effectiveness, but the fact that they depend on several steps being perfectly reliable (for example, honest management of the anonymous remailer) and on an absence of "lurker" or "sniffer" spy programs at numerous vulnerable junctures along the way. It seems odd, on the face of it, for cypherpunks to put so much faith in abstract networks and unknown sysops whose best-advertised trait is a love of masks and unaccountability instead of trusting the larger civilization around them, in which the weapon of light is so much more effective than any disguise.

214   *. . . cyber-reality's ability to reproduce the erotic atmosphere . . .* Dorian Sagan, "Sex, Lies and Cyberspace," *Wired*, January 1995. Sagan goes on to say, "Yet these masks work only if they are not true lies—that is if they accentuate the truth. On AOL, I understood more fully than ever before the origin of our word 'person.' Before the Latin *persona-*, meaning role, the word was the Etruscan *phersu*, or actor's mask."

215   *. . . anonymity can be used to serve social, as well as anti-social ends . . .* Personal correspondence to the author dated July 25, 1994, concerning deliberations with EFF officers Jerry Berman and David Johnson, about a proposed EFF official position on anonymity. The memo outlines why Godwin believes the EFF should not endorse any

legal scheme that penalizes anonymity. He provides six arguments in support of anonymity and alternatives to a legal regime that discourages anonymity. See also "Who Was That Masked Man?," *Internet World*, January 1995, 22–25. This article debates whether or not anonymity should be preserved or outlawed, concluding that, despite problems with anonymity, it should be preserved as an online option.

215   . . . *ruled that anonymity can be somewhat justified* . . . As in other privacy matters, the courts have been vague, sometimes contradictory, and always contingent in discussing when anonymity must be protected. For instance, a woman in Ohio was arrested for handing out fliers about a tax increase. Supposedly, her pamphlets were in violation of Ohio's election laws, which require a person's name and address on all leaflets (*McIntyre v. Ohio*). This incident has led many lawyers to confront the conflict between the First Amendment and the political disclosure laws of most states. In the already cited 1960 case *Talley v. Los Angeles* (a discrimination case) the Supreme Court said, "Persecuted groups and sects from time to time throughout history have been able to criticize oppressive practices and laws either anonymously or not at all." However, the Court later moved away from this view in the 1976 case *Buckley v. Valeo*, when it upheld most of the disclosure requirements written into the new federal elections law in order to ensure accountability and prevent corruption. Dissenting in *McIntyre v. Ohio Elections Commission*, Supreme Court Justice Antonin Scalia castigated the generally dishonorable aspect of concealed identity: "It facilitates wrong by eliminating accountability, which is ordinarily the very purpose of anonymity." He argued that to create legal protection for anonymous communication, absent a clear reason to expect threats, harassment, or reprisals, is a "distortion of the past that will lead to a coarsening of the future."

216   . . . *lack of any clear consensus* . . . As an experiment, the reader might try polling his or her friends. Ask (in a carefully unbiased way) whether anonymity should be protected on the same basis as free speech; then note any significant difference, on average, between the answers given by women and those given by men. While unscientific and subjective, the trial may be revealing.

216   . . . *Debating over the best placement along a spectrum* . . . A quirky analogy was suggested to me. Free speech is like Vitamin C: you know that too little can kill you, while too much will scarcely do much harm. Anonymity, on the other hand, is like a dangerous, potentially addictive, and toxic drug. It has special uses, but no one doubts that an overdose can kill a patient. Even most strong privacy adherents do not deny this. They simply believe that the crossover between benefit and toxicity is a rather high dose.

217   . . . *Which "eccentric" is more likely to be let alone?* . . . Again, we turn for a colorful illustration to the irrepressible John Perry Barlow (*Netview*, September 1995): "I come from a town in Wyoming where everybody knows everything about everybody all the time. But there you have a kind of exemption with your privacy because they know you: you may be a weirdo, but you're *their* weirdo. What's happening now is something really different—you leave a slime-trail of bits wherever you go in the modern world. And somebody can come along behind you and sweep up all those bits and create a data puppet of you that has every aspect of yourself, including your sins and peccadilloes and secret shames, but does not have the exonerating quality of being anyone's weirdo." Barlow reluctantly concludes that secrecy will be necessary in the future, because his *first* choice for a solution seems unlikely. "The answer is to get rid of the secret shame. But that's a leap we're not going to make right away."

In his 1993 book *The Costs of Privacy* (New York: A. DeGruyter), Steven L. Nock made a case that modern privacy is a response to the fact that so many strangers surround us. In our old villages, we knew the reputations of almost everyone we encountered. But today we must replace that knowledge. We do this by trying to learn more about strangers, while trying to conceal from them information about ourselves. The result is a surly arms race of scrutiny. "Privacy grows as the number of strangers grows. And since strangers tend not to have reputations, there will be more surveillance when there are more strangers. Privacy is one consequence, or cost, of growing numbers of strangers. Surveillance is one consequence, or cost, of privacy."

218   . . . *make encryption ubiquitous* . . . Quoted by Todd Lappin, "Cyber Rights in Fantasyland," *Wired*, November 1996. The quotation continues:
"Right now it's too easy for government and citizens in general to feel threatened by encryption, because most people don't have it, don't use it, and have only a vague sense of what it is. Once it becomes so commonplace that everyone just assumes that their phone calls and e-mail are encrypted—only then will we have a buffer against people who feel threatened by individual citizens having access to that kind of privacy."

218   . . . *profiled in a gushing article* . . . Josh McHugh, "Politics for the Really Cool," *Fortune*, September 1997, 172.

218   . . . *self-described cyber-libertarians* . . . Not to be confused with more moderate libertarians, such as those at the Cato Institute, who hold to principles of consensus building and gradualism (see "A *Withering Away*" at the end of chapter 9).

221   . . . *just for the fun of it* . . . There is, at present, nothing illegal about innovative games of "counter spy" being played by hobbyists, as long as no directly fraudulent crimes occur. Even the Clipper initiative would have had no effect on bands of intellectual T-cells practicing their anti-tyrant skills with other technologies, "just in case."

223   . . . *interpretation of the U.S. Constitution* . . . See Mike Godwin, "Government Eavesdropping (Thinking Clearly About Digital Telephony)," *Internet World*, September 1994, 93–95.

223   . . . *assumption that there exists a direct link between tyranny and efficiency* . . . For instance, the vaunted industrial capabilities of Nazi Germany were actually less than any of its major enemies, even though it had a head start gearing up for war. Hitler's rush to start hostilities, in 1939, and then his schedule for attacking the Soviets, in 1941, were both pushed ahead by the fact that Britain, and later the Soviet Union, once alerted to the danger, began catching up and would soon outstrip German war production. The greatest producer by far was the United States, even on a per capita basis. And yet a wretched myth persists about horrible dictatorships: "They were awful, but you gotta admit, they were efficient." See John F. Kennedy, *Why England Slept* (New York: Funk & Wagnalls, 1940), and Richard Overy, *Why the Allies Won* (London: Jonathan Cape, 1995).

224   . . . *to discover that we made an error, and correct it* . . . For instance, suppose we try to implement a transparent society and later decide that we don't like it. If free speech and citizen sovereignty are preserved, we can always step back and try an approach that emphasizes information "ownership" and encrypted anonymity. (I wonder, though, if we could do it in the opposite order. It somehow seems unlikely.)

226   *Even when it comes to tending the earth* . . . There is a long-standing myth that other cultures were better environmentalists, simply because they lived closer to the land, and because our present world civilization seems so rapacious toward natural

resources. But these differences diminish when today's environmental damage is divided up among the population on a per capita basis, and when careful analysis is made of past depredations against the earth, committed by supposedly nature-loving clans and tribes. John Perlin's *A Forest Journey* (New York: Norton, 1989) makes it clear that there is nothing new about short-sighted exploitation of resources, since people are driven more by near-term hunger than by long-term husbandry. What *is* relatively new is a widespread and growing consciousness of environmentalism among today's well-educated world population. An awareness that shows real signs of becoming powerful and habitual in the years and generations ahead. The key element appears to be a low level of ambient fear. When individuals are fearful, the environment never scores high on any scale of concern. It is when individuals can pause and think beyond near-term concerns that they begin pondering posterity.

## THE PROBLEM OF EXTORTION

228    . . . *those warnings that are backed up by a credible track record* . . . Consider the following innovative criminal scheme, an interesting turn on the old "stock market expert" swindle. An extortionist sets up one thousand assumed names and uses them to send death threats to a million people. After a year, he checks on who has died of natural or other causes. (He did nothing to induce any of the deaths—at least not directly.) Out of his one thousand encrypted aliases, the crook keeps the one hundred that had the best prediction records—the highest death rates. He then makes a second round of threats. Again a year passes and he checks which aliases are associated with the highest natural death rates, culling the ten most successful names. A year after that he is left with just with a single alias. But that one name by now has a fearsome reputation for success at targeting people for mysterious death! He then posts a final threat. Using the final name and its dreaded encrypted calling card, he demands payment of $1,000 in untraceable ecash from a million suckers in exchange for allowing them to continue living—a cheap price to most folks. For the cost of a few cleverly spammed e-mail messages, and without ever carrying out a single traceable physical act, he becomes a billionaire!

Fortunately (but alas for those of you considering pulling this scam), there are several decisive flaws to the plan. Readers are invited to figure them out.

## CHAPTER 8

231    . . . *on its way to becoming the most frightened* . . . A. Wildavsky, *American Scientist*, 67 (1979), p.32.

234    . . . *Similar mixtures of confidentiality and assigned responsibility* . . . Partial juror anonymity is well known in the scientific peer review process, whereby articles submitted to technical journals are anonymously critiqued by several experts. While this confidentiality encourages generally open appraisals of a paper, the option of unsealing the reviewers' identity is available, if suspicion of partiality is raised.

235    . . . *fringe believes such invisibility will remain possible* . . . This fantasy was reflected in the television series, *Max Headroom*, which depicted a computer-networked world of tomorrow in which many individuals chose to become "blanks"—opting out of the databases and living in a shadowy economy on the streets.

235    . . . *restrict use of the number by federal agencies* . . . The U.S. Privacy Act of 1974 (Public Law 93-579) does not go so far as to require agencies using the SSN to change to some other identifier, nor does it prevent agencies from using the SSN for

new purposes; however, it does make it unlawful for federal, state, or local governments to deny an individual rights or benefits based simply on whether a client refused to provide his or her SSN.

236 *. . . Why Should People Lie? . . .* Except that it does happen. An author I know was impersonated for years by someone who arranged book signings, gave radio interviews discussing my colleague's novels as if she had written them, and finally began signing documents in the real author's name! The impostor did real harm, yet for years no one ever thought to ask for proof that she was who she claimed to be.

239 *Am I dubious this will work as planned? . . .* Are modern encryption techniques truly ready to handle the coming needs of electronic commerce? This book is not a tome about that weighty subject. Nevertheless, it should be pointed out that many of the claims being made by proponents of e-commerce—that it will be secure, efficient, and accountable—have still to be proved. No technique has yet been developed that can simultaneously guarantee authentication, privacy, and atomicity (making sure that the transaction happens only once). When you add some of the other dangers that have been widely discussed, such as unexpected software glitches, or disgruntled software designers setting up back doors to allow undetected theft or fraud, the resulting scenario may be too frail and unreliable a foundation to depend on for the economic well-being of an entire world. Under these circumstances, people might still demand paper receipts for a long time to come. A hard copy keeps both sides of a transaction accountable, and makes it reconstructible, if volatile electronic memories unexpectedly go "poof." (More on this later.)

243 *. . . using the Social Security number . . .* Illustrating this trend, the U.S. Federal Aviation Administration is now calling for the collection of the SSNs of all air travelers, not primarily for security reasons, but in order to identify victims of accidents. Whether or not this particular request is blocked, such efforts will only multiply in the future.

247 *. . . time limits, which have been reduced . . .* A bipartisan federal commission on government secrecy, the second in the nation's history, reported that the government kept too much secret for too long, and blamed "a culture of secrecy" for fostering and perpetuating conspiracy theories. The commission proposed a National Declassification Center to oversee an opening process. Most classified material would be made public after ten years, all after thirty years. Senator Daniel Patrick Moynihan stated, "The culture of secrecy in place in the federal government will modernize only if there comes about a counterculture of openness, a climate which simply assumes that secrecy is not the starting place."

247 *. . . some kinds of transparency should be . . .* Alas, as we will see in chapter 9, it is very likely that technology will set time limits for us. Any security system that is adequate for one decade may seem like tissue during the next. The ciphers guarding old secret files and records may wind up having a natural decay rate. If so, we will all have to assume that even whispers may echo back to us, someday.

249 *By codifying the Government's power to spy invisibly . . .* Diffie seems to assume that the wealthy, the powerful, and criminals require a government-mandated back door in order to do their sneaking around, when in fact what all these groups really need is a haze to remain hidden and unaccountable from both government and the public at large.

250 *. . . an encryption tax or tariff . . .* The notion of "bit taxes" has already been raised by Walter Truett Anderson, a Canadian economist. Dr. Arthur Cordell proposed an

alternative as a method for governments to survive the information age: every digital bit of information transmitted on the Net would be taxed at some minuscule amount, say, .000000001 cents a bit, or one-billionth of a cent, on every single item of e-mail, every piece of data. Naturally, most netizens abhor this idea. Clinton administration Commerce Secretary William Daley has already said that the Internet should be considered a "tariff-free environment," but we are in early days yet, and the official tune may change when e-commerce takes over as the major cash-enthalpy flow in the economy. Encryption taxes and other ideas may or may not be practical on today's Internet, but what about the new networks being put together by the NSF, or DARPA, or consortia including IBM and MCI, whose designs are not yet finished? Perhaps one or more of these might be set aside for anonymous-encrypted traffic, while secrecy is discouraged on others? We may wind up having several realms, each with its own rules, a diversity that may lend civilization strength.

The advantage of an encryption tax over a mere bit tax is that raw bit traffic is not a deleterious commodity whose reduction might provide a social good. Rather, taxing bit flows would inherently burden and even threaten openness—like atherosclerotic plaque on the walls of a body's blood vessels. But taxing encrypted traffic is another matter entirely. One needn't create a huge bureaucracy of officials to enforce this tax, or inspect every portal of the Internet for coded messages. We would never catch or detect most cases, but a significant sampling would do. If tattle-tale audits were carried out by private individuals or competitors, that should be enough to keep things reasonably honest and above board, in much the same way that shoplifting is suppressed to irritating but bearable levels nowadays mostly by the alert eyes of other customers, not by a store's harried employees.

250 ... *same principle should be vigorously applied to government agencies* ... The tricky part would be how to make sure agencies did not writhe to evade such limitations, or simply "budget away" the added costs. Nevertheless, such a tool could be worth exploring, especially if everyone came to see it as a matter of simple equity—treating all secretkeepers equally.

252 ... *Public Feedback Regulation* ... Professor Peter Swire, *Public Feedback Regulation: Learning to Govern in the Age of Computers, Telecommunications, and the Media*, Unpublished Study, 1993. See www.osu.edu/units/law/swire.html.

257 ... *may fight for a general policy of live and let live* ... This optimistic scenario assumes that all the different types of weirdos are smart enough to see what they have in common with other weirdos. This is a supposition, and it may not happen, as we see in the darker examples given in chapter 9. In addition to tolerance of eccentricity, a world of light will also need forgiveness, a tendency to let minor transgressions slip into the past. Again, there are three ways this might be achieved: (1) mandated amnesia, as credit bureaus are now required to "forget" consumer information that is more than seven years old; (2) exhorting people to have a forgiving attitude towards others; and (3) creating a situation in which gossips and harridans find it in their own best interests to let others forget mistakes that they have outgrown, because it will be easy to turn the glare of disapproval around and shine it on the imprudent past errors of disapprovers.

Each of these three solutions has problems. Number one has limited effectiveness in dealing with specific institutions, and will not prevent banks or other companies from maintaining their own secret lists, for example, noting bankruptcies more than seven years old. Basically, solution number one tries to overcome the human drive to know things.

Number two, exhortation, has a miserable track record, when used all by itself.

Number three, reciprocal transparency, is at least partly hypothetical. Many examples show that tolerance based on self-interest plays a role in modern life. But whether the method will translate into the future, as depicted on these pages, is a view that the author freely admits to be speculative.

258   . . . *database containing reports by all the women that the young man had previously dated* . . . Again, try polling your friends about this use of "dating databases," and see if there is a difference between the responses of men and women.

260   . . . *role of producer or critic won't vanish* . . . Virginia Postrel, editor of *Reason* magazine (a libertarian journal), projects that the twenty-first century will be the "age of editors," because human potential for creativity will tap a vast reserve of billions of educated minds; the real art will be in sifting the datascape, culling and selecting, nurturing and guiding—and finally drawing the attention of a distracted multitude to something new that's worthy to rise above the general storm of new things.

260   Lee Marshall, "The World According to Eco" (interview), *Wired*, March 1997.

260   ". . . *tag commentary . . . a few parasitic bytes affixed to any data stream* . . ." Some experts dislike the term "tag commentary," and I can't blame them. For one thing, metadata concerning a particular message do not have to be "affixed to" the data itself but can flow or be stored elsewhere, yet be logically associated with their intended referent. W3C PICS and RDF are among the technology initiatives currently working along these lines. Nevertheless, for the purposes of helping a general audience visualize the concept, I have kept with the original terminology I used in 1987.

262   . . . *Percolation may have drawbacks* . . . Note that one experiment along these lines can be found at http://www.crit.org. Percolation may wind up depending on something like the Platform for Internet Content Selection (PICS). This system proposes a general labeling infrastructure for Internet traffic, while leaving the labeling *vocabulary* to the user. Some proposed uses of PICS labels are to rate levels of language, violence, nudity, and sex, or whether a product has been scanned for viruses. Publishers can label their own sites, but cannot prevent others from distributing further labels about them. PICS could also note privacy ratings. Your Web browser could flash a warning if a site doesn't match your privacy preferences. PICS shifts the burden of censorship from online publishers to the individual users. But some claim that PICS filters could be imposed at the level of proxy server or nation-state, providing a tool for censors and making it easier for countries such as China or Singapore to impose restrictions. *HotWired* columnist Simson Garfinkel described PICS as "the most effective global censorship technology ever designed."

263   *Does [Buck Henry's skit] illustrate the decadent . . . future?* . . . If so, Plato will turn out to be right in predicting that the final outcome of democracy is mob rule, followed by a takeover of his preferred approach to government; dictatorship by a "noble" elite.

266   . . . *modern observers who think we have entered an era of unpredictability* . . . See Kevin Kelly, *Out of Control* (Reading, Mass.: Addison-Wesley, 1994), and Edward Tenner, *Why Things Bite Back* (New York: Knopf, 1996).

267   . . . *a "predictions market"* . . . University of California economist Robin Hanson calls his system a "betting pool on disputed science questions, where the current odds-on favorites are treated as the current intellectual consensus. Ideas futures markets let you bet on the future settlement of a scientific controversy. [See

http://www.ideosphere.com/ and http://hanson.berkeley.edu/ideafutures.html.] But the method may have wider applications." Note: a form of predictions market was depicted in John Brunner's wonderfully prescient science fiction novel *The Shockwave Rider* in 1974, a work that illustrated principles of transparency and also invented the terminology, possibly the very concepts, of computer "viruses" and "worms."

267  . . . *Anyone claiming to have special foresight* . . . In management, the yearly performance review is supposedly a kind of predictions registry, attempting to further the careers of those who have done well. In fact, this is basic to almost all forms of accountability, as humans strive to tell the difference between those who are credible and those who, despite their superficial charismatic allure, are not.

268  . . . *lets them be applied anywhere, any time* . . . Regarding the "specificity score" of any prediction, one notes that, way back in 1798, in one of Europe's most popular books, the authors claimed to show how every verse and phrase of the Book of Revelation meticulously related to Napoleon Bonaparte and his contemporaries. Today we see the same level of blithe certainty in countless millennialist treatments of the very same biblical passages. In not a single case does the writer ponder *why* protean vagueness should be a desirable trait in prophecy.

268  . . . *society should take notice* . . . Regarding potential for a predictions registry consider the intriguing possibility of a "policymaker's dating service." It is a simple fact of life that certain charismatic types of individuals (like Kennedys) are likely to have exceptional influence in our world, by virtue of charisma, social skills, or family connections. This is bound to happen, because human beings have always been swayed by such qualities. Unfortunately, charisma and connections have little positive *or* negative correlation with being right. On the other hand, there are lots of people out there who have excellent track records for accuracy and good judgment, who will never get anywhere near a position of power because they are also irksome, funky-looking, not well connected, or hard to get along with. Our hypothetical predictions registry offers a unique possibility of *matching* these two types of individuals. Imagine if the charismatic could be paired up with those who have proved astute! What service could better help society than to unite those who are destined to be powerful with advisers who will help them to be right! (Or at least to steer them away from the most egregious blunders.)

268  . . . *fans suspensefully follow champion seers* . . . In a growing hobby of "celebrity markets," fans bet on the relative values, rising and falling, of movie star careers. This is a concrete (if trivial) example of ad hoc registries becoming a participatory sport, as well as catering to spectators.

## "THE PLAUSIBILITY MATRIX"

273  . . . *put us on more even ground* . . . . Some suggest that in a world of masks there will be safety for average citizens because the rich will be in competition with each other, and ultimately will hold one another at bay. Alas, there is no evidence that such a thing happens outside the influence of fierce social and governmental constraints. Medieval Europe, the Roman Empire, imperial China, nineteenth-century American robber barons, and countless other cases indicate that, on the contrary, aristocrats see it as in their own best interests to collude. Confronting each other head-on can be terribly risky. Yes, there are flashy feuds and "wars," but the upper classes rou-

tinely dropped all such struggles to unite at the first sign of serious competition from below. By acknowledging each other's spheres of influence, oligarchs found it possible to fleece the lower classes like sheep in a field.

275    . . . *Umberto Eco expressed this concern eloquently* . . . Lee Marshall, "The World According to Eco," *Wired*, March 1997.

276    . . . *validity of box 2, in principle* . . . Box 2 is superior only when we are talking about potential threats to constitutional freedom. But there are other troubling questions. What of the "quiet" neighbors who are spouse beaters, child abusers, white-collar thieves, and so on? Should they be spared all accountability, just because they cannot plot a coup against democracy? It is a hard question, and one that might have different answers, depending on whether you are the powerful one or the powerless victim held in the dark, private tyranny of some individual homes.

## CHAPTER 9

279    *The interested reader is encouraged* . . . Bruce Schneier, *Applied Cryptography: Protocols, Algorithms, and Source Code in C*, 2nd ed. (New York: John Wiley & Sons, 1996). Schneier is a pragmatist who has no illusions about the practical problems of implementing crypto-systems. "Why Cryptography Is Harder than It Looks," B. Schneier, *Information Security Bulletin*, vol. 2, no. 2, March 1997, pp. 31–36.

280    . . . *DNA Computer has drawn special attention* . . . "DNA Solution of Hard Computational Problems," Richard J. Lipton, *Science*, vol. 268, 28 April 1995, p. 542. Also "Molecular Computation of Solutions to Combinatorial Problems," Leonard Adelman, *Science*, vol. 266, 11 November 1994, p. 1021.

286    . . . *gnat cameras* . . . *seem plausible at this point* . . . The chief theoretical limit has to do with optics, where visual systems begin losing acuity when the size of the aperture gets too small. Actual insect eyes, for instance, have only crude image-forming capabilities, relying instead on localizing and characterizing types of motion. But this problem may not limit micro-imaging devices very much. A mobile surveillance system need only implant itself at a good vantage point, presumably in some shrouded corner with a view of some adversary, and then inflate an artificial air or gel-based lens to the size that is needed in order to concentrate enough light and escape diffraction limitations. In the long run, the point is not whether such devices are likely, or even plausible, but whether we should bet the entire farm *against* these surveillance tools ever appearing on the scene. In an open society, we will have a chance of knowing if they do arrive—and of holding their owners accountable.

287    *Stepping back from far-out speculation* . . . For more on the Witness program, see http://www.witness.org.

289    Robert Wright, *The Moral Animal: Why We Are the Way We Are: The New Science of Evolutionary Biology* (New York: Pantheon, 1994).

290    . . . *favorite human pastime* . . . What is fiction but a made-up tale that the reader chooses to believe in for a while? (Note: One recent popular novel, *The Truth Machine*, by James L. Halperin, vividly depicts the quest for an effective lie detector.)

290    . . . *a less radical midway opinion may be more typical* . . . Once again, the reader is invited to try taking an informal poll among male and female friends regarding their attitudes toward the desirability of an effective, cheaply available lie detector. Draw your own conclusions.

292 . . . *Psychiatric Aspects of Wickedness* . . . *Psychiatric Annals*, vol. 27, no. 9 (Sept. 1997). A study released in 1997 showed that 80% of the 1.7 million men and women behind bars in the U.S. had abuse or addiction problems with drugs or alcohol (Columbia Univ.).

293 *Most people are cowed by the power of large institutions* . . . See http://www.anu.edu.au/people/Roger.Clarke/DV/HumanID.html.

295 Steven E. Miller, *Civilizing Cyberspace: Policy, Power and the Information Super-highway* (Reading, Mass.: Addison-Wesley Publishing, 1996), p. 292.

295 . . . *According to one dour vision* . . . Gary T. Marx, *Undercover: Police Surveillance in America* (Berkeley: University of California Press, 1988).

298 . . . *individuals tend to gravitate towards a safe average, suppressing individuality and creativity in favour of . . . demands of an omniscient observer* . . . Philip E. Agre and Christine A. Harbs, "Social Choice About Privacy: Intelligent Vehicle-Highway Systems in the United States," *Information Technology & People*, vol. 7, no. 4 (1994).

298 . . . *Dr. Seuss's children's story* . . . Dr. Seuss, *Did I Ever Tell You How Lucky You Are?* (New York: Random House, 1973).

299 . . . *in his short story "I See You"* . . . In Damon Knight, *On Side Laughing* (New York: St. Martin's Press, 1991). Another science fiction tale depicting people exchanging privacy for participation in a new culture can be seen in the novel *Oath of Fealty*, by Larry Niven and Jerry Pournelle.

## A WITHERING AWAY

306 . . . *government that creates markets in the first place* . . . Jaron Lanier, quoted from "Karma Vertigo: Or Considering the Excessive Responsibilities Placed on Us by the Dawn of the Information Infrastructure," *Netview: Global Business Network News*, winter 1995. Although bureaucrats are often depicted as relentlessly power hungry, many officials actually share the same cautious attitude toward government's proper role, as expressed in March 1997 by Christine A. Varney of the Federal Trade Commission, at the Seventh Conference on Computers, Freedom and Privacy: "First, I believe that, in general, government should regulate only when there has been an identifiable market failure or where an important public policy goal cannot be achieved without government intervention. Second, the pace of change in the information industry is unprecedented. Government regulation, on the other hand, moves very slowly, and the predictive skills of government agencies are notoriously limited. As a result, regulatory and legislative solutions to consumer protection issues are unlikely to be either timely or sufficiently flexible with respect to the digital world at this juncture. And finally, I believe the electronic medium itself offers new opportunities for consumer education and empowerment, which in turn increases the likelihood that self-regulatory regimes will be effective."

307 . . . *paternalistic protections may prove less necessary* . . . Jeff Cooper, director of the Center for Information Strategy and Policy, contends that states have traditionally relied on five monopolies in order to maintain their sway: (1) legitimate use of violence, (2) promulgation of views through propaganda, (3) establishment of a firm currency and setting exchange rates, (4) access to cutting edge technology, and (5) expertise and credibility. Today we see the power of states eroding in four out of five of these categories. The new wired world offers vast alternatives to state propaganda, for

instance. Private currency brokers are now more important than state bankers in establishing rates of exchange. New technologies enter the civilian realm so quickly that armed forces now buy many items straight off the shelves. And expertise is spreading to the populace at large, at unprecedented rates.

The chief questions we face are (a) Do we really want the legitimate use of coercion or violence to be "deregulated" or "privatized" along with the rest? (b) Might there be plenty of jobs left for government, even if Cooper's monopolies are broken? (c) Will the loss of state control in categories 2 through 5 be a *democratic dispersal* or simply wind up giving these powers over to the hands of other elites?

In a society that is mostly transparent, former monopolies 2 through 5 may become so widely distributed, among so many players, that accumulation of tyrannical power may never become likely again. This could result in nation-states that are less relentlessly dominant in our lives than in the past. That does not mean nations will necessarily go away, or even lose great importance in helping mediate consensus approaches to solving great problems. One role they can serve is as the centripetal centers of common loyalty that bind together all the diverse, spinning "tribes" of interest we will be joining, a core identification of citizenship that people share.

## CHAPTER 10

310   . . . *initiative made by President Eisenhower* . . . The Soviets claimed that the "open skies" proposal was a step toward acquiring targeting information for a preemptive strike. Their counterproposal for limited overflights, while unsatisfactory and self-serving, might conceivably have been the basis for negotiated confidence building, but it was rejected by Washington. Special interests in both capitals had a stake in continued distrust. Nevertheless, few doubt Eisenhower's essential sincerity, or the foresight of his prediction that the alternative to openness would at best be a devastatingly expensive arms race. Several trillion dollars later, that bitter and secretive standoff has left an ecologically damaged world, barely keeping up with population growth, unable to afford truly ambitious projects such as acquisition of resources from outer space. A trillion dollars is a lot of money to spend on things that were supposed to be too scary ever to be used. Containment was effective, but an open world might have been better still.

310   . . . *democracies almost never wage war on one another* . . . Michael W. Doyle, "Liberalism in World Politics," *American Political Science Review* 80(4) (1986): 1151–69.

316   *Some propose information itself as the target.* . . . Jeffrey Cooper, "Understanding Information Warfare: Another View," from *Society and Security in the Information Age*, John Arquilla and David Ronfeldt, eds., Johns Hopkins University Press, 1998.

318   . . . *invite outsiders to test* . . . A secondary effect of such contests would be to throw government and nongovernment techies into each other's company for periods long enough for them to recognize their similarities and common ideals, and to realize that they are members of the same civilization.

319   . . . *Repression is not defensible* . . . David Rothkopf, "In Praise of Cultural Imperialism?" *Foreign Policy* (summer 1997). Rothkopf is managing director of Kissinger Associates.

319   . . . *lack of internal passport controls* . . . A possible sign of an end to this era may be seen in the fact that ticket holders on U.S. domestic airline flights are now asked to present a picture ID. Airline employees are trained in "profile watching" to alert superiors to *types* of individuals who score highly on a list of traits that are

considered to correlate with potential security risk. Some see in these measures the slow but steady approach of authoritarianism. An alternative would be to view them as awkward and desperate measures that might be eliminated if transparency tools made air travel safe from terror threats. (See the earlier discussion of risk perception.)

320    . . . *toward a true center of culpability* . . . At this point let me drop even a pretense of scholarly detachment. Since World War II, Switzerland and its fellow banking havens have sheltered lucre for the world's tax cheats, drug dealers, dictators, and mafias. In exchange for this money-laundering scam, the banks could charge large fees and, above all, get away with paying scant interest, a major unfair competitive advantage. Many Third World countries have been stripped of working capital by corrupt officials, entrenched elites, and criminal gangs. Out of these ill-gotten gains, the pittance that was not squandered—perhaps a few tens of billions of dollars— arguably rests at this moment in coffers alongside "dormant" accounts of Nazi warlords and their hapless murdered victims. One might envision those poor nations someday demanding justice—as depicted in my novel *Earth*—but real pressure can come only from the West. Recently, the bankers of Berne and Vaduz have begun loosening the ignominious shroud of secrecy just enough to eliminate some of their most disreputable clients, a few notorious drug lords, as a sop to Western governments. But this gesture may not suffice when hard-pressed U.S. and European taxpayers estimate how much of their own burden might ease if aristocratic tax cheaters had to account for their fair share.

Whether or not this scenario actually comes to pass, it is credible enough that the world's elites should go on notice. Caching their reserves in such havens may be self-defeating in the long run, creating a dossier that will later haunt them when secret lists are handed over to placate an angry world. From now on it might be better to invest the money, whether ill gotten or not, in real estate.

322    . . . *the scientific spirit is more human* . . . J. Bronowski, *Science and Human Values* (New York: Harper & Row, 1972).

## CHAPTER 11

328 . . . *a wired, global society, the concept of openness has never been more important* . . . Peter Schwartz and Peter Leyden, "The Long Boom: A History of the Future 1980–2020," *Wired*, July 1997; see also http://www.wired.com/5.07/longboom/.

328 Jaron Lanier, "Karma Vertigo: Or Considering the Excessive Responsibilities Placed on Us by the Dawn of the Information Infrastructure," *Netview: Global Business Network News*, vol. 6, no. 1, winter 1994–95.

# FOLLOW-UP

Join a critical discussion on openness. The Foresight Institute, a nonprofit educational organization examining the impact of coming technologies, will sponsor a series of online discussions on the goal of openness and its relationship to surveillance and encryption technologies in the twenty-first Century. Interested participants are invited to visit *http://crit.org/ openness* on the Web for information on these discussions, which are tentatively scheduled for June and December 1998, 1999, and 2000, featuring contributions by both advocates and opponents of transparency. Archives of past discussions will also be available.

In addition to comments or criticism of this book, some questions that might be worth pursuing are as follows:

1) What accumulations of power do people fear most and are those centers of power best controlled by blinding them or by forcing accountability on them? What real or potential power elites are getting *too little* attention nowadays?

2) Looking to history: Is there an example where a civilization failed because it was *too open*? Are there any examples when generalized secrecy helped prevent tyranny?

3) Do we need new social innovations to help unite and draw us together while we fly apart into a million little tribes? What do we need to flourish as a society in an Age of Amateurs?

• • •

None of us will have the last word on this subject. If we create a society that is dynamic, progressive, and free, our descendants are sure to find many of our abstract posturings rather quaint and amusing. That's just fine. As long as we keep raising children who are smarter and better than we are, all these problems we're agonizing over will sort themselves out in the long run.

Our brainy descendants will have other things to worry about.

# ACKNOWLEDGMENTS

*The first duty of a revolutionary is to get away with it.*

ABBIE HOFFMAN

I want to thank those who lent a kind (and critical) eye to early drafts of this book. These good folks include Stefan Jones, John Gilmore, Steve Jackson, Carl Malamud, Roger Clarke, Bruce Murray, Bruce Sterling, Chris Peterson, Robin Hanson, Xavier Fan, Martha Minow, Ann Florini, Peter Swire, Michael Foale, Gregory Benford, Joe Miller, Robert Qualkinbush, Gary T. Marx, Wendy Grossman, Steinn Sigurdsson, Jonathan R. Will, Joseph Carroll, Eric J. Sprunk, Hollis Heimbouch, Nick Arnett, Rebecca Eisenberg, Erik and Rebecca Van Riper, Mark Burgess, Jay Kunin, James Flynn, Robert Redfield, Victor Stone, Geoffrey Landis, Peter Becker, Ira Moskatel, Dina Heredia, Bear Giles, Damien Sullivan, Declan McCullagh, Jeff Cooper, and Barry Fulton. A book like this one profits immensely from the attacks and brickbats of those who disagree with it. (Isn't criticism the foremost defense against error?) Therefore, I thank those whose courteous — or caustic — disagreement revealed flaws in earlier drafts, helping make this book a better argument for transparency: Philip Agre, William Campbell, Reilly Jones, Eric Hughes, Hal Finney, Solveig Singleton, and Matt Blaze.

Kalinda Basho was meticulous as my assistant. Special thanks go to John Bell, my editor, as well as to my agent Ralph Vicinanza. Finally, I owe so much to my wife, Dr. Cheryl Brigham, who contributed wondrous labors of research, innumerable insights, and support. If the light is to shine, it must begin at home.

# INDEX